About the Author

Cary A. Jardin is a Sun Certified Java Programmer and Developer. He was born and resides in San Diego, CA, and holds a B.S. in Computer Science from California State University San Marcos, where he specialized in Neural Networks and Inter Process Communication (IPC).

His professional programming experience includes creating and deploying Web-based yellow pages for BellSouth, a distributed video application for Union Pacific Railroad, a Java-based gaming transport engine for Brighter Child Interactive, a Java client for NCR TOPEND transactional processor, and an online credit card transaction/storefront/JavaBeans application for Shielded Technologies, Inc.

Cary also holds several patents, including Random Class Security (RCS), which provides the means for highly secure communications utilizing Java technology. He is currently employed as Director of Engineering for ServNOW. He is the author of *Electronic Commerce in Java, Symantec Visual Cafe Sourcebook*, and currently teaches a Visual Café course at www.digitalthink.com.

His other interests are cycling, remote-control toys, his wife, and his baby on-the-way, although not necessarily in that order.

Trademark Acknowledgments

Acknowledgments

I would like to thank Maryrose J. Jardin for being my first-round editor, graphic artist, and wife. Thanx also go to Eric Enockson and the entire ServNow team. Finally, I would like to thank Slugger, my English Bulldog, for his patience and support.

Contents at a Glance

Table of Contents

3   Java Objects and Exceptions   95

4   Threads in the Java Platform   123

Part III: Appendices   567

A   Overview of the Certification Process   569

B   Using the CD-ROM   579

Index   583

Introduction

The *Java 1.1 Certification Training Guide* is designed for Java programmers who want to take the Sun Certified Java Programmer (310-022) and Sun Certified Java Developer (310-024) examinations offered by Sun. These two exams are sequential: the Sun Certified Java Programmer exam tests your knowledge of Java language semantics and usage and is a prerequisite for taking the Sun Certified Java Developer exam, which tests your knowledge of developing Java solutions.

Who Should Read This Book

This book is designed to help prepare experienced Java programmers who are working towards Java Certification for the Sun Certified Java Programmer and the Sun Certified Java Developer exams.

This book is your one-stop shop. It contains everything you need to know to pass both Java certification exams. The CD-ROM that accompanies this book contains testing software (written in Java) with hundreds of exam questions. The software mimics the actual exam software so you can become comfortable with the testing environment before you have to take the actual exam.

You do not need to take a class in addition to buying this book to pass the exams. However, depending on your personal study habits, you might benefit from taking a class in addition to reading the book.

The amount of information that the Java Programmer and Java Developer exams cover is immense. Topics range from computer architecture to details about OOD to GUI event models. This book covers the specific areas of knowledge required to successfully complete the Java certification process. If you are coming from a non-programming or non-Java background, you might want to purchase an additional Java reference such as *Special Edition Using Java 1.1, Third Edition* from Que or *Teach Yourself Java 1.1 in 21 Days* from Sams.

If you have anything from minimal to extensive experience with Java, this book is optimal for you. At your level, the contents of this book will provide exactly the information needed to complete the Java Certification process, as well as hone and expand your existing Java knowledge.

How This Book Helps You

This book is designed to provide the information required to complete the certification process in the order and format most closely matching that of the actual certification examinations. For instance, the Certified Programmer exam must be completed before the Certified Developer exam can be initiated. Likewise, the first section of the book focuses on Certified Programmer content, and the second section covers Certified Developer content. You'll also find helpful test hints, real-world examples, exercises, and testing software.

At points when you are reading through a chapter and say, "I know this stuff," you can begin using the book to locate the exact areas on which you need to focus. Using the following process, the book's content can be transformed from a linear, cover-to-cover content flow to a specific, non-linear presentation of content based on your specific needs.

1. **Assess your skills.** The beginning of each chapter contains a few sample test questions. Try your hand at these questions, and keep track of the ones you miss and the ones you are not 100% sure about.

2. **Jump to specific points of interest.** After the sample questions have been completed, use the reference information found in Appendix A, "Overview of the Certification Process," to direct you to a specific area of interest. Once you feel comfortable, and feel confident that you have a mastery of that specific testing area, you can test your knowledge in

the supplied practice tests in the "Practice Test" chapters, or electronically on the CD-ROM.

3. **Test your skills with a practice exam.** After you have completed a specific area, test your general knowledge to guide your next course of study. The five "Practice Test" chapters and the CD-ROM-based test tool allow you to determine the precise areas of study on which you need to focus. After a specific point of study has been flagged, you will be guided to the chapter that will best aid your study, at which point you should loop back to Step 1.

The following items outline how to use this book:

▶ **Decide how to spend your time wisely.** Pre-chapter quizzes at the beginning of each chapter test your knowledge of the objectives contained within that chapter. You can use these quizzes to gauge how much time you need to spend studying the objectives contained within each chapter. Answers to each pre-chapter quiz are found at the end of the chapter. It's not enough to guess the right answer; make sure you would be able to justify your answer before deciding to skip any material in this book.

 Objectives

▶ **Test Objectives.** Throughout this *Training Guide* you will find an icon like the one shown in the margin. This icon points out every objective you need to know to pass the exam—pay particular attention to this information.

▶ **Extensive practice test options**. Plenty of questions at the end of each chapter test your comprehension of the material. An answer list follows the questions so you can check your progress and decide what material you need to review in greater detail.

▶ **CD-ROM Test Engine.** You'll also get a chance to practice for the certification exams using the test engine on the CD-ROM. This engine was written in Java and mimics the testing environment you will encounter when you take the exam. The test engine generates new tests from a database of hundreds of questions each time you take it.

Note For a complete description of the test engine, please see Appendix B, "Using the CD-ROM."

Understanding What the Sun Certified Java Programmer Exam (310-022) Covers

The Sun Certified Java Programmer Exam (310-022) covers five main topic areas, arranged in accordance with test objectives. The following list provides a detailed outline of the material covered in the test:

1. Sun-Provided Development Tool Knowledge and Runtime Environment

   ▶ Knowledge of JDK shipped tools.

   ▶ Working understanding of the JVM technology.

2. Language Syntax Knowledge

   ▶ Proper syntax usage.

   ▶ Language-reserved words and declarations.

   ▶ Programming efficiency.

3. Language Mechanics

   ▶ The four object accessibility modifiers: `public`, `private`, `default`, and `protected`.

   ▶ Firm knowledge of language mechanics to ensure solid, scalable, and extensible implementations.

   ▶ In-depth Java language mechanics lesson.

   ▶ Specific Java mechanics of Java thread support.

4. API Knowledge

   ▶ Knowledge of Sun supplied utility classes.

▶ Specific method knowledge of the base `Object` class.

▶ Understanding of GUI development facilities.

5. Specific Applet and Application Implementation Issues

▶ Java application deployment can take two discrete routes, each with separate associated issues.

▶ An applet's home is inside a Web browser, which in turn dictates the applet's operating environment. A Java application's home is in the executing computer's operating system.

▶ Each deployment offers its own set of attributes, with neither being superior to the other. Rather, the deployments have their own qualities and abilities. The key is to know which one fits your need most precisely.

Understanding What the Sun Certified Java Developer Exam (310-022) Covers

Where the Certified Programmer exam focuses on Java programming, the Certified Developer exam focuses on the use of Java in software development. The following list provides a detailed outline of the material covered in the test:

1. Network Programming

▶ Working knowledge of TCP/IP socket usage

▶ Understanding of UDP datagram support

▶ Specific RMI deployment issues

2. Object-Oriented Design

▶ Knowledge of Java nuances that affect design patterns

▶ Understanding of how to properly model a solution

3. Java-Related Technologies

▶ Knowledge of RMI

▶ Knowledge of the Java enterprise facilities

> ▶ Knowledge of JavaBeans

> ▶ Knowledge of the Java Foundation Classes

4. Java Deployment Issues

> ▶ Understanding of various platform issues

> ▶ Knowledge of applet- and application-specific deployment issues

Hardware and Software Needed

To use all the materials in this book, you will need a computer capable of running either HotJava or a Java-enabled Web browser such as Netscape Navigator or Internet Explorer.

Tips for the Exam

Remember the following tips as you prepare for the Sun Certified Java exams:

> ▶ **Read all the Material.** All the material in this Training Guide is relevant to the two Java exams. Reading and understanding all this material is the most important step to successfully passing the exams.

> ▶ **Take the pre-chapter quizzes.** Use these quizzes to quickly assess where you need to spend the most time studying. Each chapter begins with a set of questions related to the test objectives found in that chapter. Answers to these quizzes can be found at the end of each chapter.

> ▶ **Complete all the questions in the "Review Questions" section at the end of each chapter.** These sections function as mini-tests that help you determine how well you have mastered the test objectives in each chapter. You can roughly gauge how much progress you've made with this book by comparing the results of the pre-chapter quizzes with those of the Review Questions.

> ▶ **Use the Test Engine on the CD-ROM.** Each time you use the test engine it will generate a new exam for you based on a

database of hundreds of questions. Take several complete exams, examine your scores, and get comfortable with the testing environment.

New Riders Publishing

The staff of New Riders Publishing is committed to bringing you the very best in computer reference material. Each New Riders book is the result of months of work by authors and staff who research and refine the information within its covers.

As part of its commitment to you, the NRP reader, New Riders invites your input. Please let us know if you enjoy this book and find it useful, if you have trouble with the information and examples presented, or if you have a suggestion for the next edition.

Please note, though, that the New Riders staff cannot serve as a technical resource during your preparation for the Sun Certified Java exams.

If you have a question or comment about any New Riders book, you can contact New Riders Publishing in several ways. We will respond as quickly as we can. Your name, address, or phone number will never become part of any mailing list or be used for any purpose other than to help us continue to publish the best books possible. You can write to us at:

New Riders Publishing
Attn: Publisher
201 West 103rd Street
Indianapolis, IN 46290

If you prefer, you can fax New Riders at (317) 817-7448.

You can also send e-mail to New Riders at: **tryan@mcp.com**

New Riders is an imprint of Macmillan Computer Publishing. To obtain a catalog or information, or to purchase any Macmillan Computer Publishing book, please call (800) 428-5331.

Thank you for selecting *Java 1.1 Certification Training Guide*!

Sun Java Programmer Certification

Chapter 1

Java and the Java Virtual Machine (JVM)

The word Java is often used in a confusing manner. For example, saying, "I program in Java," and, "My browser is Java-enabled" is ambiguous. The first statement refers to the Java programming language, and the second refers to the Java runtime environment, or Java Virtual Machine (JVM). This chapter focuses on the sometimes forgotten aspects of the Java technology suite, which are the Java runtime environment and the JVM.

The Java runtime environment and JVM provide Java programs the underlying framework for their cross-platform nature. For many in the industry, the Java runtime environment and JVM are the black magic pieces of the Java technology. After reading this chapter, you will know all the ins and outs of the Java runtime environment and JVM technologies.

 Objectives

▶ How the JVM executes Java programs

▶ JVM and JRE internals

▶ JVM interaction with native resources

▶ Class file composition

▶ Cross-platform characteristics of the different JREs

Test Yourself! Before reading this chapter, test yourself to determine how much study time you will need to devote to this section.

1. The JVM architecture makes the following provisions to ensure compatibility across all processors:

   A. Uses a stack-based architecture

   B. Is modeled after the lowest common denominator architecture

   C. Minimizes the use of registers

   D. A and B

   E. A and C

2. The JVM registers and stack are:

   A. 8 bits wide

   B. 16 bits wide

   C. 32 bits wide

   D. 64 bits wide

Answers are located at the end of the Chapter...

The Java Runtime Environment Makes Java Cross-Platform

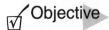 Objective

The easiest and cleanest way to describe the relationship between Java and the Java runtime environment is to compare both technologies to the way Velcro functions. For instance, if you want to temporarily mount a pair of speakers onto your computer monitor, you could attach strips of opposing pieces of Velcro to your speakers and computer, and then put the devices together. Using Velcro instead of, say, glue, gives you the ability to move the speakers at will, without any adverse effects. Velcro allows you to attach the speaker to whatever you want to attach it to, as long the object has an opposing piece of Velcro on it.

Figure 1.1

Java Velcro Effect.

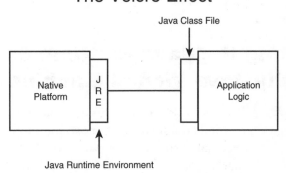

Just as Velcro requires two pieces to operate, so does Java, as displayed in Figure 1.1. A Java executable, or class file, is the first piece, and the Java runtime environment is the second. You can think of the Java runtime environment as the receptor to which the Java executable bonds. The Java runtime environment binds itself to the specific native platform and provides a shield against any platform-specific issues by eliminating machine-specific issues. This shielding is known as a *layer of indirection* for the Java executable.

At the time the executable is handed to the Java runtime environment for execution in the JVM, the application can assume a certain set of predefined functionality. It is up to the JVM to shield the application from any platform-specific dependencies. As long as the platform has a JVM affixed to it, all Java executables are able to run. In this way, the Java application binds to the JVM and the JVM, in turn, binds to the specific platform.

One of the most common oversights in the Java world is to say that Java executables can run on any platform. A more correct statement is that Java applications can run on any platform that has an accessible Java runtime environment. Not all platforms are Java-ready, but the list is growing. The Java runtime environment has been announced as a standard facility for the next generation of operating systems produced by all major vendors. For example, the next release of Windows might contain a Java runtime environment. As long as a Java runtime environment is accessible, the Java executable will run, regardless of platform. Soon there will be no distinction between what is a Java-executable and what is native code.

Relating the Java Runtime Environment and the Java Virtual Machine

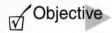 Objective

It sounds odd to say, "This executable runs on any machine with an Intel architecture." A more common statement is to say, "This executable runs on any Windows 95 platform." The difference is that the first sentence describes the machine architecture, such as Intel, Motorola, or Sun. The second makes a more specific statement about the operating system in which the executable may be run. Likewise, the JVM provides Java executables with a machine architecture to be executed on, and the runtime provides basic operating system functionality.

When there was only one version of the Java runtime environment, you could assume that any machine with a JVM would execute a Java class file. With the release of JDK 1.1, saying that a machine is Java-enabled is not enough. Current Java applications written with JDK 1.1 will not run on a JDK 1.02-*compatible* runtime, but they will run on a JDK 1.02-*compliant* JVM. The difference lies in the support files provided by the runtime environment.

Put simply, the JVM emulates a "Java Chip." It knows only how to execute the Java machine instruction set. The support classes required by Java executables, like the java.lang package, reside in the runtime environment and are fetched by the JVM as needed. In this manner, the JVM can remain common between JDK versions with only the support classes changing. Figure 1.2 illustrates how the JVM uses the files found in the runtime environment to execute a class file.

Figure 1.2

Java runtime environment interaction with the JVM.

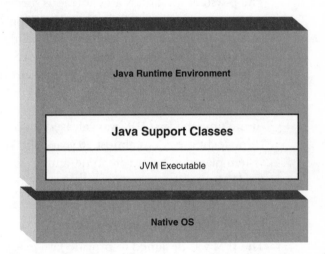

As you can see from Figure 1.2, the Java runtime environment acts as an operating system of sorts, loading required classes into the JVM for execution. In this way, the Java runtime environment acts as the interface between the native machine and the JVM. Later in this chapter, a section entitled "Executing A Class in the JVM" diagrams the complete execution of a class file to demonstrate exactly how the runtime and JVM interact. But for now, think of the JVM as a piece of the Java runtime environment, and remember that the JVM requires the facilities of the runtime to execute Java classes.

Old Technology Revisited

About 1977, a project by the name p-system was being developed at the University of California San Diego under Professor Kenneth

Bowles. The goal of the p-system project was to create a ubiquitous operating system providing a common platform for application executions through the use of a virtual machine architecture. Keep in mind this was several years before the first IBM PC, Macintosh, or Amiga hit the market. Computer architectures at the time were vastly different, and the concept of providing a solution to machine-specific, or native applications was revolutionary.

The p-system was and is an enormous success. By 1985, p-systems were running on the DEC LSI-11, the Zilog Z80, the Motorola 68000, and almost every member of the Intel 80*86 family from the 8088 to the 80386. Even today, Cabot Software of the United Kingdom continues to sell newer versions under license as a alternative for Java.

At the time the first JDK was released for public use, virtual machine technology was almost 20 years old. Without a doubt, the p-system played a major role in designing, sculpting, and stabilizing the JVM.

Cross-Platform Capabilities

The JVM was designed to provide Java executables with a standard platform for execution. However, if the JVM was only implemented on a single platform, Java technology would not offer anything more than native-compiled applications. Java's intrinsic benefits, and its ultimate ubiquity, come from the number of different platforms which provide a Java runtime environment. Today, the JVM and Java runtime environment are available on an increasing number of platforms. The following is a partial list of supported platforms:

- AS/400
- AIX
- Amiga
- FreeBSD

- HP
- Linux
- Macintosh
- MP-RAS

- ▶ NeXT
- ▶ OS/2
- ▶ Solaris

- ▶ Windows 3.1
- ▶ Windows 95
- ▶ Windows NT

JVM Architecture

 Objective ▶ The JVM is probably one of the most misunderstood technologies of the Java suite. Some say that the JVM is an interpreter, interpreting Java-compiled byte code into actual native machine calls. This statement isn't entirely false, but it is not true enough to be right. That is, the JVM is a virtual machine; it is not an interpreter, but rather an emulator.

Virtual machine technology has historically been distinct from interpreter technology. The reason lies in how and at what level the interpretation takes place. Interpreters directly map a proprietary byte code into system calls. Some map directly into machine instructions, but no attempt is made, by any interpreter, to emulate an intermediate machine architecture.

The JVM functions like an interpreter in some areas, but this comparison is not a direct one. If anything, you can generally refer to interpreters as scaled-down, simplified, and altogether less-complicated forms of a virtual machine. As you will see in the next few sections, the JVM is an entire framework for a machine architecture, not unlike Intel or Motorola. The only difference is that the JVM does not require a chip- or silicon-based implementation to operate.

JVM Examined

If you have never gone through the agony of writing programs directly to a machine's hardware, the similarities between existing silicon-based architectures and the JVM are probably not obvious to you. Nevertheless, it is important to realize the level at which the JVM executes class files. The JVM is an entire machine architecture with the capability of being implemented directly into a silicon chip.

The JVM's architecture revolves around the concept of an implementation that is not machine-specific. That is, the architecture itself makes no assumptions about the machine or silicon on which it is implemented. In this way, the JVM is the sole and autonomous entity that executes class files.

As shown in Figure 1.3, the JVM is broken into five distinct units of functionality, which all work in harmony to achieve the primary task of executing class files.

Figure 1.3

JVM Architecture.

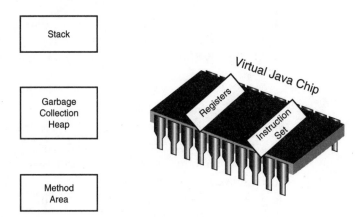

The following sections analyze the functionality of each of the five key JVM units. Throughout this discussion, keep in mind how closely the JVM maps to existing and potential silicon-based architectures.

These units are:

▶ Registers

▶ Stacks

▶ Garbage-collection heaps

▶ Method areas

▶ Instruction sets

JVM Registers and a Stack-Based Architecture

In the Intel and Motorola architectures, registers are used for almost everything, due to the fact that both architectures are register-based. Say you want to add the numbers 2 and 3. As shown in Figure 1.4, in a register-based architecture you would load the value 2 into a register (memory storage device), and then load the value 3 into another register.

Figure 1.4

Register-based operations.

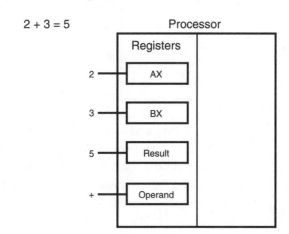

Once the values are loaded, you would load an And operation code value into yet another register to instruct the processor to perform the operation. So essentially, you would use registers as the means of communicating with the processor. However, different makes and models of processors contain various types and quantities of registries, making it impossible to create an all-encompassing virtual architecture based on registers. The solution the JVM opted for is a stack-based architecture.

The JVM was designed to function in any machine architecture while retaining the ability to be implemented directly on silicon. To achieve this, and maintain compatibility with architectures with various types and quantities of register devices, the JVM utilizes a stack-based architecture. Revisiting the 2 plus 3 problem, you can see the inherent difference between the two architectures. As shown in Figure 1.5, in a stack-based architecture the value of 2 is pushed onto a stack, then the value 3 is pushed onto the same stack, and finally the add operation code is pushed onto the same stack.

Figure 1.5

Stack-based operations.

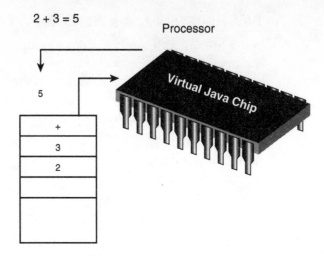

Once the values and the add instruction have all been pushed onto the stack, the processor is directed to start executing the instruction on the stack by setting a single register value to initiate execution. In this manner, the stack-based model can execute the same add operation with one register and one stack.

From the stack-based example in Figure 1.4, you can see that the JVM requires the use of a few registers. But, the usage of these registers varies drastically from the example displayed in Figure 1.5. The following describes each of the four JVM registers and its use.

JVM Registers:

- ▶ pc—The pc register is a 32-bit wide program counter. Its main responsibility is to keep track of program execution, and it is also identical to a program counter register on a register-based architecture.

- ▶ optop—The optop register is a 32-bit wide register responsible for maintaining a memory reference to the top of the operation stack.

- ▶ frame—The frame register is a 32-bit wide register responsible for providing a pointer to the current stack frame. From this stack frame, the JVM can retrieve needed operands or opcodes for stack maintenance.

▶ vars—The vars register is a 32-bit wide register responsible for providing the base offset of the local variable in the current stack frame. That is, the JVM looks to this offset to find all variables currently in the program's scope.

Single Stack Resource

As mentioned in the previous section, the entire JVM architecture revolves around a single, 32-bit wide stack resource. However, this stack is not a simple, everyday stack of 32-bit wide elements. Elements are pushed onto and popped off of the stack in the same manner as they are in a normal FIFO (First In First Out) programmatic stack. The difference lies in how the JVM stack is partitioned.

The JVM is partitioned into three separate regions. The following describes each of these regions and their roles in the larger JVM stack picture. Later, this chapter steps through the execution of a class file to demonstrate how these regions are used.

JVM Stack Regions:

▶ *local variable region*   The local variable region of the method frame provides the vars register with a base reference for accessing the local variables. All local variables are 32-bits wide, and 64-bit variables occupy two variable entries.

▶ *execution environment region*   The execution environment region of the stack frame is used to provide op-code for maintaining the methods stack frame. It also maintains pointers to the local variables, the previous stack frame, and the top and bottom of the current frame's operand region.

▶ *operand stack region*   The operand stack region contains the operands for the current method.

Garbage Collection Heap

The concept of garbage collection in Java is sometimes a difficult thing to grasp, so take a step back and compare it to how you consume groceries. You go to the store, purchase your groceries, consume your goods, and then dispose of the refuse. Now, say that everything you buy is 100% recyclable so that, once you consume an item, it goes right back to the grocery store to be restocked for another consumer. In the same way, memory resources may be consumed and then directly reused. In this way the Garbage Collection Heap device of the JVM allows for the recycling of used memory resources.

The Garbage Collection Heap device is the central facility for all memory storage devices. If your program wants to store a number, a memory device is allocated from the Garbage Collection Heap to facilitate your request. Once your program is finished with the storage device, the memory goes back to the heap for "restocking."

Restocking or garbage collection is not something defined in the JVM specification. That is, not all JVM implementations perform garbage collection in the same way. Some JVMs may restock the memory at the time it is returned to the heap. Other implementations may wait until the heap, or store, is completely empty before they restock the shelves. Either way, the Garbage Collection Heap device is responsible for allocating and reusing memory resources. How and when its duties are performed is a JVM implementation issue.

The Method Storage Area

As the name implies, the Method Storage area is the primary memory storage device for all methods found in the executing class. Later in this chapter, in the section named "Execution of a Class file," when you diagram the execution of a class file, you will revisit this area of the JVM. But for now, just think of it as the general storage device for all Java executable code.

JVM Instruction Set

The last piece of the JVM is not a region, or a device, or even a physical element of the JVM. Rather, the JVM Instruction Set is the driving entity that gives the JVM life. The Instruction Set tells the processor to perform an action. In the case of the JVM Instruction Set, those actions equate into 160 instructions, partitioned in 17 different categories.

In native-compiled programs, the executable contains that program's associated set of operations, which perform the desired functionality. The difference with Java-executable program files is that the operations contained with the file are JVM instructions and not native instructions. In this manner, Java executables are identical to normal executables, except Java executables are compiled to run on the JVM.

Note

None of the 160 instructions are testable items in either the Java Certified Programmer or Java Certified Developer examinations. For this reason, there will not be a detailed discussion of each individual instruction. However, the following is a list of JVM instructions for reference purposes.

bipush	sipush	ldc1
ldc2	ldc2w	aconst
iconst	iconst	lconst
fconst	dconst	Iliad
iload	lload	fload
dload	aload	istore
lstore	fstore	dstore
astore	astore	iinc
newarray	anewarray	multianewarray
arraylength	iaload	laload
faload	daload	aaload
caload	saload	iastore
lastore	fastore	dastore
aastore	bastore	castore
sastore	nop	pop
pop2	dup	dup2
dup_x1	dup2_x1	dup_x2

continues

dup2_x2	swap	iadd
ladd	fadd	dadd
isub	lsub	fsub
dsub	imul	fmul
dmul	idiv	ldiv
fdiv	ddiv	imod
lmod	fmod	ddiv
ineg	lneg	fneg
dneg	ishl	ishr
iushr	lshl	lshr
lshur	iand	land
ior	lor	ixor
lxor	i2l	i2f
i2d	l2i	l2f
l2d	f2i	f2l
f2d	d2i	d2l
d2f	int2byte	int2char
int2short	ifeq	iflt
ifle	ifne	ifgt
if_icmpeq	if_icmpne	if_icmplt
if_icmple	if_icmpgt	if_icmpge
lcmp	fcmpl	fcmpg
dcmpl	dcmpg	if_acmpeq
if_acmpne	goto	jsr
ret	ireturn	lreturn
freturn	dreturn	areturn
return	tableswitch	lookupswitch

putfield	getstatic	putfstatic
getfield	invokevirtual	invokestatic
invokeinterface	athrow	new
checkcast	newfromname	instanceof
verifystack	monitorenter	monitorexit
breakpoint		

Anatomy of a Class File

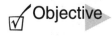 **Objective**

The structure of a class encapsulates an entire object. For this reason, class file structure is required knowledge for the Certified Programmer Examination.

You know that Java executables run on a JVM and are directly interpreted into native instructions, so now it's time to discuss the concept of a Java executable file, or class file.

In the PC world, an executable directly equates to an .exe file, and, on most platforms, executable files contain an entire program sequence. Java does things a little differently. Each executable file holds a single compiled object. One object acts as the entry point and calls supporting class files for needed functionality. For example, upon execution of an Applet, the Java runtime environment loads the main executable class and java.applet.Applet class into the JVM for execution.

Unlike native file executables, which contain a grouping of functionality in a single file, Java executables are constructed in such a way as to contain only a single object per file. In this way, each executable file is a reusable, self-contained application component. To facilitate this, the file is broken into fifteen separate Java class file regions, which are as follow:

▶ magic

▶ version

- ▶ constant_pool_count

- ▶ constant_pool[constant_pool_count - 1]

- ▶ access_flags

- ▶ this_class

- ▶ super_class

- ▶ interfaces_count

- ▶ interfaces[interfaces_count]

- ▶ fields_count

- ▶ fields[fields_count]

- ▶ methods_count

- ▶ methods[methods_count]

- ▶ attributes_count

- ▶ attributes[attribute_count]

Each region contains a different piece of the developed object. Figure 1.5 illustrates the regions of a class file. The following sections analyze each of the regions in turn.

The Magic Region

The Magic Region must contain a magic value of 0xCAFEBABE. This value simply has to be there. There is not much more to say about this region except to ask, "Why is it called magic?" It just is!

The Version Region

In anticipation of future development in Java, the class file format was created with a version stamp of sorts. The Version Region holds the version number of the compiler that created the class file. This is used to specify incompatible changes to either the format of the class file or JVM instruction set changes. In this way, the Java runtime environment can quickly and accurately determine compatibility.

The constant_pool Region

A familiar mechanism used in the class file format is to provide a region that specifies the size of another contained region. In this way, regional boundaries can be dynamically adjusted as needed. The constant_pool_count specifies the size of the next region, which is the constant_pool region.

The constant_pool contains an array of (constant_pool_count - 1) in size, which stores string constants, class names, field names, and all constants referenced in the body of the code. For each element in the constant_pool array, the first byte contains a type specifier, specifying the content of the entry. Although the type specifier values are not testable items, Table 1.1 provides the type values for reference purposes.

Table 1.1

Table of constant types.

Constant Type	Value	Storage
CONSTANT_Asciiz	1	1-byte reference tag, 2-byte length specifier, and array of bytes of that specified length
CONSTANT_Unicode	2	1-byte reference tag, 2-byte length specifier, and array of bytes of that specified length
CONSTANT_Integer	3	1-byte reference tag and 4-byte value
CONSTANT_Float	4	1-byte reference tag and 4-byte value

continues

Table 1.1   continued

Constant Type	Value	Storage
CONSTANT_Long	5	1-byte reference tag, 4-byte value containing the high bytes, and 4-byte value containing the low bytes
CONSTANT_Double	6	1-byte reference tag, 4-byte value containing the high bytes, and 4-byte value containing the low bytes
CONSTANT_Class	7	1-byte reference tag and 2-byte index into the constant_pool containing class's string name
CONSTANT_String	8	1-byte reference tag and 2-byte index into constant_pool holding the actual string value encoded using a modified UTF scheme
CONSTANT_Fieldref	9	1-byte reference tag and two 2-byte indexes
CONSTANT_Methodref	10	1-byte reference tag and two 2-byte indexes into constant_pool
CONSTANT_InterfaceMethodref	11	1-byte reference tag and two 2-byte indexes
CONSTANT_NamedType	12	1-byte tag and two 2-byte indexes into constant_pool

The access_flags Region

Chapter 2, "Java Language Internals," explores the various types of class accessor modifiers. For now, you need only know that the class accessor modifiers simply limit class users. For example, say you create a class you want to be used only by other classes you create. To limit the classes from which your class can be used, you would specify the appropriate accessor modifiers.

The access_flags region holds the class's visibility information. This information is stored as a 2-byte field that specifies 16 different values describing various properties of fields, classes, and methods. Although the access flag values are not testable items, Table 1.2 provides the flag values for reference purposes.

Table 1.2

Table of access flags.

Constant Name	Value
ACC_PUBLIC	0x0001
ACC_PRIVATE	0x0002
ACC_PROTECTED	0x0004
ACC_STATIC	0x0008
ACC_FINAL	0x0010
ACC_SYNCHRONIZED	0x0020
ACC_THREADSAFE	0x0040
ACC_TRANSIENT	0x0080
ACC_NATIVE	0x0100
ACC_INTERFACE	0x0200
ACC_ABSTRACT	0x0400

The this_class Region

During the course of a class's execution, it is sometimes necessary to present some specific information regarding internal characteristics. For this reason, the this_class provides a two-byte index into constant_pool specifying the information about the current class.

The Interfaces Region

Each class can implement any number of defined interfaces. The Interfaces Region provides all implemented interface information through a two-byte `interfaces_count` indexing the array contained in the Interfaces Region.

The Fields Region

All data members, or fields, of the currently specified class are contained within the Fields Region. That is, all stateful class information is specified in the class file by a 2-byte `fields_count` index which specifies the number of fields to be found in a field's array. Each field element has a 2-byte value of `access_flags`, two 2-byte indexes into `constant_pool`, a 2-byte attribute count, and an array of attributes.

The first index, `name_index`, holds the name of the field. The second, `signature_index`, holds the signature of the field. The last fields work in tandem to store any needed attributes about the field. In this way, field accessibility can be specified.

The Methods Region

Very similar to the Fields Region, the Methods Region contains all methods of the current class. The `methods_count` supplies the number of methods stored in the methods array. This number includes only the methods declared in the current class. The Methods Region contains an array of elements that provide complete information about the method.

Each method element contains a 2-byte `access_flags` value, 2-byte `name_index` referencing the name of the method in the `constant_pool`, 2-byte `signature_index` referencing signature information found in the `constant_pool`, 2-byte `attributes_count` containing the number of elements in the `attributes` array, and an `attributes` array. Currently, the only value that can be found in the `attributes` array is the `Code` structure, which provides the information needed to properly execute the specified method. Although the Code structure is not a testable item, the following information provides the structure for reference purposes.

Code Structure

Contained in the first two bytes of each element is the attribute_name_index. This index provides a pointer to the constant_pool supplying the name Code. The next two bytes, named attribute_length, provide the length of the Code structure, not including attribute_name_index. Actual Code-specific information begins with the next three 4-byte fields, followed by the method's op-code. max_stack contains the maximum number of entries on the operand stack during the methods execution. max_locals specifies the total number of local variables for the method. code_length is the total length of the next field, with the Code field containing op-code.

After the Code field, the Code structure provides detailed exception information for the method. This starts with the exception_table_length and exception_table, which describe each exception handler in the method code. start_pc, end_pc, and handler_pc give the starting and ending positions in which the event handler, pointed to by handler_pc, is active. catch_type, which follows handler_pc, denotes the type of exception handled.

The remainder of the Code structure is devoted to debugging information. line_number is the 2-byte line number of the method's first line of code. LocalVariableTable_attribute contains a structure used by the debugger to determine the value of local variables. The structure consists of three 1-byte values and a local_variable_table structure.

The first two fields of the structure, attribute_name_index and attribute_length, are used to describe the structure. The third contains the length of the local_variable_table. local_variable_table contains the following 2-byte fields in the following order: start_pc, length, name_index, signature_index, and slot. start_pc and length denote the offset when the variable value can be found. name_index and signature_index are indexes into constant_pool where the variable's name and signature can be found. slot denotes the position in the local method frame where the variable can be found.

The Attributes Region

Throughout Java and the JVM, provisions were made for future enhancements. For example, the Attributes Region contains all the overhead for later expansion. For example, the current class structure contains only one element in the defined Attribute array—the SourceFile structure. Nevertheless, an attributes_count field is provided just in case future elements need to be added. Although the SourceFile structure is not a testable item, the following information provides the structure for reference purposes.

The SourceFile Structure

The SourceFile structure consists of three 2-byte values. attribute_name_index indexes into the constant_pool to the entry containing the SourceFile string. attribute_length must contain a value of 2. sourcefile_index indexes into the constant_pool to the entry containing the source file name.

Executing a Class in the JVM

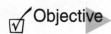 Now that you have an understanding of the JVM and the Class file format, it is time to connect the dots. You have learned the architecture of both the JVM and the Class file, but you have not yet seen how the two interact. The JVM is designed to execute JVM instructions, and the Class file is designed to provide the JVM with all the required executable information. When the two interact, a Java class is executed.

The information needed to piece together the details of a Class file execution can be found in the previous sections of this chapter. However, without studying each element of the JVM in detail, the proper execution sequence might not be clear. For this reason, here's a summary of the execution of a Class file: the Class Loader finds, verifies, and loads the class into the JVM for execution, then signals for execution to begin.

Although this summarized version of a Class file execution is streamlined, and correct, it leaves a few questions unanswered, such as the following: What is the Class Loader? What does it find and how does it do so? How does it signal the JVM to begin execution? The next two sections will discuss each of these questions in turn, beginning with a look at the Class Loader.

The Class Loader

As the name implies, the Class Loader mechanism loads classes into the JVM. All executable code placed into the JVM for execution arrives there by means of a Class Loader. However, the Class Loader's function is not as simple and trivial as you might assume. Quite to the contrary, the Class Loader is in many ways a complex, adaptable, and intelligent facility without which the JVM cannot live.

The Java runtime environment is a single entity containing subsections that each provide separate and distinct pieces for functionality. The Class Loader is likewise partitioned into subsections, each providing a specialized piece of the Class Loader puzzle. The following is a list of each of the Class Loader Internal Units and their associated performance tasks:

▶ Class File Retrieval Unit—The Class File Retrieval Unit is responsible for the retrieval of stored class files. This involves resolving the class name to the accessible class storage environment, checking with the Class Cache Unit to see if the Class Cache Unit is already in the system, and presenting the class as a stream of bytes to the Class Verification Unit.

▶ Class Cache Unit—The Class Cache Unit works in tandem with the Class File Retrieval Unit to optimize the load time of requested class files. The JVM specification makes no assumption about the cache algorithm used in the Class Cache Unit. The cache algorithm, in fact, has been an area of optimization for the various Java runtime environment implementations.

▶ Class Verification Unit—Once the class has been loaded, the Class Verification Unit verifies the validity of the loaded class. Validity checks include, but are not limited to, class file format integrity, binary compatibility of the class file and the JVM, and security violations.

▶ Class Linker Unit—After the class has been deemed safe by the Class Verification Unit, it is passed to the Class Linker Unit to retrieve any needed supporting classes. The Class Linker Unit analyzes the class's hierarchy, and dependencies, and makes subsequent calls to the Class File Retrieval Unit to load any required classes.

▶ Class Initializer Unit—At the point the Class Initializer Unit receives a class, it is ready to be loaded into the JVM for execution. The role of the Class Initializer Unit is to properly load the class regions into the JVM for execution, as shown in Figure 1.6.

Execution of a Loaded Class

To summarize the task of the Class Loader, it finds, verifies, and loads the class into the JVM for execution. At this point, the JVM Method region is loaded with all of the class's methods, the JVM Stack is loaded with class initialization, and the registers are set to the initial class execution state. All that is left is for the Class Loader to signal the JVM to begin execution.

Previously in this chapter, the operating differences between a register-based architecture and JVM's stack-based model were discussed. At the point of class execution, the JVM follows the exact model specified in that section for popping operands off the stack and pushing them onto it for execution, as shown in Figure 1.5.

Figure 1.6

Class Loader internals.

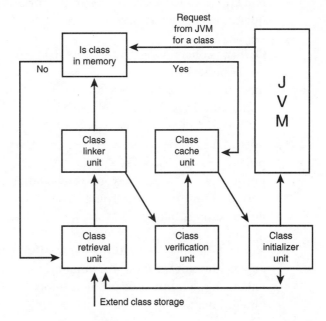

A final note about Class file execution and the JVM has to do with threads. The concept of threads was not explored in this chapter with respect to the JVM, and will not be discussed until Chapter 5, "Java API." However, you should keep in the back of your mind that the JVM architecture and Class file execution procedure discussed in this chapter can be scaled to handle an almost infinite number of simultaneously executing threads.

Various JVM Implementations

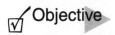 Objective

Each JVM is a little different. Knowing the various nuances is vital to development and required knowledge for the Certified Programmer Examination.

Not all computers are created equal. Likewise, not all JVMs are created equal. You have seen, through the discussion of the JVM and the Class file execution, that the JVM specification leaves room for implementation characteristics. An example is the issue of garbage collection. The JVM makes no assumptions about how unused memory resources are reallocated and placed for reuse. Issues such as these are responsible for differences in cross-JVM operation characteristics.

Garbage collection, threads, and GUI characteristics are, for Java developers, the things that go "bump" in the night. In later chapters, you will look at the threads and GUI cross-JVM implementation issues. This chapter has discussed the concept of garbage collection, but the intrinsic scheduling problem of garbage collection might not be obvious. For example, say your applications are providing some sort of real-time information, but you are having a problem. Every so often, your application stops responding for a period of time, and then comes back to life. This problem is the direct responsibility of JVM-implementation garbage collection.

Not all JVM-implementation characteristics are as obvious as your application not working. Fortunately, the JDK test suite has eliminated a large number of problem spots that plagued earlier Java development.

JDK Test Suite

Beginning with JDK 1.1, Sun has required Java runtime environment implementations to conform to the JDK Test Suite. That is, in order for a product to claim that it is "Java-enabled", it must first pass the JDK Test Suite. This initiative by Sun provides a standardization of the various Java runtime environment implementations.

Before JDK 1.1, all vendors that offered Java runtime environment support took it upon themselves to broadly interpret the JVM specifications. Specifically, issues like cross-platform thread support and GUI presentation were areas with high degrees of variation. The result was non-predictable class execution on the various runtime implementations. A quick example of this is exemplified in Windows 3.1 thread support: there is none!

The JDK Test Suite has done wonders for cross-platform implementations. Sun has also stated their dedication to ensuring conformity through licensing restrictions. If you don't conform, you don't get to use the word "Java" in your product. This is not to say that now all JVMs will be created equal, but at least they will be from the same planet.

Cross-Platform Issues

Maintaining a list of all cross-platform issues is impossible for a couple of reasons. The first reason lies in the fact that the list of platforms is in a constant state of flux. It seems as if every day news of a new Java-enabled device is hitting the streets, with no end in sight. The second reason for being unable to provide a complete list has to do with the rate of change in the Java world. New technologies are added and others deleted almost daily. This being the case, knowledge of platform-specific issues is not required on either certification exam. Nevertheless, it is invaluable information.

The following list provides some basic Java execution characteristics for a handful of platforms. Platforms excluded from this list are no less important than included entries. Rather, the included platforms simply provide the largest range of Java-enabled platforms.

▶ Window 95/Windows NT—Despite differences in display characteristics between the various browsers, Java support is relatively stable. However, garbage collection is usually performed only when all system resources are exhausted, and thread scheduling can cause a starvation state.

▶ Window 3.1—This platform has the same issues as Windows 95/Windows NT; however, threads are not supported on the 16-bit implementation.

▶ Macintosh—The major complaint for most Macintosh developers is the foreign look and feel of Java GUI elements. That is, buttons, scrollbars and other GUI elements have a PC look and feel.

▶ Various UNIX flavors—Probably the widest array of compatibility issues can be seen in the UNIX world, specifically with respect to thread scheduling. Remarkably enough, GUI presentation is relatively stable across all X-window implementations.

▶ JavaChips—JavaChips are silicon-based implementations of the Java Virtual Machine. Although a number of manufacturers are ramping up to provide these chips, it is too soon to note any operating characteristics.

Summary

All the elegance of the Java language and the beauty of the derived technologies are dependent on the JVM. In this way, the JVM is the heart of the Java technology suite.

It was stated in this chapter that Java's ubiquity is a function of the number of Java-enabled platforms. Java's ubiquity is provided by the mature and stable technology of the JVM and the Java run-time environment. However, without multiple platform implementations of the JVM and Java runtime environment, Java's intrinsic benefit ceases to exist. This chapter provided background information and details to show how the Java technology is portable across multiple platforms.

Chapter 2, "Java Language Internals," will begin to look at the higher-level technologies that ride on the ideas and implementations discussed in this chapter. However, before you run off to play with the fun stuff, take some time and test your skills. The following section provides a few sample questions that can be used to affirm your knowledge of JVM concepts. Keep in mind that a good portion of the nitty gritty details of this chapter were provided to round out your knowledge, and will not appear on either of the certification exams. The following review questions provide a good sample of what you can expect on the exams.

Review Questions

1. Which one of the following best describes the role of the JVM?

   A. An interpreter

   B. A device used to execute Applets

   C. An emulator used to execute Java machine code on a native platform

   D. A plug-in to Microsoft Internet Explorer

2. The JVM specification defines the process by which unused memory resources are collected and put onto the heap for reuse.

   A. True

   B. False

3. The JVM architecture makes the following provisions to ensure compatibility across all processors:

   A. Uses a stack-based architecture

   B. Is modeled after the lowest common denominator architecture

   C. Minimizes the use of registers

   D. A and B

   E. A and C

4. A Java runtime environment is available on Windows 3.1.

   A. True

   B. False

5. The JVM registers and stack are:

   A. 8 bits wide

   B. 16 bits wide

    C. 32 bits wide

    D. 64 bits wide

6. The Windows 3.1 Java runtime environment supports threads.

    A. True

    B. False

7. The Class file contains the following:

    A. JVM executable instructions

    B. Method naming information

    C. Field naming information

    D. All of the above

8. Classes are executed by the JVM in this manner:

    A. The ClassLoader loads the class into the JVM for execution, and then signals for execution to begin.

    B. The ClassLoader finds, verifies, and loads the class into the JVM for execution, and then signals for execution to begin.

    C. The JVM prompts the user for the class to execute.

    D. The runtime environment loads the Applet information into the JVM, and then begins the JVM process.

9. A JavaChip is:

    A. An accelerator chip designed to aid the JVM running on the native machine

    B. A chip which stores Java class files to increase ClassLoader performance

    C. A silicon implementation of the JVM

    D. The chip inside Sun's JavaStation

10. What major feature(s) was/were debuted in the JDK 1.1?

   A. JDBC

   B. RMI

   C. JavaBeans

   D. Improved AWT

   E. None of these

   F. All of these

Review Answers

1. C

2. B

3. E

4. A

5. C

6. B

7. D

8. B

9. C

10. F

Chapter 2

Java Language Internals

The Java programming language is the culmination of a number of different well-known languages. If you are from the Pascal world, you will see some glimmers of familiar syntax, like `println` and string support. However, if you are coming to Java from a C/C++, or SmallTalk background, a large portion of the syntax will feel very natural. Java is a platform-independent, concurrent, object-oriented language built to be easily palatable to all.

Before you get too far into the internals of the Java language, you need to know what this chapter, and this book for that matter, do *not* cover. The scope of this book is to get you ready to successfully complete the Sun Java Certification program. So the goal of this chapter is not to teach you how to program in the Java language. Rather, this chapter provides language syntax and usage information. For a complete tutorial/reference that teaches all aspects of programming in Java, it is recommended that you reference Que's *Special Edition Using Java 1.1, Third Edition*.

This chapter provides you with an understanding of the Java language syntax. Concepts such as reserved words, conditionals, loops, and declarations span programming language boundaries and provide the basis for learning a new language. This is exactly the scope and goal of this chapter.

 Objectives

- ▶ Contextually understand Java's reserved words

- ▶ Utilize Java's loop facilities

- ▶ Identify Java's operators

- ▶ Harness Java's conditional constructs

Test Yourself! Before reading this chapter, test yourself to determine how much study time you will need to devote to this section.

1. Given a byte with a value of 01110111, which of the following statements will produce 00111011?

   Note : 01110111 = 0x77

   A. 0x77 << 1

   B. 0x77 >> 3

   C. 0x77 >> 1

   D. 0x77 >>> 1

   E. C and D

2. An interface provides which of the following?

   A. A template for further development

   B. A mechanism for further development

   C. An alternative to class declarations

   D. A and C

   E. A and B

Answers are located at the end of the Chapter...

The Java Programming Language Defined

Many people in the industry claim that Java is very similar to C++, which isn't entirely fair. You wouldn't say that dogs and cats are similar based on the fact that they both have four legs. True, Java and C++ share a portion of common syntax and ideologies. Nevertheless, Java is a new, feature-rich language all to its own.

The Java language (originally named Oak) was initially designed for small computing devices such as Personal Digital Assistants (PDAs). Led by James Gosling, the language was formed out of the frustration of limited and proprietary development tools on the market for developing embedded solutions. After several years of toying around with the language, the capabilities of this new language began turning heads. The decision was made to move Oak from the embedded environment to the new Internet frontier where the name Java was given to this new technology.

The battle cry of the Java language development was "If you're not going to do it right, don't do it at all." In this section, you will take an in-depth look at what the Java language team of James Gosling, Bill Joy, and Guy Steele framed as the incarnation of the next generation of programming languages.

Java Reserved Words

 Objectives

Besides needing to know Java's reserved words for programming, contextual knowledge and usage of each reserved word is required information for the Certified Programmer Examination.

The syntax of any programming language revolves around the usage of predefined keys, or reserved words. That is, the goal of all languages is to express thought. Specifically, programming languages are designed to instruct the lifeless heap of iron and silicon that is a computer to do something meaningful. Reserved words form the basis for communication between the computer and programmer.

The study of programming languages, in the empirical sense, has strong ties to the mathematical sciences. Concepts such as set theory and large amounts are discrete mathematics that are required to fully analyze the empirical structure of a programming language. For now you're only interested in how the reserved words are used, and their associated functions. Knowledge of the lexical analysis of the Java programming language might be useful for compiler designers, but this sort of knowledge will not help you gain Java certification.

The following is a list of all reserved words found in the Java programming language. Following the list, a brief discussion of each will be provided to further increase your knowledge of the language. Keep in mind that reserved words are major topics of testing in the Certified Programmer Examination.

▶ abstract	▶ finally	▶ public
▶ boolean	▶ float	▶ return
▶ break	▶ for	▶ short
▶ byte	▶ goto	▶ static
▶ case	▶ if	▶ super
▶ catch	▶ implements	▶ switch
▶ char	▶ import	▶ synchronized
▶ class	▶ instanceof	▶ this
▶ continue	▶ int	▶ throw
▶ default	▶ interface	▶ throws
▶ do	▶ native	▶ transient
▶ double	▶ new	▶ try
▶ else	▶ null	▶ void
▶ extends	▶ package	▶ volatile
▶ final	▶ protected	▶ while

Abstract

The abstract reserved word acts as a modifier for class and method declarations. For example, the following code declares an abstract class containing an abstract method.

```
abstract class notMuch{
    public abstract boolean addYourCodeHere(int in);
}
```

In this example, the abstract class notMuch was declared to contain a single abstract method. Notice that there is nothing after the declaration of addYourCodeHere. The abstract method modifier provides the ability to define method signatures, without including an actual implementation. In this way, any class that wants to inherit a class that has been declared as abstract, must implement any declared abstract. Also, if a class contains any methods defined as abstract, the class must be declared as abstract. The following illustrates this dependency.

```
abstract class notMuch{
    public abstract boolean addYourCodeHere(int in);
}
class myStuff extends notMuch{
    public boolean addYourCodeHere(int in){
        return "" + in;
    }
}
```

The previous code segment declares myStuff to extend the abstract class notMuch. To then implement the inherited abstract method, the myStuff class implements the addYourCodeHere declaration. This example is syntactically correct and complete. The following, however, are both common examples of misuses of the abstract reserved word.

```
//Note: The absence of the abstract modifier.
//    As long as the class contains an abstract method
//    the Class must be declared as abstract.
class notMuch{
    public abstract boolean addYourCodeHere(int in);
}
```

```
class myStuff extends notMuch{
   public boolean addYourCodeHere(int in){
      return "" + in;
   }
}

class abstract notMuch{
   public abstract boolean addYourCodeHere(int in);
}
//Note: All abstract methods must be implemented in order to
➥inherit
//      and abstract class.
class myStuff extends notMuch{
}
```

boolean

The boolean reserved word describes a base Java data type containing a boolean value. Later in this chapter you will focus on Java data types, but for now, the following provides a brief example of boolean usage.

```
boolean test = false;
if(test)
   System.out.println("Its a Boy!");
else
   System.out.println("Its a Girl!");
```

This example declares the variable test to hold a value of false. The test variable is then used to make a decision of what message to display on the screen.

break

The break statement exits program execution out of the innermost enclosing switch, while, do, or for statements. Later in this chapter you will learn more about the concept of program loop mechanisms, which will provide the proper context for discussion of the break statement. But for now, the following example displays one of the many uses of the break statement.

```
boolean test = false;
for(;;){
   if(test)
      System.out.println("One More Time!");
   else{
      System.out.println("All Done");
      break;
   }
}
```

byte

The byte reserved word describes a base Java data type containing an 8-bit value. Later in this chapter you will focus on Java data types, but for now the following provides a brief example of byte usage.

```
byte value = -120;
System.out.println("The Value is : " + -120);
```

This example declares the variable test to hold a value of -120. The reason for setting the value to a negative number is to demonstrate the fact that Java bytes are signed, which differs from most programming languages.

case

The case reserved word is used to signify a condition handler in a multiple condition statement. Later in this chapter you will focus on Java conditional statements, but for now the following provides a brief example of the type of facility the case statement provides.

```
byte value = -120;
switch (value){
   case 1: System.out.println("Umm!");
      break;
   case 2: System.out.println("Umm, Umm!");
      break;
   case -120: System.out.println("Wow!");
      break;
}
```

In this way, the `case` statement declares a block of code as the handler for the specified value. The output from the code above would be `Wow!`, which corresponds with the `case` specified of -120.

catch

The `catch` reserved word is used to handle a raised exception. In Chapter 3, "Java Objects and Exceptions," you will focus on Java exceptions, but for now the following provides a brief example of the type of facility the `catch` statement provides.

```
String intValue = "H345";
try{
    Integer I = new Integer(intValue);
}
catch(Exception e){
    System.out.println("Invalid String Value");
}
```

This example utilizes the `catch` statement to handle a non-legal integer string passed to the `Integer` class for conversion. Based on the value of the `intValue` string, the output of this code segment would be `"Invalid String Value"`.

char

The `char` reserved word describes a base Java data type containing a 16-bit character value. Later, in the section named "Data Types," you will focus on Java data types, but for now the following provides a brief example of `char` usage.

```
char keyHit = 'D';
if(keyHit = 'D')
    System.out.println("The D Key was Hit");
else
    System.out.println("You entered a key that I have no idea
➥what to do with");
```

The example declares the variable `keyHit` to hold a value of `D`. The `keyHit` variable is then used to make a decision of what message to display on the screen.

class

The class reserved word is used to signify the declaration of a Java object called a class. All defined objects must be declared with the reserved word, class. However, the modifiers preceding the class reserved word are optional. In Chapter 3 you will take a look at class access modifiers. For now, the following example declares a public class named myStuff.

```
public class myStuff{
   char sex = 'M';
}
```

continue

The continue statement proceeds with the next iteration of an enclosing loop. Looking back to the break statement, which terminates the executing loop, the continue statement does not terminate the loop like the break. Rather, the continue statement merely skips to the next iteration of the loop. The following provides an example of the continue statement's usage.

```
boolean test = false;
for(;;){
   if(test){
      System.out.println("One More Time!");
      continue;
   }
   break;
}
```

Also, the continue statement can be directed to continue at a predefined mark.

```
i:
for(;;){
   if(test){
      System.out.println("One More Time!");
      continue i;
   }
   break;
}
```

In this example, the break statement is never reached. At the point the continue statement executes, the program skips the remaining instructions continued in the loop. Later in this chapter, in "Java Loops," Java's loop facilities will be discussed, including the intricacies of the continue statement.

default

The default reserved word is used to signify a default condition handler in a multiple condition statement. Later in this chapter, in "Java Conditional Statements," you will focus on Java conditional statements, but for now the following provides a brief example of the type of facility the case statement provides.

```
byte value = -120;
switch (value){
    case 1: System.out.println("Umm!");
        break;
    case 2: System.out.println("Umm, Umm!");
        break;
    case 3: System.out.println("Wow!");
        break;
    default:System.out.println("No Handler");
}
```

In this way, the default statement declares a block of code as the handler for the case that no other case statement matches the requirements. That is, in the above statement the value of "No Handler" would be printed, based on the fact there is no case -120: statement to handle the value of value.

do

The do reserved word is used to signify the beginning of a do loop. Later in the chapter you will fully explore Java's loop facilities and nuances. For now, the following provides a brief example of a do loop construction.

```
do{
    System.out.println("This will print once");
}while(false);
```

double

The `double` reserved word describes a base Java data type containing a 64-bit real value. Later in this chapter, in "Data Types," you will focus on Java data types, but for now the following provides a brief example of `double` usage.

```
double mrGPA = 3.9999999;
if(mrGPA >= 4.0)
    System.out.println("Wow!");
else
    System.out.println("You are a LOOSER!");
```

This example declares the variable `mrGPA` to hold a value of `3.9999999`. The `mrGPA` variable is then used to make a decision of what message to display on the screen.

else

The `else` reserved word works in tandem with the `if` reserved word to form a conditional facility. Later in this chapter, in "Java Reserved Words," you will learn Java's reserved word capabilities. However, for now the following provides an example of forming a conditional with `if` and `else`.

```
double mrGPA = 3.9999999;
if(mrGPA >= 4.0)
    System.out.println("Wow!");
else
    System.out.println("You are a LOOSER!");
```

This example uses the `if` reserved word to form a test on the `mrGPA`. The `println` statement directly under the `if` is executed in the case that the test evaluates to a `true` value. Likewise, the `else` statement signifies the statement to execute if the test is evaluated to `false`.

extends

The `extends` reserved word is used to denote the inheritance of a declared class. In this way, a declared class can specify its parent class. The following example demonstrates the extends reserved word specifying a class's parent class.

```
class sweetFruit{
    public boolean sweet = true;
}
pubic class apple extends sweetFruit{
}
```

This example declared a class called sweetFruit, which is then used to extend the declared apple class. In Chapter 3 you will look at the Java object model more closely.

final

The final reserved word can be used as a declaration modifier for either a class or a method. In general terms, the final modifier ensures that subclasses cannot modify a provided resource. In the case of a class, any class declared as final may not be subclassed. Likewise, any method declared as final may not be overloaded in a subclass. The following example provides an example of each of these uses.

```
public class junkPile{
    public boolean isFull(){
        return true;
    }
}
```

```
public final class storage extends junkPile{
    public boolean isEmpty = false;
}
```

The following two examples are provided to show improper usage of the final modifier.

```
public final class junkPile{
    public boolean isFull(){
        return true;
    }
}
```

```
//The below line will produce a compiler error,
//due to the fact a final class is being extended.
public class storage extends junkPile{
   public boolean isEmpty = false;
}

public class junkPile{
   final public boolean isFull(){
      return true;
   }
}
public class storage extends junkPile{
public boolean isEmpty = false;

   //The following line will produce a compilation error

   public boolean isFull(){
      return super();
   }
}
```

finally

The `finally` reserved word is used as a default action for an exception block. In Chapter 3 you will focus on Java exceptions, but for now the following provides a brief example of the type of facility the `finally` statement provides.

```
String intValue = "H345";
try{
   Integer I = new Integer(intValue);
}
catch(Exception e){
}
finally{
   System.out.println("This Will ALWAYS Be Printed");
}
```

This example utilizes the `finally` print a statement, regardless if an execution is thrown or not.

float

The float reserved word describes a base Java data type containing a 32-bit real value. Later in this chapter, in "Data Types," you will focus on Java data types, but for now the following provides a brief example of float usage.

```
float mrGPA = 3.9999999;
if(mrGPA >= 4.0)
   System.out.println("Wow!");
else
   System.out.println("You are a LOOSER!");
```

This example declares the variable mrGPA to hold a value of 3.9999999. The mrGPA variable is then used to make a decision of what message to display on the screen.

for

The for reserved word is used to signify the beginning of a for loop. Later in the chapter, in "Java Loops," you will fully explore Java's loop facilities and nuances. For now, the following provides a brief example of a for loop construction.

```
for(int i =0;i < 200;++i)
   System.out.println("This will print 200 times");
}
```

goto

The goto statement redirects the program execution path to a predefined mark. In this way, the goto statement may act similar to the continue statement. The only difference between the two is that the continue statement has the ability to proceed to the next iteration of an enclosing loop. The goto statement has no such ability. To the contrary, the goto statement must be used with a predefined, labeled marker. The following demonstrates the goto statement's ability to redirect program execution.

```
startagain:
for(;;){
```

```
    if(test){
       System.out.println("Lets do that again!");
       goto startagain;
    }
    break;
}
```

if

The `if` reserved word provides a conditional branching facility for Java. In other words, based on a condition that can be evaluated to either `true` or `false`, a section of code may or may not be executed. Later in this chapter, in "Java Reserved Words'" you will discuss Java's reserved word capabilities. For now, the following provides an example of forming a conditional with `if` and `else`.

```
Boolean allGood = true;
if(allGood)
    System.out.println("All is Good!");
```

This example uses the `if` reserved word to form a test on the `all-Good` boolean value. The `println` statement directly under the `if` is executed in the case that the test evaluates to a `true` value.

implements

The `implements` reserve word may be appended onto a class declaration to specify the `interfaces` that `class` utilizes. In this way, Java has the ability to multiply inherent features from other classes. This will be discussed more in Chapter 3. For the time being, the following provides an example of the `implements` reserve word usage.

```
interface appTemplate {
    public void in(String data);
    public String getOut()
    public void runMe();
}

public class myApp implements appTemplate{
    private Sting inData = "";
    private Sting outData = "";
```

```
    public void in(String data){
        inData = data;
    }
    public String getOut(){
        return outData;
    }
    public void runMe(){
        outData = "Hello World";
    }
}
```

In this example, the interface specified three methods that are to be implemented by any class that wants to use its facility. The class myApp implements the interface by providing implementations for all methods specified by the interface. A class can implement any number of interfaces. However, an implementation must be provided for all declared methods, in all utilized interfaces.

import

The import reserved word includes a specified class file into the currently defined class. In this way, the containing class file may reference classes not directly declared with the body of the class file. The following demonstrates this principle.

```
import java.util.Hashtable;

public class storage extends Hashtable{

}
```

This example imports the Hashtable class from the java.util package. Notice that once the class has been imported, the class may then be referred to as Hashtable. The corollary to this statement is demonstrated in the following example where the import statement is not used.

```
public class storage extends java.util.Hashtable{

}
```

Both uses are correct. However, the first one is more common, and more convenient if the class will be referenced more than once.

instanceof

The instanceof statement provides a very powerful feature, but is not commonly used. instanceof is used to test to see if an object is an instance of a certain class. This concept might seem a little abstract, but think of the ability to take in a parameter of a generic object type, and then look into that object to find ancestry information. The following method does just that.

```
public class lookInto{
    public static void whatIsThis(Object in){
        if(Object instanceof Integer)
           System.out.println("This Object is an Integer");
        else
        if(Object instanceof Float)
           System.out.println("This Object is an Float");
        else
        if(Object instanceof Boolean)
           System.out.println("This Object is an Boolean");
        else
        if(Object instanceof byte[])//Note: All arrays are Objects
in Java.
           System.out.println("This a byte array");
    }
}
```

int

The int reserved word describes a base Java data type containing a 32-bit integer value. Later in this chapter, "Data Types," you will focus on Java data types, but for now the following provides a brief example of int usage.

```
int numberOfKids = 4;
if(numberOfKids >= 4)
   System.out.println("Wow! You have been busy!");
```

This example declares the variable numberOfKids to hold a value of 4. The numberOfKids variable is then used to make a decision of what message to display on the screen.

interface

The interface reserve word is used to define a template from which future classes may base development. In this way, Java has the ability to multiply inherent features from other classes. The following provides an example of the interface reserve word usage.

```
interface appTemplate {
   public void in(String data);
   public String getOut()
   public void runMe();
}

public class myApp implements appTemplate{
   private Sting inData = "";
   private Sting outData = "";

   public void in(String data){
      inData = data;
   }
   public String getOut(){
      return outData;
   }
   public void runMe(){
      outData = "Hello World";
   }
}
```

In this example the interface specified three methods that are to be implemented by any class that wants to use its facility. The class myApp implements the interface by providing implementations for all methods specified by the interface. A class can implement any number of interfaces. However, an implementation must be provided for all declared methods, in all utilized interfaces.

native

When, in the course of development, there comes a need to use natively implemented procedures, the native reserved words make it so. That is, when you want to call a procedure in a natively compiled library, the native reserved word provides the ability to prototype an external implementation. The following example is a `native` prototype example, which can be found in `java.lang.awt.image.ColorModel.java` package.

```
/* Throw away the compiled data stored in pData */
private native void deletepData();
```

new

The `new` reserved word is used to dynamically create new objects. `new` may also be viewed as a memory resource allocation operator, but the first definition is more Java-savvy. That is, Java does not have a concept of de-allocation of memory. So, to say that `new` is a memory allocation operator would imply the existence of a de-allocation, which does not exist. The following example demonstrates the `new` operator.

```
Hashtable h;
h = new Hashtable(10);
```

null

The `null` reserved word provides a constant signifying the absence of value. For example a string might contain the value `""`, which is an empty string. However, the string can also be set to `null`, signifying that the string contains no value whatsoever. The following provides a brief demonstration of this fact.

```
String A = "";
String B = null;
if(A == null)
   System.out.println("A = null");

if(B == null)
   System.out.println("B = null");
```

The example above would produce the output A = null; however, the output B = null would not be displayed.

package

The package reserved word is used to denote a class's membership in a defined group. In Chapter 3 you will learn more about the packaging of objects. But for now, a loose definition of a package is a simple collection of classes. The following example declares a class to be a member of the example package.

```
package example;

public class funWithNumbers{
    public Sting One = "One";
    public Sting Two = "Two";
    public Sting Three = "Three";
    public Sting Four = "Four";
}
```

protected

The protected reserved word is used to denote class, method, and field level access control. Specifically, the protected modifier is used to limit class, method, and field level access to members of the current package. You will get knee-deep into access modifiers in Chapter 3. For now the following provides an example of class and method usage of the protected reserved word.

```
package example;

protected class funWithNumbers{
public Sting One = "One";
    public Sting Two = "Two";
    public Sting Three = "Three";
    public Sting Four = "Four";
}
```

This defined class is declared as protected. This means that only other members of the example package can use and subclass the funWithNumbers class.

```
package example;
```

```
public class funWithNumbers{
    protected One = "One";
    protected String theStuff(){
        return "myStuff";
    }
}
```

The class defined in this example is declared as `public`. This means that the class is visible to all classes. However, the field `One` and the method `theStuff` are declared as protected, effectively limiting their visibility to the `example` package.

private

The `private` reserved word is used to denote class, method, and field level access control. Specifically, the `private` modifier is used to limit class, method, and field level to the currently defined class file. The following provides an example of class and method usage of the `private` reserved word.

```
package example;

private class funWithNumbers{
    public Sting One = "One";
    public Sting Two = "Two";
    public Sting Three = "Three";
    public Sting Four = "Four";
}

public class funWithNumbers extends funWithNumbers{
    private String theStuff(){
        return "myStuff";
    }
}
```

This defined class is declared as `private`, and then is followed by a `public` class definition. Notice the `public` class extends the `private` class. This is only possible if these two files are declared with the same class file. Furthermore, the `funWithNumbers` class declares a private field and method, which are only visible within the `funWith-Numbers` class.

public

The public reserved word is used to denote class, method, and field level access control. Specifically, the public modifier is used to completely open access to all. In other words, the private modifier limited access to the currently defined class file, and public is the antithesis. public provides wide open access to all declared classes, methods, and fields. The following provides an example of class and method usage of the public reserved word.

```
public class funWithNumbers extends funWithNumbers{
    public String theStuff(){
        return "myStuff";
    }
}
```

This defined class is declared as public, allowing open access to all class inheritance, visible method calls, and field usage.

return

The return reserved word is used to exit from a containing method body. That is, the return statement is used to return program execution to the calling method. The following demonstrates this capability.

```
public String returnOne(){
    return "One";
}
```

In this code, the return reserved word is used to return a String value of One to the calling method.

short

The short reserved word describes a base Java data type containing a 16-bit integer value. Later in this chapter, in "Data Types," you will focus on Java data types, but for now the following provides a brief example of short usage.

```
short numberOfKids = 4;
if(numberOfKids >= 4)
    System.out.println("Wow! You have been busy!");
```

This example declares the variable numberOfKids to hold a value of
4. The numberOfKids variable is then used to make a decision of
what message to display on the screen.

static

The static reserved word is used as a field and method modifier
to specify a permanent nature. Fields and methods declared as
static are guaranteed to exist only in a single memory location at
a time, regardless of the number of instances. For example, every
time you create a new class, a memory region is declared for every
non-static field. If the field is declared as static, all instances of
the class share the same variable memory storage region. In this
way, static methods and fields remain constant throughout all
instances of a class.

Another nice feature about static methods and fields is their ability to be accessed without creating an instance of the class. The
following example demonstrates this case.

```
public class javaConst{
    public static int coolFactor = 10;
    public static Sting getCaffeineLevel(){
        return "Real HIGH!";
    }
}
public class myClass{
    public void printMe(){
        System.out.println("Cool Factor = " +
➥javaConst.coolFactor);
        System.out.println("Caffeine Level is "+
➥javaConst.getCaffeineLevel());
    }
}
```

Notice in this example that coolFactor and getCaffeineLevel() were
accessed without creating a new instance of the class javaConst.
Rather, all static methods and fields can be accessed by merely
directly referencing the class name.

super

The super reserved word provides direct access to a class's parent class. In this way, subclassed classes may access parent methods even if the subclass overloads the desired method. The following example shows a common use of the super reserved word.

```
public class helpMe{
   public void callPolice{
   System.out.println("Let Me Call the Police!");
   }
}

public class help extends helpMe{
   public void callPolice{
      System.out.println("I think We should Call the Police!");
   }
   public void doSomthing(){
      super.callPolice();
   }
}
```

In this example, the outcome of a call to doSomthing would be Let Me Call the Police!

switch

The switch reserved word is used to signify a multiple condition statement. Later in this chapter, in "Java Conditional Statements," you will focus on Java conditional statements, but for now the following provides a brief example of the type of facility the switch statement provides.

```
byte value = -120;
switch (value){
   case 1: System.out.println("Umm!");
      break;
   case 2: System.out.println("Umm, Umm!");
      break;
   case -120: System.out.println("Wow!");
      break;
}
```

In this way, the switch statement defines a facility for the checking of value against predefined handlers. The output from the code above would be Wow!, which corresponds with the case specified of -120.

synchronized

The synchronized reserved word provides thread method serialization facilities. Chapter 4, "Threads in the Java Platform," will focus on Java thread support and proper use of the synchronized reserved word. For now, the following is a sample synchronized method declaration.

```
public synchronized String get(int index){
    return b[I];
}
```

this

The this reserved word provides direct access to the resources of the current class. In this way, a subclassed class may provide a reference to itself. The following example shows a common use of the this reserved word.

```
public class helpMe{
    public void callPolice{
        System.out.println("Let Me Call the Police!");
    }
}

public class help extends helpMe{
    public void callPolice{
        System.out.println("I think We should Call the Police!");
    }
    public void doSomthing(){
        this.callPolice();
    }
}
```

In this example, the outcome of a call to doSomthing would be I think We should Call the Police!

throw

The throw reserved word raises an exception. Through the throw mechanism, a method has the ability to raise an exception to signify an invalid state. The following provides a brief taste of the throw mechanism.

```
public void doConversion(int convertMe) throws Exception {
    if (convertMe != 1220)
        throw(new Exception("Invalid value"));
}
```

throws

The throws reserved word is used to denote a method that raises one or more exceptions. Through the throws method modifier, a method has the ability to raise any number of exceptions. The following provides a brief taste of the throws mechanism.

```
public void doConversion(int convertMe) throws Exception {
    if (convertMe != 1220)
        throw(new Exception("Invalid value"));
}
```

transient

The transient reserved word provides a way to specify non-persistent class information. That is, when a class is presented to a persistent storage subsystem, all fields specified as transient will not be committed to storage. For example, in the following class, the field saveMe will be saved to persistent storage, but ingoreMe will not be saved.

```
public class storage{
    public int savMe = 3;
    public transient int ingoreMe = 5;
}
```

try

The try reserve word is used to signify the beginning of an exception block. The world of Java exceptions is covered in depth in Chapter 3. For now, the following provides a brief taste of the try block.

```
String intValue = "H345";
try{
    Integer I = new Integer(intValue);
}
catch(Exception e){
    System.out.println("Invalid String Value");
}
```

void

The void reserved word is used to denote a method that does not return a value. In this way, a method proceeded by a void specifier can be viewed as a procedure. Likewise, a method not preceded by a void specifier can be viewed as a function. The following example demonstrates the usage of the void specifier.

```
public void doMe(){
    System.out.println("Hello!");
}
```

volatile

The volatile reserved word provides a facility for the synchronization of local thread variables with the master variable pool. That is, Java provides threads the ability to maintain local copies of shared variables to expedite execution. However, this means that the thread must reconcile the local variable with the master resource at a synchronization point. So to save having to manually reconcile local variables, the volatile reserved word can be used to direct the JVM to automatically handle such a facility. The following provides an example of a volatile field.

```
static volatile int count = 2;
```

while

The while reserved word is used to signify the beginning of a while loop, and the ending condition of a do loop. Later in the chapter, in "Java Conditional Statements," you will fully explore Java's loop facilities and nuances. For now, the following provides a brief example of a while loop construction.

```
while(false){
   System.out.println("This will never be  printed");
}
```

Data Types

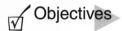 Knowing how Java stores and handles primitive data types is valuable for optimized development and required knowledge for the Certified Developer Examination.

All programming languages provide a set of standard devices for storing data. The difference comes when you start looking at what types of storage devices are provided, how large the storage elements are, and how much freedom you have in converting these between the different types of storage devices. For example, most incarnations of the Basic programming language provide a single numeric storage device to hold integer and real values. Other languages like C provide four different integer, and two real storage devices. In this example, Java could be classified as similar to C for data storage devices, but different enough from other languages to justify an in-depth analysis.

Java provides eight primitive data types, each providing its own distinct role. The following provides a list of all Java primitive data types and a discussion of each. Although some aspects of each data type may overlap, knowing each data type and what are legal data type conversions is imperative exam information.

▶ short

▶ byte

- ▶ int

- ▶ long

- ▶ char

- ▶ boolean

- ▶ float

- ▶ double

short

The short data type provides an integer 16-bit storage device with a valid range of -32768 to 32767. Table 2.1 is a quick reference conversion chart for the short data type.

Table 2.1

short Conversion Chart.

Convert To	Legal	Requires Cast
byte	Yes	Yes
int	Yes	No
long	Yes	No
float	Yes	No
double	Yes	No
char	Yes	No
boolean	No	N/A

byte

The byte data type provides an integer 16-bit storage device with a valid range of -128 to 127. Table 2.2 provides a quick reference conversion chart for the byte data type.

Table 2.2

byte Conversion Chart.

Convert To	Legal	Requires Cast
short	Yes	No
int	Yes	No
long	Yes	No
float	Yes	No
double	Yes	No
char	Yes	No
boolean	No	N/A

int

The int data type provides an integer 32-bit storage device with a valid range of -2147483648 to 2147483647. Table 2.3 provides a quick reference conversion chart for the int data type.

Table 2.3

int Conversion Chart.

Convert To	Legal	Requires Cast
short	Yes	Yes
byte	Yes	Yes
long	Yes	No
float	Yes	No
double	Yes	No
char	Yes	Yes
boolean	No	N/A

long

The long data type provides an integer 64-bit storage device with a valid range of -9223372036854775808 to 9223372036854775807.

Table 2.4 provides a quick reference conversion chart for the long data type.

Table 2.4

long Conversion Chart.

Convert To	Legal	Requires Cast
short	Yes	Yes
byte	Yes	Yes
int	Yes	Yes
float	Yes	No
double	Yes	No
char	Yes	Yes
boolean	No	N/A

char

The char data type provides an integer 16-bit storage device with a valid range of 0 to 65536. Table 2.5 provides a quick reference conversion chart for the char data type.

Table 2.5

char Conversion Chart.

Convert To	Legal	Requires Cast
short	Yes	Yes
byte	Yes	Yes
int	Yes	Yes
long	Yes	Yes
float	Yes	Yes
double	Yes	Yes
boolean	No	N/A

boolean

The `boolean` data type provides an integer 1-bit storage device representing `true` and `false` values. Table 2.6 provides a quick reference conversion chart for the `boolean` data type.

Table 2.6

boolean Conversion Chart.

Convert To	Legal	Requires Cast
short	No	N/A
byte	No	N/A
int	No	N/A
long	No	N/A
float	No	N/A
double	No	N/A
char	No	N/A

float

The `float` data type provides an integer 64-bit storage device that is specified in IEEE Standard for Binary Floating-Point Arithmetic, ANSI/IEEE Std. 754-1985 (IEEE, New York). Table 2.7 provides a quick reference conversion chart for the `float` data type.

Table 2.7

float Conversion Chart.

Convert To	Legal	Requires Cast
short	Yes	Yes
byte	Yes	Yes
int	Yes	Yes
long	Yes	Yes
double	Yes	No
char	Yes	Yes
boolean	No	N/A

double

The double data type provides an integer 32-bit storage device that is specified in IEEE Standard for Binary Floating-Point Arithmetic, ANSI/IEEE Std. 754-1985 (IEEE, New York). Table 2.8 provides a quick reference conversion chart for the double data type.

Table 2.8

float Conversion Chart.		
Convert To	Legal	Requires Cast
short	Yes	Yes
byte	Yes	Yes
int	Yes	Yes
long	Yes	Yes
float	Yes	Yes
char	Yes	Yes
boolean	No	N/A

Operators

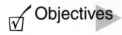 Objectives

Java provides an assortment of operators to aid development, all of which are required knowledge for the Certified Programmer Examination.

In the statement 1 + 1 = 2, the number 1 is an *operand* and the + is the *operator*. Operators are specific tasks, or comparisons, that take in an operator and produce a result. The plus sign is an operator that takes in two parameters, adds them together, and returns the value. Java provides a large body of operators that can be broken down into five classifications based on their function: arithmetic, relational, bit-manipulation, assignment, and miscellaneous.

Some of the operators you will probably recognize right off the bat, others you may struggle with. For example, the + operator is addition, which might be obvious, = is assignment, which might be as obvious, and >>> is the zero-filled right-shift operator that only a rocket scientist might recognize.

Java evaluates all expressions in a left-to-right fashion, which is fairly standard. Likewise, Java conforms to mainstream operator support. However, explicit knowledge of all Java operators is required to successfully pass the Certified Java Programmer exam. The following is a list of all five operator types, with a description of each operation. After the list you will find a discussion of each of the five operator groups.

Java Arithmetic Operators:

+	Addition operator
-	Subtraction operator
*	Multiplication operator
/	Division operator
%	Modulus operator

Java Relational Operators:

>	Greater than operator
<	Less than operator
>=	Greater than or equal to operator
<=	Less than or equal to operator
!=	Not equal to operator
==	Equal to operator
!	Not operator
&&	AND operator
¦¦	OR operator

Java Bit-Manipulation Operators:

~	Complement operator
&	AND operator
¦	OR operator

^	Exclusive OR operator
<<	Left shift
>>	Right shift
>>>	Right Zero Filled shift

Java Assignment Operators:

=	Assignment
++	Increment and assign
—	Decrement and assign
+=	Add and assign
-=	Subtract and assign
*=	Multiply and assign
/=	Divide and assign
%=	Take modulus and assign
¦=	OR and assign
&=	AND and assign
^=	Exclusive OR and assign
<<=	Left shift and assign
>>=	Right shift and assign
>>>=	Zero filled right shift and assign

Java Miscellaneous Operators:

(type)	Convert to type
instanceof	Is instance of a class?
new	Creates a new object
? :	If...Then selection

Java Arithmetic Operators

Java's arithmetic operators are fairly mundane. In fact, most of them you would expect to find on an ordinary calculator. Addition, subtraction, multiplication, division, and modulus functions comprise the arithmetic operators. However, as mundane as the arithmetic operators may be, Tables 2.9 provide an example usage of each operator.

Table 2.9

Operand Type Acceptance.

byte	short	int	long	character	boolean	String	float	double
Addition Operand (i = 2 + 3;)								
Yes	Yes	Yes	Yes	No	No	Yes	Yes	Yes
Subtraction Operand (i = 2 - 3;)								
Yes	Yes	Yes	Yes	No	No	No	Yes	Yes
*Multiplication Operand Type Acceptance (i = 2 * 3;)*								
Yes	Yes	Yes	Yes	No	No	No	Yes	Yes
Division Operand Type Acceptance (i = 2 / 3;)								
Yes	Yes	Yes	Yes	No	No	No	Yes	Yes
Modulus Operand Type Acceptance (i = 2 % 3;)								
Yes	Yes	Yes	Yes	No	No	No	Yes	Yes

Java Relational Operators

Relational operators provide the means for comparison between two different variables or constants. As with the arithmetic operators, the relational operators are very much straightforward. However, lumped into this category are Java's logical operators. Unless you come from a C background, the logical operators might seem foreign. But not to fear, the following tables (2.10 to 2.18) will provide a discussion of each of the nine relational operators.

Table 2.10

Greater Than Operand Type Acceptance.

byte	short	int	long	character	boolean	String	float	double
Yes	Yes	Yes	Yes	Yes	No	No	Yes	Yes

The greater-than operator is used to test magnitude difference between two operands. The following example can be read, "if 2 is greater than 3."

```
if(2 > 3){}
```

Table 2.11

Less Than Operand Type Acceptance.

byte	short	int	long	character	boolean	String	float	double
Yes	Yes	Yes	Yes	Yes	No	No	Yes	Yes

The less-than operator is used to test magnitude difference between two operands. The following example can be read, "if 2 is less than 3."

```
if(2 < 3){}
```

Table 2.12

Greater Than or Equal to Operand Type Acceptance.

byte	short	int	long	character	boolean	String	float	double
Yes	Yes	Yes	Yes	Yes	No	No	Yes	Yes

The greater-than-or-equal-to operator is used to test magnitude difference between two operands. The following example can be read, "if 2 is greater than or equal to 3."

```
if(2 >= 3){}
```

Table 2.13

Less Than or Equal to Operand Type Acceptance.

byte	short	int	long	character	boolean	String	float	double
Yes	Yes	Yes	Yes	Yes	No	No	Yes	Yes

The less-than-or-equal-to operator is used to test magnitude difference between two operands. The following example can be read, "if 2 is less than or equal to 3."

```
if(2 <= 3){}
```

Table 2.14

Not Equal to Operand Type Acceptance.

byte	short	int	long	character	boolean	String	float	double
Yes	Yes	Yes	Yes	Yes	Yes	Yes	Yes	Yes

The not-equal operator is used to test equality between operands. Besides the above specified legal primitive types, the not equal operator can be used to test object reference equivalence. The following example can be read, "if 2 is not equal to 3."

```
if(2 != 3){}
```

Table 2.15

Equal to Operand Type Acceptance.

byte	short	int	long	character	boolean	String	float	double
Yes	Yes	Yes	Yes	Yes	Yes	Yes	Yes	Yes

The equal operator is used to test equality between operands. Besides the above specified legal primitive types, the equal operator can be used to test object reference equivalence. The following example can be read, "if 2 is equal to 3."

```
if(2 == 3){}
```

Table 2.16

Logical Not Operand Type Acceptance.

byte	short	int	long	character	boolean	String	float	double
No	No	No	No	No	Yes	No	No	No

The logical-not operator denotes logical negation. The following example can be read, "if true is equal to not false."

```
if((true) == (!false)){}
```

Table 2.17

Logical And Operand Type Acceptance.

byte	short	int	long	character	boolean	String	float	double
No	No	No	No	No	Yes	No	No	No

The logical and operator denotes logical dependence. The following example can be read, "if a equals a, and b equals b."

```
if((a==a ) && (b==b)){}
```

Table 2.18

Logical Or Operand Type Acceptance.

byte	short	int	long	character	boolean	String	float	double
No	No	No	No	No	Yes	No	No	No

The logical or operator denotes logical non-dependence. For example, the following example can be read, "if a equals a, or b equals b."

```
if((a==a ) ^^ (b==b)){}
```

Java Bit-Manipulation Operators

Bit-manipulation operators deal with the movement and manipulation of binary information. For example, the complement operator(~) has the ability to flip all the bits contained in a primitive data type. Knowing what to use and where is entirely dependent on your need. However, bit-manipulation operators are definite testable items. For this reason, the following sections provide detailed information on each of the seven Java bit-manipulation operators.

~ Complement Operator

The complement operator is used to do a full bit flip. That is, what bits were 0 will be set to 1, and likewise what bits were 1 will be set to 0. The following provides an example usage of the complement operator.

```
byte i  = 0xFF; // i = 11111111
i = ~i;
//i = 00000000
```

& AND Operator

The AND operator directly compares each bit of two elements in turn. If the two bits being analyzed are both 1s, then the resultant bit will be 1. If either of the bits are 0s, then the resultant bit will be a 0. The following provides an example usage of the AND operator.

```
byte i  = 0x0F; // i = 00001111
byte j  = 0xF0; // i = 11110000

byte result = i & j;
//result = 00000000
```

| OR Operator

The OR operator directly compares each bit of two elements in turn. If either bit is a 1, then the resultant bit will be a 1. The following provides an example usage of the OR operator.

```
byte i  = 0x0F; // i = 00001111
byte j  = 0xF0; // i = 11110000

byte result = i ¦ j;
//result = 11111111
```

^ Exclusive OR Operator

The Exclusive OR operator compares each bit of two elements in turn. If either bit is a 1 and the other is 0, then the resultant bit will be a 1. If both bits are 1, or if both bits are 0, the result is a 0. The following provides an example usage of the Exclusive OR operator.

```
byte i  = 0x1F; // i = 00011111
byte j  = 0xF0; // i = 11110000

byte result = i ^ j;
//result = 11101111
```

<< Left Shift Operator

The left shift operator is used to shift all bits to the left by the specified positions. The bits added from the left will be zeros, and the excess bits on the left will be truncated. The following provides an example usage of the left shift operator.

```
byte i  = 0xFF; // i = 11111111
byte result = i << 2;
//result = 11111100
```

>> Right Shift Operator

The right shift operator is used to shift all bits to the right by the specified number of positions. The bits added to the left side will be the same value as the leading sign bit. That is, if the sign bit is set, all bits padded from the left will be 1s. Likewise, if the sign bit is not set, all bits padded from the left will be 0s. The following provides an example usage of the right shift operator.

```
byte i  = 0xF0; // i = 11110000
byte result = i >> 2;
//result = 11111100
```

>>> Right Zero Filled Shift Operator

The right zero filled shift operator is used to shift all bits to the right by the specified positions. The bits added to the left side will be 0, regardless of the leading sign bit. The following provides an example usage of the right shift operator.

```
byte i  = 0xF0; // i = 11110000
byte result = i >>> 2;
//result = 00111100
```

Java Assignment Operators

Java's assignment operators can be viewed in two categories. The first category contains new operators. The second group is nothing more than previously discussed operators with an equal sign appended to them. To minimize the amount of redundant information, you will look at each of the two categories in varying detail.

The first category of Java assignment operators provides basic assignment and shorthand notation. That is, the base assignment operator (=), which assigns value A to value B, as demonstrated here.

```
B = A;
```

The other two elements in the first category of Java assignment operators provide common shorthand for incrementing and decrementing a value, as the following example explains.

```
A++; // A++ is the same as A = A + 1;
A--; // A-- is the same as A = A - 1;
```

The second group of Java assignment operators can best be described as previously discussed operators with an assignment coupled to them. Although this definition might not seem intuitive at this point, once you have seen a couple of these hybrid operators their meaning will be crystal clear. The following list provides a brief example of each hybrid assignment operator.

 Note

> Java's compound assignment operators are more efficient than their expanded notation.

+=   Add and assign:

```
A += 2; // A += 2 is the same as A = A + 2;
```

-=   Subtract and assign:

```
A -= 2; // A -= 2 is the same as A = A - 2;
```

*=   Multiply and assign:

```
A *= 2; // A *= 2 is the same as A = A * 2;
```

/= Divide and assign:

```
A /= 2; // A /= 2 is the same as A = A / 2;
```

%= Take modulus and assign:

```
A %= 2; // A %= 2 is the same as A = A % 2;
```

¦= OR and assign:

```
A ¦= 0xFF; // A ¦= 0xFF is the same as A = A ¦ 0xFF;
```

&= AND and assign:

```
A &= 0xFF; // A &= 0xFF is the same as A = A & 0xFF;
```

^= Exclusive OR and assign:

```
A ^= 0xFF; // A ^= 0xFF is the same as A = A ^ 0xFF;
```

<<= Left shift and assign:

```
A <<= 2; // A <<= 2 is the same as A = A << 2
```

>>= Right shift and assign:

```
A >>= 2; // A >>= 2 is the same as A = A >> 2
```

>>>= Zero filled right shift and assign:

```
A >>>= 2; // A >>>= 2 is the same as A = A >>> 2
```

Java Miscellaneous Operators

The last group of Java operators consists of a collection of various types of operators. The only thing these operators share is the fact that they each have nothing in common with one another. For this reason you will look at each individually.

The cast operator is used to convert between various variable types. Earlier, in the "Data Types" section, the cast operator was used to show how primitive data types could be converted to other primitive types. However, the final operator of the miscellaneous group is the selection operator, which is demonstrated in the following example.

```
float f = 1.34;
int i = (int)f; //The variable f is casted into an int.
```

The instanceof and new operators found in the Miscellaneous group have previously been defined in the section "Java Reserved Words" earlier in this chapter. However, the final operator of the Miscellaneous group is the selection operator, which is demonstrated in the following example.

```
int i  = ?(2==3):2:4;
//is equivalent to
if( 2 == 3)
    i == 2;
else
    i == 4;
```

Java Conditional Statements

 Objective

Java provides a set of standard condition statement constructs. Nevertheless, each form of Java conditional statement is required knowledge for the Certified Java Programmer Examination.

A conditional statement provides the program with the ability to make a discussion that will alter the program's path of execution. Another way to look at a conditional statement is as a fork in the road. One path goes one way, the other goes a different way; which way to follow is based on your decision. Conditional statements allow programs the ability to branch based on an evaluated decision.

An if statement is the section of code that decides whether to go left or right. The if statement is used to guide an application to one of two execution paths based on a Boolean decision. For example, a simple conditional might test to see if an error has occurred. If yes, exit the program. Otherwise, continue processing. The following are the two acceptable formats for the if statement.

```
if ( boolean expression ){
statement
...
}

if ( boolean expression ){
  statement
```

```
   ...
}
else{
   statement
   ...
}
```

The following example will always print `"All Good"`.

```
if( true ){ //the decision
   //if the decision true path
   System.out.println("All Good");
}
else{
   //if the decision false path
   System.out.println("Bad, Real Bad");
}
```

The `switch` statement provides the identical purpose as the `if` statement. In fact, any `switch` statement can be rewritten as an `if`, and vice versa. `switch` is sometimes called a decision tree; given one variable, execution can take multiple paths. The following provides the valid `switch` syntax.

```
Switch( expression ){

   case value: {}
   ...
   default : {}
}
```

The following example will always print `"X = 2"`.

```
int X = 2;

switch( X ){
   //Based on the Value of X, one of the following will be per-
➥formed.
case 1:{
            System.out.println("X = 1");
            break;
         }

   case 2:{
```

```
            System.out.println("X = 2");
            break;
    }
  //If all else fails, execute the default section
default:{
  System.out.println("X = " + X);


    }
}
```

For the most part, the if statement is more widely used. The switch provides a specialized form of conditional, where the if can be used for anything. When to use which is completely up to you, just remember that any switch statement can be written as an if. Most newcomers to programming find that the if statement is more like English syntax, and prefer its use. Even many experienced programmers still only use if statements because they make the code more readable to a broader spectrum of readers. In the end, it simply boils down to your own personal preference.

Java Loops

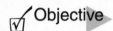 Objective ▶ Knowledge of all forms of Java loops facilities is required knowledge for the Certified Java Programmer Examination.

Without the ability to loop, a computer would be as useless as a pen with no ink. The fact is that computers derive their entire computing power from the ability to quickly loop, or iterate, through a series of instructions. Without loops, code would be much more difficult to write and less flexible. For example, think how you would write a program to count to 10 without a loop. You probably would write 10 lines that print out the numbers from 1 to 10, instead of one print statement that printed the counter of a loop. Computers have always had, and will always have, the ability to loop through a block of instructions. The Java loop statements are merely the methods to access this functionality.

The for loop in Java and C/C++ is the most common. In C/C++ there is no choice. There are other loops in Java, but the for loop remains supreme. The legal syntax for a for loop in Java is:

```
for(initialization; loop condition ; increment ){
      code to be looped
}
```

The following example prints a count from 0 to 29.:

```
//Count from 0 to 29
for(int i = 0; i < 30; ++i){
    System.out.println("i = " + i);
}
```

The `for` loop's general form provides an iterative loop. This means that each time the loop is executed, a counter maintains the number of times the loop has been executed. The `while` loop has no such iteration mechanism; it has a simple Boolean decision of when to terminate the loop. The syntactical valid form of `while` is as follows:

```
while (condition){
    code to be looped
}
```

The following example will print `loop forever` until either your machine dies, or you terminate the process.

```
while (true){
    System.out.println("loop forever");
}
```

Notice in the `while` loop how the decision to continue to loop is made at the beginning of the loop. What if you wanted to make that decision after the loop had executed? The `do` loop provides a "post decision" loop to facilitate this need. The following is the correct syntax for a `do` loop:

```
do {
    code to loop
} while(condition)
```

The following example will print `This will print once` once.

```
do{
    System.out.println("This will print once");
}while(false);
```

Loops in many ways are not as cut-and-dried as conditional statements. First, there are more loops to choose from than conditionals. Second, although one loop can take the place of the other loops, like the if and switch statements, the readability is diminished. For example, the for loop can represent a while loop, but the while loop implementation more closely represents true English grammar. If you are coming from the C/C++ world, you will probably only use the for loop. If you are coming from a Pascal background, you might use all loops equally. In the end, it once again boils down to personal preference.

Summary

At the level of reserved words and operators, many languages can appear similar. Java, in particular, encapsulates ideologies and syntax from many different languages. In this chapter, the Java language syntax and most all of the fundamental pieces of the language were presented. With this knowledge under your belt, you are primed and ready to experience what is driving flocks of programmers to Java.

This chapter presented the building blocks of the Java language. Chapter 3 will build on this knowledge by exploring the world of Java objects and exceptions.

The following section provides ten practice questions to aid your comprehension of the material presented in this chapter. Firm knowledge of language syntax is primary to the Certified Developer Exam, and you are urged to use the following questions to test your knowledge before you move on. If you are like most developers and are saying to yourself, "I know this stuff!" ignore your gut feeling and proceed with the practice questions. The questions presented in the exam are sure to stump even the most experienced developer.

Review Questions

1. Which of the following is not a reserved word?

    A. NULL

    B. switch

    C. catch

    D. instanceof

    E. None of these

2. Given a byte with a value of 01110111, which of the following statements will produce 00111011?

    Note : 01110111 = 0x77

    A. 0x77 << 1

    B. 0x77 >> 3

    C. 0x77 >> 1

    D. 0x77 >>> 1

    E. C and D

3. The statement A %= 3; can best be described as

    A. A equals A divided by 3

    B. A equals A in 3 digit percentage form

    C. A equals A modulus 3

    D. None of the above

4. What is the error in the following code?

```
public class myClass{
    public abstract void myfunction();
}
```

    A. public abstract void myfunction();

    B. public class myClass{

    C. No error

5. An interface provides which of the following?

    A. A template for further development

    B. A mechanism for further development

    C. An alternative to class declarations

    D. A and C

    E. A and B

6. Which of the following best describes the public class modifier?

    A. Allows only classes in the current package to use its facilities

    B. Allows other classes to subclass it

    C. Opens the class up for usage and subclassing to all

    D. A and B

7. A package is?

    A. A collection of interfaces

    B. A collection of classes

    C. A way to provide naming for a group of related classes

    D. All of the above

8. Which of the following is NOT a primitive Java data type?

    A. `int`

    B. `boolean`

    C. `float`

    D. `double`

    E. `long`

9. If there is an error in the following code, what is it?

```
public class myClass{
    public String myfunction(){
        String out = "Hello";
        int i = 0xff;
        i >>>= 4;
        out += i;
        return(out ¦ i);
    }
}
```

    A. `i >>>= 4;`

    B. `out += i;`

    C. `return(out ¦ i);`

    D. No error

10. The `throws` reserved word provides which of the following?

    A. Raises an exception

    B. Triggers an event

    C. Defines the exception(s) a method can raise

    D. Defines the exception a method can raise

Review Answers

1. A

2. E

3. C

4. B

5. E

6. C

7. D

8. B

9. C

10. C

Answers to Test Yourself Questions at Beginning of Chapter

1. D

2. A

C h a p t e r

Java Objects and Exceptions

One of the stranger things about C/C++ is the ability to write pure C code, but call the code *objectized*. That is, the primary feature that C++ added to C was object support. However, C++ is backwards-compatible with C. In this way, you could write non-objectized code, run it through a C++ compiler, and call it C++. This is not the case with Java.

In Java everything is an object. If you want to create a simple program to say "Hello World," you have to create an object which encapsulates the program. For example, the following is a simple "Hello World" program.

```java
public class helloWorld{
    public static void main(String args[]) {
        System.out.println("Hello World");
    }
}
```

The above declares a `class`, or object, named `helloWorld`, in which the only method of the class displays the string `Hello World`. This might seem like a meaningless example, but the point is that everything in Java is an object.

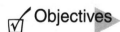 Objectives

- ▶ Object declarations and usage

- ▶ Casting between objects

- ▶ Java exceptions

- ▶ Specific knowledge of the reserved words `class`, `extends`, `public`, `private`, `protected`, `final`, `throw`, and `throws` is required for this chapter and can be found in Chapter 2, "Java Language Internals."

Test Yourself! Before reading this chapter, test yourself to determine how much study time you will need to devote to this section.

1. What modifier would be used to limit a method's visibility to only the currently defined class?

   A. public

   B. private

   C. protected

   D. static

2. What modifier would be used to limit a method's visibility to only the other classes and subclasses in the current package?

   A. public

   B. private

   C. protected

   D. static

Answers are located at the end of the Chapter...

Java Objects

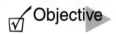 **Objective**   Java is an object-oriented language. Knowing how to declare and use objects is vital to development and required knowledge for the Certified Programmer Examination.

Unlike most concepts in computer science that you can point to and say, "This. This is what it looks like," objects are slightly more elusive. Java's essence lies in object technology; mastering Java requires comprehensive knowledge of objects and the object-oriented paradigm.

Almost every programming language has the notion of a grouping of data elements. For example, Pascal supports a record, C supports a struct, and database-centric languages, such as Delphi, PowerBuilder, and Visual Basic, utilize records in a database table. Each of these examples serves the common purpose of grouping together pieces of information into a single device. Once the device is created, or formed, the device can be referenced as a single element all to itself, and each element it contains can likewise be referenced individually. This type of data element grouping is generally referred to as data encapsulation.

Data encapsulation is the cornerstone of Object theory, but object theory takes data encapsulation to the next step. That is, encapsulating a group of data elements into a single entity provides one-stop access to the stored information. Above and beyond the access of data elements, an object has the ability to store code to access, modify, and present the stored information. The following example provides a simple object, or class, for the storage of personal weight information.

```
public class myWeight{
    public int weight;
    public int goalWeight;
    public int numberOfPoundsLeft;
}
```

The class in this code encapsulated three separate elements of information into a single unit named myWeight. Everything in the above example could be facilitated without the use of any object-oriented methodologies. However, the following example uses an object's ability to encapsulate code and data into a single element.

```java
public class myWeight{
    public int weight;
    public int goalWeight;
    public int numberOfPoundsLeft;
    public String lostWeight(int howMuch){
        weight -= howMuch;
        numberOfPoundsLeft -= howMuch;

        if(numberOfPoundsLeft <= 0)
            return "You Did IT!!!!";
        else
            return "Keep on going. Only " + numberOfPoundsLeft
➡+ " pounds left.";
    }
    public String gainedWeight(int howMuch){
        weight += howMuch;
        numberOfPoundsLeft += howMuch;

        return "The point of this is to LOOSE weight!";
    }

}
```

As you can see from the previous example, objects allow data and code to be encapsulated into a single entity, which leads directly into the accepted definition of an object: A single extensible, reusable, self-contained unit of data and code encapsulation.

Declaring a Class

Declaring a class in Java is very straightforward, and requires little more than some rote memorization. The following declares a class named firstClass which extends Object.

```java
public class firstClass extends Object{
}
```

As you can see, there are three pieces of the class declaration, beginning with the reserved word public and ending with Object.

The following diagrams and defines each of the key elements of a class declaration.

▶ Class Visibility and Access—`public`, `protected`, `default`, or `final`

▶ Class Naming—`firstClass`

▶ Class Inheritance—`final`, `extends Object`

Class Visibility and Access

 Firm understanding of Java's method and object visibility modifiers is required knowledge for the Certified Programmer Examination.

In Chapter 2, the concept of class visibility was discussed, but only at preliminary level. Drilling down deeper into the subject of class visibility, you need to focus on the two key factors defining the visibility of a class. These are: "Who has access to use the class?", and "Who has access to inherit the class's properties?". The answers to these questions lie in the complete understanding of the four visibility modifiers: `public`, `private`, `protected`, and default. Table 3.1 provides a quick overview of each of the supported class visibility modifiers.

Table 3.1

Table of class visibility modifiers.	
Modifier	Visibility
`public`	Unrestricted
`protected`	Accessible only from within the package, but extensible anywhere
`default`	Accessible and extensible only from within the package
`private`	Accessible only from within declared class file

The first and most unrestricted class visibility modifier is `public`. Classes that are declared as `public` have no restrictions on visibility and usage. For example, the following example declares a public class named myPublicClass.

```
public myPublicClass{
    public int useMe;
}
```

Declaring the myPublicClass class as public allows the class to be extended, as demonstrated below.

```
public myNewPublicClass extends myPublicClass {
    public int useMe;
}
```

Likewise, public classes have unrestricted access, as the example demonstrates.

```
public myTestClass {
    public myPublicClass useMe;
}
```

The protected and default modifiers offer varying degrees of visibility for declared classes. Both these modifiers rely on the concept of packages which will be covered later in this chapter. For now, Table 3.1 provides a sense of what these two modifiers offer; this information will be expanded upon later.

Lastly, the private modifier forbids other classes from sub-classing, or using the defined class.

Class Inheritance

The concept of data encapsulation was discussed earlier in this chapter, as well as the standard object facilities. One of the most important concepts to understand is that an object's ability to encapsulate information and code into a single entity provides the mechanism for object inheritance.

Inheritance is a concept everyone is familiar with. As human-beings we inherit a legacy of generic characteristics from previous generations. Eye color, hair color, height, and even weight are inherited from your parental genetic code. Likewise, your parents' genetic code was inherited from their parents, and so on. In this way, a hierarchy of genetic characteristics is constructed.

In Java, an object is the product of prior generations. However, to avoid the "chicken and the egg" problem, you should know that all Java objects are the product of the `java.lang.Object` class. That is, all Java-created classes have at least one parent class, which is `Object`. The following provides a list of the characteristics which are inherited by all Java classes.

Public Methods of `java.lang.Object`:

- ▶ `Object clone()` Creates a copy of the current class.

- ▶ `boolean equals(Object)` Checks to see if the passed class reference is equal to the current class.

- ▶ `void finalize()` Specifies a method to be performed when this class is garbage collected.

- ▶ `Class getClass()` Returns the `java.lang.Class` object of this class.

- ▶ `int hashCode()` Returns a hashcode for this class. This method is used with the `java.util.Hastable` class.

- ▶ `void notify()` Notifies a single waiting thread on a change in condition of another thread. This method will be covered in depth in Chapter 5, "Java API."

- ▶ `void notifyAll()` Notifies all of the threads waiting for a condition to change. This method will be covered in depth in Chapter 5.

- ▶ `String toString()` Returns a string that represents the value of this object.

- ▶ `void wait()` Waits to be notified by another thread of a change in this class. This method will be covered in depth in Chapter 5.

- ▶ `void wait(long)` Waits to be notified by another thread of a change in this class, or the specified time has elapsed. This method will be covered in depth in Chapter 5.

▶ wait(long,int) Waits to be notified by another thread of a change in this class, or the specified time has elapsed. This method will be covered in depth in Chapter 5.

Listing 3.1 provides a demonstration of object inheritance. In this example, a set of three standard banking functions are formed into a objectized representation. Located in the source are comments describing each piece of functionality.

Listing 3.1 Class inheritance

```java
//Base Class holds the amount
class transaction{
   public int amount;
   public transaction(int Amount){
      amount = Amount;
   }
}
//Withdraw inherits transaction
class withdraw extends transaction{
   public int from;
   //Overrides base constructor
   public withdraw(int Amount, int From){
      super(Amount);
      from = From;
   }
}
public class bankApp{
   public static void main(String args[]) {
      //Create a new withdraw object
      withdraw W = new withdraw(78,2);
      //print the Amount
      sysytem.out.println("The Amount is " + W.amount);
      //print the From Account
      sysytem.out.println("From Account " + W.from);
      //print the Amount
```

```
        sysytem.out.println("The Objects String " + W.toString());


    }
}
```

Figure 3.1 provides an object diagram of the classes formed in Listing 3.1. Notice how `transaction` class inherits all of `Object`'s public members, and likewise withdraw inherits all of `Object`'s and transaction's members.

Figure 3.1

*Complete class
structure diagram
for Listing 3.1.*

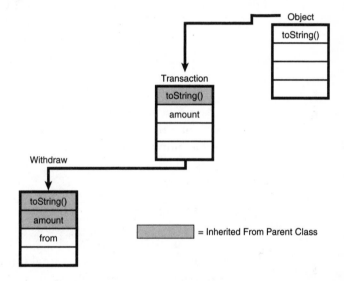

= Inherited From Parent Class

In spite of this inheritance, it is not beneficial to allow future generations access to internal support functions. For this reason, Java provides a set of member modifiers which restrict inheritance and usage. For example, Listing 3.1 declares all members as `public` to ensure complete inheritance and usage. The following list provides a detailed description of each of these modifiers.

▶ `public`   The `public` modifier specifies full inheritance and usage rights to all accessing and inheriting classes.

▶ `private`   Almost an exact opposite of the `public` modifier, the `private` modifier is only accessible to other members of the current class. That is, a member that is declared as `private` does not exist for any class other than the current class.

▶ default The default modifier, referred to as "package," only allows classes in the current package access to specified members.

▶ final The final modifier forbids any future generations from overriding the specified member.

Constructors and Creation Order

Look back to Listing 3.1 and find the method named transaction in the transaction class. As you can see, this method is used to initialize the initial value of the amount member. More generally, the transaction method is called an *object constructor*. That is, an object constructor is a method that is called when a new instance of an object is created.

An object is a single autonomous entity which contains specific, contextual information. For example, the following object encapsulates a single employee's data file.

```java
public class employee{
    public int numMonthWithCompany;
    public boolean newHire;
}
```

The numMonthWithCompany denotes the total number of months the employee has been with the company. Also, the newHire field flags the existence of a new employee. With this implementation, external code will need to accompany the object in order to properly set the newHire flag. However, the following example utilizes an object constructor to set both the numMonthWithCompany and the newHire flag.

```java
public class employee{
    public int numMonthWithCompany;
    public boolean newHire;
    //The following is the constructor,
    //which will be called when a new instance
    //of the object is created.
    public employee(int Months){
        newHire = Months == 0;
        numMonthWithCompany = Months;
    }
}
```

Constructors provide the means to adapt an object to its runtime environment. In this way, more generic objects can be created which contain the ability to morph themselves into various configurations based on a specific need. A good analogy to a constructor is the birth of a baby. Upon the baby being "constructed," or born into the world, sensory input defines its initial condition. Usually, a newborn is so overwhelmed with sensory input that screaming is its normal defined output. However, it might be possible to modify the environment in which the newborn is first exposed to, in an attempt to modify the screaming behavior. In programming terms, modify the constructor input to change the initial state.

The concept of a child giving birth to its parents sounds inherently strange. However, in some programming languages that is exactly the case, specifically with the programmatic concept of creation order defining when objects are created, as well as when their constructors are called.

As shown in Figure 3.2, there is a direct hierarchy of parental objects for every object. Also, you can see that each object relies on functionality found in parental objects. This being the case, when a new object is created, all supporting parental objects must also be created. More concretely, if each object has its own constructor, each object in the hierarchy must execute its constructor whenever a child object is created. Figure 3.2 illustrates the creation of the defined objects in Listing 3.2.

As you can see from Figure 3.2, Java implements a top-down creation policy. That is, the top-most parent in the object hierarchy is created first, sequentially followed by each subsequent parent until the bottom-most object is created. This is demonstrated in Listing 3.2

Figure 3.2

*Complete class
structure diagram
for Listing 3.2.*

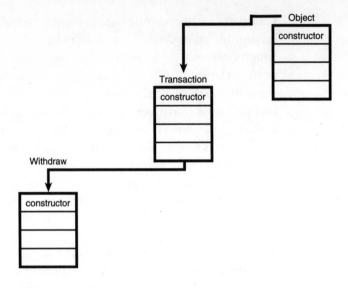

Listing 3.2   Class construction

```
class SayHello{
    public SayHello(String in){
        System.out.println(in);
    }
}


class Class1{

    public Class1(){
        System.out.println("Class1");
    }
}


class Class2 extends Class1{

    public SayHello S = new SayHello("Class2 Member");
    public Class2(){
        super();
```

```
                System.out.println("Class2");
        }
    }


class Class3 extends Class2{
    public SayHello SE = new SayHello("Class3 Member");
    public Class3(){
        super();
        System.out.println("Class3");
    }
}


public class creationOrder {


    public static void main(String args[]) {
        Class3 C = new Class3();
        System.out.println("All Done");
        System.out.println("(press Enter to exit)");
        try {
            System.in.read();
        } catch (Exception e) {
            return;
        }
    }
}
```

The main body of the code in Listing 3.2 creates a Class3 object.
Based on the top-down policy of Java, the proper creation would
be Class1, Class2, and then Class3. The following program output
proves this to be the case.

```
Class1
Class2 Member
Class2
Class3 Member
Class3
All Done
(press Enter to exit)
```

Java creation order policy can be summarized by, "The parent must be created before the child," which makes intrinsic sense based on the order of nature. A child must have parents in order to be born, and a class is guaranteed to have its parent's resources available upon execution of the constructor.

Implementing Interfaces and Abstract Method

Thus far, the concept of an object has been defined as an encapsulation of data and code. However, what if you merely want to define an object, but not populate the encapsulated content? That is, say you are creating a file folder to contain important documents. You would undoubtedly create a folder for each appropriate heading. Then, as you receive documents you can put them into the predefined folders. In this way, you are predefining the storage of your information. Java supports the concept of predefining methods without supplying an implementation.

For example, the following defines a base class named `ticTacToe` which defines three methods. However, no implementation is supplied for any of the three methods. In this way, the class is defining a mechanism for inherited objects to implement.

```
public class ticTacToe{
public void X(int pos){}
  public void O(int pos){}
public boolean gameOver(){
    return false;
  }
}
```

This example utilizes the brute force method of declaring a template for future objects. Although this approach might work, it is not the most efficient mechanism to achieve the goal. The following code example defines the same object template using the `abstract` and `interface` definitions.

```
public abstract class ticTacToe{
   public abstract void X(int pos);
```

```
    public abstract void O(int pos);
    public abstract boolean gameOver(int pos);
}
public interface ticTacToe{
    public void X(int pos);
    public void O(int pos);
    public boolean gameOver(int pos);
}
```

Both the `abstract` and `interface` methods of defining object templates produce similar results. However, the two methods contain drastically different side effects. Chapter 11, "Creating Java APIs," will discuss the difference between the `abstract` and `interface` methods of defining object templates. But, in an attempt to summarize a future discussion: A class can inherit only one class, but it can implement as many interfaces as it desires.

In many cases, a single object cannot encapsulate all of the various pieces involved in a solution. More commonly, solutions are grouped into distinct units of objects called *packages*. Each package can contain one or more individual classes. However, a package is a single unit of encapsulated classes.

In Java, a package is a grouping of classes which are commonly used together. On the usage side, a package allows for multiple classes to be imported into a class with a single import statement. For example, the following imports all of the classes found in the common Java IO facilities.

```
import java.io.*;
```

From the development perspective, a package can define a partition of thought. For example, if you were creating a banking application, you might choose to store all banking-related classes in a single package. The following defines a class named `withdraw` to reside in the `banking` package.

```
package banking;
public class withdraw{
    public int amount;
}
```

Object Casting

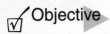 Objective

Java's dynamically extensible nature requires complete knowledge of object casting facilities. For this reason, object casting knowledge is required for the Certified Programmer Examination.

Casting, in the typical programmatic usage, refers to the translation between one storage device and another. Chapter 2, "Java Language Internals," discussed the concept of casting from numerical storage devices, such as int and float. Translating 1.00 into 1 is a logical and useful translation of a numeric value. Casting of classes is equally useful and logical, but requires a bit more thought.

Classes are storage devices, just like an int or a float. However, as stated earlier in this chapter, every class contains at least one parent. Thus, the complexity of casting between objects is a function of the number of parents a class has. For example, Figure 3.3 displays a graph showing two classes sharing a single parent. For each class in the hierarchy there is a separate set of legal casts.

Figure 3.3

Two classes share a single parent.

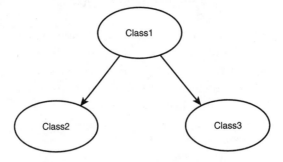

In order to simplify and classify the vast commutations and permutations of various object castings, Java provides the following two laws governing the actions of object casting.

▶ Casting Down

▶ Casting Up

Casting Down

Casting down refers to the directional casting that narrows the containing storage device. For example, casting from a long to an int would narrow the amount of storage required to store the numeric value. When casting objects, narrowing more specifically refers to the narrowing of functionality from a subclass to a parent. Casting down, more appropriately called "unsafe casting," narrows functionality from a subclass and converts the object into a parental class.

Based on the nature of casting down, not all operations are legal at runtime. For example, the following code defines Class2 and Class3 to share a common parent.

```
class Class1{}
class Class2 extends Class1{}
class Class3 extends Class1{}
```

The following code example provides an example of each case in which the Class1, Class2, and Class3 could be casted into one another. Granted, not all class hierarchies are this simplistic, nevertheless all down-casting scenarios can be broken into the following cases.

Always legal:

```
Class1 mysteryClass = new Class2;
Class2 MyClass = (Class2) mysteryClass;
```

Always legal:

```
Class1 mysteryClass = new Class3;
Class3 MyClass = (Class3) mysteryClass;
```

Compilation error and never legal:

```
Class1 mysteryClass = new Class3;
Class2 MyClass = (Class2) mysteryClass;
```

Possibly legal—if and only if "mysteryClass = new Class3;":

```
Class3 MyClass = (Class3) mysteryClass;
```

Possibly legal—if and only if `"mysteryClass = new Class2;"`:

```
Class2 MyClass = (Class2) mysteryClass;
```

Casting Up

Unlike casting down, casting up is always legal and valid. However, it takes a little practice to spot an up-casting usage. Revisiting the numerical casts, casting from an `int` to a `long` is an example of an up cast. Likewise, casting from a subclassed class to a parent class is always legal, thus the nickname "safe cast."

To demonstrate the classification of up casting operations, the following classes provide a simplistic class hierarchy. Once again, not all hierarchies will be this simple, but all can be localized to serve as a model.

```
class Class1{}
class Class2 extends Class1{}
class Class3 extends Class2{}
```

Always legal:

```
Class2 mysteryClass = new Class2;
Class1 MyClass = (Class1) mysteryClass;
```

Always legal:

```
Class3 mysteryClass = new Class3;
Class1 MyClass = (Class1) mysteryClass;
```

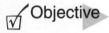 Java's exceptions provide a powerful facility for the trapping and propagation of runtime error. Knowing how to catch, handle, and declare exceptions is crucial for effective Java development and is required knowledge for the Certified Programmer Examination.

Exceptions

Simply put, an exception is an object that is created to signify an event. For example, if at some time a section of code tries to execute a division by zero, an exception will be raised to notify of the error. In this way exceptions provide a mechanism for the handling of runtime errors.

Normally, when an object is defined it is assigned a specific name. However, in the case of exceptions, an object is created before a specific name has been assigned. Think of it as a ball that is thrown into the sky. When the ball is airborne, no one person retains ownership of the ball, and in a sense it is free. But when the ball makes its descent to the earth, it can either be caught or plunge to the ground. If it is caught, the ball then is the property of the person who caught the ball. An exception does not possess an owner until the exception is caught, at which time the exception is handled. Otherwise, the uncaught exception will be propagated to the calling block of code.

To more fully understand the concept of an exception, it is imperative to analyze the handling and throwing of exceptions individually.

Handling Exceptions

Revisiting the ball analogy, all exceptions must be caught. Programmatically speaking, "caught" can be defined as a `try...catch` block. For example, the following code catches an exception, which is thrown by a call to `System.in.read()`.

```
try {
   System.in.read();
} catch (Exception e) {
   return;
}
```

Chapter 2, "Java Language Internals," discusses the proper syntax for both the `try` and `catch` facilities. Additionally, Chapter 2 discusses the use of the `finally` facility which provides clean-up after a `try` block has been executed. However, for this discussion, the specific point of interest regarding `try` blocks lies in the how a `try` block is executed, and the specific exception which may be thrown.

Program Flow with Exceptions

When a program reaches the `try` statement, execution continues through the course of the supplied statements. In the case of the previous example, the statement executed inside the try block is `System.in.read()`. If this statement executes without an exception, program execution proceeds to the next line following the `try...catch` block. However, if an exception is raised, the statement within the `catch` block will be executed. Following the raised exception, program execution will proceed to the next line following the `try...catch` block.

In the following example, the `finally` statement is used to execute a clean-up statement after the execution of the try block. Whether an exception is raised or not, program execution cannot leave the `try...catch` block without executing. The result being that the output bye-bye is guaranteed to be output every time the `try...catch` block is executed.

```
try {
    System.in.read();
} catch (Exception e) {
    return;
}
finally{
    System.out.println("bye-bye");
}
```

Handling Specific Exceptions

Thus far, all examples provided have been catching the generic base class for all exceptions named `Exception`. For example, the following code catches the generic `Exception`.

```
try {
    System.in.read();
}catch (IOException e){
    System.out.println("IO exception");
} catch (Exception e) {
    return;
}
```

This example first attempts to catch the specific IOException thrown by the System.in.read(). In the case that System.in.read() throws an exception other than the IOException, the generic Exception is caught. In this manner, Java provides the ability to catch specific, contextual exceptions, or provide a generic handler. The following is a list of the standard Java exceptions. Each is thrown to signify a specific event, and each is a subclass of Exception. The following is a complete list of the standard exceptions thrown by java.lang members provided for example purposes only—they will not appear on the test.

▶ ArithmeticException

▶ ArrayIndexOutOfBounds Exception

▶ ArrayStoreException

▶ ClassCastException

▶ ClassNotFoundException

▶ CloneNotSupported Exception

▶ Exception

▶ IllegalAccessException

▶ IllegalArgumentException

▶ IllegalMonitorState Exception

▶ IllegalStateException

▶ IllegalThreadState Exception

▶ IndexOutOfBoundsException

▶ InstantiationException

▶ InterruptedException

▶ NegativeArraySize Exception

▶ NoSuchFieldException

▶ NoSuchMethodException

▶ NullPointerException

▶ NumberFormatException

▶ RuntimeException

▶ SecurityException

▶ StringIndexOutOfBounds Exception

Throwing Exceptions

Using the reserved word `throw`, which is specified in Chapter 2, custom exceptions and Java-supplied exceptions can be created. In the following example, the method throws an `Exception` to signify an invalid parameter value. Notice the parameter passed to the constructor of the `Exception` object. This parameter is used to provide a textual message explaining the exception, and will be explained in full in Chapter 5, "Java API."

 Note

> The process by which an exception comes into being is called *throwing* an exception. That is, programmatically Java provides the ability for you to create your own exceptions, or propagate uncaught exceptions. In both cases, the reserved words `throw` and `throws` are employed to facilitate the creation and propagation of exceptions.

```java
public void doSomeThing(int Value)throws Exception{
   if(Value < 0)
      throw new Exception("Bad Value");
   return;
}
```

In the previous example, the method declaration includes the reserved word `throws`. This signifies to the Java compiler that the defined method can throw an exception of type `Exception`. Any number of exceptions can be thrown from a single method. However, all potentially thrown exceptions must be handled by the calling method. The following code is an example of how to propagate an uncaught exception.

```java
public void doSomeThing()throws Exception{
   try {
      System.in.read(); // Throws IOException
   }catch (RuntimeException e){
      System.out.println("IO exception");
   }
   //Exception not caught, propagate up the call stack.
}
```

Summary

To many outside the object-oriented world, the idea of storing data and code in a single, accessible device doesn't seem all that important. It isn't until concepts such as inheritance and exceptions are presented that the true appreciation of objects can be assimilated. Java is a true object-oriented language, and in this chapter you learned why.

As stated in this chapter, everything is an object. Unlike C++, which provides programmers the ability to implement non-object solutions, Java requires all to conform to the object-oriented paradigm. Everything from pure data containers to code libraries are encapsulated into objects. The contents of this chapter focused on how to use and create your own objects.

Exceptions provide a facility to handle runtime errors. This chapter discussed exceptions, and how they can be used to inform of and handle various runtime occurrences. Included in this discussion were examples of the `try`, `catch`, `finally`, `throw`, and `throws` language facilities.

In Chapter 4, "Threads in the Java Platform," objects will be expanded to include threads and multiple objects executing simultaneously. This is not to say that the knowledge gained from this chapter is just a prelude to Chapter 4. Rather, this chapter contains core testable information. All the concepts and details found in this chapter constitute a good 60% of the Certified Programmer Examination. Knowing the information found in this chapter is crucial to successfully passing the Certified Programmer Examination. For this reason, the following exam questions are provided to give samples of what you can expect on the exams, and what to potentially revisit.

Review Questions

1. The following code listing contains one error, which is:

```
public abstract class myClass{
    public abstract fun(int Value){}
}
```

   A. public abstract class myClass

   B. public abstract fun(int Value){}

   C. Incomplete class definition

   D. Class must contain a constructor

2. Which answer best describes the following object hierarchy?

```
class class1{}
class class2 extends class1{}
class class3 extends class3{}
```

   A. class3's parent class is class2, and class2's parent class is class1.

   B. class3's parent class is class2, class2's parent class is class1, and class1's parent is Object.

   C. class1's parent class is class2, and class2's parent class is class3.

   D. class1's parent class is class2, class2's parent class is class3, and class3's parent is Object.

3. What modifier would be used to limit a method's visibility to only the currently defined class?

   A. public

   B. private

   C. protected

   D. static

4. What modifier would be used to limit a method's visibility to only the other classes and subclasses in the current package?

   A. public

   B. private

   C. protected

   D. static

5. The following defines an object hierarchy.

```
class class1{}
class class2 extends class1{}
class class3 extends class3{}
```

When is the following method valid?

```
public class3 castMe(class1 ref){
   return (class3)ref;
}
```

   A. Always

   B. Never

   C. If and only if ref references an class3 object

   D. If and only if ref references an class2 object

6. The following defines an object hierarchy.

```
class class1{}
class class2 extends class1{}
class class3 extends class3{}
```

When is the following method valid?

```
public class1 castMe(class3 ref){
   return (class1)ref;
}
```

   A. Always

   B. Never

C. If and only if ref references an class3 object

D. If and only if ref references an class2 object

7. What is the output of the following try...catch block?

```
try{
    int I;
    return;
}catch(Exception e){
    System.out.println("I am Here");
    return;
}finally{
    System.out.println("Hello Nurse!");
}
```

A. Hello Nurse!

B. No output

C. I am Here

D. Depends on the creation of the int I;

8. The following code contains a single error, which is

```
public class myClass{
    public void testMe(int Value){
        throw new Exception("Throw ME!");
    }
}
```

A. public class myClass{

B. public void testMe(int Value){

C. throw new Exception("Throw ME!");

D. No Error. You are trying to trick me!

9. A method may only implement a single interface.

A. True

B. False

10. A method may only extend a single class.

    A. True

    B. False

Review Answers

1. B

2. A

3. B

4. C

5. C

6. A

7. A

8. C

9. B

10. A

Chapter

Threads in the Java Platform

This chapter requires good working knowledge of Java classes, class declaration, and object-oriented design. You should also have an understanding of the content discussed in Chapter 3, "Java Objects and Exceptions," to fully comprehend the focus of this chapter.

This chapter focuses on creating, using, and coexisting with Java threads. Chapter 3 described an object as an autonomous entity in which data and code can be encapsulated. If you stop and think about what this statement means, you will come to the realization that each object is a self-contained executable. That is, an object contains all the data and code needed to be a self-contained program. The concept of threads puts this principle to the test by allowing each object to execute individually.

If you are from a UNIX programming background, forking a separate process is second nature. Having multiple processes running simultaneously is not a new concept, but threads aren't truly separate processes. At the JVM level, threads are merely separate execution paths sharing memory address space.

In this chapter, you will learn not only how to use threads in Java, but also the issues surrounding Java threads. Concepts such as thread scheduling, synchronization, and native thread implementations are all topics of discussion in this chapter. By the conclusion of this chapter you will be a master of concurrent Java programming.

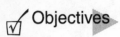 Objectives

▶ What constitutes a thread

▶ Thread priority and scheduling

▶ Writing concurrent code

Test Yourself! Before reading this chapter, test yourself to determine how much study time you will need to devote to this section.

1. How are thread priority and thread scheduling related?

   A. They aren't.

   B. It depends on the thread scheduling algorithm used to implement the JVM.

   C. Thread priority is specified when a thread is to be executed next.

   D. Thread priority is used to determine the next thread to execute from the waiting thread pool.

2. The Runnable interface is used for what?

   A. A marathon

   B. Defining a thread

   C. Defining a class that can be executed by a thread

   D. Defining a class to execute a new thread

Answers are located at the end of the Chapter...

What Is a Thread?

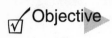 Objective

Knowing how to declare and use Java threads is required knowledge for the Certified Programmer Examination.

Each object is a self-contained, programmatic entity, which implies that each object can run independently of other executing objects. A Java thread is an object that can run concurrently with the main application flow and other threads.

A general classification of a thread is a process, or lightweight process, that can be concurrently executed in a shared memory space with other threads. In some environments, this definition of threads loosely translates into separately executing applications, with some overhead to allow each application access to a shared memory pool.

There are many different flavors of threads, but for now the goal is to master Java-flavored threads. Later in this chapter, you will learn how and why Java threads interact with the various native platform thread implementations, but for now you'll learn about creating Java threads.

What are Threads Good For?

Consider an applet that displays an animation sequence while presenting the user with an arbitrary GUI. It is not common practice to have the user wait until the animation is loaded and completed until he can use the interface. On the contrary, the animation is considered a background task, where allowing the user to use the interface is the foremost priority. This and many other concurrent execution needs can be solved with a thread implementation.

Threads as a development tool have been around for a long time. However, it wasn't until the release of Windows 95 that threads began ringing in the ears of the general computer market. The marketing ploy presented by Microsoft stated that, "Your applications will run faster with our new thread support." This statement isn't far from true. Proper use of the thread paradigm allows a

computer to schedule different thread executions, based on resource utilization. That is, if one thread is waiting for information
to be fetched from the hard drive, another thread can be executed on the free CPU cycles. In this way, threads increase the performance of application execution by optimizing machine resources.

On a low level, threads break applications down into a finer granularity for the optimization of resources. On a high, and program-
mer-friendly level, threads provide your programs with the ability to
do multiple things at once. Revisiting the animation in the applet
GUI, a thread provides the ability to execute the loading and presenting of the animation as a separate task. Other uses include
"spawning" a separate thread to complete a complicated processing
task, using a thread as a background media loader, and creating
individual threads to handle client requests in a server application.
Regardless of the application, Java thread support provides ready-
to-use facilities to optimize any process.

Creating a Thread

As you will see, the basic framework for a thread is identical to the
creation of a class. The only differences are semantic overhead
and a few required methods. The following is a complete definition of a thread called runMeTOO.

```java
public class runMeTOO implements Runnable {

   public  Thread This_Thread = null;

   public void start(){

      if (This_Thread == null){

         //Creates a new thread to be executed
         This_Thread = new Thread(this);
         //Starts the new thread and calls run()
         This_Thread.start();
      }
   }

   public void stop(){
```

```
        //Terminate the thread
        if (This_Thread != null)
            This_Thread.stop();
        This_Thread = null;
    }

    public void run(){

    //Your Code Here!

    }
}
```

As bare as the previous might look, this skeleton is the standard base building block for all Java threads. To understand this skeleton fully, each piece must be analyzed in turn, starting with class declaration.

Thread Class Definition

The first line of the skeleton class begins with the declaration of the new thread class.

```
public class runMeTOO implements Runnable
```

What makes this declaration assume the characteristics of a thread lies in the implementation of the runnable interface. However, do not think of the runnable interface as the entire mechanism for a Java thread. To the contrary, a runnable interface merely provides a standard execution point for java.lang.Thread. That is, the runnable interface requires only that the run() method be implemented. There is nothing in the runnable interface that defines the characteristics of a thread. java.lang.Thread requires a class to implement the runnable interface in order to execute the class as a thread.

Creating and Starting a Thread

In the skeleton thread definition class, a single field was defined as follows:

```
public  Thread This_Thread = null;
```

The variable This_Thread is used to hold a reference to the Thread class responsible for executing the currently defined runnable interface. Confused? The concept of a class being executed by a separate, contained class might seem a little odd. But, the light begins to dawn when the concept is broken down into its principle elements.

The following start() method is responsible for executing the current thread.

```
public void start(){

    if (This_Thread == null){

        //Creates a new thread to be executed
        This_Thread = new Thread(this);
        //Starts the new thread and calls run()
        This_Thread.start();
    }
}
```

As you can see, there is more to the start() method than a simple call. In fact, the start() method is creating a new Thread class by passing in a reference to the currently defined runMeTOO class, and then calling the start() method of the newly constructed Thread class. In this way, the new Thread is initialized, or constructed, to execute the runMeTOO class. In Chapter 5, "Java API," the complete Thread class will be explored. However, for now accept the idea that you cannot create a working Thread class without a runnable interface, and that the Thread class contains a start()method which begins the execution of the constructed Thread class.

Stopping a Thread

For various reasons, having the ability to stop a thread's execution is essential. For example, when an application or applet needs to terminate, all threads must be stopped. For this reason, Java threads contain a stop() method call to terminate a thread's execution.

The following code, provided in the previous thread skeleton, provides an all-in-one thread termination facility:

```
public void stop(){

    //Terminate the thread
    if (This_Thread != null)
        This_Thread.stop();
    This_Thread = null;
}
```

As you can see, the heart of the stop() method lies in a call to This_Thread.stop(), which is calling java.lan.Thread.stop(). Chapter 5 will further discuss the operating characteristics of the stop() method call. Nevertheless, this skeleton code can be generically used to terminate a thread's execution.

Your Code Here!

The final piece required in developing your own thread is your code. This is a small detail, but one that is ultimately important. In the skeleton thread code provided, the following run() method denotes where to put your code:

```
public void run(){

  //Your Code Here!

  }
```

The run() method gets invoked when the thread's start() method is invoked. Once invoked, the run() method will execute until one of the following run() termination conditions occurs:

▶ run() terminates naturally. In the case where a thread has a predetermined task to perform, after the task is completed the run() method will return.

▶ The stop() method is called. As mentioned before, the stop() method terminates a thread's execution. This termination directly translates into exiting the run() method.

▶ External JVM event. In extreme cases, events such as garbage collection and paging to a new HTML page in a browser may temporarily terminate all running threads.

Because the defined thread skeleton is a class in itself, you have free rein to add any fields and methods required to facilitate your thread's functionality. However, the thread's main execution branch must be defined within the run() method.

Executing a Thread

Once a thread has been defined, execution can be initiated with only two lines of code. For example, the following code creates and executes the thread runMeTOO:

```
runMeTOO  T1 = new runMeTOO();
T1.start();
```

In this code, a variable named T1 was defined and initialized to be of type runMeTOO. The variable was then used to call the runMeTOO class's start() method, which in turn creates a new Thread object.

An alternative method that can be used to begin a new thread's execution is demonstrated in the following example:

```
Thread  T1 = new Thread(new runMeTOO());
T1.start();
```

This method begins by creating a Thread object and constructing it with a new instance of the runMeTOO implementation of the runnable interface. Once the Thread has been created, the method start() in java.lang.Thread is invoked to execute the thread. This method provides more direct access to the actual thread object executing the runnable interface.

Both methods of executing a new thread essentially facilitate the same task. Both create and execute the defined runnable interface, but each provides a separate way to reference the running thread. However, both methods do succeed in the task of executing a specified thread, which will run until normally or abnormally terminated.

Real World Example

In an attempt to provide an example of how threads can be used, Listing 4.1 demonstrates a server-side Java thread use. In the example, the server sits and listens for connections from arbitrary client applications. Once a connection has been made, a thread is spawned to handle each client connection.

Listing 4.1   Thread Example—Loop-Back Server!

```java
import java.util.Hashtable;
import java.util.Enumeration;
import java.net.*;
import java.io.*;



class ClientChild implements Runnable
{
   //Socket to Client Connection
   public  Socket  Child;
   //Placeholder if the thread can be destroyed
   public  boolean Dead        = true;
   //Reference to current thread
   public  Thread Child_Thread = null;


   //Constructor
   public ClientChild(Socket child){
       Child = child;
   }


   //Start-up new thread
   public void start(){
     if (Child_Thread == null){
        Child_Thread = new Thread(this);
        Child_Thread.start();
     }
   }
```

```java
//Stop the currently executing thread
public void stop(){
    if (Child_Thread != null)
        Child_Thread.stop();
    Child_Thread = null;
}


//Main Application Loop.
//Loop-Back all Data! Fun!
public void run(){
    Dead = false;
    System.out.println("New Client Created");
    try{
        DataInputStream ClientIn = new DataInputStream(
                Child.getInputStream());
        OutputStream ClientOut = Child.getOutputStream();
//create a socket to localhost
        Socket ToMe = new Socket("127.0.0.1",6253);
        DataInputStream ServerIn = new DataInputStream(
                ToMe.getInputStream());
        OutputStream ServerOut = ToMe.getOutputStream();

        for(;;){

            if(ClientIn.available() != 0){
                byte tmp[] = new byte[ClientIn.available()];
                ClientIn.readFully(tmp);
                ServerOut.write(tmp);
                ServerOut.flush();
            }

            if(ServerIn.available() != 0){
                byte tmp[] = new byte[ServerIn.available()];
                ServerIn.readFully(tmp);
```

continues

Listing 4.1　Continued

```
                    ClientOut.write(tmp);
                    ClientOut.flush();
                }
            }
        }catch(Exception e){
            Dead = false;
            return;
        }
    }
}


//Main Server Class
class PAServer extends Object{
    //Main Server Socket
    private      ServerSocket SRVR;
    //New Child Socket
    private      Socket Child;

    //Contains all the threads
    private      Hashtable ThreadStorage;
    private      ClientChild child_proc;

    //Main Server Loop
    public void run(){

        if(!BindServer())
            return;

        //Create Thread Storage
        ThreadStorage = new Hashtable(10);
        System.out.println("Loop-Back Server Running");

        for(;;){
            //Get A new client connection - blocking call
            if((Child = AcceptClient()) == null)
                break;
```

```
            child_proc = new ClientChild(Child);
            ThreadStorage.put(Child.getInetAddress(),child_proc);
            child_proc.Dead = false;
            child_proc.start();
            //Clean out all dead threads
            DoGC();
        }
        //terminate nicely
        try{
            SRVR.close();
        }catch (Exception ex){
            //there is a problem exit
            System.out.println("Termination Error");
            return;
        }
    }


    private void DoGC(){

        ClientChild tmp_child;
        Object key;
        for (Enumeration e = ThreadStorage.keys() ;
    ➥e.hasMoreElements();){
            key = e.nextElement();
            if(ThreadStorage.get(key) != null){
                tmp_child = (ClientChild) ThreadStorage.get(key);
                if(tmp_child.Dead){
                    tmp_child.stop();
                    ThreadStorage.remove(key);
                }
            }
        }
    }
```

continues

Listing 4.1 Continued

```
        private  boolean BindServer(){
           int PORT = 6253;

           System.out.println("Binding Port = " + PORT);

           try{
               SRVR = new ServerSocket(PORT);
           }catch (Exception ex){
               //there is a problem exit
               System.out.println("Binding Error");
               return(false);
           }
           return(true);
        }


       private Socket AcceptClient(){
          Socket tmp;
          //accept on the port - this will block until a client is
➥accepted
          try{
              tmp = SRVR.accept();
          }catch (Exception ex){
              //there is a problem exit
              System.out.println("Accept Error");
              return(null);
          }
          return(tmp);
       }
    }

    //Main Public Launcher
    public class CSPassiveAgent {
```

```
public static void main(String args[]) {
    PAServer Server = new PAServer();
    Server.run();
}
}
```

Although Listing 4.1 does little more than a recursive loop-back, it lays the framework for any socket-based server application. That framework is to use a separate thread for each new client request.

Thread Scheduling and Priority

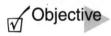 With multiple thread execution, simultaneous timing issues come into play. For this reason, knowing about Java's thread scheduling facilities is required knowledge for the Certified Programmer Examination.

Threads provide the ability to concurrently execute separate execution branches. From the programmatic level, a thread can be created to go down one path, while other program logic explores another. However, the number of threads that can be concurrently executed is not a function of the number of processors contained in the local machine. This leads to the conclusion that threads need to take turns executing.

As discussed in Chapter 1, "Java and the Java Virtual Machine (JVM)," the JVM is an entire computer architecture. Included in the architecture are hooks to support separately executing threads. However, unless a Java application is running on a Java-Chip, a native JVM implementation must cope with the needs of concurrently executing threads. This, in turn, means that the thread implementation is dependent on the native operating system support. For example, Windows 3.1 does not have a concept of threads, which explains why the Windows 3.1 JVM does not support threads.

A native microprocessor is able to execute only a single instruction at a time. The fact that various operating systems and Java provide thread support for concurrent execution does not change this fact. Rather, Java applications rely on JVM thread scheduling to execute multiple threads, and thread priority to determine which gets executed first.

Thread Scheduling

The entire concept of thread scheduling boils down to two questions: "What determines when the thread will be executed?" and, "Once a thread's execution window has elapsed, what determines when the thread will be executed again?" Both of these questions eventually equate to a structure which holds waiting threads and the policy for selecting the next execution thread.

Consider the case of three threads waiting to be executed. In the case where the threads are stored in a stack model, the first thread will run until completion without yielding to the other threads. This condition is called a *starvation* state, because the two waiting threads are not receiving execution cycles.

Not all thread scheduling techniques are that blatant, and most work with minimal starvation states. However, you should be aware that the actual thread scheduling algorithm used in any given JVM implementation is not specified in the JVM specification. This fact has a good side and a bad side. The good side is that if it is not specified, it is not a testable item. The bad side is that if you are creating an application that relies on a certain scheduling algorithm, you are out of luck. However, to help aid your understanding of scheduling algorithms, Listing 4.2 provides a mechanism to test a scheduling algorithm on any given platform.

Listing 4.2   Thread Scheduling Test.

```
import java.util.*;


class singleThread implements Runnable
{
    public Thread Child_Thread = null;
```

```java
public String MyName;
public int CalcPrimeOf;

public singleThread(String Name, int PrimeOf){
    MyName = Name;
    CalcPrimeOf = PrimeOf;
}

public void start(){
  if (Child_Thread == null)
  {
    Child_Thread = new Thread(this);
    Child_Thread.start();
  }
}

public void stop(){
  if (Child_Thread != null)
    Child_Thread.stop();
  Child_Thread = null;
}

public boolean IsPrime(long in){

    boolean prime = true;
    System.out.println(MyName + " Testing - " + in);
    for(long i = 2; i <= (in / 2);++i){
        if((in % i) == 0){
            prime = false;
            break;
        }
    }
    return prime;
}
```

continues

Listing 4.2 Continued

```
    public void run(){

        int NumberOfTimeToRun = (int)(Integer.MAX_VALUE *
➡Math.random());

        for(int i = 0;i < NumberOfTimeToRun;++i){
            try{
                //Sleep for enough time to let others have some
➡fun.
                int SleepFor = 4;
                System.out.println(MyName + " Going to Sleep for"
+
                 SleepFor + " milliseconds");
                Thread.sleep(SleepFor);
            }
            catch(Exception e){}
            IsPrime(CalcPrimeOf);
        }
        System.out.println(MyName + " Done!");
    }
}

public class threadTest {

    public static void main(String args[]) {

        Hashtable storage = new Hashtable(10);
        //create 10 threads;
        for(int i = 0;i < 10;++i)
            storage.put(new Integer(i), new Thread(
                new singleThread("Thread " + i, i * 365)));

        //Startup the Threads
        for(int i = 0;i < 10;++i){
```

```
            Thread tmp = (Thread)storage.get(new Integer(i));
            //tmp.setPriority(i+1);
            tmp.start();
        }


        //join up with all the threads
        //Startup the Threads
        for(int i = 0;i < 10;++i){
            Thread tmp = (Thread)storage.get(new Integer(i));
            try{
                tmp.join();
            }catch(Exception e){}
        }

    }
}
```

Listing 4.3 is a test run of the application defined in Listing 4.2. The output was generated on a dual Pentium 120MHz running Windows NT 4.0 and the Symantec JIT enhanced JVM. Notice the repeating cycle displaying a queue-based, round-robin scheduling algorithm.

Listing 4.3   Thread Scheduling Test Output Run.

```
Thread 3 Testing - 1095
Thread 9 Testing - 3285
Thread 1 Testing - 365
Thread 7 Testing - 2555
Thread 5 Testing - 1825
Thread 0 Testing - 0
Thread 4 Testing - 1460
Thread 2 Testing - 730
Thread 6 Testing - 2190
Thread 8 Testing - 2920
Thread 3 Going to Sleep for 4 milliseconds
Thread 9 Going to Sleep for 4 milliseconds
Thread 1 Going to Sleep for 4 milliseconds
```

continues

Listing 4.3 Continued

```
Thread 7 Going to Sleep for 4 milliseconds
Thread 5 Going to Sleep for 4 milliseconds
Thread 0 Going to Sleep for 4 milliseconds
Thread 4 Going to Sleep for 4 milliseconds
Thread 2 Going to Sleep for 4 milliseconds
Thread 6 Going to Sleep for 4 milliseconds
Thread 8 Going to Sleep for 4 milliseconds
Thread 3 Testing - 1095
Thread 9 Testing - 3285
Thread 1 Testing - 365
Thread 7 Testing - 2555
Thread 5 Testing - 1825
Thread 0 Testing - 0
Thread 4 Testing - 1460
Thread 2 Testing - 730
Thread 6 Testing - 2190
Thread 8 Testing - 2920
```

Thread Priority

A corollary concept to thread scheduling is thread priority. When you have an understanding of thread scheduling, the concept of thread priority seems intuitively logical. For example, two threads are waiting to be executed, but one is of more importance to you. Thread priority defines the order in which threads are selected for execution.

At a programmatic level, you, the developer, have an idea of the type of processing each thread will perform, and the level of importance associated with each task. The Java language provides a mechanism by which a priority can be set for each running thread. The setPriority() method found in java.lang.Thread provides the following call structure:

```
setPriority(int newPriority)
```

In this structure, the newPriority must be within the integer range of 1 to 10, with 10 being the highest priority. For example, a background processing thread would be set to a priority of 3, whereas an application-critical thread would be set to 10. Keep in mind, however, that Java does not make any claim to the thread scheduling algorithm used in any given JVM implementation. Furthermore, without knowing the scheduling algorithm definition, the characteristics of a given thread priority are impossible to define.

Listing 4.4 is a test run of the application defined in Listing 4.2, with priority setting turned on. The output was generated on a dual Pentium 120MHz running Windows NT 4.0 and the Symantec JIT enhanced JVM (the same machine as Listing 4.3.). In comparison to the run provided in Listing 4.3, the order has decayed from a distinct queue-based, round-robin scheduling algorithm to a more complicated thread execution order. This signifies a priority-based thread selection and an availability-based scheduling algorithm.

Listing 4.4   Thread Scheduling With Priority Test Output Run.

```
Thread 6 Testing - 2190
Thread 4 Testing - 1460
Thread 0 Going to Sleep for 4 milliseconds
Thread 1 Testing - 365
Thread 8 Testing - 2920
Thread 2 Going to Sleep for 4 milliseconds
Thread 3 Testing - 1095
Thread 4 Going to Sleep for 4 milliseconds
Thread 6 Going to Sleep for 4 milliseconds
Thread 5 Testing - 1825
Thread 7 Testing - 2555
Thread 0 Testing - 0
Thread 9 Testing - 3285
Thread 1 Going to Sleep for 4 milliseconds
Thread 8 Going to Sleep for 4 milliseconds
Thread 2 Testing - 730
```

continues

Listing 4.4 Continued

```
Thread 3 Going to Sleep for 4 milliseconds
Thread 4 Testing - 1460
Thread 6 Testing - 2190
Thread 5 Going to Sleep for 4 milliseconds
Thread 7 Going to Sleep for 4 milliseconds
Thread 0 Going to Sleep for 4 milliseconds
Thread 9 Going to Sleep for 4 milliseconds
Thread 1 Testing - 365
Thread 8 Testing - 2920
Thread 2 Going to Sleep for 4 milliseconds
Thread 3 Testing - 1095
Thread 4 Going to Sleep for 4 milliseconds
Thread 6 Going to Sleep for 4 milliseconds
Thread 5 Testing - 1825
Thread 7 Testing - 2555
Thread 0 Testing - 0
Thread 9 Testing - 3285
Thread 1 Going to Sleep for 4 milliseconds
Thread 8 Going to Sleep for 4 milliseconds
Thread 2 Testing - 730
Thread 3 Going to Sleep for 4 milliseconds
Thread 4 Testing - 1460
Thread 6 Testing - 2190
Thread 5 Going to Sleep for 4 milliseconds
Thread 7 Going to Sleep for 4 milliseconds
Thread 0 Going to Sleep for 4 milliseconds
Thread 9 Going to Sleep for 4 milliseconds
Thread 1 Testing - 365
Thread 8 Testing - 2920
Thread 2 Going to Sleep for 4 milliseconds
Thread 6 Going to Sleep for 4 milliseconds
Thread 4 Going to Sleep for 4 milliseconds
Thread 5 Testing - 1825
Thread 3 Testing - 1095
Thread 7 Testing - 2555
```

```
Thread 0 Testing - 0
Thread 8 Going to Sleep for 4 milliseconds
Thread 9 Testing - 3285
Thread 6 Testing - 2190
Thread 4 Testing - 1460
Thread 2 Testing - 730
Thread 1 Going to Sleep for 4 milliseconds
Thread 5 Going to Sleep for 4 milliseconds
Thread 3 Going to Sleep for 4 milliseconds
Thread 7 Going to Sleep for 4 milliseconds
Thread 0 Going to Sleep for 4 milliseconds
```

Programming with Concurrent Execution Paths

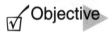 Objective   Multi-thread application takes full advantage of the concurrent processing capabilities of modern operating systems. For this reason, knowing how to use threads to create concurrent applications is required knowledge for the Certified Programmer Examination.

Developing without the use of threads or multiple processes might seem logically simpler than developing with multiple threads. Without threads, program execution is linear and can easily be represented in a flow diagram. Development with threads, on the other hand, is not as easily represented. Instead of having a single linear execution path, you need to contend with multiple, connected linear execution paths. Nevertheless, concurrent thread programming is still a scaled model of the traditional development paradigm.

In the traditional computing model, programs contain a finite set of instructions executed in a sequential order. If you break a thread-based program into its main parts, the traditional computing model is maintained. However, it is maintained not for the program as a whole, but rather for each separate executing thread. For example, in every one of the sample thread applications presented in this chapter, two distinct execution paths are defined. Each example contains a thread execution path and a main program execution path. In themselves, all paths conform to the traditional computing model. It is only when the application is looked at as a whole that a divergence from the traditional computing model takes place.

Whenever something deviates from traditional methods, a feeling of uncertainty is sure to follow. Many developers are reticent to probe into concurrent thread-based development for fear of a drastic increase in development complexity. Concurrent thread-based development is not inherently more difficult, just different. However, the key is how to manage it in a concurrent world.

In this chapter, you have learned how to declare and use threads to aid program development. This next section focuses on the elements needed to facilitate multiple threads coexisting peacefully. Also, given the fact that threads share a common memory space, this section will show you how to facilitate Inter-Thread Communication (ITC.)

One at a Time!

Thus far, the sample threads presented in this chapter have been fairly simplistic. That is, they all have been fairly self-sufficient, to the extent that the threads look like small, self-contained execution blocks—more appropriately called *mutually exclusive* execution blocks. A thread that minds its own business and does not share any resources with other executing threads, is a mutually exclusive thread. It is a common belief that most threads and thread designs use mutually exclusive threads. However, whenever a thread uses a common resource, like standard output, that thread is no longer mutually exclusive, but *collaborative.*

The reason for the distinction between the two types of threads has to do with the level of complexity and support required to execute a particular thread. For example, if a thread is totally mutually exclusive then it is essentially an entirely separate process, and not a thread. However, threads, by definition, have the ability to share resources, including memory resources. For this reason, a facility must be provided to facilitate proper thread interaction and coordination. In Java, thread resources are coordinated through a set of facilities that provide a "One Thread at a Time" programmatic device.

To give you a brief idea about why threads need to be coordinated and generally guarded from one another, think about this scenario: one thread creates an object for another to use. To clarify terms, the first thread is viewed as the *producer*, and the second is the *consumer*. Without knowing when the producer will be ready for the consumer, an error state may result from the producer not having a resource ready for the consumer. In this case, the producer and consumer threads must be coordinated in order to ensure proper data delivery. In Java, this coordination is provided by a set of serialization facilities.

Class Serialization

Class-level serialization ensures that only one thread at a time has privileges to execute a class's methods. For example, the following class defines two methods to be synchronized, meaning only one thread can be granted execution access at a time.

```
class multiThreadResource{
    private static int counter = 0;

    public static synchronized void increment(){
        counter++;
    }

    public static synchronized void decrement(){
        counter--;
    }
}
```

By defining each method as synchronized, only one thread can execute increment() and decrement() at a time. For example, one thread executes the increment(), while at the same time a second thread tries to execute decrement(). The second thread will wait until the first thread has exited the increment() method, thus guaranteeing single-thread execution of synchronized methods, and providing class-level thread serialization of shared methods.

Execution Block Serialization

In some cases, it is not necessary to serialize access to an entire group of methods. Rather, only a certain section contains volatile instructions. For this reason, the synchronized reserved word can be used for block-level serialization.

The following example demonstrates the use of the block synchronized device to limit thread access to a specified block of code:

```
class multiThreadResource{
    private Object O = new Object();
    private int counter = 0;

    public void increment(){
        synchronized(O){
            counter++;
        }
    }
}
```

In this example, Object O is used as a locking device for the synchronized statement. That is, when a thread comes to the synchronized statement, Object O is checked for a lock status. If it is locked, meaning another thread is in the volatile section, the thread will block until the lock has been released. The actual mechanism by which the object is locked and released will be covered in the next section. However, at the synchronized call level, object-level locks are not visible.

Inter-Thread Communication

One of the most powerful features of thread technology is the ability to share memory space with other threads. That is, two threads have the ability to share a single memory variable. This is even more so the case where individual processes require sophisticated Inter-Process Communication (IPC) facilities to transmit information. Threads can readily exchange information through a shared memory object to facilitate Inter-Thread Communication (ITC).

To provide an example of how to facilitate ITC, imagine two threads processing away. At some point, one of the threads may want to access the other thread's status. To facilitate this, an object is created to hold the current state of the processing thread. When the state changes, the object's information is updated. Likewise, the monitoring thread can simply look into the object at any time to determine the status.

The idea of two threads sharing a single object to facilitate communication is very straightforward. The confusion comes into play when all of the "what-if" scenarios are examined. For example, what if the monitor thread is trying to obtain status at the exact same time the other thread is updating the status? This particular "what if" is a general case for the core of all ITC problem spots, and one that does not have a clear, defined answer. So, instead of answering the question, in this case it is easier to eliminate the need for the question. That is, Java provides a mechanism to allow a thread to lock or unlock a resource to prevent such a problem. This mechanism comes in the shape of wait and notify facilities.

Wait()

Both the wait() and notify() methods are members of java.lang.Object. Chapter 5 will cover the complete object class, but for this discussion all that is needed is the knowledge of the wait() method.

Simply put, the wait() method will block until another thread makes a call to notify. For example, Listing 4.5 defines ITC class to transmit strings.

Listing 4.5   Wait/Notify Example.

```
public class sendString{
    private String Data = "";
    public synchronized void sendMessage(String toSend){
        Data = toSend;
        notify();
    }
    public synchronized Sting getMessage(){
        return Data;
    }
}
```

Through this defined class, a monitor thread can retrieve current thread status for a producer thread. Furthermore, the monitor would make a call to the sendString class's wait() method to be notified of a new producer state.

Notify()

With functionality as closely tied as wait() and notify(), it is hard to define one without stepping on the toes of the other. As you can see from the discussion of the wait() facility, notify() notifies a single thread blocking on a call to wait(). There are some different versions of the notify() method that will be covered in Chapter 5. Nevertheless, a good example of notify() usage can be found in the sendMessage() method of Listing 4.5.

Summary

Threads are wonderful things. That is not a rhetorical statement, but a pure fact. Through the use of threads you can process multiple execution branches at once. If this concept doesn't currently seem all that powerful, give it some time. Threads provide the means to implement elegant solutions to some ugly problems.

In this chapter you learned how to create, execute, and use threads for general use. However, training yourself to think in terms of threads is equivalent to the object-oriented learning curve. Once you have it, it clicks, but getting there is the tough part. The good news is that thread-specific questions comprise only 5 to 10 percent of the Certified Java Programmer Exam.

It was not the goal of this chapter to make you an overnight expert of Java thread design. Rather, this chapter presented the general framework that composes Java thread technology. The following questions provide a sample set of actual certification questions to assess your skills in Java thread facilities.

Review Questions

1. Which statement best describes the following class?

```
class dataCenterResource{
    private static String  data = "";

    public static synchronized void setString(String in){
        data = in;
}

    public static synchronized String getString(){
        return data;
    }
}
```

   A. The class is a simple storage device for a string.

   B. The class is a simple storage device for multiple threads to access a single string.

   C. The class provides a mechanism by which only one thread can get or set the stored string value at a time.

   D. The class provides a mechanism by which only multiple threads can get or set the stored string value.

2. The wait() call does which of the following?

   A. Blocks until a thread terminates

   B. Blocks until notified by another thread

   C. Blocks until the object is ready for access

   D. Blocks a thread until all other threads have terminated

3. How are thread priority and thread scheduling related?

   A. They aren't.

   B. It depends on the thread scheduling algorithm used to implement the JVM.

    C. Thread priority is specified when a thread is to be executed next.

    D. Thread priority is used to determine the next thread to execute from the waiting thread pool.

4. The `Runnable` interface is used for what?

    A. A marathon

    B. Defining a thread

    C. Defining a class that can be executed by a thread

    D. Defining a class to execute a new thread

5. Which statement best defines the following code segment? Note: `myClass` implements `Runnable`.

```
Thread  T1 = new Thread(new myClass());
T1.start();
```

    A. Thread T1 is created and executed.

    B. Thread T1 is constructed to contain the `Runnable` interface `myClass`, and it executes the `myClass` `run()` method.

    C. A compilation error will occur at T1.start();.

    D. Thread T1 is constructed to contain the Runnable interface myClass, and it executes the Thread run() method.

6. The JVM specification specifies the thread scheduling used.

    A. True

    B. False

7. Which of the following terminates a thread's execution?

    A. Calling the `stop()` method

    B. An external JVM event

    C. A thread returning from its `run()` method

    D. All of the above

8. All threads created in Java are mutually exclusive.

    A. True

    B. False

9. The `wait()` and `notify()` methods are defined in what class?

    A. `String`

    B. `Thread`

    C. `Object`

    D. Runnable

10. The `wait()` and `notify()` methods are members of what class?

    A. `String`

    B. `Thread`

    C. `Object`

    D. All of the above

Review Answers

1. C

2. B

3. B

4. C

5. B

6. B

7. D

8. B

9. C

10. D

Chapter 5

Java API

This chapter will present the fundamentals of the Java Class Libraries. In order to fully comprehend the discussed topics, it is recommended that you read Chapter 2, "Java Language Internals," and Chapter 3, "Java Objects and Exceptions." Specifically, this chapter examines Java Class Library class methods, fields, and constructors.

An object is a reusable encapsulation of data and code. So, wouldn't it be nice if someone took the time and created a whole slew of different objects to aid in development? That is exactly what the Java Class Libraries provide. Everything from the base object class to a Hashtable is provided, free of charge with the JDK.

In the original release of the JDK, there were only a handful of class packages. Then Java 1.1 hit the street with a plethora of new package facilities. Everything from a basic stack storage device to 3D graphics API is available to aid any aspect of development. The Java Class Library is growing, and potentially always will in Java's push to further aid application development.

In this chapter, a handful of key Java Class Library packages will be discussed. Due to the size of the Java Class Library, not all can be covered. However, the handful of packages selected are testable items. This is not to say knowledge of the entire Library isn't useful, rather the selected packages merely reflect the Java Certified Programmer Exam. Chapters 12, "JFC and Java Media Kit," through 14, "Additional Java Technologies," will discuss some key technologies found in the Java Class Library, but for now the following packages will be the focus of this chapter.

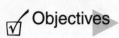 Objectives

▶ `java.lang`

▶ `java.util`

▶ `java.AWT`

Test Yourself! Before reading this chapter, test yourself to determine how much study time you will need to devote to this section.

1. Which of the following is NOT a method of `java.lang.Object`?

   A. `wait()`

   B. `equals(Object)`

   C. `getHashCode()`

   D. `notify()`

2. `java.util.EventObject` is the parent class of `java.awt.AWTEvent`.

   A. True

   B. False

Answers are located at the end of the Chapter...

java.lang

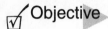 Objective

As the name implies, the java.lang package is an assortment of Java required and standard classes. For example, contained within the java.lang package is object, which is the base class for all Java-defined objects. This is not to say that all java.lang contained classes are of the importance of object. Rather, the classes found in java.lang are critical to programming in Java.

The following is a list of all classes contained in java.lang. A good majority of the classes will sound familiar to you, while others may sound obscure. Classes like String and Thread may sound familiar, and others like ClassLoader may seem a little more obscure. In either case, the following classes are the foundation building blocks for all Java development:

▶ Boolean	▶ Object
▶ Byte	▶ Process
▶ Character	▶ Runtime
▶ Class	▶ SecurityManager
▶ ClassLoader	▶ Short
▶ Compiler	▶ String
▶ Double	▶ StringBuffer
▶ Float	▶ System
▶ Integer	▶ Thread
▶ Long	▶ ThreadGroup
▶ Math	▶ Throwable
▶ Number	▶ Void

 Objective

As useful and vital as all of these classes are, only a handful contain testable information. For this reason, not all of the classes contained in the java.lang package will be discussed in this chapter. Rather, the following specific subset will be analyzed in an attempt to precisely identify crucial areas of required knowledge for the Certified Programmer Exam:

▶ Number

▶ Object

▶ String

▶ System

▶ Thread

Number

The Number class provides a base class for all Java data type objects. That is, for every primitive data type provided by Java, a class is provided to encapsulate the associated data type's functionality. These data type objects are all in turn derived from the Number class, which provides a basis for the data type encapsulation facilities. For example, all of the following classes are derived from Number and are contained within java.lang.

▶ Boolean

▶ Byte

▶ Character

▶ Double

▶ Float

▶ Integer

▶ Long

▶ Short

Each of these classes represents numeric values, by virtue of being derived from the Number class. Likewise, custom numeric encapsulation classes can be formed by deriving from the Number class. The following provides detailed constructor and method information for the Number class.

Constructors

The Number class contains only a single constructor, with the following signature.

```
public Number()
```

Methods

The Number class contains the following methods, most of which are abstract. Notice how the members merely facilitate the extraction of various primitive data types. This provides homogeneous data retrieval and conversion facilities.

- ► public byte byteValue()   Returns the encapsulated numeric value as a byte.

- ► public abstract double doubleValue()   Returns the encapsulated numeric value as a double.

- ► public abstract float floatValue()   Returns the encapsulated numeric value as a float.

- ► public abstract int intValue()   Returns the encapsulated numeric value as an int.

- ► public abstract long longValue()   Returns the encapsulated numeric value as a long.

- ► public short shortValue()   Returns the encapsulated numeric value as a short.

Object

As mentioned in Chapter 3 all classes are derived from java.lang.object. In this way, object is the parent of all Java classes. The point being, knowledge of the facilities inherited by all Java classes is fundamental, and required to get the most out of the Java Class Library facilities.

The following sections provide an inventory of the provided elements which object presents.

Constructors

The Object class contains only a single constructor, with the following signature.

```
public Object()
```

Methods

Resource locking, presentation, and manipulation devices can be found in Object's methods. This set of methods in turn provides a common set of tools to manipulate class resources. The Object class contains the following methods.

▶ `protected native Object clone() throws CloneNotSupportedException`   Creates a duplicate class to the current class.

▶ `public boolean equals(Object obj)`   Checks to see if the passed object reference refers to the current class.

▶ `protected void finalize() throws Throwable`   Called by garbage collection before the resource is put on the heap for reuse.

▶ `public final native Class getClass()`   Returns the class object which defines the current class.

▶ `public native int hashCode()`   Returns a hash code value for the specific instance of the current class.

▶ `public final native void notify()`   Notifies a single thread blocked in a wait() call, as discussed in Chapter 4, "Threads in the Java Platform."

▶ `public final native void notifyAll()`   Notifies all threads blocked in a wait() call.

▶ `public String toString()`   Returns a string representation of the object.

▶ `public final void wait() throws InterruptedException` Blocks indefinitely until notified by a separate thread, as discussed in Chapter 4.

▶ `public final native void wait(long timeout) throws InterruptedException` Blocks for the specified amount of time, or until notified by a separate thread, as discussed in Chapter 4.

▶ `public final void wait(long timeout, int nanos) throws InterruptedException` Blocks for the specified amount of time, or until notified by a separate thread.

String

In Java, all string assignment and manipulation facilities are provided by means of the `String` class. That is, Java strings are implemented around the `String` class, to the extent that the following lines of code are equivalent.

```
String MyString = "Hello";
```

is equal to

```
String MyString = new String("Hello");
```

Seeing how the `String` class provides all string storage and manipulation facilities for Java, it is prudent to have a firm grasp of the `String` class. For this reason, the following sections dissect all constructors and methods provided by the `String` class.

Constructors

The `String` class provides a series of constructors targeted to aid in conversion of various data formats. For example, a separate constructor is supplied for constructing a string from both a character and byte array. In this way, various data sources can be used to construct a `String` class.

The following provides a list of all constructors for the `String` class:

▶ `public String()` Creates an empty string.

▶ `public String(byte bytes[])` Creates the string based off the supplied byte array, encoded in the default platform character set.

▶ public String(byte ascii[], int hibyte)   Creates the string based off the supplied byte array, ASCII-encoded and filled with the supplied hi-order byte.

▶ public String(byte bytes[], int offset, int length)   Creates the string based off the supplied byte array, encoded in the default platform character set. The offset and length define the subset of the byte array used for the construction.

▶ public String(byte ascii[], int hibyte, int offset, int count)   Creates the string based off the supplied byte array, ASCII-encoded and filled with the supplied hi-order byte. The offset and length define the subset of the byte array used for the construction.

▶ public String(byte bytes[], int offset, int length, String enc) throws UnsupportedEncodingException   Creates the string based off the supplied byte array, ASCII-encoded in the specified scheme. The offset and length define the subset of the byte array used for the construction.

▶ public String(byte bytes[], String enc) throws UnsupportedEncodingException   Creates the string based off the supplied byte array, ASCII-encoded in the specified scheme.

▶ public String(char value[])   Creates a string from the specified character array.

▶ public String(char value[], int offset, int count)   Creates a string from the specified character array. The offset and length define the subset of the char array used for the construction.

▶ public String(String value)   Creates a clone of the specified string.

▶ public String(StringBuffer buffer)   Creates a new string based off the contents of the specified StringBuffer class.

Methods

The methods found in the String class provide an assortment of functionality. Everything from character-level string manipulation to pattern-searching methods is encapsulated in the String class. The following provides a complete list of all methods found in the String class:

▶ `public char charAt(int index)` Returns the character at the specified index.

▶ `public int compareTo(String anotherString)` Compares two strings on the basis of a character-by-character analysis.

▶ `public String concat(String str)` Concatenates the specified string to the end of this string.

▶ `public static String copyValueOf(char data[])` A static method to create a string from character array.

▶ `public static String copyValueOf(char data[],int offset, int count)` A static method to create a string from character array. The offset and length define the subset of the char array used for the construction.

▶ `public boolean endsWith(String suffix)` Tests if this string ends with the specified suffix.

▶ `public boolean equals(Object anObject)` Returns true if the specified object reference is equal to the current string instance.

▶ `public boolean equalsIgnoreCase(String anotherString)` Returns true if the specified string is equal to the currently stored string value.

▶ `public byte[] getBytes()` Converts the currently defined string into a byte array.

▶ `getBytes(String)` A static method to convert a method into a byte array.

▶ `public void getChars(int srcBegin, int srcEnd, char dst[], int dstBegin)` Loads the specified character array with the requested subset of characters.

▶ `public int hashCode()` Returns a hash code for this string.

▶ `public int indexOf(int ch)` Returns the index within this string of the first occurrence of the specified character.

▶ `public int indexOf(int ch, int fromIndex)` Returns the index within this string of the first occurrence of the specified character, starting the search at the specified index.

▶ `public int indexOf(String str)` Returns the index within this string of the first occurrence of the specified substring.

▶ `public int indexOf(String str, int fromIndex)` Returns the index within this string of the first occurrence of the specified substring, starting at the specified index.

▶ `public native String intern()` Returns a standard representation for the string object.

▶ `public int lastIndexOf(int ch)` Returns the index within this string of the last occurrence of the specified character.

▶ `public int lastIndexOf(String str)` Returns the index within this string of the last occurrence of the specified character, searching backward starting at the specified index.

▶ `public int lastIndexOf(String str, int fromIndex)` Returns the index within this string of the right-most occurrence of the specified substring.

▶ `public int lastIndexOf(String str, int fromIndex)` Returns the index within this string of the last occurrence of the specified substring.

▶ `public int length()` Returns the length of this string.

▶ `public boolean regionMatches(boolean ignoreCase, int toffset, String other, int ooffset, int len)` Returns true if the two specified regions match.

▶ `public boolean regionMatches(int toffset, String other, int ooffset, int len)` Returns true if the two specified regions match.

▶ `public String replace(char oldChar, char newChar)` Replaces all occurrences of the specified character with the provided replacement.

▶ `public boolean startsWith(String prefix)` Returns true if the string begins with the specified prefix.

▶ `public boolean startsWith(String prefix, int toffset)` Returns true if the string begins with the specified prefix.

▶ `public String substring(int beginIndex)` Returns a substring beginning at the specified index position.

▶ `public String substring(int beginIndex, int endIndex)` Returns a substring defined by the specified begin and end index positions.

▶ `public char[] toCharArray()` Converts this string to a new character array.

▶ `public String toLowerCase()` Converts this string to lower-case.

▶ `public String toLowerCase(Locale locale)` Converts all of the characters in this string to lowercase using the rules of the given local value.

▶ `public String toString()` Returns a reference to the current object.

▶ `public String toUpperCase()` Converts this string to upper-case.

▶ `public String toUpperCase(Locale locale)` Converts all of the characters in this string to uppercase using the rules of the given locale.

▶ `public String trim()` Removes white space from both ends of this string.

▶ `public static String valueOf(boolean b)` Returns the string representation of the `Boolean` argument.

- ▶ public static valueOf(char c)   Returns the string representation of the character argument.

- ▶ public static String valueOf(char data[])   Returns the string representation of the char array argument.

- ▶ public static String valueOf(char data[], int offset, int count)   Returns the string representation of a specific subarray of the char array argument.

- ▶ public static String valueOf(double d)   Returns the string representation of the double argument.

- ▶ public static String valueOf(float f)   Returns the string representation of the float argument.

- ▶ public static String valueOf(int i)   Returns the string representation of the int argument.

- ▶ public static String valueOf(long l)   Returns the string representation of the long argument.

- ▶ public static String valueOf(Object obj)   Returns the string representation of the Object argument.

System

java.lang.System provides a melting pot of various vital Java application functionality. Facilities like standard in, standard out, and garbage collection can be found in the system, along with all other runtime-specific facilities. In general, the System class provides a static resource for accessing JVM and environment-present facilities.

The following sections present a complete list of all resources contained within the System class. It should be noted that all defined facilities within the System class are meant to be accessed as static members. That is, the System class cannot be instantiated. Rather, all members can be accessed as static members.

Fields

The System class provides direct access to standard out, standard in, and standard error streams through the following static field references.

▶ `public static final PrintStream err` The standard error output stream

▶ `public static final InputStream in` The standard input stream

▶ `public static final PrintStream out` The standard output stream.

Methods

The System class contains a number of static methods for accessing various aspects of the JVM and runtime environment. The following is a complete list of all methods found in the System class.

▶ `public static native void arraycopy(Object src, int src_position, Object dst, int dst_position, int length)` Copies an array from the specified source array to the specified destination.

▶ `public static native long currentTimeMillis()` Returns the current time in milliseconds.

▶ `public static void exit(int status)` Terminates the currently running Java Virtual Machine.

▶ `public static void gc()` Runs the garbage collector.

▶ `public static Properties getProperties()` Returns current system properties.

▶ `public static String getProperty(String key)` Returns the current system property matching the specified key.

▶ `public static String getProperty(String key, String def)` Returns the current system property matching the specified key. If the property is not found, the specified default is returned.

▶ `public static SecurityManager getSecurityManager()` Returns the system security interface.

▶ `public static native int identityHashCode(Object x)` Returns the same hash code for the given object as would be returned by the default method `hashCode()`, whether or not the given object's class overrides `hashCode()`.

▶ `public static void load(String filename)` Loads the specified file name as a dynamic library.

▶ `public static void loadLibrary(String libname)` Loads the system library specified by the `libname` argument.

▶ `public static void runFinalization()` Runs the finalizing methods for all objects waiting to be garbage collected. Can be called before Java exits to ensure safe cleanup.

▶ `public static void setErr(PrintStream err)` Redirects standard error output stream.

▶ `public static void setIn(InputStream in)` Redirects standard input stream.

▶ `public static void setOut(PrintStream out)` Redirects standard output stream.

▶ `public static void setProperties(Properties props)` Sets the system properties to the `Properties` argument.

▶ `public static void setSecurityManager(SecurityManager)` Sets the system security.

Thread

Chapter 4, "Threads in the Java Platform," thoroughly discussed the use and declaration of Java threads. However, specific internal `Thread` class information was put off until this chapter. The following sections provide a complete anatomy of the `java.lang.Thread` class.

Fields

As discussed in Chapter 4, each Java thread may be set with an associated property. This property in turn defines the priority in which the thread is to be executed. The `Thread` class provides three symbolic constant thread priorities for ease of use:

▶ `MAX_PRIORITY` Maximum thread priority

▶ `MIN_PRIORITY` Minimum thread priority

▶ `NORM_PRIORITY` Default thread priority

Constructors

The construction of threads in Chapter 4 was limited to a single constructor call. However, Java threads provide a mechanism to partition threads into groupings, and provide names for each individual thread. The following list of constructors provides the means to create, name, and organize thread resources.

▶ `public Thread()` Creates a new thread.

▶ `public Thread(Runnable target)` Creates a new thread initialized with the specified `Runnable` interface.

▶ `public Thread(Runnable target, String name)` Creates a new thread initialized with the specified `Runnable` interface. The `name` parameter is used to assign a name to the newly created thread.

▶ `public Thread(String name)` Creates a new thread with the specified name.

▶ `public Thread(ThreadGroup group, Runnable target)` Creates a new thread initialized with the specified `Runnable` interface. The `group` parameter is used to add the newly created thread into the specified thread group.

▶ `public Thread(ThreadGroup group, Runnable target, String name)` Creates a new thread initialized with the specified `Runnable` interface. The `group` and `name` parameters are used to add a newly created thread into the specified thread group with the given name.

▶ public Thread(ThreadGroup group, String name)   Creates a new thread with the specified name and in the specified group.

Methods

All of the methods contained within the Thread class provide access to thread execution and identity information. Chapter 5 provided limited insight to the complete scope of provided facilities. The following provides a complete list of methods provided in the Thread class.

▶ public static int activeCount()   Returns the current number of active threads in the current thread group.

▶ public void checkAccess()   Checks thread permissions to modify this thread's properties.

▶ public native int countStackFrames()   Counts the number of stack frames in this thread.

▶ public static native Thread currentThread()   Returns a reference to the currently executing thread object.

▶ public void destroy()   Terminates the thread without any cleanup.

▶ public static void dumpStack()   Prints a call-stack trace to the standard output stream for the current thread instance.

▶ public static int enumerate(Thread tarray[])   Loads an array of all active threads in the current group.

▶ public final String getName()   Returns the current thread's name.

▶ public final int getPriority()   Returns the current thread's priority.

▶ public final ThreadGroup getThreadGroup()   Returns the current thread's thread group.

▶ public void interrupt()   Interrupts the current thread's execution.

▶ `public static boolean interrupted()`   Returns true if the current thread has been interrupted.

▶ `public final native boolean isAlive()`   Returns true if the current thread is executing.

▶ `public final boolean isDaemon()`   Returns true if the current thread has been spawned as a daemon thread.

▶ `public boolean isInterrupted()`   Returns true if the current thread has been interrupted.

▶ `public final void join() throws InterruptedException` Blocks until the current thread has terminated.

▶ `public final synchronized void join(long millis) throws InterruptedException`   Blocks until either the current thread has terminated or the specified time has expired.

▶ `public final synchronized void join(long millis, int nanos)`   Throws `InterruptedException` blocks until either the current thread has terminated or the specified time has expired.

▶ `public final void resume()`   Resumes a thread that has been suspended.

▶ `public void run()`   The thread's main execution block. This function is only used when a thread is constructed without a `Runnable` interface.

▶ `public final void setDaemon(boolean on)`   Sets the current thread to be either a daemon or user thread.

▶ `public final void setName(String name)`   Sets the name of the current thread.

▶ `public final void setPriority(int newPriority)`   Sets the priority of the current thread.

▶ `public static native void sleep(long millis) throws InterruptedException`   Puts the currently running thread into a dormant state for the specified amount of time.

▶ `public static void sleep(long millis, int nanos) throws InterruptedException` Puts the currently running thread into a dormant state for the specified amount of time.

▶ `public native synchronized void start()` Begins execution of either the current thread's `run()` method, or the specified `Runnable` interface.

▶ `public final void stop()` Terminates the current thread.

▶ `public final synchronized void stop(Throwable o)` Terminates the current thread.

▶ `public final void suspend()` Suspends this thread.

▶ `public String toString()` Returns thread's name, priority, and thread group.

▶ `public static native void yield()` Causes the currently executing thread to pause, allowing other threads to process.

java.util

The `java.util` package provides an array of useful development resources. Classes such as `Stack`, `Hashtable`, and `TimeZone`, that provide helpful and time-saving programmatic devices, are designed to expedite development. These devices are not necessary hi-tech facilities. Rather, the `java.util` package provides a utility belt of tools to aid Java development.

The following is a list of all classes contained in `java.util`. A good majority of the classes will sound familiar to you, while others may sound obscure. Classes like `Stack` and `Date` may sound familiar, and others like `Observable` may seem a little more obscure.

- ▶ BitSet
- ▶ Calendar
- ▶ Date
- ▶ Dictionary
- ▶ EventObject
- ▶ GregorianCalendar
- ▶ Hashtable
- ▶ ListResourceBundle
- ▶ Locale
- ▶ Observable

- ▶ Properties
- ▶ PropertyResourceBundle
- ▶ Random
- ▶ ResourceBundle
- ▶ SimpleTimeZone
- ▶ Stack
- ▶ StringTokenizer
- ▶ TimeZone
- ▶ Vector

As useful as these classes are, only a handful contain direct testable information. For this reason, not all of the classes contained in the java.util package will be discussed in this chapter. Rather, the following specific subset will be analyzed in an attempt to precisely identify crucial areas of required knowledge for the Certified Programmer Exam.

- ▶ EventObject
- ▶ Hashtable

EventObject

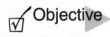 Objective

Beginning with JDK 1.1, java.util.EventObject became the base class for most Java events. Events such as AWTEvent and ActionEvent both rely on the facilities provided by the EventObject class for tracking the source of a fired event.

The following sections diagram the members of the EventObject class.

Fields

The EventObject class provides only a single, protected field that references the source object for the current EventObject class. The field's definition is as follows.

▶ `protected transient Object source`   Provides access to the defined origin of the current event.

Constructors

The `EventObject` class contains only a single constructor, with the following signature.

▶ `public EventObject(Object source)`   Creates a new `EventObject` instance to contain a reference to the event's origin.

Methods

The `EventObject` class provides two methods for the retrieval and presentation of the contained source field. The following discusses each of the methods.

▶ `public Object getSource()`   Retrieves the reference to the event's origin.

▶ `public String toString()`   Returns a string representation of the current `EventObject`.

Hashtable

Objective

`java.util.Hashtable` has become the universal Java data storage device, and for good reason. Objects can simply be put into the table and then retrieved with a single call. The beauty and utility of the `Hashtable` class cannot be overstated. The `Hashtable` class is Java's generic object storage and retrieval device.

As with most programmatic tools, the reason for the wide use of the `Hashtable` class can be explained in three words: it is simple. The following sections provide a complete discussion of the members contained within the `Hashtable` class.

Constructors

The `Hashtable` class contains only a set of three constructors, with the following signatures. Each of the three constructors provides an added level of control over the creation and growth of the hashtable.

▶ `public Hashtable()` Constructs the hashtable initialized with the default initial capacity and growth factor.

▶ `public Hashtable(int initialCapacity)` Constructs the hash-table initialized with the defined initial capacity and default growth factor.

▶ `public Hashtable(int initialCapacity,float loadFactor)` Constructs the hashtable initialized with the defined initial capacity and growth factor.

Methods

The `Hashtable` class provides a set of methods for the storage and retrieval of object resources. The following is a complete list of methods found in the `Hashtable` class.

▶ `public synchronized void clear()` Empties the hashtable.

▶ `public synchronized Object clone()` Creates a duplicate `Hashtable` object.

▶ `public synchronized boolean contains(Object value)` Returns true if the specified object is contained as a data element within the hashtable.

▶ `public synchronized boolean containsKey(Object key)` Returns true if the specified object is contained as a key element within the hashtable.

▶ `public synchronized Enumeration elements()` Returns a list of all contained data elements.

▶ `public synchronized Object get(Object key)` Returns the object with the specified key object.

▶ `public boolean isEmpty()` Returns true if the hashtable contains no elements.

▶ `public synchronized Enumeration keys()` Returns a list of all contained key elements.

▶ `public synchronized Object put(Object key, Object value)` Adds a new element into the hashtable associated with the specified key value.

▶ `protected void rehash()` Rehashes the contents of the hashtable into a hashtable with a larger capacity.

▶ `public synchronized Object remove(Object key)` Removes the key and its corresponding object from this hashtable.

▶ `public int size()` Returns the number of elements in the hashtable.

▶ `public synchronized String toString()` Returns a string representation of the hashtable.

java.awt

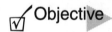 Objective ▶

The Abstract Windowing Toolkit (AWT) contains all Java GUI components and layout facilities. In fact, any graphical element presented in a Java GUI probably originated from a class provided in the AWT. Put simply, the AWT provides Java with its GUI development facilities.

The following list provides a complete list of classes contained within the `java.awt` package. A majority of the classes will sound familiar to you, while others might sound obscure.

▶ AWTEvent	▶ CheckboxMenuItem
▶ AWTEventMulticaster	▶ Choice
▶ BorderLayout	▶ Color
▶ Button	▶ Component
▶ Canvas	▶ Container
▶ CardLayout	▶ Cursor
▶ Checkbox	▶ Dialog
▶ CheckboxGroup	▶ Dimension

- ▶ Event
- ▶ EventQueue
- ▶ FileDialog
- ▶ FlowLayout
- ▶ Font
- ▶ FontMetrics
- ▶ Frame
- ▶ Graphics
- ▶ GridBagConstraints
- ▶ GridBagLayout
- ▶ GridLayout
- ▶ Image
- ▶ Insets
- ▶ Label
- ▶ List
- ▶ MediaTracker
- ▶ Menu
- ▶ MenuBar

- ▶ MenuComponent
- ▶ MenuItem
- ▶ MenuShortcut
- ▶ Panel
- ▶ Point
- ▶ Polygon
- ▶ PopupMenu
- ▶ PrintJob
- ▶ Rectangle
- ▶ ScrollPane
- ▶ Scrollbar
- ▶ SystemColor
- ▶ TextArea
- ▶ TextComponent
- ▶ TextField
- ▶ Toolkit
- ▶ Window

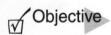 **Objective** ▶ As useful as these classes are, only a handful contain direct testable information. For this reason, not all of the classes contained in the java.awt package will be discussed in this chapter. Rather, the following specific subset will be analyzed in an attempt to precisely identify crucial areas of required knowledge for the Certified Programmer Exam.

- ▶ AWTEvent
- ▶ Event

AWTEvent

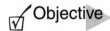

Beginning with JDK 1.1, `java.util.AWTEvent` is the base class for all Java AWT-defined events. `AWTEvent` provides a standard encapsulation for all GUI-based events. The following sections diagram the members of the `AWTEvent` class.

Fields

`AWTEvent` provides a series of static constants used for the distinguishing of specific GUI events. For example, the `KEY_EVENT_MASK` field is used to test if the current event was generated in response to a key being hit on the keyboard.

The following provides a complete list of all defined fields for the `AWTEvent` lass.

- ▶ `ACTION_EVENT_MASK`   The action event mask

- ▶ `ADJUSTMENT_EVENT_MASK`   The adjustment event mask

- ▶ `COMPONENT_EVENT_MASK`   The component event mask

- ▶ `CONTAINER_EVENT_MASK`   The container event mask

- ▶ `FOCUS_EVENT_MASK`   The selecting focus event mask

- ▶ `ITEM_EVENT_MASK`   The event mask for selecting item events

- ▶ `KEY_EVENT_MASK`   The event mask for selecting key events

- ▶ `MOUSE_EVENT_MASK`   The event mask for selecting mouse events

- ▶ `MOUSE_MOTION_EVENT_MASK`   The event mask for selecting mouse motion events

- ▶ `RESERVED_ID_MAX`   The maximum value for reserved AWT event IDs

- ▶ `TEXT_EVENT_MASK`   The event mask for selecting text events

- ▶ `WINDOW_EVENT_MASK`   The event mask for selecting window events.

Constructors

Two constructors are provided by the `AWTEvent` class. The first provides support for JDK 1.0-style events, and the second initializes a new event object with a data `Object` and type code. The complete signatures for these events are as follows.

▶ `public AWTEvent(Event event)` Creates an `AWTEvent` object from the parameters of a 1.0-style event.

▶ `public AWTEvent(Object source, int id)` Creates an `AWTEvent` object with the specified source object and type.

Methods

A set of methods is provided by the `AWTEvent` class to facilitate event routing and identification. The following is a complete list of all methods contained within the `AWTEvent` class.

▶ `protected void consume()` Sets the consumed flag to signify that the event has been handled.

▶ `public int getID()` Returns the event type.

▶ `protected boolean isConsumed()` Returns `true` if the event has been handled.

▶ `public String paramString()` Returns the parameter string associated with the creation of the current class.

▶ `public String toString()` Returns a string representation of the object.

Event

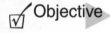 Objective

As mentioned earlier, there are two objects that define the event model framework in JDK 1.1 and later; these are `java.util.EventObject` and `java.awt.AWTEvent`. However, the pre-JDK 1.1 event model for all events consists of one object: `java.AWT.Event`.

Fields

 Objective

Even though the java.AWT.Event class is not readily used in current Java development efforts, its presence persists in legacy code and in the Certified Programmer Exam. For this reason, the following provides a complete anatomy of the java.AWT.Event.

Unlike the java.awt.AWTEvent class, which provides classification for contained event information, the Event class tries to cram all possible AWT events into a single class. To facilitate this, the Event class provides the following field constants to decipher stored event information.

- ▶ ACTION_EVENT Signifies an action event.

- ▶ ALT_MASK The alt modifier constant.

- ▶ arg An arbitrary argument.

- ▶ BACK_SPACE The Back Space key.

- ▶ CAPS_LOCK The Caps Lock action key.

- ▶ clickCount The number of consecutive clicks.

- ▶ CTRL_MASK The control modifier constant.

- ▶ DELETE The Delete key.

- ▶ DOWN The down arrow action key.

- ▶ END The End action key.

- ▶ ENTER The Enter key.

- ▶ ESCAPE The Escape key.

- ▶ evt The next event.

- ▶ F1 The F1 function action key.

- ▶ F10 The F10 function action key.

- ▶ F11 The F11 function action key.

- ▶ F12 The F12 function action key.

- ▶ F2 The F2 function action key.

- ▶ F3 The F3 function action key.

- ▶ F4 The F4 function action key.

- ▶ F5 The F5 function action key.

- ▶ F6 The F6 function action key.

- ▶ F7 The F7 function action key.

▶ F8   The F8 function action key.

▶ F9   The F9 function action key.

▶ GOT_FOCUS   A component gained the focus.

▶ HOME   The Home action key.

▶ id   The type of this event. This value maps directly to one of the defined constant field identifiers.

▶ INSERT   The Insert key.

▶ key   The key code that was pressed in a keyboard event.

▶ KEY_ACTION   The action key press keyboard event.

▶ KEY_ACTION_RELEASE   The action key release keyboard event.

▶ KEY_PRESS   The key press keyboard event.

▶ KEY_RELEASE   The key release keyboard event.

▶ LEFT   The left arrow action key.

▶ LIST_DESELECT   A list was deselected.

▶ LIST_SELECT   A List was selected.

▶ LOAD_FILE   A file loading event.

▶ LOST_FOCUS   A component lost the focus.

▶ META_MASK   The meta modifier constant.

▶ modifiers   The state of the modifier keys.

▶ MOUSE_DOWN   The mouse down event.

▶ MOUSE_DRAG   The mouse drag event.

▶ MOUSE_ENTER   The mouse enter event.

▶ MOUSE_EXIT   The mouse exit event.

▶ MOUSE_MOVE   The mouse move event.

▶ MOUSE_UP   The mouse up event.

▶ NUM_LOCK   The NumLock action key.

▶ PAUSE   The Pause action key.

▶ PGDN   The Page Down action-key.

▶ PGUP   The Page Up action key.

▶ PRINT_SCREEN   The PrintScreen action key.

▶ RIGHT   The right arrow action key.

▶ SAVE_FILE   A file saving event.

▶ SCROLL_ABSOLUTE   The absolute scroll event.

▶ SCROLL_BEGIN   The scroll begin event.

▶ SCROLL_END   The scroll end event.

▶ SCROLL_LINE_DOWN   The line down scroll event.

▶ SCROLL_LINE_UP   The line up scroll event.

▶ SCROLL_LOCK   The ScrollLock action key.

▶ SCROLL_PAGE_DOWN   The page down scroll event.

▶ SCROLL_PAGE_UP   The page up scroll event.

▶ SHIFT_MASK   The shift modifier constant.

▶ TAB   The Tab key.

▶ target   The target component.

▶ UP   The up arrow action key.

▶ when   The time stamp.

▶ WINDOW_DEICONIFY   The de-iconify window event.

▶ WINDOW_DESTROY   The destroy window event.

▶ WINDOW_EXPOSE   The expose window event.

▶ WINDOW_ICONIFY   The iconify window event.

▶ WINDOW_MOVED   The move window event.

▶ x   The x coordinate of the event.

▶ y   The y coordinate of the event.

Constructors

java.awt.Event provides three constructors for the initialization of specific event information. The following provides a list of each of these constructors.

▶ public Event(Object target, int id, Object arg)   Constructs an event with the specified target component, event type, and argument.

▶ `public Event(Object target, long when, int id, int x, int y, int key, int modifiers)` Constructs an event with the specified target component, time stamp, event type, x and y coordinates, keyboard key, state of the modifier keys, and an argument set to null.

▶ `public Event(Object target, long when, int id, int x, int y, int key, int modifiers, Object arg)` Constructs an event with the specified target component, time stamp, event type, x and y coordinates, keyboard key, state of the modifier keys and argument.

Methods

A set of methods are provided by the `Event` class to present the encapsulated event information. The following is a complete list of all methods contained within the `Event` class.

▶ `public boolean controlDown()` Returns `true` if the Control key is depressed.

▶ `public boolean metaDown()` Returns `true` if the meta key is depressed.

▶ `protected String paramString()` Returns the parameter string of this event.

▶ `public boolean shiftDown()` Returns `true` if the Shift key is depressed.

▶ `public String toString()` Returns the string representation of this event's values.

▶ `public void translate(int x, int y)` Translates an event relative to the given component.

Summary

The entire Java Class library is huge, and getting larger. It is true that a large class library aids development, but, at the same time, the size of a class library adds additional amounts of information to learn. Bigger is not always better, and in the case of the Java Programmer Certification this is definitely true.

In this chapter you learned the specific class signatures required for the successful completion of Java Programmer Certification. The extent of knowledge required for the completion of Java Programmer Certification is a far cry from mastery of the entire Java Class Library, or even the highlighted classes. Rather, the knowledge required to complete the Java Programmer Certification is limited to a general feel for each highlighted class.

The following questions provide an example set of actual Certification questions to assess your skills in the Java Class Library.

Review Questions

1. A Hashtable is what?

    A. A generic object storage device.

    B. A generic data storage device.

    C. A deprecated facility from JDK 1.0

    D. Not supported in JDK 1.0.

2. Which of the following is NOT a method of `java.lang.Object`?

    A. `wait()`

    B. `equals(Object)`

    C. `getHashCode()`

    D. `notify()`

3. The `java.lang.String` class provides methods for finding substrings within the contained string.

    A. True

    B. False

4. `Float`, `Double`, and `Byte` have which of the following in common?

    A. They represent numeric values.

    B. They are derived from Number.

    C. They have a primitive data type counterpart.

    D. All of the above.

5. `java.util.EventObject` is the parent class of `java.awt.AWTEvent`.

    A. True

    B. False

6. `java.lang.Thread` utilizes which of the following methods to relinquish a processing slot to another thread?

   A. `Sleep()`

   B. `Wait()`

   C. `yield()`

7. `java.awt.AWTEvent` contains a constructor to aid in porting the `Event` class to the post-JDK 1.1 event model.

   A. True

   B. False

8. The `java.lang.System` class must be instantiated in order to use its facilities.

   A. True

   B. False

9. The `java.lang.System` class contains which of the following fields?

   A.   Standard in

   B.   Standard out

   C.   Standard error

   D.   All of the above

10. Which of the following members is used to find the type of event encapsulated in a `java.awt.Event` class?

   A.   `getEventType()`

   B.   `isMouseEvent()`

   C.   `getParameters()`

   D.   `id`

Review Answers

1. A

2. C

3. A

4. D

5. A

6. C

7. A

8. B

9. D

10. D

Chapter 6

JDK Supplied Tools

Back in the early days of Java—before Cafe, Visual Cafe, Mojo, or even Visual J++—all Java development was done through a text editor and JDK supplied tools. That's right, no Integrated Development Environments (IDEs), just raw command line functionality. Today, development is done for the most part in an IDE or visual development tool that puts a layer between JDK tools and the developer. However, the JDK supplied tools have not gone away, they have just been assimilated.

Even today, with all of the visual development tools and code generators, the need still arises to manually use the JDK-supplied command line tools. In fact, tools like `javadoc` and `jar` are only accessible by directly invoking the JDK supplied command line tool. For this reason, the Certified Java Programmer exam contains a set of JDK tool specific questions.

In this chapter, a subset of the tools found in the JVM will be discussed. The other tools supplied in the JDK are of importance for various aspects of development, but are not explicit testable material. However, all tools discussed in this chapter are directly testable items.

This chapter will discuss the following JDK supplied tools:

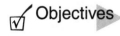 Objectives

- ▶ `javac`

- ▶ `java`

- ▶ `appletviewer`

- ▶ `javadoc`

Test Yourself! Before reading this chapter, test yourself to determine how much study time you will need to devote to this section.

1. What variations of the java tool are provided in the JDK?

   A. javag

   B. javag_w

   C. java_w

   D. A and B

   E. All of the Above

2. `javac -depend myClass.java` will cause which of the following to happen?

   A. `myClass.java` to be compiled.

   B. All depended classes of `myClass.java` to be compiled.

   C. A and B

   D. None of the Above

JDK Supplied Compiler javac

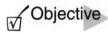Objective ▶ A development environment wouldn't be much without a compiler, and the JDK wouldn't be anything without a Java compiler. For this reason, the JDK is shipped with two separate compilers, javac and javac_g.

> ▶ javac [options] filename.java ...

> ▶ javac_g [options] filename.java ...

javac and javac_g are identical from a usage standpoint. However, where the difference comes into play is in the optimization arena. javac_g is designed to produce unoptimized code suitable to use with debuggers.

The following sections provide a detailed look at the usage of javac and javac_g. However, because javac_g's usage is identical to javac, all subsequent discussions will focus on javac. javac_g's usage is indistinguishable from javac, and can be used as a direct replacement for all subsequent examples and discussions.

.java to .class

javac compiles Java source code from a .java file, and produces JVM executable .class files. This raw source to executable is directly analogous to compiling .c files to .exe, or any source file to natively executable format. However, the compilation process for Java source files is different from conventional languages.

Java has the ability to dynamically load and use different classes during execution. On a compilation level, this means that not all the code is linked into a single executable. Rather, each class contains its own executable .class file. For example Listing 6.1 defines three separate classes which compose a single application. In the traditional way of looking at these classes, the executable code for each class would be compiled and linked into a single executable, but that's not Java-"trinsic." Each class is its own separate object, and is contained in its own separate executable. Thus, the result from the compilation of the following code example is three separate class files.

Listing 6.1 Listing of threadTest.java.

```java
import java.util.*;

class multiThreadResource{
    private Object O = new Object();
    private int counter = 0;

    public void increment(){
        synchronized(O){
            counter++;
        }
    }
}


class singleThread implements Runnable
{
    public Thread Child_Thread = null;
    public String MyName;
    public int CalcPrimeOf;

    public singleThread(String Name, int PrimeOf){
        MyName = Name;
        CalcPrimeOf = PrimeOf;
    }

    public void start(){
      if (Child_Thread == null)
      {
        Child_Thread = new Thread(this);
            Child_Thread.start();
      }
    }

    public void stop(){
      if (Child_Thread != null)
        Child_Thread.stop();
```

```
            Child_Thread = null;
    }


   public boolean IsPrime(long in){

        boolean prime = true;
        System.out.println(MyName + " Testing - " + in);
        for(long i = 2; i <= (in / 2);++i){
            if((in % i) == 0){
                prime = false;
                break;
            }
        }
        return prime;
    }


   public void run(){

        int NumberOfTimeToRun = (int)(Integer.MAX_VALUE *
Math.random());


        for(int i = 0;i < NumberOfTimeToRun;++i){
            try{
                //Sleep for enough time to let others have some
➥fun.
                int SleepFor = 4;
                System.out.println(MyName + " Going to Sleep for "
                    + SleepFor + "milliseconds");
Thread.sleep(SleepFor);
            }
            catch(Exception e){}
            IsPrime(CalcPrimeOf);
        }
        System.out.println(MyName + " Done!");
    }
}
```

continues

Listing 6.1 Continued

```
public class threadTest {

    public static void main(String args[]) {

        Hashtable storage = new Hashtable(10);
        //create 10 threads;
        for(int i = 0;i < 10;++i)
            storage.put(new Integer(i), new Thread(new
                singleThread("Thread " + i, i * 365)));

        //Startup the Threads
        for(int i = 0;i < 10;++i){
            Thread tmp = (Thread)storage.get(new Integer(i));
            tmp.setPriority(i+1);
            tmp.start();
        }

        //join up with all the threads
        //Startup the Threads
        for(int i = 0;i < 10;++i){
            Thread tmp = (Thread)storage.get(new Integer(i));
            try{
                tmp.join();
            }catch(Exception e){}
        }
    }
}
```

Generated class files from the compilation of threadTest.java:

```
multiThreadResource.class
singleThread.class
threadTest.class
```

Finding the Classes

So, each class has an associated .class file. However, javac and java don't require all .class files to be present in the current compilation of execution directory (which will be discussed later in this chapter). Rather, javac and java rely on the CLASSPATH environment variable as a package search path.

Chapter 3, "Java Objects and Exceptions," presented a concept of a class, or object naming space. More specifically, Chapter 3 explained the concept of a package containing a grouping of classes and/or other packages. What wasn't described is exactly how classes are located to be executed or compiled, which is exactly the role of the CLASSPATH environment variable.

The CLASSPATH environment variable specifies the location of various packages on your development, or execution environment. For example, the following is an example of a CLASSPATH environment variable. Each path defined will be searched sequentially for the existence of any imported Classes. Further, javac and java support the concept of .ZIP files containing various packages. The .ZIP files, are looked upon as directories and handled in the same manner.

```
CLASSPATH=.;C:\JAVA\LIB\CLASSES.ZIP;D:\weblogic\classes-
jdk102;d:\mct.3e\lib\mct3_0.zip;e:\website\java\classes;
g:\VisualCafe\java\lib;g:\Cafe\java\charts
```

Command Line Usage

javac does not have many command line parameters, but the few it has are powerful and make javac a flexible command line compilation tool. The following diagrams each command line option for javac.

Complete List of Support javac command line options:

- ▶ -classpath Specifies the ClassPath

- ▶ -d Redirects output to the specified directory

- ▶ -encoding Uses the specified character encoding

- ▶ -g   Enables debug

- ▶ -nowarn   Ignore all warnings

- ▶ -O   Optimizes the compilation

- ▶ -verbose   Print all class resolutions

- ▶ -depend   Update all dependencies

- ▶ -J   Set a specified system parameter

-classpath

As mentioned earlier in this section, the CLASSPATH environment variable specifies the package search path for javac. However, it is sometimes beneficial to explicitly specify the package search path used for compilation. For this reason, the -classpath command line parameter specifies package search path to be used for the compilation.

When the -classpath command line parameter is specified, the supplied search path effectively overrides the CLASSPATH environment variable. For this reason, the valued provided in the -classpath parameter must conform to the semicolon path notation. That is, each path, including the current working directory and all subsequent package directories, must be specified in entirety separated by a semicolon. For example, the following specifies a package search path containing the current directory and an arbitrary path.

```
javac -classpath .;C:\tools\java\classes ...
```

-d—Output Directory

If -classpath allows you to specify the class input directories, it is logical to include a parameter to specify the output directory. For this reason, the -d parameter provides the ability to specify the output path for all compiled .class files. For example, the command invokes the javac compiler with the -d parameter specifying all created .class files are to be written to the C:\output directory.

```
javac -d C:\output Hello.java
```

-encoding—Encoding Type

The -encoding parameter allows you to specify the specific character encoding scheme used in the compilation of your classes. Specifically, this option allows you to use such internationalized coding schemes as EUCJIS\SJIS. However, if this option is not specified, then the platform default converter is used.

-g—Debug On

The existence of debugging information in .class files greatly contributes to the size of the file. For this reason, the -g parameter allows you to enable such debug information. For example, the following example compiles a class with all debugging options on. Omitting the -g parameter instructs javac not to include the extra debugging information.

```
javac -g Hello.java
```

-nowarn—No Warnings For Me

For a variety of different reasons, javac may display various warning messages to flag a possible error. This is not to say that the produced warnings prohibit the complete compilation and linkage of the source file(s). Rather, a warning is displayed to flag a piece of code which may possibly be a problem spot. For example, when compiling Java JDK 1.0 programs in a JDK 1.1+ javac, a number of deprecated warnings appear to inform of an incorrect usage. The code will still compile, javac will just complain about the code. For this reason, the -nowarn option informs javac not to display any warning messages.

-O—Bigger and Faster

The -O parameter is used to optimize the execution speed of the produced .class file by inlining static, final, and private methods. However, the down side to this optimization is that .class files will be inherently larger.

-verbose—Show Me Everything

For a variety of different reasons, knowing what java is loading, and compiling can be beneficial. To supply this benefit, the -verbose parameter instructs java to output all classes being compiled and linked.

-depend—Compile Everything

As shown in Chapter 2, "Java Language Internals," a class can have any given number of parents. Which leads to an issue of compilation complexity. As you can imagine, compiling all parent classes for all used classes can be a time intensive task. The solution being, the -depend parameter which allows access to specify the level of compilation to take place. That is, with the -depend parameter all recursively dependent files will be sequentially recompiled. Omitting the -depend parameter directs javac to only recompile any directly dependent, missing, or out of date .class files.

-J—Include a Parameter

The -J parameter provides the facility to store Java runtime directives directly in the class file. That is, by using the -J parameter, parameters for the java runtime tool may be embedded directly into the created class file.

Java Command Line Execution with java

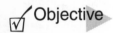

As stated in Chapter 1, "Java and the Java Virtual Machine," applets are executed in a browser, and applications are executed from the command line. However, what wasn't mentioned is exactly how Java applications are invoked from the command line, which is by using the JDK supplied java command line tool.

▶ java [*options*]   classname <args>

▶ java_g [*options*]   classname <args>

▶ javaw [ ]   classname <args>

▶ javaw_g [*options*]   classname <args>

java, java_g, javaw, and javaw_g are all variations of the base tool. The java command line tool executes the specified Java application in a normal, or traditional, way. That is, optimized class execution with an associated output console window. However, some usages may not wish to execute the specified class with the supplied optimization, thus java_g. Likewise, other bundled usages may require the specified class to be executed with an external console window, javaw. Finally, there may be even other usages which require neither optimization or an application console window, javaw_g.

The supplied variations of the java command line tool provide many variations to suite specific class execution needs. Nevertheless, much like javac and javac_g which utilize the same command line parameter, so do the variations of the java command line tool. The following sections will present a complete set of command line options supported by each of the three java command line tool variations.

Command Line Usage

The java command line tool executes a specified class file with a virgin operating environment. Since this the case, it is not surprising that the java command line tool provides a variety of parameters to tweak the operating environment, which is to execute the specified class. The following sections describe each of the supported command line parameters.

A complete list of support java command line options follows:

- ▶ -debug   Enable debug

- ▶ -cs, -checksource   Verify latest source version

- ▶ -classpath path   Specify CLASSPATH

- ▶ -mx x   Sets the maximum size of the memory allocation pool

- ▶ -ms x   Sets the startup size of the memory allocation pool

▶ -noasyncgc Specifies no asynchronous garbage collection

▶ -prof Print profiling information

▶ -version Displays Java version numbers

▶ -help Provides brief command line option help

▶ -ss x Sets the size C stack

▶ -oss x Sets the size Java stack size

▶ -t Prints JVM trace information

▶ -v, -verbose Displays all class resolutions

▶ -verify Turns ClassLoader verification on

▶ -verifyremote Forces all remote classes to be verified

▶ -verbosegc Display garbage collection statistics

▶ -D Sets a specified JVM variable

Debug Enabled

Another supplied JDK tool is called jdb, or Java debugger. The
-debug parameter sets up the appropriate execution hooks to use
the jdb tool. The following provides an example usage.

```
java -debug myClass
```

Check Source Files

The -cs, a -checksource parameter, compares the modification
time of the source file, with the creation time of the associated
.class file. If the .class file is found to be older than the source file,
the class is recompiled before it is used. This process holds for all
classes utilized by the specified Execution class. The following provides an example usage.

```
java -cs myClass
```

Specifying the CLASSPATH

The -classpath parameter provides the ability to override the set CLASSPATH environment variable. The syntax and usage is identical to the -classpath parameter presented earlier in this chapter for the javac.

Maximum Memory Allocation Pool Size

The -mx x parameter provides the means to set the maximum size of the memory allocation pool (the garbage collected heap). The specified value x following the -mx parameter determines the maximum number of bytes, kilobytes, or megabytes, depending on the supplied value. The following provide sample usages.

```
java -mx 1000 myClass
```

sets the maximum size of the memory allocation pool to 1000 bytes.

```
java -mx 10k myClass
```

sets the maximum size of the memory allocation pool to 10 kilobytes.

```
java -mx 10m myClass
```

sets the maximum size of the memory allocation pool to 10 megabytes.

Startup Memory Allocation Pool Size

The -ms x parameter allows to explicitly set the startup size of the memory allocation pool (the garbage collected heap). The specified value x following the -ms parameter determines the original number of bytes, kilobytes, or megabytes depending on the supplied value. However, if the -ms x parameter is omitted the default startup size is 1 megabyte. The following provide sample usages.

```
java -ms 1000 myClass
```

sets the startup size of the memory allocation pool to 1000 bytes.

```
java -ms 10k myClass
```

sets the startup size of the memory allocation pool to 10 kilobytes.

```
java -ms 10m myClass
```

sets the startup size of the memory allocation pool to 10 megabytes.

Manual Garbage Collection

The -noasyncgc parameter turns off automatic garbage collection. However, if automatic garbage collection is disabled the responsibility to run garbage collection falls on the developer. If -noasyncgc parameter is specified and garbage collection is not explicitly called within the application, garbage collection will only be run when all memory resources have been consumed.

No Class Garbage Collection

The -noclassgc parameter instructs the garbage collection mechanism to not reclaim unused classes in memory. If the -noclassgc parameter is omitted garbage collection will reclaim all unused class memory resources.

Enable Profiling

The Java Runtime has the ability to produce profile information pertaining to the execution of any given class, including execution time and resource usage. To enable this feature, the -prof must accompany either java_g, or javaw_g command line tools. By default, profile information is stored in .\java.prof. The following provide sample usages.

```
java_g -prof myClass
javaw_g -prof myClass
```

writes all profile information to .\java.prof.

```
java_g -prof: .\myrun.prof myClass
javaw_g -prof: .\myrun.prof myClass
```

writes all profile information to .\myrun.prof.

The following is a partial listing of a profile file:

```
count                       callee                    caller             time
   68         java/lang/String.<init>([C)V               <unknown caller>        15
   68    java/lang/System.arraycopy(Ljava/la    java/lang/String.<init>([C)V         0
   68          java/lang/Object.<init>()V       java/lang/String.<init>([C)V         0
   24    java/util/Vector.elementAt(I)Ljava/ java/awt/Menu.getItem(I)Ljava/awt/M     0
   17    java/util/Vector.ensureCapacity(I)V java/util/Vector.addElement(Ljava/l     0
   16          java/lang/Object.<init>()V     java/awt/MenuComponent.<init>()V       0
   16          java/lang/Object.<init>()V        java/awt/Color.<init>(I)V           0
   16          java/lang/Object.<init>()V     java/util/HashtableEntry.<init>()V     0
   16    java/util/HashtableEntry.<init>()V   java/util/Hashtable.put(Ljava/lang/    0
   16    java/util/Hashtable.put(Ljava/lang/            <unknown caller>            0
   16         java/lang/String.hashCode()I    java/util/Hashtable.put(Ljava/lang/    0
   15     java/awt/MenuComponent.<init>()V    java/awt/MenuItem.<init>(Ljava/lang    0
   15          java/awt/Color.<init>(I)V       java/awt/Color.<init>(III)V          0
   15    java/awt/MenuComponent.removeNotify   java/awt/Menu.removeNotify()V         0
   13          java/awt/Color.<init>(III)V     java/awt/Color.<clinit>()V           0
   12    java/awt/Menu.add(Ljava/awt/MenuIte java/awt/Menu.add(Ljava/lang/String     0
   12    java/awt/Toolkit.getDefaultToolkit(    java/awt/MenuItem.addNotify()V        0
   12    java/awt/MenuComponent.getParent()L sun/awt/win32/MMenuItemPeer.<init>(     0
   12    sun/awt/win32/MMenuItemPeer.dispose java/awt/MenuComponent.removeNotify     0
   12    java/awt/MenuItem.<init>(Ljava/lang java/awt/Menu.add(Ljava/lang/String     0
   12         java/awt/MenuItem.addNotify()V      java/awt/Menu.addNotify()V        16
   12    java/awt/Menu.getItem(I)Ljava/awt/M      java/awt/Menu.addNotify()V         0
   12    sun/awt/win32/MToolkit.createMenuIt      java/awt/MenuItem.addNotify()V    16
   12          java/lang/Object.<init>()V     sun/awt/win32/MMenuItemPeer.<init>(     0
   12    java/awt/Menu.getItem(I)Ljava/awt/M      java/awt/Menu.removeNotify()V      0
   12    java/util/Vector.addElement(Ljava/l java/awt/Menu.add(Ljava/awt/MenuIte     0
   12    sun/awt/win32/MMenuItemPeer.create( sun/awt/win32/MMenuItemPeer.<init>(    16
   12    sun/awt/win32/MMenuItemPeer.<init>( sun/awt/win32/MToolkit.createMenuIt    16
   10    sun/awt/win32/MFramePeer.insets()Lj
```

Display Tool Version Number

The -version parameter displays the build version information for the java command line tool.

Get Help

The -help parameter displays the parameter help information for the java command line tool.

Set Maximum C Stack Size

The -ss *x* parameter allows you to explicitly set the size of the C stack for each created thread to the value specified in *x*. The specified value *x* following the -ss parameter determines the C stack size in number of bytes, kilobytes, or megabytes depending on the supplied value. The following provide sample usages.

```
java -ss 1000 myClass
```

sets the size C stack size to 1000 bytes.

```
java -ss 10k myClass
```

sets the size C stack size to 10 kilobytes.

```
java -ss 10m myClass
```

-oss x

sets the size C stack size to 10 megabytes.

Set Maximum Java Stack Size

The -ss *x* parameter allows you to explicitly set the size of the Java stack for each created thread to the value specified in *x*. The specified value *x* following the -ss parameter determines the Java stack size in number of bytes, kilobytes, or megabytes depending on the supplied value. The following provide sample usages.

```
java -oss 1000 myClass
```

sets the size Java stack size to 1000 bytes.

```
java -oss 10k myClass
```

sets the size Java stack size to 10 kilobytes.

```
java -oss 10m myClass
```

sets the size Java stack size to 10 megabytes.

Enable Execution Tracing

The -t parameter enables tracing for the execution of the specified class. However, the –t parameter only works with the java_g command line tools. The following provides a sample usage.

```
java_g -t myClass
```

Example trace information:

```
0          0execute_java_constructor new java/lang/ThreadGroup =>
➥java.lang.ThreadGroup@15030B8/159CBE0
0 Entering
Entering java.lang.ThreadGroup.<init>(ThreadGroup.java:52)
Entering java.lang.Object.<init>(Object.java:29)
     0          0execute_java_constructor new java/lang/String =>
➥java.lang.String@15030C8/159CC28
0 Entering
Entering java.lang.String.<init>(String.java:84)
Entering java.lang.Object.<init>(Object.java:29)
0 Entering
Entering java.lang.System.<clinit>(System.java:73)
0 Entering
Entering java.io.FileDescriptor.<clinit>(FileDescriptor.java:42)
Entering java.io.FileDescriptor.<init>(FileDescriptor.java:34)
Entering java.lang.Object.<init>(Object.java:29)
Entering java.io.FileDescriptor.<init>(FileDescriptor.java:34)
Entering java.lang.Object.<init>(Object.java:29)
Entering java.io.FileDescriptor.<init>(FileDescriptor.java:34)
Entering java.lang.Object.<init>(Object.java:29)
Entering java.io.FileInputStream.<init>(FileInputStream.java:67)
Entering java.io.InputStream.<init>(InputStream.java:34)
Entering java.lang.Object.<init>(Object.java:29)
Entering java.lang.System.getSecurityManager(System.java:101)
Entering java.io.BufferedInputStream.<init>(BufferedInputStream.
➥java:76)
Entering java.io.FilterInputStream.<init>(FilterInputStream.
➥java:41)
Entering java.io.InputStream.<init>(InputStream.java:34)
Entering java.lang.Object.<init>(Object.java:29)
Entering java.io.FileOutputStream.<init>(FileOutputStream.
➥java:72)
Entering java.io.OutputStream.<init>(OutputStream.java:33)
Entering java.lang.Object.<init>(Object.java:29)
Entering java.lang.System.getSecurityManager(System.java:101)
```

```
Entering java.io.BufferedOutputStream.<init>(BufferedOutputStream.
➡java:60)
Entering java.io.FilterOutputStream.<init>(FilterOutputStream.
➡java:41)
Entering java.io.OutputStream.<init>(OutputStream.java:33)
Entering java.lang.Object.<init>(Object.java:29)
Entering java.io.PrintStream.<init>(PrintStream.java:61)
Entering java.io.FilterOutputStream.<init>(FilterOutputStream.
➡java:41)
Entering java.io.OutputStream.<init>(OutputStream.java:33)
Entering java.lang.Object.<init>(Object.java:29)
Entering java.io.FileOutputStream.<init>(FileOutputStream.java:72)
Entering java.io.OutputStream.<init>(OutputStream.java:33)
Entering java.lang.Object.<init>(Object.java:29)
```

Enable Verbose Loading of Class Resources

The -v and -verbose parameters provide means to keep track of
each class that is loaded into the JVM. The following provides a
sample usage.

```
java_g -t myClass
```

Example Verbose Class Loading Information:

```
[Loaded java/awt/peer/MenuBarPeer.class from
➡D:\CAFE\JAVA\BIN\...\..\bin\..\JAVA\LIB\CLASSES.ZIP]
[Loaded sun/awt/win32/MMenuBarPeer.class from
➡D:\CAFE\JAVA\BIN\...\..\bin\..\JAVA\LIB\CLASSES.ZIP]
[Loaded sun/awt/win32/MMenuPeer.class from
➡D:\CAFE\JAVA\BIN\...\..\bin\..\JAVA\LIB\CLASSES.ZIP]
[Loaded sun/awt/win32/MMenuItemPeer.class from
➡D:\CAFE\JAVA\BIN\...\..\bin\..\JAVA\LIB\CLASSES.ZIP]
[Loaded sun/awt/ScreenUpdater.class from
➡D:\CAFE\JAVA\BIN\...\..\bin\..\JAVA\LIB\CLASSES.ZIP]
[Loaded sun/awt/ScreenUpdaterEntry.class from
➡D:\CAFE\JAVA\BIN\...\..\bin\..\JAVA\LIB\CLASSES.ZIP]
[Loaded java/awt/Graphics.class from
➡D:\CAFE\JAVA\BIN\...\..\bin\..\JAVA\LIB\CLASSES.ZIP]
[Loaded sun/awt/win32/Win32Graphics.class from
➡D:\CAFE\JAVA\BIN\...\..\bin\..\JAVA\LIB\CLASSES.ZIP]
[Loaded java/awt/Event.class from
➡D:\CAFE\JAVA\BIN\...\..\bin\..\JAVA\LIB\CLASSES.ZIP]
[Loaded java/awt/peer/TextAreaPeer.class from
```

```
⮕D:\CAFE\JAVA\BIN\..\..\bin\..\JAVA\LIB\CLASSES.ZIP]
[Loaded java/lang/IllegalMonitorStateException.class from
⮕D:\CAFE\JAVA\BIN\..\..\bin\..\JAVA\LIB\CLASSES.ZIP]
```

Enable Byte-Code Verification

As mentioned in Chapter 1, "Java and the Java Virtual Machine," the JVM performs a byte-code verification algorithm on all loaded classes. The -verify option applies the same a byte-code verification algorithm to the specified class. However, only the classes execution paths will be verified and not unused pieces of code.

Enable Remote Byte-Code Verification

Similar to the -verify parameter, the -verifyremote performs a byte-code verification algorithm on all classes loaded with class-loader mechanism. By default, the java command line assumes the -verifyremote policy.

Disable Byte-Code Verification

The -noverify parameter disables the default remote byte-code verification algorithm through the classloader mechanism. In a sense, the -noverify parameter turns off the byte-code verification mechanism of the JVM.

Display Garbage Collection

Similar to the -verbose parameter, the -verbosegc parameter displays information pertaining to the garbage collector mechanism. With -verbosegc parameter, a statement is printed each time the garbage collector mechanism is executed.

Edit JVM Properties

The -D parameter allows for name/value modification of Java class field constants. For example, the following executes the java command line tool and sets the value of awt.button.color to blue. The java command line tool allows for any number of such name/value properties.

```
Java_g -Dawt.button.color=blue
```

Applet Command Line Execution with Appletviewer

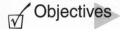 Objectives ▶

It is true that applets require a browser to execute operate, and they do inherit their operating environment from whichever breed of browser the applet is being executed from. However, this does not mean that applet development or deployment require the use of a large, commercial browser. Rather, just as the `java` command line tool provided a means to execute Java classes, the `appletviewer` tool provides an execution platform for applets.

The following provides usage and command line parameters for the `appletviewer` utility. A single call to `appletviewer` may execute multiple applet windows, depending on the number of URLs provided on the command line.

```
appletviewer [ options ] urls ...
appletviewer -debug myApplet.html yourApplet.html
```

Complete List of appletviewer command line options:

▶ `-debug` Enables debugging by executing the Applet(s) in the `jdb` command line tool.

▶ `-encoding` Specifies the encoding name for the Applet's HTML file.

▶ `-J` Can be used to specify a parameter to the Java runtime. The parameters supported correspond with the parameters for the `java` tool. Also multiple parameters can be specified, but all must begin with `-J`.

Auto Documentation with javadoc

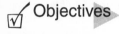 Objectives ▶

Traditionally in development, source code documentation is usually for internal use only. However, `javadoc` changes all that. Imagine a tool which contains enough logic to search through source code files, and produce a complete API documentation. This is not to say that `javadoc` "auto documents" source class files, but rather `javadoc` allows for a clear presentation of comments embedded in the source.

javadoc provides a means for the developer to contextually express implementation details directly inside source file. That is, inside a source file comments, embedded HTML documentation can be provided. However, before an example can be presented, the style of javadoc comments must be explained.

javadoc command line format:

```
javadoc [ options ] [ package ¦ source.java ]
```

JavaDoc Source Comments

The basic premise of javadoc is to scour through a class's source code and hunt out comments, which are then contextually analyzed. However, not all comments embedded inside a source code file are automatically recognized by javadoc. Rather, only "doc" comments are exposed.

A doc comment is signified by a comment which begins with the /** character string. For example, the following provides a doc comment for a declared method.

```
/**
 * This is My Method!
 */
public void myMethod(){
}
```

Any plain text or HTML commands specified in a doc comment are exposed verbatim in the generated Class API documentation.

Supported javadoc Tags

Besides just plain text and HTML comments, javadoc provides a series of specialized tags to aid documentation. The following provides a complete list of these tags and their associated usage.

```
/**
 * Place Class or Interface tags here
 */
public myClass{
```

```
/**
 * Method or Field Documentation Tags here
 */
  public myClass(){
  }
}
```

Class and Interface Documentation Tags:

▶ @author (name-text)   Inserts an author entry into the generate documentation. Multiple @author tags are supported.

▶ @version (version-text)   Inserts a version entry into the generate documentation, specifying the software version.

▶ @see (classname)   Inserts a hyperlink entry in the see portion of the documentation.

▶ @since (since-text)   Inserts a since entry specifying the du-
  ration which the specified class or interface has been available.

▶ @deprecated (deprecated-text)   Inserts a since entry signifying that the class or interface is no longer supported.

Method and Field Documentation Tags:

▶ @param (parameter-name description)   Inserts an entry in
  the generated documentation describing the specified method parameter.

▶ @return (description)   Inserts an entry in the generated
  documentation describing the return value.

▶ @exception (fully-qualified-class-name description)   Inserts
  an entry in the generated documentation describing the
  specified exception thrown.

▶ @see (classname)   Inserts a hyperlink entry in the see portion of the documentation.

▶ @since since-text   Inserts a since entry specifying the dura-
  tion which the specified field or method has been available.

▶ `@deprecated` (deprecated-text)   Inserts a `since` entry signifying that the field or method is no longer supported.

JavaDoc Command Line Options

 **Objectives**

The `javadoc` command line tool provides a number of options to modify the process, and information used to generate the documentation. The following is a complete list of the command line options available.

`javadoc` Command Line Options:

▶ `-classpath` *path*   Identical to the `java`, `javac`, and `appletview-er` tools, the `-classpath` option specifies the `CLASSPATH` used by `javadoc` to resolve class references.

▶ `-public`   Generates documentation for public classes and members only.

▶ `-protected`   Generates documentation for `public` and `pro-tected` classes and members only.

▶ `-private`   Generates documentation for all classes and members.

▶ `-Jflag`   Identical to the `appletviewer` tool, the `-J` option sets runtime system specific variables. For example, the following example specifies that 32MB of memory is allocated to hold the generated documentation.

`javadoc -J-mx32m -J-ms32m <classes> ...`

▶ `-encoding` *name*   Used to specify the encoding name for the specified source file, such as EUCJIS\SJIS.

▶ `-docencoding` *name*   Specify the encoding scheme used for the generated HTML.

▶ `-version`   Enables the generation of version information based off the `@version` tags.

▶ `-author`   Enables the generation of author information based off the `@author` tags.

▶ -noindex   Instructs javadoc not to generate an index.html page.

▶ -notree   Instructs javadoc not to generate an tree.html page.

▶ -d *directory*   Specifies the directory in which to place all generated files.

▶ -verbose   Enables a complete account of the generation process to be generated.

▶ -nodeprecated   Does not generate deprecated information.

Summary

The Java Developer Kit is designed to provide all the tools needed to develop applets and applications in Java. To accomplish this, a large set of tools are provided to facilitate key tasks, like compiling source code. Everything from two different flavors of a compiler to five different varieties of Java runtime tools can be found in the JDK. However, intimate knowledge of each tool is not required for Java development, and definitely not required for the Java Programmer Certification.

In this chapter a subset of JDK supplied tools was presented. From these discussions, you gained a complete working knowledge of each tool and the function those tools play in the JDK. However, wrote memorization of this content is not required or warranted. Rather, the Java Certification Exam focuses on a fairly static group of tool-specific questions. The trick is knowing what to study.

The following questions provide an example set of actual Certification questions to assess your skills in Java Class Library.

Review Questions

1. In the java tool, the `-verbose` tool does which of the following?

    A. Displays the explicit loading of each class.

    B. Generates information regarding how many times a method has been called.

    C. Informs when garbage collection is performed.

    D. The option has been deprecated.

2. With `javadoc`, which of the following denotes a `javadoc` comment.

    A. `//*`

    B. `/*Begin`

    C. `/**`

    D. `//Begin`

3. What variations of the java tool are provided in the JDK?

    A. `javag`

    B. `javag_w`

    C. `java_w`

    D. A and B

    E. All of the above

4. `appletviewer` only retrieves classes found in the CLASSPATH environment variable.

    A. False

    B. True

5. `javac -depend myClass.java` will cause which of the following to happen?

    A. `myClass.java` to be compiled.

    B. All depended classes of myClass.java to be compiled.

    C. A and B

    D. None of the above

6. Which `javadoc` tag is used denote a comment for a method parameter.

    A. `@paramter`

    B. `@value`

    C. `@param`

    D. `@method`

7. `java_w` provides which of the following feature?

    A. Executes a specified class.

    B. Executes a specified class without optimization

    C. Executes a specified class in its own separate window

    D. Executes a specified class without an associated console window

8. The `@deprecated` `javadoc` tag is used to denote deprecated classes, interfaces, or members.

    A. True

    B. False

9. The `appletviewer` has facilities to execute multiple applets at a time by allowing for which of the following?

    A. Multiple applets defined in the HTML

    B. Multiple URL's to be provided on the command line

    C. Providing a window to select desired applets

    D. A and B

10. `java_g` is used for which of the following?

    A. Executing a class with optimization turned off

    B. Using the jdb tool

    C. Compiling the specified source without optimization

    D. A and B

Review Answers

1. A

2. C

3. E

4. B

5. C

6. C

7. D

8. A

9. D

10. D

Chapter

Certified Programmer Practice Test #1

7

The scope of this chapter is to provide detailed test information for the Certified Java Programmer Examination. For this reason, it is required that you should read chapters 1-6 before proceeding.

By now, you know that the Certified Java Programmer examination covers a large body of material. Everything from JVM issues to reserved words to AWT events is covered in the exam. Without a doubt, the scope of knowledge required for you to succeed is by no means trivial. For this reason, knowing the specifics on which you should focus is crucial, and those specifics are the focus of this chapter.

As in school when a teacher has a "what will be on the test" lecture, this chapter provides a picture of the Certified Java Programmer Examination. Beginning with a general study check list and ending with a practice exam, this chapter is devoted to providing a general feel of the Certified Java Programmer examination. This chapter will provide the following resources for the Certified Java Programmer Examination:

 Objectives

- ▶ Study Guide and Check List

- ▶ Practice Exam and Answers

Countdown to Certification

With Chapters 1 through 6 behind you, you are ready to start thinking about sitting for the exam. For many, the idea of sitting for any exam instills an element of fear. If you've read all the previous material, you have the knowledge to take the test. All that is left is to practice.

The following sections set the stage for taking the Certified Java Programmer examination. When reading these sections, begin to prepare yourself mentally for what you can expect from the exam. Above all, relax; this is just a test.

What to Expect from the Exam

Put bluntly, the test is not trivial. Keep in mind that it is designed to validate your skills as a programmer, and not just test your rote memorization. Armed with the knowledge learned in this book, you will be amply prepared. Nevertheless, it helps to frame the composition and setting of the examination.

The Java certification exams are proctored by Sylvan Prometric. If you have never taken an exam from Sylvan Prometric before, the experience will be a new one. This is because the exam is completely proctored by computer, with no human interaction at all. Answers are entered directly into the computer and evaluated in real time. At the end of the exam, you will receive a summary of your score, broken down by question category. There is no waiting for the results in the mail; rather, you get instant examination feedback.

The idea of taking a test on the computer may conjure up ideas of simple true/false and multiple-choice questions. However, the Sylvan Prometric examination facility allows for short answer as well as simple true/false and multiple-choice questions. The true/false and multiple-choice questions require fairly straightforward responses, but the short answer questions are not as simple. That is, the short answer questions require you to input your answer exactly as the test's answer key appears. You will learn how to handle these types of questions later in this chapter.

How to Manage the Testing Procedure

The actual testing process isn't all that complicated. You sit in front of a machine and try to answer questions for a couple hours. However, getting the most out of the testing facility is usually ignored when your entire focus is trying to pass the test at hand. For this reason, you should take some time and cover the key features of the Sylvan Prometric exam to help you manage the examination process.

The fact that the Sylvan Prometric exam is proctored on a computer provides some intrinsic benefits. The following is a list of features and helpful testing hints that will ease and optimize the testing process. Also, the CD-ROM accompanying the book provides a mock-up testing facility equivalent to the Prometric system.

Keys To Managing Sylvan Prometric Examinations:

▶ Skip It—The testing application allows you to skip questions. This facility cannot be used simply to ignore answering desired questions, but rather allows you to revisit questions later. You can use this option to put certain questions off until the end of the test. That is, if you skip a question, the testing application will prompt you again for an answer before the examination session is completed.

▶ Flag It—When testing, there are always questions that you would like to revisit, or for which you are just not entirely sure of the answers. For this reason, the testing application allows you to flag questions. When desired, you can pull up a list of flagged questions so you can revisit the desired question. This tool is invaluable for questions that are either pivotal for other questions, or for questions you are not quite sure about. In either case, the ability to flag a question for later review is definitely a testing asset.

▶ Answer It—As stated earlier, the Certification exam is comprised of true/false, multiple choice, and short answer questions. Answer as many questions as you can, and if you are not sure of the question flag it for later review. If you are completely at a loss, skip it and keep the question in mind when answering the other questions. In most cases, you will find a question that alludes to the correct answer of the un-answered question.

Preparation Checklist

The following list provides a checklist of topics that are covered in the Programmer Certification exam. You should be comfortable with each of the topics found in list and ready to answer specific questions on each. Glance over the list both before you take the provided practice exam, and before you sit for the actual test. This will get your Java gears turning, and put you in the proper mind-set to successfully complete the exam.

Programmer Certification Exam Study Checklist:

▶ The relationship between the JVM and the Java runtime.

▶ How the Java runtime is invoked for an applet.

▶ How the Java runtime is invoked for an application.

▶ What are the Java reserved words?

▶ What are the Java operators?

▶ How to use the Java bit manipulation operators.

▶ What are the Java conditionals?

▶ How Java conditionals modify the execution path.

▶ Handling Java exceptions.

▶ How Java exceptions modify the execution path.

▶ How Java exceptions are created.

▶ How to declare a Java class.

▶ How to declare an applet.

▶ How to declare an application.

▶ The behaviors of the class visibility modifiers.

▶ The behaviors of the method visibility modifiers.

▶ Java class inheritance and access.

▶ Declaring Java threads.

▶ InterThread communication.

▶ Executing a thread.

▶ Thread scheduling and priority.

▶ Java garbage collection execution.

▶ What are the Javadoc comment tags?

▶ What are the command line options for java?

▶ Using the JDK 1.1+ event model.

▶ The components of the AWT.

▶ How to use the facilities of java.util.

▶ Locking objects.

▶ Members of java.lang.Object.

▶ Members of java.lang.String.

▶ Members of java.lang.Number.

▶ Members of java.lang.Integer.

If you traversed this list with only a slight level of uncertainty, go ahead and dive into the practice test. On the other hand, if you are now questioning your total Java knowledge, take some time and revisit the topics you are not quite sure of, and then take the test. As you can see, the test is all-encompassing of the Java language, and requires a fairly high level of knowledge. Very few Java programmers could go through the preceding list and feel certain about each and every topic. Don't feel bad if you find yourself at a loss; it is a common feeling.

Practice Examination

The following exam and answers are provided as a companion to the testing software found on the accompanying CD-ROM. However, the detailed description of each of the answers is not included on the CD-ROM. The test that follows is one of three tests provided on the CD-ROM, and provides a printed and portable study device. With that said, best of luck.

1. The wait() and notify() methods are members of what class?

   A. String

   B. Thread

   C. Object

   D. All Of the above

2. Given a byte with a value of 01110111, which of the following statements will produce 00111011?

   Note: 01110111 = 0x77

   A. 0x77 << 1;

   B. 0x77 >> 3;

   C. 0x77 >> 1;

   D. 0x77 >>> 1;

   E. C and D

3. The following application contains a single error.

```
public class myClass{
    public static void main(String args[]){
        for(int i=0; i < 4345;++i){
            if((i % 2) == 0)
                System.out.println("This is fun");
            else
                System.out.println("Not it isn't");
        }
        (new System()).out.println("The End");
```

```
      }
}
```

Which line contains the error?

   A. for(int i=0; i < 4345;++i){

   B. if((i % 2) == 0)

   C. public static void main(String args[]){

   D. (new System()).out.println("The End");

4. A package is

   A. A collection of interfaces

   B. A collection of classes

   C. A way to provide naming for a group of related classes

   D. All of the above

5. The JVM architecture makes the following provisions to ensure compatibility across all processors:

   A. Uses a stack-based architecture

   B. Is modeled after the lowest common denominator architecture

   C. Minimizes the use of registers

   D. A and B

   E. A and C

6. A JavaChip is

   A. An accelerator chip designed to aid the JVM running on the native machine

   B. A chip that stores Java class files to increase ClassLoader performance

   C. A silicon implementation of the JVM

   D. The chip inside Sun's JavaStation

7. What major feature(s) was/were debuted in the JDK 1.1?

   A. JDBC

   B. RMI

   C. JavaBeans

   D. Improved AWT

   E. None of these

   F. All of these

8. Which of the following is not a reserved word?

   A. NULL

   B. switch

   C. catch

   D. instanceof

   E. None of these

9. A Java runtime environment is available for Windows 3.1.

   A. True

   B. False

10. The statement A %= 3; can best be described as:

   A. A equals A divided by 3.

   B. A equals A in 3 digit percentage form.

   C. A equals A modulus 3.

   D. None of the Above.

11. Which one of the following best describes the role of the JVM?

   A. An interpreter

   B. A device used to execute applets

C. An emulator used to execute Java machine code on a native platform

D. A plug-in to Microsoft Internet Explorer

12. The class file contains the following:

A. JVM executable instructions

B. Method naming information

C. Field naming information

D. All of the above

13. The following code may contain a single error. If it does, what is that error?

```
public class myClass{
     public abstract void myfunction();
     public static void main(String args[]){
         for(int j=0;i < 12;++j){
             for(int i=0; i < 4345;++i)
                     System.out.println("This is fun");
             // Run the garbage collector.
             System.out.println("Executing the garbage col-
lector");
         }
     }
}
```

A. public abstract void myfunction();

B. public class myClass{

C. No Error

14. An interface provides which of the following?

A. A template for further development

B. A mechanism for further development

C. An alternative to class declarations

D. A and C

E. A and B

15. The following defines an object hierarchy.

```
class class1{

    public static int myValue = 2;
}

class class2 extends class1{

    public static int yourValue = 3;

    public int ourValue(){

        return myValue + yourValue;
    }
}
class class3 extends class1{
    public static int theirValue = 5;
    public int ourValue(){

        return myValue + theirValue;
    }

}
public class myClass{

    public static class3 castMe(class1 in){
        return (class3)in;
    }
    public static void main(String args[]){
        class3 v = castMe(new class1());
    }
}
```

When does the following method cause an error/exception?

```
public static class3 castMe(class1 in){
        return (class3)in;
    }
```

A. At compilation

B. Never

   C. If and only if `in` references a `class3` object

   D. If and only if `in` references a `class2` object

16. Which of the following best describes the public class modifier?

   A. Allows only classes in the current package to use its facilities

   B. Allows other classes to subclass it

   C. Opens the class up for usage and subclassing to all

   D. A and B

17. Which of the following is *not* a primitive Java data type?

   A. `int`

   B. `bool`

   C. `float`

   D. `double`

   E. `long`

18. The following code contains one error.

```java
public class myClass{
   public String myfunction(){
      String out = "Hello";
      int i = 0xff;
      i >>>= 4;
      out += i;
      return(out | i);
   }
}
```

   A. i >>>= 4;

   B. out += i;

   C. return(out | i);

   D. It's all good!

19. The throws reserved word provides which of the following?

    A. Raises an exception

    B. Triggers an event

    C. Defines the exceptions a method can raise

    D. Defines the exception a method can raise

20. The following code listing contains one error.

```java
public abstract class myClass{
    public static boolean IsPrime(long in){
        boolean prime = true;
        for(long i = 2; i <= (in / 2);++i){
            if((in % i) == 0){
                prime = false;
                break;
            }
        }
        return prime;
    }
    public abstract void fun(int Value){};
}
```

What is the error?

    A. `public abstract class myClass`

    B. `public abstract void fun(int Value){};`

    C. Incomplete class definition

    D. Class must contain a constructor

21. Please complete the following source, so that if the value of A is equal to B then return A×B, otherwise return 0;

```java
public class myClass{
    public return int myFun(int A, int B){
        //Your Single Line of Code Here!
    }
}
```

Enter answer here:_____

22. Which following answer best describes the following object hierarchy?

```
class class1{

    public static int myValue = 2;
}

class class2 extends class1{

    public static int yourValue = 3;

    public int ourValue(){

        return myValue + yourValue;
    }
}
class class3 extends class2{
    public static int theirValue = 5;
    public int ourValue(){
        return myValue + theirValue;
    }

}
```

   A. class3's parent class is class2, and class2's parent class is class1.

   B. class3's parent class is class2, class2's parent class is class1, and class1's parent is Object.

   C. class1's parent class is class2, and class2's parent class is class3.

   D. class1's parent class is class2, class2's parent class is class3, and class3's parent is Object.

23. What is the output of the following try...catch block?

```
public class tryme {
    public static void main(String args[]) {

        try{
            int I;
            return;
        }catch(Exception e){
```

```
              System.out.println("I am Here");
              return;
          }finally{
              System.out.println("Hello Nurse!");
          }


      }
}
```

A. Hello Nurse!

B. No output

C. I am Here

D. Depends on the creation of the int I;

24. What modifier would be used to limit a method's visibility to only the currently defined class?

    A. public

    B. private

    C. protected

    D. static

25. The following defines an object hierarchy.

```
class class1{

    public static int myValue = 2;
}

class class2 extends class1{

    public static int yourValue = 3;

    public int ourValue(){

        return myValue + yourValue;
    }
}
class class3 extends class1{
    public static int theirValue = 5;
    public int ourValue(){
```

```
            return myValue + theirValue;
        }


    }
    public class myClass{

        public static class1 castMe(class2 in){

            return (class1)in;
        }
        public static void main(String args[]){
            class1 v = castMe(new class2());
        }
    }
```

When does the following method cause an error/exception?

```
public static class1 castMe(class2 in){
return (class1)in;
    }
```

A. At compilation

B. Never

C. If and only if in references a class3 object

D. If and only if in references a class2 object

26. Which statement best describes the following class?

```
public class dataCenterResource{
  private static Sting  data = "";
  public static synchronized void setString(String in){

    data = in;

  }
  public static synchronized String getString(){

    return data;

  }

}
```

A. The class is a simple storage device for a string.

B. The class is a simple storage device for multiple threads to access a single string.

C. The class provides a mechanism by which only one thread can get or set the stored string value at a time.

D. The class provides a mechanism by which only multiple threads can get or set the stored string value.

27. What modifier would be used to limit a method's visibility to only the other classes in the current package and subclasses?

A. public

B. private

C. protected

D. static

28. Given the following code listing:

```java
public class myClass{


    //Your Declaration HERE!{
        try {
            System.in.read();
        } catch (IOException e) {
            return;
        }
    }

    public static void main(String args[]) {
        System.out.println("My console application");
        System.out.println("");
        System.out.println("(press Enter to exit)");
        waitForKey();
    }

}
```

At the specified location, provide a method declaration with the following properties:

Name: `waitForKey`

Input Parameters: None

Return Value: None

Visibility: All classes, including subclasses, in the current package.

Enter answer here:_____

29. The JVM registers and stack are:

    A. 8 bits wide

    B. 16 bits wide

    C. 32 bits wide

    D. 64 bits wide

30. Which of the following members is used to find the type of event encapsulated in a `java.awt.Event` class?

    A. `getEventType()`

    B. `isMouseEvent()`

    C. `getParameters()`

    D. `id`

31. A class can have only a single parent.

    A. True

    B. False

32. The `wait()` call does which of the following?

    A. Blocks until a thread terminates

    B. Blocks until notified by another thread

    C. Blocks until the object is ready for access

    D. Blocks a thread until all other threads have terminated

33. Classes are executed by the JVM in this manner:

    A. The ClassLoader loads the class into the JVM for execution and then signals for execution to begin.

    B. The ClassLoader finds, verifies, and loads the class into the JVM for execution and then signals for execution to begin.

    C. The JVM prompts the user for the class to execute.

    D. The runtime environment loads the applet information into the JVM and then begins the JVM process.

34. How are thread priority and thread scheduling related?

    A. They aren't.

    B. It depends on the thread scheduling algorithm used to implement the JVM.

    C. Thread priority is specified when a thread is to be executed next.

    D. Thread priority is used to determine the next thread to execute from the waiting thread pool.

35. java_g is used for which of the following?

    A. Executing a class with optimization turned off.

    B. Using the jdb tool.

    C. Compiling the specified source without optimization.

    D. A and B.

36. The wait() and notify() methods are defined in what class?

    A. java.lang.String

    B. java.lang.Thread

    C. java.lang.Object

    D. java.lang.Runnable

37. The `Runnable` interface is used for what?

    A. A marathon

    B. Defining a thread

    C. Defining a class that can be executed by a thread

    D. Defining a class to execute a new thread

38. The `java.lang.System` class contains which of the following fields?

    A. Standard In

    B. Standard Out

    C. Standard Error

    D. All of the above

39. The JVM specification defines the process by which unused memory resources are collected and put onto the heap for reuse.

    A. True

    B. False

40. In the `java` tool, the `-verbose` tool does which of the following?

    A. Displays the explicit loading of each class.

    B. Generates information regarding how many times a method has been called.

    C. Informs when garbage collection is performed.

    D. The option has been deprecated.

41. Given the following code segment:

```
import java.util.Hashtable;
import java.util.Enumeration;
import java.net.*;
import java.io.*;
```

```
class myClass implements Runnable
{
//Reference to current thread
   public  Thread Child_Thread = null;
   //Start-up new thread
   public void start(){
      if (Child_Thread == null){
         Child_Thread = new Thread(this);
         Child_Thread.start();
      }
   }
   //Stop the currently executing thread
   public void stop(){
      if (Child_Thread != null)
         Child_Thread.stop();
      Child_Thread = null;
   }
   public void run(){
      for(int i = 0;i < 4556;++i);
   }
}
//Main Public Launcher
public class CSPassiveAgent {
   public static void main(String args[]) {
      Thread  T1 = new Thread(new myClass());
      T1.start();
   }
}
```

Which statement best defines the following code segment?

```
Thread T1 = new Thread(new myClass());
T1.start();
```

A. Thread T1 is created and executed.

B. Thread T1 is constructed to contain the Runnable interface myClass, and it executes the myClass run() method.

C. A compilation error will occur at T1.start();.

D. Thread T1 is constructed to contain the Runnable interface myClass, and it executes the Thread run() method.

42. The JVM specification specifies the thread scheduling used.

    A. True

    B. False

43. Which of the following terminates a thread's execution?

    A. Calling the stop() method

    B. An external JVM event

    C. A thread returning from its run() method

    D. All of the above

44. A Hashtable is what?

    A. A generic object storage device

    B. A generic data storage device

    C. A deprecated facility from JDK 1.0

    D. Not supported in JDK 1.0

45. Which javadoc tag is used to denote a comment for a method parameter?

    A. @parameter

    B. @value

    C. @param

    D. @method

46. java.util.EventObject is the parent class of java.awt.AWTEvent.

    A. True

    B. False

47. All threads created in Java are mutually exclusive.

   A. True

   B. False

48. A class may only implement a single interface.

   A. True

   B. False

49. The following defines an object hierarchy.

```
class class1{
public static int myValue = 2;
}
class class2 extends class1{
public static int yourValue = 3;
public int ourValue(){
return myValue + yourValue;
    }
}
class class3 extends class1{
    public static int theirValue = 5;
    public int ourValue(){
return myValue + theirValue;
    }
}
class class4 extends class1{
}
public class myClass{
public static class2 castMe(class3 in){
return (class2)in;
    }
    public static void main(String args[]){
        class2 v = castMe(new class4());
    }
}
```

When does the following method cause an error/exception?

```
public static class2 castMe(class3 in){
        return (class2)in;
    }
```

A. At compilation

B. Never

C. If and only if in references a `class3` object

E. If and only if in references a `class2` object

50. Which of the following is *not* a method of `java.lang.Object`?

A. `wait()`

B. `equals(Object)`

C. `getHashCode()`

D. `notify()`

51. `Float`, `Double`, and `Byte` have which of the following in common?

A. They represent numeric values.

B. They are derived from Number.

C. They have a primitive data type counterpart.

D. All of the above.

52. The `java.lang.String` class provides methods for finding substrings within the contained string.

A. True

B. False

53. `java.lang.Thread` utilizes which of the following methods to relinquish the thread instance's processing slot to another thread?

A. `Sleep()`

B. `Wait()`

C. `yield()`

54. `java.awt.AWTEvent` contains a constructor to aid in porting the Event class to the post-JDK 1.1 event model.

    A. True

    B. False

55. What modifier would be used to limit a method's visibility to all other classes and subclasses?

    A. `public`

    B. `private`

    C. `protected`

    D. `final`

56. With javadoc, which of the following denotes a javadoc comment?

    A. `//*`

    B. `/*Begin`

    C. `/**`

    D. `//Begin`

57. What variations of the Java tool are provided in the JDK?

    A. `javag`

    B. `javag_w`

    C. `java_w`

    D. A and B

    E. All of the above

58. `appletviewer` only retrieves classes found in the `CLASSPATH` environment variable.

    A. False

    B. True

59. `javac -depend myClass.java` will cause which of the following to happen?

    A. `myClass.java` to be compiled

    B. All dependent classes of `myClass.java` to be compiled

    C. A and B

    D. None of the above

60. `java_w` performs which of the following actions?

    A. Executes a specified class

    B. Executes a specified class without optimization

    C. Executes a specified class in its own separate window

    D. Executes a specified class without an associated console window

61. The `@deprecated` javadoc tag is used to denote deprecated classes, interfaces, or members.

    A. True

    B. False

62. The `appletviewer` has facilities to execute multiple applets at a time by allowing for which of the following?

    A. Multiple applets defined in the HTML

    B. Multiple URLs to be provided on the command line

    C. Providing a window to select desired applets

    D. A and B

63. Which of the following assignment statements is invalid?

    A. `float f = 435;`

    B. `long l = 054;`

C. `double d = 0x77578;`

D. None of the above

64. Which of the following assignment statements is invalid?

A. `double d = 45456.444;`

B. `long l = 45784;`

C. `int i = 1;`

D. `int j = (int)d;`

65. Convert the following statement into its octal equivalent.

```
int i = 16;
//Octal Declaration HERE!
```

Enter octal declaration here:_____

66. Given the following code segment:

```
class class1{
    public class1(){
        System.out.println("class1");
    }
}
class class2 extends class1{
    public class2(){
        System.out.println("class2");
    }
}
class class3 extends class2{
    public class3(){
        System.out.println("class3");
    }
}
public class tryme {
    public static void main(String args[]) {
        System.out.println("In main");
        class3 c = new class3();
    }
}
```

In what order will the output be produced?

A. class3, class2, class2, In main

B. class1, class2, class3, In main

C. In main, class1, class2, class3

D. In main, class3, class2, class1

67. Which of the following best describes when a variable becomes available for reclamation by the garbage collector?

A. After the variable is out of a method's scope

B. After you use it

C. Upon returning from the containing method block

D. When the variable is no longer referenced anywhere in the JVM

68. Given the following code listing:

```
public class tryme {
  public static void main(String args[]) {
    int maincount = 0;
    outer:for(int i=0;i < 5;++i)
          middle:for(int j=0;j < 5;++j)
              inner:for(int k=0;k < 5;++k){
                      System.out.println("Hello - " +
➥++maincount);
                      if((k%5) ==0)
                          break outer;
    }
      }
}
```

Which of the following is the last line of output?

A. Hello - 25

B. Hello - 5

C. Hello - 1

D. Hello - 10

69. What is the numeric range for a Java int?

    A. -(2^31) to (2^31)

    B. -(2^16) to (2^16 - 1)

    C. 0 to (2^32)

    D. -(2^31) to (2^31 - 1)

70. Given the following HTML applet declaration:

```
<APPLET URL codebase = "/" archive="Myapplet.zip"
➥CODE="Myapplet.class" WIDTH=500 HEIGHT=300>
<PARAM NAME="USERID" VALUE="DAD001">
</APPLET>
```

    Provide an assignment statement that assigns the value held in the "USERID" parameter to a string named "UserId".

Enter answer here:_____

71. Given the following code listing:

```
public class tryme {
 public static void main(String args[]) {
  int maincount = 0;
  outer:for(int i=0;i < 5;++i)
     middle:for(int j=0;j < 5;++j)
         inner:for(int k=0;k < 5;++k){
                 System.out.println("Hello - " +
➥++maincount);
                 if((k%5) == 0)
                     continue middle;
         }


 }
```

    Which of the following is the last line of output?

    A. Hello - 25

    B. Hello - 5

    C. `Hello - 1`

    D. `Hello - 10`

72. What modifier would be used to disallow subclasses from overriding a declared method?

    A. `public`

    B. `private`

    C. `protected`

    D. `final`

73. Given the following code listing:

```
public String whatIsThis(Object myObject){

        //Your Conditional HERE
            return "It is an Integer";
    return "No Idea";
    }
```

Provide a single `if` statement such that `It is an Integer` is returned if `myObject` is an integer.

Enter code here:_____

74. Given the following code listing:

```
public boolean isThisRunnable(Object myObject){

        //Your Conditional HERE
        return true;
    return false;
    }
```

Provide a single `if` statement such that `true` is returned if `myObject` implements the `Runnable` interface.

Enter code here:_____

75. Which of the following statements would equate to false, given the following declaration?

```
String s1 = "Hello";
String s2 = "Hello";
```

    A. s1 == s2

    B. s1.equals(s2)

    C. s1 = s2

    D. None of the above

76. The following defines an object hierarchy.

```
class class1{

    public static int myValue = 2;
}

class class2 extends class1{

    public static int yourValue = 3;

    public int ourValue(){

        return myValue + yourValue;
    }
}
class class3 extends class1{
    public static int theirValue = 5;
    public int ourValue(){

        return myValue + theirValue;
    }

}
public class myClass{

    public static class3 castMe(class1 in){
        return (class3)in;
    }
    public static void main(String args[]){

}
}
```

When does the following method cause an error/exception?

```
public static class3 castMe(class1 in){
        return (class3)in;
    }
```

A. At compilation

B. Never

C. If in references a class3 object

E. If in references a class2 object, or it references a class1 object

77. What modifier would be used to limit a method's visibility to all classes and subclasses in the same package?

A. public

B. private

C. protected

D. final

E. None—default

78. What is the output of the following try...catch block?

```
public class tryme {
    public static void main(String args[]) {

        try{
            int I;
            throw(new Exception("Hello Nurse"));
            return;
        }catch(Exception e){
            System.out.println("I am Here");
            return;
        }finally{
            System.out.println("Hello Nurse!");
        }

    }
}
```

A. Hello Nurse!

B. No output

C. I am Here

D. A and C

79. Which of the following is not a reserved word?

A. Integer

B. int

C. interfaceof

D. instanceof

E. goto

80. Given the following code listing:

```
public class tryme {
 public static void main(String args[]) {
  int maincount = 0;
  try{
      outer:for(int i=0;i < 5;++i)
              middle:for(int j=0;j < 5;++j)
                  inner:for(int k=0;k < 5;++k){
                      System.out.println("Hello - " +
  ++maincount);
                      if((k%5) == 0)
                          throw(new Exception());
                  }
  }
  catch(Exception e){
  }
 }
}
```

Which of the following is the last line of output?

A. Hello - 25

B. Hello - 5

    C. `Hello - 1`

    D. `Hello - 10`

81. Enter the complete main method declaration required for a Java executable class.

Enter answer here:_____

82. Which of the following base data types does not have a corresponding class wrapper?

    A. `int`

    B. `byte`

    C. `float`

    D. `void`

    E. None of the above

83. What modifier would be used to disallow a class's member to be overridden?

    A. `public`

    B. `private`

    C. `protected`

    D. `final`

    E. None—default

84. What is the numeric range for a Java byte?

    A. `0` to `(2^8)`

    B. `-(2^7)` to `(2^7 - 1)`

    C. `-(2^8)` to `(2^8 - 1)`

    D. `0` to `(2^16)`

85. `java -0` is used for which of the following?

   A. Executing a class in the debugging facility

   B. Executing a class with all profiling options on

   C. Executing a class with optimization turned on

   D. Executing a class with a specified object stream

86. Given a byte with a value of 11110111, which of the following statements will produce 00111011?

   Note: 01110111 = 0x77

   A. 0x77 << 1;

   B. 0x77 >> 3;

   C. 0x77 >> 1;

   D. 0x77 >>> 1;

   E. C and D

87. Which of the following assignment statements is invalid?

   A. double d = 45456.444;

   B. long l = 45784;

   C. int i = new Integer(44);

   D. int j = (int)d;

88. Which of the following statements would equate to true, given the following declaration:

   ```
   boolean b1 = true;
   boolean b2 = false;
   ```

   A. s1 == s2

   B. s1 & s2

   C. s1 ¦ s2

   D. s1 ¦¦ s2

89. What exception is thrown by the read() method of an InputStream?

   A. Exception

   B. IOException

   C. ReadException

   D. None of the above

90. Are you brain fried?

   A. Yes

   B. No

Answers and Discussion

The following provides the answers to of all sample test questions, followed by a brief discussion of the correct answer.

1. D   wait() and notify() methods provide a mechanism to facilitate object-level resource locking. For this reason, wait() and notify() are members of the Object class.

2. E   The difference between 01110111and 00111011 is a single bit shift to the right. Since the leading bit is a 0, both the >> and >>> operators work identically. However, if the leading bit was 1, the >> and >>> would have different results.

3. D   The System class is intended to be used as a static class. For this reason, declaring a new instance of System would cause a compilation error.

4. D   Java packages provide a grouping facility for classes and interfaces.

5. E   In an effort to minimize the number of registers needed by the JVM architecture, a stack-based model was employed.

6. C   Despite how cool a Java-flavored potato chip might sound, the JavaChip is a silicon implementation of the JVM.

7. F   The jump from JDK 1.02 to JDK 1.1 encapsulates an explosion of functionality. JDBC, RMI, JavaBeans, and an improved AWT event model are only a few of the new features.

8. A   NULL is not a reserved word, but null is.

9. A   The Windows 3.1 platform does have an accessible Java runtime environment; it doesn't support threads but it works.

10. C   The % operator performs a modulus operation. Therefore "A %= 3;" can best be described as A equals A modulus 3.

11. C   The JVM is an emulator used to execute Java machine code on a native platform.

12. D   A Java class file contains JVM executable instructions, method naming information, and field naming information.

13. B   Any class that contains an abstract method declaration must be declared as abstract.

14. D

15. C   class3 is a child of class1. Therefore, casting a class1 reference into a class3 reference will only succeed if the reference points to a class3 object.

16. C   The public class modifier opens the class up for usage and subclassing to all.

17. B   bool is not a primitive data type, but Boolean is.

18. C   The binary or operator (¦) cannot be used on a string object.

19. C   The throws reserved word is used to declare the exception(s) a given method produces.

20. B   The purpose of an abstract class is to forward declare the method. Providing the braces ({}) actually implements the method with no instruction, thus making it non-abstract.

21. `return (A==B)? AxB ¦ 0;`

22. A   There are 2 ways to state class hierarchy. The first is top down, "class1 is the parent class of class2, and class2 is the parent class of class3." The second is bottom up, "class3's parent class is class2, and class2's parent class is class1".

23. A   Under normal operating conditions, the declaration "int I;" will not throw an exception. For this reason, I am Here will never be output. However, the finally block of any try…catch block will always be throw. Meaning, the above code won't execute the catch block, but it will execute the finally block, for an output of Hello Nurse!.

24. B

25. B   class2 is a child of class1. Therefore, casting a class2 reference into a class1 reference will always succeed.

26. C   The class provides a mechanism by which only one thread can get or set the stored string value at a time. In this way, the class provides a single reader, single writer facility.

27. C   protected limits a method's visibility to only the other classes and subclasses in the current package.

28. public void waitForKey(){}

29. C   The JVM registers and stack are 32 bits wide.

30. D   The id field holds the code associated with the nature of the java.awt.Event instance.

31. A   Java supports only single object inheritance.

32. C

33. B

34. B   The thread priority signifies the presidencies of any given thread. However, the use of thread priority depends on the thread-scheduling algorithm used to implement the JVM.

35. D   The java_g executes the specified class with optimization turned off so that it may be executed in the jdb tool.

36. D `wait()` and `notify()` methods provide a mechanism to facilitate object-level resource locking. For this reason `wait()` and `notify()` are members of the `Object` class.

37. C The Runnable interface is used to define a target for the `Thread` class.

38. D The `java.lang.System` class is the gatekeeper for all system/process specific resources, including `Standard In`, `Standard Out`, and `Standard Error`.

39. B The JVM specification does NOT define the process by which unused memory resources are collected and put onto the heap for reuse.

40. A The `-verbose` option displays the explicit loading of each class.

41. B Runnable interfaces are called Thread targets. In this case, `Thread T1` is constructed to contain the Runnable interface `myClass`, and it executes the `myClass` `run()` method.

42. B The JVM specification does not specify the thread scheduling used.

43. D Calling the `stop()` method, an external JVM event, and the thread returning from its `run()` method can all terminate a thread's execution.

44. A

45. C The `@param` tag is used to document the input parameter of the associated class.

46. A All JDK 1.1+ event objects, including `java.awt.AWTEvent` are derived from `java.util.EventObject`.

47. B Mutually exclusive threads are processes. All Java threads have the ability to share common memory resources and objects, making them non-mutually exclusive.

48. B A class is allowed to implement as many interfaces as desired.

49. B   class3 and class2 share a common parent, class1. However, it is not legal to cast between siblings.

50. C   GetHashCode() is not a method contained with java.lang.Object, but hashCode() is.

51. D   Float, Double, and Byte represent numeric values, are derived from Number, and have a primitive data type counterpart.

52. A   java.lang.String contains a substring method, which provides a means for finding sub-strings within the contained string.

53. C   The yield() method of java.lang.Thread relinquishes a processing slot to another thread.

54. A   java.awt.AWTEvent contains a constructor to aid in porting the Event class to the post-JDK 1.1 event model.

55. A   public limits a method's visibility to all other classes and subclasses.

56. C   /** denotes a javadoc comment.

57. E   javag, javag_w, and java_w are all provided variations of the base JDK java command line tool.

58. A   The appletviewer can be directed to look at a specified code base via the codebase Applet tag parameter.

59. C   The -depend command line option forces javac to perform a compilation to include all supporting classes.

60. D   The java_w command line tool executes a specified class, without an associated console window, to allow more seamless integration.

61. A   The @deprecated javadoc tag is used to denote deprecated Classes, Interfaces, or Members.

62. C   By Allowing multiple URL's to be provided on the command line, the appletviewer has facilities to execute multiple applets at a time.

63. D   All of the supplied assignment statements are valid.

64. C   The conversion between a `long` and an `int` requires a cast.

65. `int i = 16` is equal to `int j = 020;`

66. C   Java's construction order is from bottom up. Thus, the order would be `In main, class1, class2, class3`.

67. D   The whole trick behind garbage collecting is to determine when a variable is no longer needed. In Java this is achieved by a reference count. When a variable is no longer referenced, it is eligible for garbage collection.

68. B   Since `0` mod `5` is `0`, the inner loop is only executed once. However, the outer loop is executed to fruition. Thus, the final line of output would be `Hello - 5`.

69. D   Java `int`'s are signed, 32-bit values. Thus, the numeric range of an int is `-(2^31)` to `(2^31 - 1)`.

70. `String UserId = getParam("USERID")`

71. A   Since `0` mod `5` is `0`, the inner loop is only executed once. However, the outer and middle loops are executed to fruition. Thus the final line of output would be `Hello - 25`.

72. D   The final modifier disallows subclasses from overriding a declared method.

73. `if(myObject instanceof Integer)`

74. `if(myObject interfaceof Runnable)`

75. C   The statement "s1 = s2" is a declaration, and not a Boolean operation. Thus, "s1 = s2" would equate to a `false` value.

76. E   Casting from a parent class to a subclass is legal but may cause a runtime exception. In this case, a runtime exception would be thrown if `in` references a `class2` object, or `in` references a `class1` object.

77. E   The "default", or package modifier is used to limit a method's visibility to all classes and subclasses in the same package.

78. C   Since an exception is intentionally thrown in the try...catch block, both the `catch` and `finally` blocks are executed. Thus, the output would be `I am Here` followed by `Hello Nurse!`.

79. A   Integer is a class found in java.lang, and not a reserved word.

80. C   Since `0` mod `5` is `0`, the inner loop is only executed once, and then throws an exception. The final line of output would be `Hello - 1`.

81. `public void main(String Args[]){}`

82. E   Beginning with JDK 1.1, all base types have a corresponding class wrapper.

83. D   The `final` modifier is used to disallow a class's member to be overridden.

84. B   Java bytes are 8-bit signed structures with a discrete range from $-(2^7)$ to $(2^7 - 1)$.

85. C   `java -O` is used for executing a Class with full optimization turned on.

86. D   The difference between `01110111` and `00111011` is a single bit shift to the right. However, since the leading bit is a 1 the `>>>` operators must be used to zero fill the shift.

87. C   An `int` variable cannot hold a reference to an `Integer` class.

88. D   Since `b2` is `false`, the only statement which would produce a true value is `b1 || b2`.

89. B   An `IOException` if thrown by the `read()` method of `java.io.InputStream`.

90. I know I am, so the answer is a big YES!

Where To Go From Here

As you can see from the questions presented in this chapter, the Certified Java Programmer examination covers a vast region of information. Everything from reserved words to construction order is asked, and asked in detail. However, now that you have completed the practice exam you have a better understanding of what constitutes a Certified Java Programmer.

This chapter presented a checklist of exam topics, and a complete 90 question exam. If you completed the entire practice exam without even breaking a sweat, congratulations. It is now time for you to call one of the Sylvan Prometric test facilities listed in Appendix A, and make your appointment to sit for the real Certified Java Programmer examination. On the other hand, if you were not certain of the material covered in the examination, use the examination software provided on the CD-ROM to better hone your skills.

Chapter 8

Certified Programmer Practice Test #2

The scope of this chapter is to provide detailed test information for the Certified Java Programmer Examination. For this reason, it is required that you should read all subsequent chapters before proceeding. Please read the introductory testing material found at the beginning of Chapter 7, "Certified Programmer Practice Test #1," before taking this exam.

This chapter will provide the following resources for the Certified Java Programmer Examination:

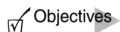 Objectives

▶ Study Guide and Check List

▶ Practice Exam and Answers

Specifics of the Certification Exam environment include:

▶ Proctored entirely by computer.

▶ No external material allowed in the testing area.

▶ The exam is comprised of true/false, multiple choice, and short answer questions.

▶ Results are presented immediately after the exam is completed.

Practice Examination

The following practice exam and answers are provided as a companion to the testing software found on the accompanying CD-ROM. However, the detailed description of each of the answers is not included on the CD-ROM. The test that follows is one of three tests provided on the CD-ROM, and provides a printed, portable study device. With that said, best of luck.

1. java_w executes a specified Class...

    A. without optimization.

    B. in its own separate window.

    C. without an associated console window.

2. Given the following declaration, which of the following statements would equate to true?

   Boolean b1 = true;

   Boolean b2 = false;

    A. b1 == b2

    B. b1 ¦¦ b2

    C. b1 ¦& b2

    D. b1 && b2

3. Which of the following assignment statements is invalid?

    A. `long l = 587.65;`

    B. `float f = 54.7;`

    C. `double d = 0x42672;`

    D. All of the above

4. In the same package, what modifier would be used to limit a method's visibility to all classes and subclasses?

    A. `final`

    B. `private`

    C. `protected`

    D. `public`

    E. `default`

5. Given the following code segment:

```
class classC extends classA{

    public classC(){
        System.out.println("C");
    }
}

class classA{

    public classA(){
        System.out.println("A");
    }
}


class classB extends classC{

    public classB(){
        System.out.println("B");
```

```
            }
       }


   public class ABC {

       public static void main(String args[]) {

            System.out.println("Main");
            classB c = new classB();


       }
   }
```

In what order will the output be produced?

A. C, B, B, Main

B. Main, A, C, B"

C. Main, A, B, C

D. Main, A, B, A

6. **Enter the complete main method declaration required for a java executable class.**

Enter answer here:_____

7. **Given the following code listing:**

```
   public class tryme {

       public static void main(String args[]) {

   int counter = 0;
    outer:for(int i=0;i < 4;++i)
           middle:for(int j=0;j < 4;++j)
                inner:for(int k=0;k < 4;++k){
       System.out.println("Hello - " + ++counter);
       if((k%4) ==0)
           break outer;


       }
   }
```

Which of the following is the last line of output?

A. `Hello at - 8`

B. `Hello at - 4`

C. `4`

D. `8`

8. To disallow a class's member to be overridden, use modifier...

   A. `public`

   B. `default`

   C. `protected`

   D. `final`

   E. `private`

9. Given the following HTML Applet declaration:

   ```
   <APPLET URL codebase = "/" archive="Myapplet.zip"
   ➥ CODE="Myapplet.class" WIDTH=450 HEIGHT=222>
   <PARAM NAME="PASSWORD" VALUE="78tre">
   </APPLET>
   ```

   Provide an assignment statement which assigns the value held in the `"PASSWORD"` parameter to a string named `"PASSWORD"`.

Enter answer here:_____

10. To disallow subclasses from overriding a declared method, use modifier...

    A. `public`

    B. `private`

    C. `final`

    D. `status`

11. Given the following code listing:

```
public String whatIsThis(Object myToy){

        //Your Conditional HERE
        return "It is an Integer";
return "No Idea";
    }
```

Provide a single if statement such that "It is an Integer" is returned if myToy is an Integer.

Enter code here:_____

12. By allowing _____, the appletviewer has facilities to execute multiple applets at a time.

    A. multiple applets defined in the HTML

    B. multiple URL's to be provided on the command line

    C. a window to select desired applets

    D. None of the above.

13. The following defines an object hierarchy.

```
class classA{
public static int myNum = 2;
}
class classB extends classA{
public static int yourNum = 3;
public int ourValue(){
return myNum + yourNum;
    }
}
class classC extends classA{
public static int theirNum = 5;
public int ourNum(){
return myNum + theirNum;
    }
}

public class myClass{
public static classC castMe(classA in){
        return (classC)in;
```

```
        }
public static void main(String args[]){
}
}
```

When does the following method cause an error/exception?

```
public static classC castMe(classA in){
        return (classC)in;
    }
```

A. At compilation

B. If in references a classC object

C. If in references a classD object

D. If in references a classB object, or in references a classA object

14. Convert the following statement into its octal equivalent.

```
int i = 16;
//Octal Declaration HERE!
```

Enter octal declaration here:_____

15. Given the following code listing:

```
public class tryme {
public static void main(String args[]) {
int maincount = 0;
try{
        outer:for(int i=0;i < 5;++i)
            middle:for(int j=0;j < 5;++j)
                inner:for(int k=0;k < 5;++k){
                        System.out.println("No more - " +
➥ ++maincount);
                        if((k%5) == 0)
                            throw(new Exception());
        }
            }
            catch(Exception e){
            }
        }
    }
```

Which of the following is the last line of output?

A. `No more - 1000`

B. `No more - 100`

C. `No more - 10`

D. `No more - 1`

16. A variable becomes available for reclamation by the garbage collector...

    A. After the variable is out of a method's scope.

    B. When the variable is no longer referenced anywhere in the JVM.

    C. Upon returning from the containing method block.

    D. After you use it.

17. The _____ base data type(s) has/have a corresponding class wrapper.

    A. `int`

    B. `byte`

    C. `float`

    D. `int and byte`

    E. `int, byte, and float`

18. What is the numeric range for a Java int?

    A. `0 to (2^32)`

    B. `-(2^31) to (2^31)`

    C. `-(2^31) to (2^31 - 1)`

    D. `-(2^15) to (2^15 - 1)`

19. What is the numeric range for a Java byte?

    A. 0 to (2^8)

    B. 0 to (2^16)

    C. -(2^8) to (2^8 - 1)

    D. -(2^7) to (2^7 - 1)

20. What major feature(s) was/were debuted in the JDK 1.1?

    A. JDBC

    B. RMI and JavaBeans

    C. JavaBeans and improved AWT

    D. JDBC and JavaBeans

    E. JDBC, RMI, JavaBeans, and improved AWT

21. Which of the following is not a reserved word?

    A. NULL

    B. switch

    C. catch

    D. null

    E. instanceof

22. The @deprecated javadoc tag denotes deprecated classes, interfaces, or members.

    A. True

    B. False

23. The statement "A /= 7;" can best be described as?

    A. A equals A divided by 7

    B. A equals A modulus 7.

C. A equals A in 7 digit percentage form.

D. None of the Above

24. The wait() call does which of the following?

    A. Blocks until the object is ready for access

    B. Blocks until notified by another thread

    C. Blocks until a thread terminates

    D. Blocks a thread until all other threads have terminated

25. The public class modifier...

    A. is rarely used.

    B. Allows other classes to subclass it.

    C. Allows only classes in the current package to use its facilities.

    D. Opens the class up for usage and subclassing to all.

26. Classes are executed by the JVM in this manner:

    A. The ClassLoader loads the class into the JVM for execution, and then signals for execution to begin.

    B. The JVM prompts the user for the class to execute.

    C. The ClassLoader finds, verifies, and loads the class into the JVM for execution, and then signals for execution to begin.

    D. The runtime environment loads the Applet information into the JVM, and then begins the JVM process.

27. Which of the following assignment statements is invalid?

    A. int i = 415;

    B. int i = 1;

    C. long l = 2782;

    D. int j = (int)d;

28. The `wait()` and `notify()` methods are defined in what class?

    A. `java.lang.String`

    B. `java.lang.Thread`

    C. `java.lang.Object`

    D. `java.lang.Runnable`

29. A package is...

    A. A collection of interfaces.

    B. A collection of classes.

    C. A way to provide naming for a group of related classes.

    D. All of the above.

30. The JVM specification defines the process by which unused memory resources are collected and put onto the heap for reuse.

    A. True

    B. False

31. _____ is used to find the type of event encapsulated in a `java.awt.Event` class.

    A. `getEventType()`

    B. `isMouseEvent()`

    C. `getParameters()`

    D. `id`

32. A Java runtime environment supports threads on Windows 3.1.

    A. True

    B. False

33. A class can only have a single parent.

    A. True

    B. False

34. Given the following code listing:

```
public class tryme {
public static void main(String args[]) {
int maincount = 0;
    outer:for(int i=0;i < 5;++i)
      middle:for(int j=0;j < 5;++j)
          inner:for(int k=0;k < 5;++k){
                  System.out.println("Hello - " +
➥++maincount);
                  if((k%5) == 0)
                      continue middle;
          }
      }
}
```

    Which of the following is the last line of output?

    A. Hello - 25

    B. Hello - 5

    C. 25

    D. 5

35. The numeric range for a Java short is...

    A. -(2^16) to (2^16)

    B. -(2^31) to (2^31 - 1)

    C. -(2^15) to (2^15 - 1)

    C. 0 to (2^16)

36. `java.util.EventObject` is the parent class of `java.awt.AWTEvent`.

    A. True

    B. False

37. How are thread priority and thread scheduling related?

    A. Thread priority is used to determine the next thread to execute from the waiting thread pool.

    B. It depends on the thread-scheduling algorithm used to implement the JVM.

    C. Thread priority is specified when a thread is to be executed next.

38. What is the output of the following try...catch block?

```
public class SeeMe {

    public static void main(String args[]) {

        try{
            int I;
            throw(new Exception("Me?"));
            return;
        }catch(Exception e){
            System.out.println("Do you see");
            return;
        }finally{
            System.out.println("Me?");
        }

    }
}
```

    A. Me?

    B. Do you see

    C. No output

    D. A and B

39. What is the Runnable interface used for?

    A. A marathon

    B. Defining a class that can be executed by a thread

    C. Defining a class to execute a new thread

    D. Defining a thread

40. Java supports only single object inheritance.

    A. True

    B. False

41. The JVM's role is a(an)…

    A. interpreter.

    B. device used to execute applets.

    C. Microsoft Internet Explorer plug-in.

    D. emulator used to execute Java machine code on a native platform.

42. What is the output of the following try…catch block?

```java
public class fun4all {

    public static void main(String args[]) {

        try{
            int I;
            return;
        }catch(Exception e){
            System.out.println("Lets have fun!");
            return;
        }finally{
            System.out.println("We love Java");
        }

    }
}
```

    A. Lets have fun!

    B. We love Java

    C. No output

    D. Depends on the creation of the int I;

43. If the following code contains a single error, what is it?

```
public class myClass{
public abstract void mytrash();
public static void main(String args[]){
for(int j=0;i < 9;++j){
            for(int i=0; i < 365;++i)
                    System.out.println("Fun with Java");
// Run the garbage collector.
                System.out.println("Running garbage collector");
        }
    }
}
```

A. public class myClass{

B. public abstract void mytrash();

C. No Error

44. The following defines an object hierarchy.

```
class classA{
public static int myValue = 2;
}
class classB extends classA{
public static int yourValue = 3;
public int ourValue(){
return myValue + yourValue;
    }
}
class classC extends classA{
public static int theirValue = 5;
public int ourValue(){
return myValue + theirValue;
    }
}
public class myClass{
public static classA castMe(classB in){
        return (classA)in;
    }
public static void main(String args[]){
        classA v = castMe(new classB());
    }
}
```

When does the following method cause an error/exception?

```
public static classA castMe(classB in){
        return (classA)in;
    }
```

A. At compilation.

B. If and only if in references a classC object.

C. If and only if in references a classB object.

D. It doesn't cause an error/exception.

45. The following defines an object hierarchy.

```
class class1{
    public static int myNumber = 2;
}
class class2 extends class1{
    public static int yourNumber = 3;
    public int ourNumber(){
        return myNumber + yourNumber;
    }
}
class class3 extends class1{
    public static int theirNumber = 5;
    public int ourNumber(){
        return myNumber + theirNumber;
    }
}
public class myClass{
    publicstatic class3 castMe(class1 in){
        return (class3)in;
    }
    public static void main(String args[]){
        class3 v = castMe(new class1());
    }
}
```

When does the following method cause an error/exception?

```
public static class3 castMe(class1 in){
        return (class3)in;
    }
```

A. If and only if in references a class2 object

B. If and only if in references a class3 object

C. At compilation

D. Never

46. Which of the following statements would equate to false, given the following declaration:

String s1 = "Cake";

String s2 = "Cake";

A. `s1 == s2`

B. `s1.equals(s2)`

C. `s1 = s2`

D. None of the Above

47. Given the following code listing:

```
public class myClass{
   //Your Declaration HERE!{
       try {
           System.in.read();
       } catch (IOException e) {
           return;
       }
   }
   public static void main(String args[]) {
       System.out.println("My console application");
       System.out.println("");
       System.out.println("(press Enter to exit)");
       holdMe();
   }
}
```

At the specified location, provide a method declaration with the following properties.

Name: `holdMe`

Input Parameters: None

Return Value: None

Visibility: All classes, including subclasses, in the current package

Enter answer here:_____

48. To ensure compatibility across all processors, the JVM architecture makes the following provision(s):

   A. Uses a stack-based architecture

   B. Minimizes the use of registers

   C. Is modeled after the lowest common denominator architecture

   D. A and B

   E. A, B, and C

49. The following code listing contains one error, which is...

```
public abstract class myClass{
   public static boolean IsPrime(long in){
        boolean prime = true;
        for(long i = 2; i <= (in / 2);++i){
            if((in % i) == 0){
                prime = false;
                break;
            }
        }
        return prime;
    }
   public abstract void fun(int Value){};
}
```

   A. `public abstract void fun(int Value){};`

   B. `public abstract class myClass`

   C. Incomplete class definition

   D. Class must contain a constructor

50. Please complete the following source, so that if the value of "P" is equal to "Q" then return P x Q, otherwise return 0;

```
public class myClass{
    public return int myTest(int P, int Q){
        //Your Single Line of Code Here!
    }
}
```

Enter answer here:_____

51. Which following answers best describes the following object hierarchy?

```
class class1{
    public static int myValue = 2;
}
class class2 extends class1{
    public static int yourValue = 3;
    public int ourValue(){
        return myValue + yourValue;
    }
}
class class3 extends class2{
    public static int theirValue = 5;
    public int ourValue(){
        return myValue + theirValue;
    }
}
```

    A. class3's parent class is class2, class2's parent class is class1, and class1's parent is Object.

    B. class1 is the parent class of class2, and class2 is the parent class of class3.

    C. class1's parent class is class2, class2's parent class is class3, and class3's parent is Object.

    D. None of the above.

52. The lass file contains

    A. JVM executable instructions

    B. Method naming information

    C. Field naming information

    D. A and B

    E. A, B, and C

53. What modifier would be used to limit a method's visibility to only the currently defined class?

    A. static

    B. private

    C. protected

    D. public

54. An interface provides which of the following?

    A. A mechanism to facilitate multiple inheritance

    B. A template for further development

    C. An alternative to class declarations

    D. A and B

    E. A and C

55. Which statement best describes the following class?

```
public class dataCenterRe{
    private static String  data = "";
    public static synchronized void setStr(String in){
        data = in;
    }
    public static synchronized String getStr(){
        return data;
    }
}
```

    A. The class is a simple storage device for multiple threads to access a single string.

    B. The class is a simple storage device for a string.

    C. The class provides a mechanism by which only one thread can get or set the stored string value at a time.

    D. The class provides a mechanism by which only multiple threads can get or set the stored string value.

56. Which of the following is NOT a primitive Java data type?

    A. `float`

    B. `int`

    C. `double`

    D. `bool`

57. To limit a method's visibility to only the other classes in the current package and subclasses, use modifier...

    A. `protected`

    B. `private`

    C. `static`

    D. `public`

58. The `throws` reserved word...

    A. Defines the exception a method can raise.

    B. Defines the exception(s) a method can raise.

    C. Raises an exception.

    D. Triggers and event.

59. The JVM registers and stack are:

    A. 32 bits wide

    B. 8 bits wide

C. 16 bits wide

D. 4 bits wide

60. The -verbose tool in the Java tool...

    A. Informs when garbage collection is performed.

    B. Displays the explicit loading of each class.

    C. Generates information regarding how many times a method has been called.

    D. The option has been deprecated.

61. Given the following code segment:

```
import java.util.Hashtable;
import java.util.Enumeration;
import java.net.*;
import java.io.*;
class myClass implements Runnable
{
//Reference to current thread
    public  Thread Child_Thread = null;
    //Start-up new thread
    public void start(){
        if (Child_Thread == null){
            Child_Thread = new Thread(this);
            Child_Thread.start();
        }
    }
    //Stop the currently executing thread
    public void stop(){
        if (Child_Thread != null)
            Child_Thread.stop();
        Child_Thread = null;
    }
    public void run(){
        for(int i = 0;i < 4556;++i);
    }
}
//Main Public Launcher
public class CSPassiveAgent {
    public static void main(String args[]) {
```

```
        Thread  T1 = new Thread(new myClass());
    T1.start();
  }
}
```

Which statement best defines the following code segment?

```
Thread  T1 = new Thread(new myClass());
    T1.start();
```

A. Thread T1 is created and executed.

B. A compilation error will occur at T1.start();.

C. Thread T1 is constructed to contain the Runnable interface myClass, and it executes the myClass run() method.

D. Thread T1 is constructed to contain the Runnable interface myClass, and it executes the Thread run() method.

62. Float, Double, and Byte all

A. are derived from Number.

B. represent numeric values.

C. have a primitive data type counterpart.

D. All of the above

63. The JVM specification does specify the thread scheduling used.

A. True

B. False

64. java.awt.AWTEvent contains a constructor to aid in porting the Event class to the post-JDK 1.1 event model.

A. True

B. False

65. A Hashtable is...

    A. a deprecated facility from JDK 1.0.

    B. a generic data storage device.

    C. a generic object storage device.

    D. All of the above.

66. With javadoc, which of the following denotes a javadoc comment?

    A. /**

    B. /*

    C. /*/*

    D. //*

67. All threads created in Java are not mutually exclusive.

    A. True

    B. False

68. What variations of the Java tool are provided in the JDK?

    A. javag

    B. javag_w

    C. java_w

    D. All of the above

    E. None of the above

69. A class can not implement more than one interface.

    A. True

    B. False

70. The following defines an object hierarchy.

```
class class1{
    public static int myValue = 2;
}
class class2 extends class1{
    public static int yourValue = 3;
    public int ourValue(){
      return myValue + yourValue;
    }
}
class class3 extends class1{
    public static int theirValue = 5;
    public int ourValue(){
      return myValue + theirValue;
    }
}
class class4 extends class1{
}
public class myClass{
  publicstatic class2 castMe(class3 in){
        return (class2)in;
    }
    public static void main(String args[]){
        class2 v = castMe(new class4());
    }
}
```

When does the following method cause an error/exception?

```
public static class2 castMe(class3 in){
        return (class2)in;
    }
```

A. At compilation

B. If and only if in references an class3 object

C. If and only if in references an class2 object

D. Never

71. Which of the following is NOT a method of
    `java.lang.Object`?

    A. `getHashCode()`

    B. `equals(Object)`

    C. `wait()`

    D. None of the above

72. Which of the following is not a reserved word?

    A. `interfaceof`

    B. `Integer`

    D. `instanceof`

    E. `goto`

73. The `java.lang.String` class provides methods for finding sub-
    strings within the contained string.

    A. True

    B. False

74. Which of the following terminates a thread's execution?

    A. Calling the `stop()` method

    B. An external JVM event

    C. A thread returning from its `run()` method

    D. All of the above.

75. To limit a method's visibility to all other classes and subclass-
    es, use modifier...

    A. `final`.

    B. `private`.

    C. `statical`.

    D. `public`.

76. Given a byte with a value of 01110111, which of the following statements will produce 00111011?

    Note : 01110111 = 0x77

    A. 0x77 << 1;

    B. 0x77 >>> 1;

    C. 0x77 >> 1;

    D. B and C

    E. None of the above

77. What is java_g used for?

    A. Executing a class with optimization turned off

    B. Using the jdb tool

    C. All of the above

    D. None of the above

78. Given a byte with a value of 11110111, which of the following statements will produce 00111011?

    Note : 01110111 = 0x77

    A. 0x77 >> 1;

    B. 0x77 >>> 1;

    C. 0x77 >> 1;

    D. B and C

    E. None of the above

79. appletviewer only retrieves classes found in the CLASSPATH environment variable.

    A. True

    B. False

80. Which of the following will happen when happenjavac -depend myClass.java?

   A. compile myName.java

   B. myClass.java to be compiled

   C. All dependent classes of myClass.java to be compiled.

   D. A and B

   E. A and C

81. Which of the following assignment statements is invalid?

   A. double d = 45256.834;

   B. long l = 45184;

   C. int j = (int)d;

   D. int i = new Integer(46);

82. Given the following code listing:

```
public boolean isThisRunnable(Object gameTwo){
        //Type Conditional HERE
             return true;
    return false;
    }
```

   Provide a single if statement such that true is returned if gameTwo implements the Runnable interface.

Enter code here:_____

83. What exception(s) is/are thrown by the read() method of an InputStream?

   A. Exception

   B. IOException

   C. ReadException

   D. All of the above

84. `java.lang.Thread` utilizes _____ to relinquish the thread instance's processing slot to another thread.

    A. `Sleep()`

    B. `yield()`

    C. `Wait()`

    D. All of the above

    E. None of the above

85. The `wait()` and `notify()` methods are members of what class?

    A. `String`

    B. `Thread`

    C. `Object`

    D. All of the above

86. Which javadoc tag is used to denote a comment for a method parameter?

    A. `@param`

    B. `@value`

    C. `@method`

    D. `@parameter`

87. The following application contains a single error.

```
public class myClass{

    public static void main(String args[]){

        for(int i=0; i < 8975;++i){
            if((i % 2) == 0)
                System.out.println("I like Java");
            else
                System.out.println("I don't like Java");
        }
        (new System()).out.println("Done");
```

```
      }
  }
```

Which line contains the error?

A. `for(int i=0; i < 8975;++i){`

B. `(new System()).out.println("Done");`

C. `public static void main(String args[]){`

D. `if((i % 2) == 0)`

88. `java.lang.System` class contains which of the following fields?

A. `Standard In`

B. `Standard Out`

C. `Standard Error`

D. `Standard In and Standard Out`

E. `Standard In, Standard Out, and Standard Error`

89. What is a JavaChip?

A. A chip that stores Java class files to increase ClassLoader performance

B. An accelerator chip designed to aid the JVM running on the native machine

C. The chip inside Sun's JavaStation

D. A silicon implementation of the JVM

E. None of the above

90. What does `java -0` execute?

A. A class with optimization turned on

B. A class with all profiling options on

C. A class in the debugging facility

D. None of the above

Answers and Discussion

The following provides a complete list of all sample test question answers, followed by a brief discussion of the correct answer.

1. C   The `java_w` command line tool executes a specified class without an associated console window, to allow more seamless integration.

2. B   Since b2 is `false`, the only statement which would produce a `true` value is `"b1 || b2"`.

3. A   A long must hold an integer value.

4. E   The "default", or package modifier is used to limit a method's visibility to all classes and subclasses in the same package.

5. B   Java's construction order is from bottom up. Thus, the order would be `Main, A, C, B`.

6. `public void main(String Args[]){}`

7. B   Since `0` mod `4` is `0`, the inner loop is only executed once. However, the outer loop is executed to fruition. Thus, the final line of output would be `Hello · 4`.

8. D   The final modifier is used to disallow a class's member to be overridden.

9. `String PASSWORD = getParam("PASSWORD")`

10. C   The final modifier disallows subclasses from overriding a declared method.

11. `if(myToy instanceof Integer)`

12. B   By allowing multiple URL's to be provided on the command line, the `appletviewer` has facilities to execute multiple applets at a time.

13. D   Casting from a parent class to a subclass is legal, but may cause a runtime exception. In this case, a runtime exception would be thrown if `in` references a `classB` object, or `in` references a `classA` object.

14. `int i = 16` is equal to `int j = 020;`

15. D   Since `0 mod 5` is `0`, the inner loop is only executed once, and then throws an exception the final line of output would be `No more - 1`.

16. B   The whole trick behind garbage collecting is to determine when a variable is no longer needed. In Java, this is achieved by a reference count. When a variable is no longer referenced, it is eligible for garbage collection.

17. E   Beginning with JDK 1.1, all base types have a corresponding class wrapper (Answer E).

18. C   Java `int`'s are signed, 32 bit values. Thus, the desecrate range of an `int` is $-(2^{31})$ to $(2^{31} - 1)$.

19. D   Java bytes are 8-bit signed structures with a discrete range from $-(2^7)$ to $(2^7 - 1)$.

20. E   The jump from JDK 1.02 to JDK 1.1 encapsulates an explosion of functionality. JDBC, RMI, JavaBeans, and an improved AWT event model lists only a few of the new features.

21. A   `NULL` is not a reserved word, but `null` is.

22. A   The `@deprecated` javadoc tag is used to denote deprecated classes, interfaces, or members.

23. A   The `/` operator performs a division operation. Therefore `"A /= 7;"` can best be described as A equals A divided by 7.

24. B   The wait() call blocks until notified by another thread.

25. D   The `public` class modifier opens the class up for usage and subclassing to all.

26. C   Classes are executed by the JVM in the following manner: The ClassLoader finds, verifies, and loads the class into the JVM for execution, and then signals for execution to begin.

27. B   The conversion between a `long` and an `int` requires a cast.

28. C wait() and notify() methods provide a mechanism to facilitate object-level resource locking. For this reason, wait() and notify() are members of the Object class.

29. D Java packages provide a grouping facility for classes and interface.

30. B The JVM specification does NOT define the process by which unused memory resources are collected and put onto the heap for reuse.

31. D The id field holds the code associated with the nature of the java.awt.Event instance.

32. B The Windows 3.1 platform does have an accessible Java runtime environment, but it doesn't support threads.

33. A Completely true, Java supports only single object inheritance.

34. A Since 0 mod 5 is 0, the inner loop is only executed once. However, the outer and middle loops are executed to fruition. Thus the final line of output would be Hello - 25.

35. C Java shorts are signed 16 bit values. So, the desecrate range of a short is $-(2^{15})$ to $(2^{15} - 1)$.

36. A All JDK 1.1+ event objects, including java.awt.AWTEvent, are derived from java.util.EventObject.

37. B The thread priority signifies the presidencies of any given thread. However, the use of thread priority depends on the thread-scheduling algorithm used to implement the JVM.

38. C Since an exception is intentionally thrown in the try…catch block, both the catch and finally blocks are executed. Thus, the output would be Do you see followed by Me?.

39. B The Runnable interface is used to define a target for the Thread class.

40. A True, Java supports only single object inheritance.

41. D   The JVM is an emulator used to execute Java machine code on a native platform.

42. B   Under normal operating conditions, the declaration `"int I;"` will not throw an exception. For this reason, `Lets have fun!` will never be output. However, the `finally` block of any try...catch block will always be thrown. Meaning, the above code won't execute the `catch` block, but it will execute the `finally` block, for an output of `We love Java`.

43. A   Any class that contains an abstract method declaration must be declared as abstract.

44. D   `classB` is a child of `classA`. Therefore, casting a `classB` reference into a `classA` reference will always succeed.

45. B   `class3` is a child of `class1`. Therefore, casting a `class1` reference into a `class3` reference will only succeed if the reference points to a `class3` object.

46. C   The statement `"s1 = s2"` is a declaration, and not a Boolean operation. Thus, `"s1 = s2"` would equate to a `false` value.

47. `public void holdMe(){)`

48. D   In an effort to minimize the number of registers needed by the JVM architecture, a stack-based model was employed.

49. A   The purpose of an abstract class is to forward declare the method. Providing the braces (`{}`) actually implements the method with no instruction, and thus making it non-abstract.

50. `return (P==Q)? PxQ : 0;)`

51. B   `class1` is the parent class of `class2`, and `class2` is the parent class of `class3`. The second way to say this is: class3's parent class is `class2`, and class2's parent class is `class1`.

52. E   A Java class file contains JVM executable instructions, method naming information, and field naming information.

53. B   The `private` visibility modifier limits a method's visibility to only the currently defined class.

54. D   An interface provides a mechanism to facilitate multiple inheritance and a template for future development.

55. C   The class provides a single reader, single writer facility.

56. D   `bool` is not a primitive data type, but Boolean is.

57. A   `protected` limits a method's visibility to the other classes in the current package and subclasses only.

58. B   The `throws` reserved word is used to declare the exception(s) a given method produces.

59. A   The JVM registers and stack are 32 bits wide.

60. B   The `-verbose` option displays the explicit loading of each class.

61. C   `Runnable` interfaces are called thread targets. In this case, Thread `T1` is constructed to contain the `Runnable` interface `myClass`, and it executes the `myClass` `run()` method.

62. D   `Float`, `Double`, and `Byte` are derived from `Number`, represent numeric values, and have a primitive data type counterpart.

63. B   The JVM specification does not specify the thread scheduling used.

64. A   `java.awt.AWTEvent` contains a constructor to aid in porting the `Event` class to the post-JDK 1.1 event model.

65. C   `java.util.Hastable` is a generic object storage device.

66. A   `/**` denotes a javadoc comment.

67. A   Mutually exclusive threads are processes. All Java threads have the ability to share common memory resources and objects, making them non-mutually exclusive.

68. D   `javag`, `javag_w`, and `java_w` are all provided variations of the base JDK `java` command line tool.

69. B   A class is allowed to implement as many interfaces as desired.

70. A class3 and class2 share a common parent, class1. However, it is never legal to cast between siblings and will cause a compilation error.

71. A GetHashCode() is not a method contained with java.lang.Object, but hashCode() is.

72. B Integer is a class found in java.lang, and not a reserved word.

73. A java.lang.String contains a substring method, which provides a means for finding sub-strings within the contained string.

74. D Calling the stop() method, an external JVM event, and the thread returning from its run method can all terminate a thread's execution.

75. D public limits a method's visibility to all other classes and subclasses.

76. D The difference between 01110111 and 00111011 is a single bit shift to the right. Since the leading bit is a 0, both the >> and >>> operators work identically. However, if the leading bit was 1, the >> and >>> would have different results (see question 78).

77. C The java_g executes the specified class with optimization turned off so that it may be executed in the jdb tool.

78. B The difference between 01110111 and 00111011 is a single bit shift to the right. However, since the leading bit is a 1 the >>> operators must be used to zero fill the shift.

79. B The appletviewer can be directed to look at a specified code base via the codebase applet tag parameter.

80. D The -depend command line option forces javac to perform a compilation to include all supporting classes.

81. D An int variable cannot hold a reference to an Integer class.

82. if(gameTwo interfaceof Runnable)

83. **B**   An `IOException` is thrown by the `read()` method of `java.io.InputStream`.

84. **B**   The `yield()` method of `java.lang.Thread` relinquishes a processing slot to another thread.

85. **D**   `notify()` and `wait()` methods provide a mechanism to facilitate object-level resource locking. For this reason `notify()` and `wait()` are members of the `Object` class.

86. **A**   The `@param` tag is used to document the input parameter of the associated class.

87. **B**   The `System` Class is intended to be used as a static class. For this reason, declaring a new instance of `System` would cause a compilation error.

88. **E**   The `java.lang.System` class is the gatekeeper for all system/process specific resources, including `Standard In`, `Standard Out`, and `Standard Error`.

89. **D**   The JavaChip is a silicon implementation of the JVM.

90. **A**   `java -0` is used for executing a class with full optimization turned on.

Where To Go From Here

As you can see from the questions presented in this chapter, the Certified Java Programmer examination covers a vast amount of information. Everything from reserved words to construction order is asked, and asked in detail. However, now that you have completed the practice exam you have a better understanding of what constitutes a Certified Java Programmer.

This chapter presented a checklist of exam topics, and a complete 90-question exam. If you completed the entire practice exam without even breaking a sweat, congratulations. It is now time for you to call one of the Sylvan Prometric test facilities listed in Appendix A, and make your appointment to sit for the real Certified Java Programmer examination. On the other hand, if you were not certain of the material covered in the examination, use the examination software provided on the CD-ROM to better hone your skills.

Chapter 9

Certified Programmer
Practice Test #3

The scope of this chapter is to provide detailed test information for the Certified Java Programmer Examination. For this reason, it is required that you should read all subsequent chapters before proceeding. Please read the introductory testing material found at the beginning of Chapter 7, "Certified Programmer Practice Test #1," before taking this exam.

This chapter will provide the following resources for the Certified Java Programmer Examination:

 Objectives

▶ Study Guide and Check List

▶ Practice Exam and Answers

Specifics of the Certification Exam Environment include:

▶ Proctored entirely by computer

▶ No external material allowed in the testing area

▶ The exam is comprised of true/false, multiple choice, and short answer questions

▶ Results are presented immediately after the exam is completed

Practice Examination

The following practice test and answers are provided as a companion to the testing software found on the accompanying CD-ROM. However, the detailed description of each of the answers is not included on the CD-ROM. The test that follows is one of three tests provided on the CD-ROM, and provides a printed, portable study device. With that said, best of luck.

Practice Test

1. Which of the following members is used to find the type of event encapsulated in a `java.awt.Event` class?

   A. `id`

   B. `getEventType()`

   C. `isMouseEvent()`

   D. `getParameters()`

2. The `@deprecated` javadoc tag cannot denote deprecated classes, interfaces, or members.

   A. True

   B. False

3. A class can only have a single parent.

    A. True

    B. False

4. The wait() call does which of the following?

    A. Blocks until a thread terminates

    B. Blocks until notified by another thread

    C. Blocks until the object is ready for access

    D. Blocks a thread until all other threads have terminated

5. What is the numeric range for a Java short?

    A. -(2^16) to (2^16)

    B. -(2^15) to (2^15 - 1)

    C. -(2^31) to (2^31 - 1)

    C. 0 to (2^16)

6. Classes are executed by the JVM in this manner:

    A. The ClassLoader loads the class into the JVM for execution, and then signals for execution to begin.

    B. The JVM prompts the user for the class to execute.

    C. The ClassLoader finds, verifies, and loads the class into the JVM for execution, then signals for execution to begin.

    D. The runtime environment loads the Applet information into the JVM, and then begins the JVM process.

7. How are thread priority and thread scheduling related?

    A. It depends on the thread-scheduling algorithm used to implement the JVM.

    B. Thread priority is specified when a thread is to be executed next.

C. Thread priority is used to determine the next thread to execute from the waiting thread pool.

D. They aren't.

8. The `wait()` and `notify()` methods are defined in what class?

A. `java.lang.String`

B. `java.lang.Thread`

C. `java.lang.Object`

D. `java.lang.Runnable`

9. The `Runnable` interface is used for what?

A. A marathon

B. Defining a thread

C. Defining a class to execute a new thread

D. Defining a class that can be executed by a thread.

10. The JVM specification does not define the process by which unused memory resources are collected and put onto the heap for reuse.

A. True

B. False

11. Which one of the following best describes the role of the JVM?

A. An interpreter

B. A device used to execute applets

C. An Microsoft Internet Explorer plug-in

D. An emulator used to execute Java machine code on a native platform

12. The class file contains

    A. JVM executable instructions

    B. Method naming information

    C. Field naming information

    D. All of the above

    E. None of the above

13. The following code might contain an error.

```
public class myClass{

    public abstract void mytrash();

    public static void main(String args[]){

        for(int j=0;i < 9;++j){
            for(int i=0; i < 365;++i)
                    System.out.println("Fun with Java");

            // Run the garbage collector.
            System.out.println("Running garbage collector");
        }
    }
}
```

    If there is an error, what is it?

    A. public class myClass{

    B. public abstract void mytrash();

    C. No Error

14. An interface provides which of the following?

    A. A mechanism to facilitate multiple inheritance

    B. A template for future development

    C. An alternative to class declarations

D. A and B

E. A and C

15. The following defines an object hierarchy.

```
class class1{

    public static int myNumber = 2;
}

class class2 extends class1{

    public static int yourNumber = 3;

    public int ourNumber(){

        return myNumber + yourNumber;
    }
}

class class3 extends class1{

    public static int theirNumber = 5;

    public int ourNumber(){

        return myNumber + theirNumber;
    }

}

public class myClass{

  publicstatic class3 castMe(class1 in){
      return (class3)in;
  }

  public static void main(String args[]){
      class3 v = castMe(new class1());
  }

}
```

When does the following method cause an error/exception?

```
public static class3 castMe(class1 in){
        return (class3)in;
   }
```

A. At compilation

B. Never

C. If and only if in references an `class2` object

E. If and only if in references an `class3` object

16. Which of the following is NOT a primitive Java data type?

A. `int`

B. `boolean`

C. `float`

D. `double`

E. `bool`

17. Given the following code listing:

```
public class myClass{


    //Your Declaration HERE!{
        try {
            System.in.read();
        } catch (IOException e) {
            return;
        }
    }

    public static void main(String args[]) {
        System.out.println("My console application");
        System.out.println("");
        System.out.println("(press Enter to exit)");
        holdMe();
    }

}
```

At the specified location, provide a method declaration with the following properties.

Name: `holdMe`

Input Parameters: None

Return Value: None

Visibility: All classes and subclasses in the current package.

Enter answer here:_____

18. The `throws` reserved word...

    A. Raises an exception.

    B. Triggers an event.

    C. Defines the exception a method can raise.

    D. Defines the exception(s) a method can raise.

19. The following code listing contains one error, which is...

```
public abstract class myClass{

    public static boolean IsPrime(long in){

        boolean prime = true;
        for(long i = 2; i <= (in / 2);++i){
            if((in % i) == 0){
                prime = false;
                break;
            }
        }
        return prime;
    }

    public abstract void fun(int Value){};

}
```

    A. `public abstract class myClass`

    B. Class must contain a constructor

C. Incomplete class definition

D. `public abstract void fun(int Value){};`

20. Please complete the following source, so that if the value of "P" is equal to "Q" then return P x Q, otherwise return 0;

```
public class myClass{

    public return int myTest(int P, int Q){
        //Your Single Line of Code Here!
    }


}
```

Enter answer here:_____

21. Which answer best describes the following object hierarchy?

```
class class1{

    public static int myValue = 2;
}

class class2 extends class1{

    public static int yourValue = 3;

    public int ourValue(){

        return myValue + yourValue;
    }
}

class class3 extends class2{

    public static int theirValue = 5;

    public int ourValue(){
        return myValue + theirValue;
    }

}
```

A. class3's parent class is class2, class2's parent class is class1, and class1's parent is Object.

B. class3's parent class is class2, and class2's parent class is class1.

C. class1 is the parent class of class2, and class2 is the parent class of class3.

D. class1's parent class is class2, class2's parent class is class3, and class3's parent is Object.

E. B and C.

22. What is the output of the following try...catch block?

```
public class tryme {

    public static void main(String args[]) {

        try{
            int I;
            return;
        }catch(Exception e){
            System.out.println("Howdy");
            return;
        }finally{
            System.out.println("Hello");
        }

    }
}
```

A. Howdy

B. Hello

C. No output

D. Depends on the creation of the int I;

23. What modifier would be used to limit a method's visibility to only the currently defined class?

A. static

B. private

C. protected

D. public

24. The following defines an object hierarchy.

```
class class1{

    public static int myValue = 2;
}

class class2 extends class1{

    public static int yourValue = 3;

    public int ourValue(){

        return myValue + yourValue;
    }
}

class class3 extends class1{

    public static int theirValue = 5;

    public int ourValue(){

        return myValue + theirValue;
    }

}

public class myClass{

    public static class1 castMe(class2 in){
        return (class1)in;
    }

    public static void main(String args[]){
        class1 v = castMe(new class2());
    }

}
```

When does the following method cause an error/exception?

```java
public static class1 castMe(class2 in){
        return (class1)in;
    }
```

A. At compilation

B. If and only if in references a class3 object

C. If and only if in references a class2 object

D. Never

25. Which statement best describes the following class?

```java
public class dataCenterRe{
    private static String  data = "";

    public static synchronized void setStr(String in){

        data = in;

    }

    public static synchronized String getStr(){

        return data;

    }

}
```

A. The class is a simple storage device for a string.

B. The class is a simple storage device for multiple threads to access a single string.

C. The class provides a mechanism by which only multiple threads can get or set the stored string value.

D. The class provides a mechanism by which only one thread can get or set the stored string value at a time.

26. Which of the following statements would equate to false, given the following declaration?

String s1 = "Hello";

String s2 = "Hello";

    A. `s1 = s2`

    B. `s1.equals(s2)`

    C. `s1 == s2`

    D. None of the above

27. What modifier would be used to limit a method's visibility to only the other classes in the current package, and subclasses?

    A. `static`

    B. `private`

    C. `protected`

    D. `public`

28. `java.lang.System` class contains which of the following fields?

    A. `Standard In`

    B. `Standard Out`

    C. `Standard Error`

    D. All of the above

    E. None of the above

29. The JVM registers and stack are:

    A. 4 bits wide

    B. 8 bits wide

    C. 16 bits wide

    D. 32 bits wide

30. In the java tool, the -verbose tool...

    A. Informs when garbage collection is performed.

    B. Generates information regarding how many times a method has been called.

    C. Displays the explicit loading of each class.

    D. Indicates that the option has been deprecated.

31. Given the following code segment:

```
import java.util.Hashtable;
import java.util.Enumeration;
import java.net.*;
import java.io.*;


class myClass implements Runnable
{
//Reference to current thread
   public  Thread Child_Thread = null;

   //Start-up new thread
   public void start(){
      if (Child_Thread == null){
         Child_Thread = new Thread(this);
         Child_Thread.start();
      }
   }

   //Stop the currently executing thread
   public void stop(){
      if (Child_Thread != null)
         Child_Thread.stop();
      Child_Thread = null;
   }

   public void run(){
      for(int i = 0;i < 4556;++i);
   }
}

//Main Public Launcher
```

```
public class CSPassiveAgent {

   public static void main(String args[]) {

      Thread  T1 = new Thread(new myClass());
      T1.start();
   }
}
```

Which statement best defines the following code segment?

```
Thread  T1 = new Thread(new myClass());
      T1.start();
```

A. Thread T1 is created and executed.

B. A compilation error will occur at T1.start();.

C. Thread T1 is constructed to contain the Runnable interface myClass, and it executes the myClass run() method.

D. Thread T1 is constructed to contain the Runnable interface myClass, and it executes the Thread run() method.

32. Which of the following is not a reserved word?

A. int

B. Integer

C, interfaceof

D. instanceof

E. goto

33. The JVM specification does not specify the thread scheduling used.

A. True

B. False

34. Which of the following terminates a thread's execution?

    A. An external JVM event

    B. Calling the stop() method

    C. A thread returning from its run() method

    D. All of the above

    E. None of the above

35. What is a Hashtable?

    A. a generic object storage device

    B. a generic data storage device

    C. a deprecated facility from JDK 1.0

    D. None of the above

36. Which javadoc tag is used to denote a comment for a method parameter?

    A. @parameter

    B. @param

    C. @value

    D. @method

37. All threads created in Java are not mutually exclusive.

    A. True

    B. False

38. Given a byte with a value of 11110111, which of the following statements will produce 00111011?

Note : 01110111 = 0x77

    A. 0x77 << 1;

    B. 0x77 >>> 1;

C. 0x77 >> 1;

D. 0x77 <<< 1;

E. C and D

39. A class can implement more than one interface.

A. True

B. False

40. The following defines an object hierarchy.

```
class class1{

    public static int myValue = 2;
}

class class2 extends class1{

    public static int yourValue = 3;

    public int ourValue(){

        return myValue + yourValue;
    }
}

class class3 extends class1{

    public static int theirValue = 5;

    public int ourValue(){

        return myValue + theirValue;
    }

}

class class4 extends class1{

}

public class myClass{
```

```
publicstatic class2 castMe(class3 in){
    return (class2)in;
}

public static void main(String args[]){
    class2 v = castMe(new class4());
}

}
```

When does the following method cause an error/exception?

```
public static class2 castMe(class3 in){
    return (class2)in;
}
```

A. At compilation

B. If and only if in references a class3 object

C. If and only if in references a class2 object

D. Never

41. Which of the following is NOT a method of `java.lang.Object`?

A. `wait()`

B. `equals(Object)`

C. `hashCode()`

D. `getHashCode()`

42. `Float`, `Double`, and `Byte` all...

A. represent numeric values.

B. are derived from Number.

C. have a primitive data type counterpart.

D. A and C.

E. All of the above.

43. The `java.lang.String` class does not provide methods for finding substrings within the contained string.

    A. True

    B. False

44. `java.awt.AWTEvent` contains a constructor to aid in porting the `Event` class to the post-JDK 1.1 event model.

    A. True

    B. False

45. What modifier would be used to limit a method's visibility to all other classes and subclasses?

    A. `static`

    B. `private`

    C. `public`

    D. `final`

46. With javadoc, which of the following denotes a javadoc comment?

    A. `//*`

    B. `/**`

    C. `/*/*`

    D. `//##`

47. `java_g` is used for which of the following?

    A. Executing a class with optimization turned off

    B. Using the `jdb` tool

    C. A and B.

    D. None of the above.

48. What variations of the java tool are provided in the JDK?

    A. javag

    B. javag_w

    C. java_w

    D. A and C

    E. A, B, and C

49. `appletviewer` only retrieves classes found in the CLASSPATH environment variable.

    A. False

    B. True

50. javac -depend `myClass.java` will cause which of the following to happen?

    A. `myClass.java` to be compiled

    B. compile `myName.java`

    C. All dependent classes of `myClass.java` to be compiled

    D. A and B

    E. None of the above

51. java_w executes a specified...

    A. class

    B. class without optimization

    C. class in its own separate window

    D. class without an associated console window

52. The `appletviewer` has facilities to execute multiple applets at a time by allowing for which of the following?

    A. Multiple applets defined in the HTML

    B. Allowing multiple URL's to be provided on the command line

    C. Providing a window to select desired applets

    D. A and B

53. Which of the following assignment statements are valid?

    A. `float f = 985;`

    B. `long l = 036;`

    C. `double d = 0x82576;`

    D. All of the above

    E. None of the above

54. Convert the following statement into its octal equivalent.

    ```
    int i = 16;
    //Octal Declaration HERE!
    ```

Enter Octal declaration here:_____

55. Given the following code segment:

    ```
    class class1{

        public class1(){
            System.out.println("ONE");
        }
    }

    class class2 extends class1{

        public class2(){
            System.out.println("TWO");
        }
    }
    ```

```
class class3 extends class2{

    public class3(){
        System.out.println("THREE");
    }
}


public class oneToThree {

    public static void main(String args[]) {

        System.out.println("In main");
        class3 c = new class3();

    }
}
```

In what order will the output be produced?

A. `Three, Two, Two, In main`

B. `ONE, TWO, THREE, In main`

C. `In main, ONE, TWO, THREE`

D. `In main, ONE, TWO, ONE`

56. Which of the following best describes when a variable becomes available for reclamation by the garbage collector?

    A. After the variable is out of a method's scope

    B. After you use it

    C. Upon returning from the containing method block

    D. When the variable is no longer referenced anywhere in the JVM

    E. A and C

57. Given the following code listing:

```
public class tryme {
```

```
public static void main(String args[]) {

    int maincount = 0;
    outer:for(int i=0;i < 5;++i)
            middle:for(int j=0;j < 5;++j)
                inner:for(int k=0;k < 5;++k){
                        System.out.println("Stop at - "
+ ++maincount);

                        if((k%5) ==0)
                            break outer;
                }
    }
}
```

Which of the following is the last line of output?

   A. Stop at - 25

   B. Stop at - 5

   C. 5

   D. 10

58. What is the numeric range for a Java int?

   A. 0 to (2^32)

   B. -(2^31) to (2^31)

   C. -(2^31) to (2^31 - 1)

   D. -(2^15) to (2^15 - 1)

59. Given the following HTML applet declaration:

```
<APPLET URL codebase = "/" archive="Myapplet.zip"
CODE="Myapplet.class"
 WIDTH=450 HEIGHT=222>
<PARAM NAME="LOGIN" VALUE="78tre">
</APPLET>
```

Provide an assignment statement which assigns the value held in the "LOGIN" parameter to a string named "LOGIN".

Enter answer here:_____

60. What modifier would be used to disallow subclasses from overriding a declared method?

    A. `public`

    B. `private`

    C. `final`

    D. `status`

61. Given the following code listing:

```
public String whatIsThis(Object myToy){

        //Your Conditional HERE
    return "It is an Integer";
    return "No Idea";
    }
```

Provide a single `if` statement such that `It is an Integer` is returned if `myToy` is an `Integer`.

Enter code here:_____

62. Given the following code listing:

```
public boolean isThisRunnable(Object myGame){

        //Your Conditional HERE
        return true;
        return false;
    }
```

Provide a single `if` statement such that `true` is returned if `myGame` implements the `Runnable` interface.

Enter code here:_____

63. The following defines an object hierarchy.

```
class class1{

    public static int myNum = 2;
}
```

```
class class2 extends class1{

    public static int yourNum = 3;

    public int ourValue(){

        return myNum + yourNum;
    }
}

class class3 extends class1{

    public static int theirNum = 5;

    public int ourNum(){

        return myNum + theirNum;
    }

}

public class myClass{

    public static class3 castMe(class1 in){
        return (class3)in;
    }

    public static void main(String args[]){
}

}
```

When does the following method cause an error/exception?

```
public static class3 castMe(class1 in){
        return (class3)in;
    }
```

A. At compilation

B. If in references a class3 object

C. If in references a class2 object, or in references a class1 object

D. Never

64. What modifier would be used to limit a method's visibility to all classes and subclasses in the same package?

   A. public

   B. default

   C. protected

   D. final

   E. private

65. Given the following code listing:

```
public class tryme {

    public static void main(String args[]) {

        int maincount = 0;

        try{
            outer:for(int i=0;i < 5;++i)
                    middle:for(int j=0;j < 5;++j)
                        inner:for(int k=0;k < 5;++k){
                            System.out.println("Hello - " +
➥++maincount);
                                if((k%5) == 0)
                                    throw(new Exception());


                        }
        }
        catch(Exception e){
        }
        }
}
```

Which of the following is the last line of output?

   A. 10

   B. Hello - 100

   C. Hello - 1

   D. Hello - 10

66. Enter the complete main method declaration required for a java executable class.

Enter answer here:_____

67. Which of the following base data types has a corresponding class wrapper?

    A. int

    B. byte

    C. float

    D. All of the above

    E. None of the above

68. What modifier would be used to disallow a class's member to be overridden?

    A. public

    B. final

    C. protected

    D. private

    E. default

69. What is the numeric range for a Java byte?

    A. 0 to (2^8)

    B. 0 to (2^16)

    C. -(2^8) to (2^8 - 1)

    D. -(2^7) to (2^7 - 1)

70. java -0 is used for executing a...

    A. class in the debugging facility.

    B. class with all profiling options on.

    C. class with optimization turned on.

    D. class with a specified object stream.

71. Which of the following assignment statements is invalid?

    A. `double d = 45256.834;`

    B. `long l = 45184;`

    C. `int j = (int)d;`

    D. `int i = new Integer(46);`

72. Which of the following statements would equate to `true`, given the following declaration?

    Boolean b1 = true;

    Boolean b2 = false;

    A. `b1 ¦¦ b2`

    B. `b1 && b2`

    C. `b1 ¦& b2`

    D. `b1 == b2`

73. What exception is thrown by the `read()` method of an `Input-Stream`?

    A. `Exception`

    B. `ReadException`

    C. `IOException`

    D. None of the above

74. `java.lang.Thread` utilizes which of the following methods to relinquish the thread instance's processing slot to another thread?

    A. `yield()`

    B. `Wait()`

C. Sleep()

D. None of the above

75. The wait() and notify() methods are members of what class?

A. Object

B. Thread

C. String

D. All of the above

76. Given a byte with a value of 01110111, which of the following statements will produce 00111011?

Note : 01110111 = 0x77

A. 0x77 << 1;

B. 0x77 >>> 1;

C. 0x77 >> 1;

D. B and C

E. A and C

77. The following application contains a single error.

```
public class myClass{

    public static void main(String args[]){

        for(int i=0; i < 8975;++i){
            if((i % 2) == 0)
                System.out.println("I like Java");
            else
                System.out.println("I don't like Java");
        }
        (new System()).out.println("Done");
    }
}
```

Which line contains the error?

A. `for(int i=0; i < 8975;++i){`

B. `(new System()).out.println("Done");`

C. `public static void main(String args[]){`

D. `if((i % 2) == 0)`

78. The JVM architecture makes the following provisions to ensure compatibility across all processors:

A. Minimizes the use of registers

B. Uses a stack based architecture

C. Is modeled after the lowest common denominator architecture

D. A and B

E. A and C

79. A JavaChip is:

A. A silicon implementation of the JVM

B. A chip which stores Java class files to increase Class-Loader performance

C. An accelerator chip designed to aid the JVM running on the native machine

D. The chip inside Sun's JavaStation

80. What major feature(s) was/were debuted in the JDK 1.1?

A. JDBC

B. RMI

C. JavaBeans

D. Improved AWT

E. All of these

F. None of these

81. Which of the following is not a reserved word?

    A. `instanceof`

    B. `switch`

    C. `catch`

    D. `NULL`

    E. `null`

82. A Java runtime environment is not available on Windows 3.1.

    A. True

    B. False

83. The statement `"A %= 5;"` can best be described as what?

    A. A equals A divided by 5

    B. A equals A modulus 5.

    C. A equals A in 5 digit percentage form.

    D. None of the above

84. Given the following code listing:

```
public class tryme {

  public static void main(String args[]) {

    int maincount = 0;
    outer:for(int i=0;i < 5;++i)
        middle:for(int j=0;j < 5;++j)
        inner:for(int k=0;k < 5;++k){
          System.out.println("Hello - " + ++maincount);
          if((k%5) == 0)
            continue middle;
```

```
            }
        }
    }
```

Which of the following is the last line of output?

A. `Hello - 25`

B. `Hello - 5`

C. `25`

D. `5`

85. Which of the following best describes the public class modifier?

    A. Opens the class up for usage and subclassing to all.

    B. Allows other classes to subclass it

    C. Allows only classes in the current package to use its facilities

    D. A and B

    E. A and C

86. `java.util.EventObject` is not the parent class of `java.awt.AWTEvent`.

    A. True

    B. False

87. Which of the following assignment statements is invalid?

    A. `int i = 1;`

    B. `double d = 84456.435;`

    C. `long l = 32789;`

    D. `int j = (int)d;`

88. What is the output of the following try...catch block?

```
public class tries {

public static void main(String args[]) {

    try{
        int I;
        throw(new Exception("Grass"));
        return;
    }catch(Exception e){
        System.out.println("Dogs like to eat");
        return;
    }finally{
        System.out.println("Grass");
    }

}
}
```

    A. Grass

    B. No output

    C. Dogs like to eat

    D. A and C

89. A package is:

    A. A collection of classes

    B. A collection of interfaces

    C. A way to provide naming for a group of related classes

    D. All of the above

90. A class can have multiple parents.

    A. True

    B. False

Answers and Discussion

The following is a complete list of all sample test question answers followed by a brief discussion of the correct answer.

1. A   The id field holds the code associated with the nature of the java.awt.Event instance.

2. B   The @deprecated javadoc tag is used to denote deprecated classes, interfaces, or members.

3. A   Java supports only single object inheritance (Answer A).

4. B   The wait() call blocks until notified by another thread.

5. B   Java shorts are signed, 16 bit values. So, the desecrate range of a short is $-(2^{15})$ to $(2^{15} - 1)$.

6. C   Classes are executed by the JVM in the following manner: The ClassLoader finds, verifies, and loads the class into the JVM for execution, and then signals execution to begin.

7. A   The thread priority signifies the presidencies of any given thread. However, the use of thread priority depends on the thread-scheduling algorithm used to implement the JVM.

8. C   wait() and notify() methods provide a mechanism to facilitate object-level resource locking. For this reason, wait() and notify() are members of the Object class.

9. D   The Runnable interface is used to define a target for the Thread class.

10. A   The JVM specification does NOT define the process by which unused memory resources are collected and put onto the heap for reuse.

11. D   The JVM is an emulator used to execute Java machine code on a native platform.

12. D   A Java class file contains JVM executable instructions, method naming information, and field naming information.

13. **A** Any class that contains an abstract method declaration must be declared as abstract.

14. **D** An interface provides a mechanism to facilitate multiple inheritance and a template for future development.

15. **D** class3 is a child of class1. Therefore, casting a class1 reference into a class3 reference will only succeed if the reference points to a class3 object.

16. **E** bool is not a primitive data type, but boolean is.

17. `public void holdMe(){}`

18. **D** The throws reserved word is used to declare the exception(s) a given method produce.

19. **D** The purpose of an abstract class is to forward declare the method. Providing the braces ({}) actually implements the method with no instruction, thus making it non-abstract.

20. `return (P==Q)? PxQ ¦ 0;)`

21. **E** There are two ways to state class hierarchy. The first is top down, class1 is the parent class of class2, and class2 is the parent class of class3. The second is bottom up, class3's parent class is class2, and class2's parent class is class1.

22. **B** Under normal operating conditions, the declaration "int I;" will not throw an exception. For this reason, Howdy will never be outputed. However, the finally block of any try…catch block will always be throw. Meaning, the given code won't execute the catch block, but it will execute the finally block, for an output of Hello.

23. **B** The private visibility modifier limits a method's visibility to only the currently defined class.

24. **D** class2 is a child of class1. Therefore, casting a class2 reference into a class1 reference will always succeed.

25. **D** The class provides a single reader, single writer facility.

26. A The statement "s1 = s2" is a declaration, and not a Boolean operation. Thus, "s1 = s2" would equate to a `false` value.

27. C protected limits a method's visibility to only the other classes and subclasses in the current package.

28. D The `java.lang.System` class is the gatekeeper for all system/process specific resources, including `Standard In`, `Standard Out`, and `Standard Error`.

29. D The JVM registers and stack are 32 bits wide.

30. C The `-verbose` option displays the explicit loading of each class.

31. C Runnable interfaces are called thread targets. In this case, Thread T1 is constructed to contain the Runnable interface myClass, and it executes the myClass run() method.

32. B Integer is a class found in java.lang, and not a reserved word.

33. A The JVM specification does not specify the thread scheduling used.

34. D Calling the stop() method, an external JVM event, and the thread returning from its run method can all terminate a thread's execution.

35. A java.util.Hashtable is a generic object storage device.

36. B The @param tag is used to document the input parameter of the associated class.

37. A Mutually exclusive threads are processes. All Java threads have the ability to share common memory resources and objects, making them non-mutually exclusive.

38. B The difference between 01110111 and 00111011 is a single bit shift to the right. However, since the leading bit is a 1 the >>> operators must be used to zero fill the shift.

39. A A class is allowed to implement as many interfaces as desired.

40. A `class3` and `class2` share a common parent, `class1`. However, it is never legal to cast between siblings and will cause a compilation error.

41. D `GetHashCode()` is not a method contained with `java.lang.Object`, but `hashCode()` is.

42. E `Float`, `Double`, and `Byte` represent numeric values, are derived from `Number`, and have a primitive data type counterpart.

43. B `java.lang.String` contains a `substring` method that provides a means for finding sub-strings within the contained string.

44. A `java.awt.AWTEvent` contains a constructor to aid in porting the `Event` class to the post-JDK 1.1 event model.

45. C `public` limits a method's visibility to all other classes and subclasses.

46. B `/**` denotes a javadoc comment.

47. C The `java_g` executes the specified class with optimization turned off so that it may be executed in the `jdb` tool.

48. E `javag`, `javag_w`, and `java_w` are all provided variations of the base JDK `java` command line tool.

49. A No, the `appletviewer` can be directed to look at a specified code base via the `codebase` applet tag parameter.

50. D The `-depend` command line option forces `javac` to perform a compilation to include all supporting classes.

51. D The `java_w` command line tool executes a specified class, without an associated console window, to allow more seamless integration.

52. B By allowing multiple URL's to be provided on the command line, the `appletviewer` has facilities to execute multiple applets at a time.

53. D All of the supplied assignment statements are valid.

54. int i = 16 is equal to int j = 020;

55. C Java's construction order is from bottom up. Thus, the order would be In main, ONE, TWO, THREE.

56. D The whole trick behind garbage collecting is to determine when a variable is no longer needed. In Java, this is achieved by a reference count. When a variable is no longer referenced, it is eligible for garbage collection.

57. B Since 0 mod 5 is 0, the inner loop is only executed once. However, the outer loop is executed to fruition. Thus, the final line of output would be Stop at - 5.

58. C Java int's are signed, 32 bit values. Thus, the desecrate range of an int is $-(2^31)$ to $(2^31 - 1)$.

59. String LOGIN = getParam("LOGIN")

60. C The final modifier disallows subclasses from overriding a declared method.

61. if(myToy instanceof Integer)

62. if(myGame interfaceof Runnable)

63. C Casting from a parent class to a subclass is legal, but may cause a runtime exception. In this case, a runtime exception would be thrown if in references a class2 object, or in references a class1 object.

64. B The "default", or package modifier is used to limit a method's visibility to all classes and subclasses in the same package.

65. C Since 0 mod 5 is 0, the inner loop is only executed once, and then throws an exception, the final line of output would be Hello - 1.

66. public void main(String Args[]){}

67. D Beginning with JDK 1.1, all base types have a corresponding class wrapper.

68. B The final modifier is used to disallow a class's member to be overridden.

69. **D**   Java bytes are 8-bit signed structures with a discrete range from $-(2^7)$ to $(2^7 - 1)$.

70. **C**   java -0 is used for executing a class with full optimization turned on.

71. **D**   An int variable cannot hold a reference to an Integer class.

72. **A**   Since b2 is false, the only statement which would produce a true value is b1 ¦¦ b2.

73. **C**   An IOException is thrown by the read() method of java.io.InputStream.

74. **A**   The yield() method of java.lang.Thread relinquishes a processing slot to another thread.

75. **D**   notify() and wait() methods provide a mechanism to facilitate object-level resource locking. For this reason notify() and wait() are members of the Object class.

76. **D**   The difference between 01110111 and 00111011 is a single bit shift to the right. Since the leading bit is a 0, both the >> and >>> operators work identically. However, if the leading bit were 1, the >> and >>> would have different results.

77. **B**   The System Class is intended to be used as a static class. For this reason, declaring a new instance of System would cause a compilation error.

78. **D**   In an effort to minimize the number of registers needed by the JVM architecture, a stack-based model was employed.

79. **A**   Despite how cool a Java flavored potato chip might sound, the JavaChip is a silicon implementation of the JVM.

80. **E**   The jump from JDK 1.02 to JDK 1.1 encapsulates an explosion of functionality. JDBC, RMI, JavaBeans, and an improved AWT event model list only a few of the new features.

81. **D**   NULL is not a reserved word, but null is.

82. B   The Windows 3.1 platform does have an accessible Java runtime environment; it doesn't support threads but it works.

83. B   The `%` operator performs a modulus operation. Therefore `"A %= 5;"` can best be described as A equals A modulus 5.

84. A   Since `0 mod 5` is `0`, the inner loop is only executed once. However, the outer and middle loops are executed to fruition. Thus the final line of output would be `Hello - 25`.

85. A   The `public` class modifier opens the class up for usage and subclassing to all.

86. B   All JDK 1.1+ event objects, including `java.awt.AWTEvent` are derived from `java.util.EventObject`.

87. A   The conversion between a `long` and an `int` requires a cast.

88. C   Since an exception is intentionally thrown in the `try…catch` block, both the `catch` and `finally` blocks are executed. Thus, the output would be `Dogs like to eat` followed by `Grass`.

89. D   Java packages provide a grouping facility for classes and interfaces.

90. B   Java supports only single object inheritance.

Where To Go From Here

As you can see from the questions presented in this chapter, the Certified Java Programmer examination covers a vast amount of information. Everything from reserved words to construction order is asked, and asked in detail. However, now that you have completed the practice exam you have a better understanding of what constitutes a Certified Java Programmer.

This chapter presented a checklist of exam topics, and a complete 90 question exam. If you completed the entire practice exam without even breaking a sweat, congratulations. It is now time for you to call one of the Sylvan Prometric test facilities listed in Appendix

A, and make your appointment to sit for the real Certified Java Programmer examination. On the other hand, it you were not certain of the material covered in the examination, use the examination software provided on the CD-ROM to better hone your skills.

The remainder of this book is dedicated to the Certified Java Developer examination, which requires the successful completion of the Certified Java Programmer examination. For this reason, you should not proceed into the following chapter until you have successfully passed the Certified Java Programmer examination.

P a r t 2

Sun Java Developer Certification

Chapter 10

Network Programming

The contents of this chapter focus on network programming or what is also called Java Inter-Process Communication (IPC). For most developers, there is something intrinsically brilliant about having two machines talk to each other. Whether it be two processes on the same box, two machines side-by-side, or two machines in different parts of the world, Inter-Process Communication (IPC) is a major feat of technology. Java IPC provides the painless means to facilitate true distributed processing.

 Objectives

- ▶ The use of UDP and TCP/IP facilities to gain access to legacy systems.

- ▶ Understand the workings of the java.net package facilities.

- ▶ Working knowledge of RMI for deployment of Java to Java applications.

Note The Certified Developer Exam is much different than the Programmer Exam. To pass the Developer Exam you do not need to memorize facts, rather you need to understand broad concepts and show hands-on programming experience. For these reasons there are not any Test Yourself quizzes or end-of-chapter questions in this section of the book.

The OSI Model, and IP, TCP, and UDP Protocols

This section defines the Open System Interconnection (OSI) seven-layer networking model—which is the basis for explaining all computer protocols—and then describes three pivotal protocols:

- ▶ Internet Protocol (IP)

- ▶ Transmission Control Protocol (TCP)

- ▶ User Datagram Protocol (UDP)

The OSI Model

The Open System Interconnection (OSI) reference model is a general model for describing computer communications. Figure 10.1 presents the standard representation of this model which organizes communication protocols into seven distinct layers.

Beginning with the bottom-most layers, and filtering up to the application presentation layer, the OSI model is the standard mechanism for describing all modern computer protocols. The following sections are devoted to providing an in-depth explanation of each of these layers. However, for the purposes of IPC and the Java Certification exam, only layers 4, 5, 6, and 7 are of substantial importance. Nevertheless, all seven layers are presented to provide contextual background.

Figure 10.1

*OSI seven-layer
network model.*

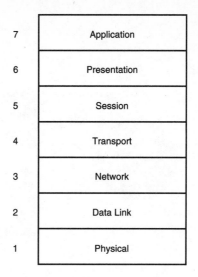

7	Application
6	Presentation
5	Session
4	Transport
3	Network
2	Data Link
1	Physical

The Physical Layer

The simplest way to describe the Physical Layer of the OSI model is to say that it's concerned with the bare copper. That is, the Physical Layer defines the requirements that must be met by the physical wire connecting one computer to another. Whether it is a RJ45, fiber link, or even radio modem, the Physical Layer is responsible for transmitting and receiving bits between computers. Figure 10.2 shows some more details of the physical layer on a networked computer.

The Data Link Layer

Riding on top of the Physical Layer is the Data Link Layer (see Figure 10.3). Usually, the Data Link Layer provides support for a Network Interface Card (NIC) and a device driver. To the operating system and all applications in general, the Data Link Layer is the gatekeeper to the Physical Layer and intern to the external network. It is in the Physical Layer that physical network protocols, such as Ethernet, fit into the OSI model.

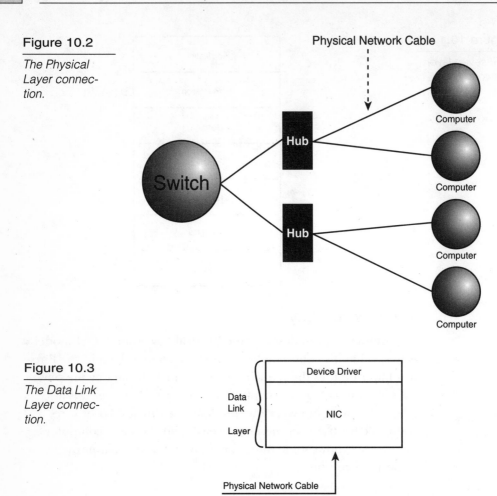

Figure 10.2

The Physical Layer connection.

Figure 10.3

The Data Link Layer connection.

The Network Layer

The Network Layer is the first physical layer above the Device Driver Layer (see Figure 10.4). Essentially, the Network Layer is the first protocol above the raw information retrieved from the Device Driver/Data Link Layer.

The Data Link layer is mainly concerned with the delivery of packets on the locally connected network. It is the responsibility of the Network Layer to provide end-to-end delivery facilities across multiple networks. Specifically, the Network Layer is comprised of three protocols in the TCP/IP protocol suite: IP, ICMP, and IGMP.

Figure 10.4

*The Network
Layer connection.*

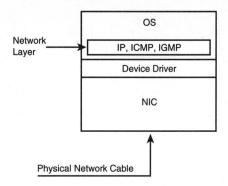

The Transport Layer

Herein begins the real interface for IPC. Both UDP and TCP are located in the confines of the Transport Layer (see Figure 10.5). However, the Transport Layer's role is different for each of these protocols. In theory, the Transport Layer is supposed to provide end-to-end error control for all protocol families. But, in the case of UDP, which provides no such error control facilities, the Transport Layer is almost a clear pass-through. Nevertheless, the Transport Layer is the first layer of the entire OSI model that is directly accessible to Java, and is the primary focus of this chapter.

Figure 10.5

*The Transport
Layer connection.*

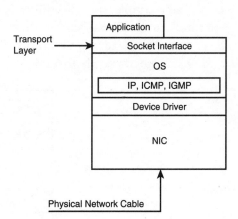

The Session Layer

The Session Layer is responsible for providing connection sequencing and maintenance for connection-oriented protocols such as TCP. Later in this chapter, the concept of connection and connection-less communications will be discussed in full detail.

However, as Figure 10.6 displays, the Session Layer can generally be assumed to be the final level of processing before the user application gains control of the data.

Figure 10.6

The Session Layer connection.

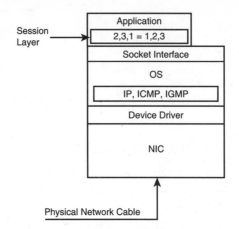

The Presentation Layer

Once the Session Layer orders the data stream into a coherent structure of data, the Presentation Layer is responsible for modifying the data into a platform dependent orientation (see Figure 10.7). For example, Intel machines store integer values in a different way than Motorola. Therefore, the Presentation Layer would be responsible for manipulating all integer values into the orientation of the executing platform.

Figure 10.7

The Presentation Layer connection.

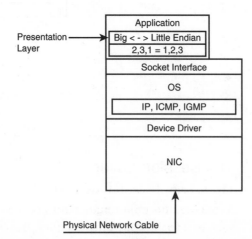

The Application Layer

The final and top-most layer of the OSI model is the Application Layer (see Figure 10.8). As the name implies, this is the actual application that utilizes the network resource. For example, in a Web server the logic that actually fetches and spits out a specified URL would be contained in the application layer.

Figure 10.8

The Application Layer connection.

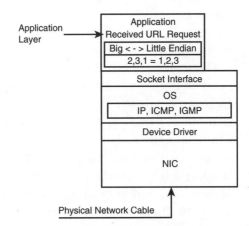

IP—The Heart of the Internet

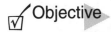

Knowing how to use the features of Java to facilitate client/server communication opens up the abilities of the Java platform, and is required knowledge to become a Certified Java Developer.

All Internet technologies rely on the base communication facilities of the Internet Protocol (IP). However, there are some characteristics of the IP that you might not expect, like the fact that IP does not guarantee the delivery of the transmitted data. Nevertheless, IP provides the base-level network protocol infrastructure which, in many ways, makes IP the heart of the Internet.

IP lives at layer 3, the Network Layer, of the OSI model. By definition, IP provides a communication facility one level above actual NIC level communication. At that level, IP is responsible for providing a single continuous conduit for transportation. To facilitate this continuous path, IP must include the infrastructure to appropriately route packets of information from point A to point B.

At the point that a higher-layered protocol passes information to the IP layer, it assumes that the data will be transported to the specified destination. However, it does not count on the delivery of that packet. That is, IP provides a connection-less, best effort transport of the specified data. Later, in the section "UDP—The OneTime Protocol," the concept of a connection-less communication will be discussed. For now, focus on the "best effort" characteristic of IP.

Figure 10.9 demonstrates the path of an IP packet through a network. In Figure 10.9, the source and destination computers are denoted by name rather than by the appropriate IP numbers for each computer. The IP numbers are unique addresses used by the IP protocol to deliver information to the appropriate recipient, and denote the machine from which the packet originated. IP's entire function is to transport the associated data packet from one IP address to another. However, IP does not make any guarantees of the timely and safe delivery of each packet. For example, Figure 10.10 shows router D being down on the network. In such a case, IP still attempts to send its outgoing packets to the designated router D, but, on failure, IP simply gives up. Thus, the term, "Best Effort Delivery."

Figure 10.9

The journey of an IP packet.

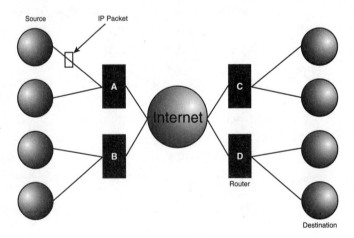

Figure 10.10

The hindered journey of an IP packet.

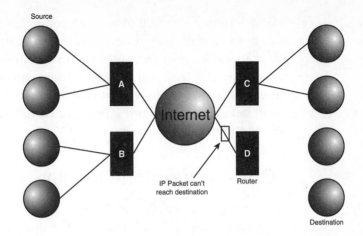

UDP—The One-Time Protocol

To understand how UDP works, think about your conversations with others. Some conversations involve an active dialog between two or more individuals, while others are comprised of a simple statement and a response. For example, stating the question "Are you hungry?" requires only a simple response, "No." In this way, there are two distinct forms of conversation, dialogs and acknowledgments. In the IP protocol world, these two types of conversations are analogies to the connection-oriented TCP and the connection-less protocol UDP.

With UDP, packets transmitted are not guaranteed to be delivered, and do not maintain a connection after the first packet has been received. In this way, UDP is a simple protocol wrapper around IP in the sense of being "Best Effort," connection-less protocol.

However, where there is simplicity there is speed, and the primary strength of UDP is its speed. Each unit of data sent, known as a datagram, is in itself an entire self-contained message. In this way, the underlying network infrastructure does not have to waste overhead in setting up a facility for a continuing conversation, or guaranteeing datagram delivery. Rather, UDP datagrams can be streamed out of a producer application for the rapid consumption of a consumer application.

UDP lends itself very well to network communication applications such as streaming audio, video, and a slue of other non-critical applications. Later in section "IPC with Datagrams," you will learn how to use UDP to its full advantage when you create a chat application. For now, remember that UDP is a connection-less, Best Effort delivery protocol not intended to supply a facility for reliable communication dialogs.

TCP—Connection-Oriented

Transmission Control Protocol (TCP) provides a reliable, connection-based transport of information. For this reason, TCP is the predominate protocol of Internet technologies. However, TCP rides on top of IP, and IP is merely a "Best Effort" delivery protocol with no capability of facilitating a reliable communication dialog. Unlike UDP, that provides a thin wrapper around the IP transport facilities, TCP provides a stable, session-oriented mechanism for reliable communication.

TCP provides the following value-added features to the IP.

▶ Guaranteed Packet Delivery

▶ Proper Data Packet Presentation

▶ Session Support

The following sections explore each of these features in detail.

Guaranteed Packet Delivery

One of the features that TCP adds to IP (thus TCP/IP) is the capability to guarantee the delivery of packets. Keep in mind that the word "guarantee" is used very loosely. Provided that nothing has happened to the physical network media—Layer 1—TCP/IP will verify that the specified information packet is properly delivered to the receiving end.

Proper Data Packet Presentation

When a data packet is sent out via UDP and IP, the transit time for the packet is unknown. Consider the case where a single packet is transmitted from one machine to another. The time the packet takes to make its journey is a random function of network utilization and media clarity. Further, since each packet is sent independently, each packet has its own associated transit time. The fact that each packet's transit time is independent leads to a problem known as *packet sequencing*. A problem not handled by IP, but solved by TCP.

Computer A has 10 packets to send to computer B. Computer A sends out the packets in logical order from packet 0 to packet 9. However, since the transit time for each packet is independent, it is possible that computer B could receive packet 9 before it receives packet 0. In modern IP networks, this occurrence is highly unlikely, but nevertheless possible and needs to be addressed.

Since IP is only concerned with the transportation of a single packet, not a series of packets, no sequencing facilities are provided. The same holds for UDP, to the extent that datagrams may be received out of order. However, by definition TCP is not only concerned with the delivery of a single packet, but also with the delivery of a series of packets, which constitutes a data coherent communication.

To solve the data sequencing problem, TCP prepends a sequence number to the outgoing packet. In this way, each packet has its own identity and sequence position. This sequence number is then used by the receiving computer to properly re-sequence the received information into the original form.

Session Support

Datagrams are a one-time means of transmitting data, but not all communication is that simple. For example, a client application could send a request to a database as a single datagram. However, it is more often the case that data communication must maintain a contextual conversation of information.

In the traditional sense of client/server applications, the server maintains a contextual conversation with each attached client. That is, multiple clients can be doing a variety of different things. One client might be asking the server to fulfill a request, while another is in the process of retrieving information. In this context, each client application must be treated as a separate conversation, and with TCP that means a separate connection.

UDP clients listen for a single packet from any arbitrary source. There is no concept of an ongoing conversation within the UDP definition. However, TCP offers the ability to initiate a connection in such a way as to secure a private means of communication between the two computers. Each connection is a distinct, ongoing conversation that is not terminated until the connection is physically closed. This conversation, or session, support is a feature provided by TCP to provide the mechanism by which two computers can engage in an ongoing, private conversation.

IPC with Datagrams

Datagrams are a rudimentary form of communication. Datagrams are not reliable, and cannot easily provide a means for a statefull conversation. Nevertheless, UDP is a practical and speedy application for the use of nonpacket-critical applications. That is, UDP provides a rapid IPC transport for non-critical applications.

From a coding perspective, creating an application to utilize UDP IPC is very straightforward, but it wasn't always like that. If this is your first experience creating an IPC application, count your blessings. As all C/C++ programmers will attest to, Java makes IPC easy. However, before you set down the path to code you first IPC application, there are a few key concepts that you need to assimilate.

Port A port is a specific communication line unique to an application. Specifically, valid port numbers are between 0 and 65535. HTTP has a port number, as does FTP and Email (SMTP/POP3). In order for your IPC applications to communicate with one another, a common arbitrary port must be agreed upon.

Binding a Port Binding a Port is just like a phone. That is, if you don't pick it up, you can't talk to anyone. Similarly, binding a port refers to the process by which a specific IP address is made ready to communicate on a specific port, like picking up the phone and waiting to hear a voice. However, since a port is a specific communication line unique to an application, only one application can be bound at a time.

Listening on a Port   Once an application has bound the port, it can then listen for information to be received from other applications/computers. This is usually achieved by blocking the application flow to wait for incoming information. During the time the application is blocking a call to receive information, the application's state is said to be "Listing on a Port."

The following section provides Java-specific UDP ICP implementation knowledge, followed by a brief example. Keep in mind while reading this material that the Coding Assignment in the Certified Developer Exam may very well call on you to implement and justify an IPC application.

Java Datagram Support

Java provides clean facilities for the creation of datagram applications. Knowledge of such facilities, and how to use them, is required knowledge to become a Certified Java Developer.

Java is a truly object-oriented language, so it should be no surprise that Java's treatment of UDP datagrams comes in the form of an object library. Specifically, `java.net` contains objects for accessing both UDP and TCP facilities. However, this section focuses on the presentation of the UDP datagram objects found in `java.net`.

Within `java.net` there are three primary classes which provide the complete suite of UDP functionality. These classes are as follows.

- ▶ `java.net.DatagramPacket`

- ▶ `java.net.DatagramSocket`

- ▶ `java.net.MulticastSocket`

Each class offers its own distinct functionality, as well as its own distinct usage. The following sections discuss each of these facilities' internals, including usage and context information.

java.net.DatagramPacket

`java.net.DatagramPacket` provides a facility for the containment of incoming and outgoing. Depending on how the object is created depicts the incoming or outgoing behavior. The morphing of an input to output buffer is facilitated by two separate and distinct constructors.

The first constructor for `java.net.DatagramPacket` presented in the following only requires an initial buffer and size. Since this construct initializes `java.net.DatagramPacket` to be an input buffer, no destination or port information is required

```
public DatagramPacket(byte ibuf[],
                      int ilength)
```

Example:

```
DatagramPacket incoming = new DatagramPacket(new byte[100],100);
```

The second constructor for `java.net.DatagramPacket` presented in the following only requires an initial buffer and size.

```
public DatagramPacket(byte ibuf[],
                      int ilength,
                      InetAddress iaddr,
                      int iport)
```

Example:

```
PipeOut.send(new DatagramPacket(input,input.length,
             InetAddress.getByName("DestMachine"),MyPortNum));
```

Once the `java.net.DatagramPacket` instance has been created, the following methods provide access to encapsulated data.

▶ `public synchronized InetAddress getAddress()` Retrieves the IP address of sending or receiving machine, depending if the `java.net.DatagramPacket` is an incoming or outgoing device.

▶ `public synchronized int getPort()` Retrieves the local or remote port from which the `java.net.DatagramPacket` is sent or received.

▶ `public synchronized byte[] getData()`   Returns the data held within the `java.net.DatagramPacket` instance. If the `java.net.DatagramPacket` instance was used for receiving a datagram, the data returned will be the received datagram data.

▶ `public synchronized int getLength()`   Returns the length of the data to be sent or the length of the data received.

▶ `public synchronized void setAddress(InetAddress iaddr)`   Sets the destination IP address of the encapsulated datagram.

▶ `public synchronized void setPort(int iport)`   Sets the destination port number of the outgoing datagram.

▶ `public synchronized void setData(byte ibuf[])`   Sets the data buffer used to hold outgoing and incoming datagram data.

▶ `public synchronized void setLength(int ilength)`   Sets the maximum incoming and outgoing data size. This value must be between 1 and the size of the provided data buffer.

Later sections in this chapter, "Example Chat Facility Using `java.net.DatagramSocket`" and "Example Chat Facility Using `java.net.MulticastSocket`," demonstrate the usage of `java.net.DatagramPacket` method and constructors.

java.net.DatagramSocket

`java.net.DatagramPacket` class provides an encapsulation of all required datagram information, like the destination and the message. However, the `java.net.DatagramPacket` class does not provide the actual transport mechanism. The `java.net.DatagramSocket` class provides direct access to the UDP network facilities for the transport of `java.net.DatagramPackets`.

As discussed in the "IPC with Datagrams" section, the general order of operation for constructing a network communication device is to bind a port to an IP address, and then listen on the port. What wasn't discussed was how to select the IP address and port to facilitate the communication. The `java.net.DatagramSocket` class provides a series of constructors to provide a direct mechanism for the selection of both the IP address and port to which the communication resource is to be associated.

The first constructor for the java.net.DatagramSocket class provides absolutely no control of the port or IP address used to create the UDP resource. As shown in the following example, this constructor does not utilize any parameters to specific port or IP address. Instead, any available port is used to create the UDP resource on the machine's default IP address. The following provides the constructor declaration and sample usage.

```
public DatagramSocket() throws SocketException
```

Example:

```
try{
    DatagramSocket myPipe = new DatagramSocket();
}
catch(SocketException e){
    System.out.println("Could not bind a local port - " + e);
}
```

For most applications, a common port must be agreed upon by both the client and server applications. For example, HTTP servers and browsers have agreed on port number 80 for data transfer (HTTP uses TCP/IP.) For this reason, a second constructor is provided by java.net.DatagramSocket allowing a port to be specified. The following provides the constructor declaration and sample usage of constructing a java.net.DatagramSocket with a specified port.

```
public DatagramSocket(int port) throws SocketException
```

Example:

```
try{
    //bind port 6789 to the default IP address
    DatagramSocket myPipe = new DatagramSocket(6789);
}
catch(SocketException e){
    System.out.println("Could not bind a local port - " + e);
}
```

The final constructor provided by java.net.DatagramSocket provides the ability to select both the port and IP address used to create the UDP communication network. However, unless you are creating an application to run on a server that terminates multiple IP address-es, this constructor is overkill. That is, most machines only respond to a single address. In such case, the IP address is a constant for all running applications. However, some server applications provide the ability to handle multiple IP addresses. In that case, the follow-ing constructor should be used.

```
public DatagramSocket(int port, InetAddress laddr) throws
SocketException
```

Example:

```
try{
   //bind port 6789 to the default IP address
   DatagramSocket myPipe = new DatagramSocket(6789,
      InetAddress.getLocalHost());
}
catch(SocketException e){
   System.out.println("Could not bind a local port - " + e);
}
```

Once the `java.net.DatagramSocket` instance has been created, the following methods provide access to the newly created UDP com-munication resource.

▶ `public void send(DatagramPacket p) throws IOException`   Transmits the specified `DatagramPacket` on the defined port and IP address. An `IOException` is thrown if a transmission error is encountered.

▶ `public synchronized void receive(DatagramPacket p) throws IOException`   Receives an incoming `DatagramPacket` on the defined port and IP address. Once the `receive` call is invoked, it will block until an incoming datagram is received, the speci-fied time-out interval elapsed, of an `IOException` is thrown signifying an error. In this case, the incoming message is larg-er than the size specified within the `DatagramPacket`, the data-gram will be truncated to fit into the specified storage area.

▶ `public InetAddress getLocalAddress()`   Specifies the local address to which the `DatagramSocket` is bound.

▶ `public int getLocalPort()` Specifies the local port to which the `DatagramSocket` listens.

▶ `public synchronized void setSoTimeout(int timeout) throws SocketException` Sets the time-out period used to interrupt a blocking call to receive. A specified non-zero time-out period will call all subsequent `receive` calls to block for the specified amount of time in milliseconds. A value of `0` will cause the receive call to block indefinitely. By default, the time-out period is set to `0`.

▶ `public synchronized int getSoTimeout() throws SocketException` Returns the currently specified time-out interval.

▶ `public void close()` Closes the datagram socket resource.

The section "Example Chat Facility Using `java.net.Datagram Socket`," later in this chapter, demonstrates the usage of `java.net.DatagramSocket` method and constructors.

java.net.MulticastSocket

The stateless, unreliable nature of the UDP protocol has been discussed throughout the course of this chapter. However, a very powerful feature of a UDP `multicast` facility has not yet been explored. A typical client/server application assumes one client for every server, but, with UDP `multicast`, a single server may fulfill multiple clients.

In the previously discussed `java.net.DatagramSocket` class, the assumption is made that a datagram originates from a single IP address, that also holds `java.net.MulticastSocket`. The difference between the two types of UDP facilities surfaces is in the destination of outgoing packets. As displayed in Figure 10.11, the `java.net.DatagramSocket` class assumes that outgoing datagrams are destined for a specific IP address, where `java.net.MulticastSocket` assumes a group of IP addresses.

Figure 10.11

Single IP destination versus Multicast group.

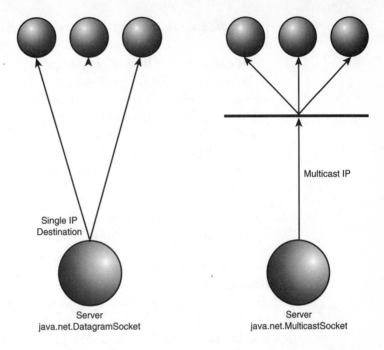

Multicast IP

Single IP
Destination

Server
java.net.DatagramSocket

Server
java.net.MulticastSocket

The following is a list of constructors and methods for the java.net.MulticastSocket class. The similarities between the java.net.MulticastSocket and java.net.DatagramSocket class are evident, except for the notion of a locally bound IP address. In fact java.net.MulticastSocket is a subclass of java.net.Datagram Socket, relies on java.net.DatagramSocket to provide the base communication facilities, and provides only a handful of specialized methods.

▶ public MulticastSocket() throws IOException   Creates a multicast socket on any available local port.

▶ public MulticastSocket(int port) throws IOException   Creates a multicast socket on the specified port.

▶ public InetAddress setInterface() throws SocketException Specifies the IP address to use for the current MulticastSocket instance.

▶ public InetAddress getInterface() throws SocketException Returns the IP address of the current MulticastSocket instance.

▶ `public void setTTL(byte ttl) throws IOException` Multicast datagrams are sent out onto a shared communication channel for all to hear. However, in a large or disbursed network of listeners, it might take the datagram a considerable amount of time to reach all listeners. For this reason, each multicast datagram has the ability to die after a specified number of network hops. Specifically, this specified number of network hops is called a TTL (Time To Live) value. `setTTL` specifies the TTL value for all outgoing multicast datagrams. The value must be between 0 and 255.

▶ `public byte getTTL() throws IOException` Returns the TTL value for all outgoing multicast datagams.

▶ `public void joinGroup(InetAddress mcastaddr) throws IOException` Joins the specified multicast group. A multicast group is specified by a class D IP address. Specifically IP, any IP address in the range from `224.0.0.1` to `239.255.255.255` may be used to specify a multicast group. Also, it is legal to join more than one group at a time.

▶ `public void leaveGroup(InetAddress mcastaddr) throws IOException` Unregisters from the specified multicast group.

▶ `public synchronized void send(DatagramPacket p, byte ttl) throws IOException` Transmits the datagram to all specified multicast groups with the specified TTL value. It is not required to join a destination group before transiting to the group.

The section "Example Chat Facility Using `java.net.MulticastSocket`," later in this chapter, demonstrates the usage of `java.net.MulticastSocket` method and constructors.

Example Chat Facility Using java.net.DatagramSocket

In an effort to begin tying all of the concepts surrounding IPC together, the following presents an example chat application using standard UDP datagrams. Figure 10.12 shows a general flow diagram describing the general application flow.

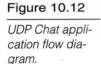

Figure 10.12

UDP Chat application flow diagram.

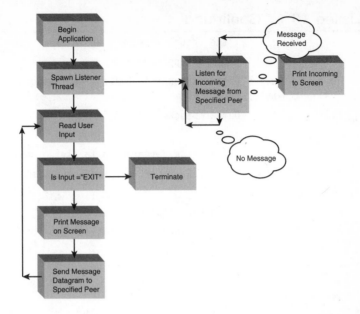

As Figure 10.12 demonstrates, there are two distinct application flows: one for the main user loop and the other listens to the socket. Listing 10.1 provides a brief example of how IPC with UDP datagrams can be facilitated. You can also find this application on the accompanying CD-ROM in the code/chapter10/UDP directory.

Listing 10.1   How IPC with UDP datagrams can be facilitated.

```java
import java.net.DatagramSocket;
import java.net.DatagramPacket;
import java.net.InetAddress;

//Create a listener thread.
class ListenForAPacket extends Thread{

    //Port to listen to
    public int ListenToPort = 0;

    //Sit in a loop waiting for a datagram
    public void run(){
        //The actual size of the incoming data will modify
```

continues

Listing 10.1 Continued

```java
                        //the actual size, but an initial value still needs
                        //to be supplied.
                        DatagramPacket incoming = new DatagramPacket(new
➥byte[100],100);
                        DatagramSocket PipeIn;
                        try{
                            //Set a datagram up to listen on the specifed port;
                            PipeIn = new DatagramSocket(ListenToPort);
                        }
                        catch(Exception e){
                                System.out.println("Error binding port - " + e);
                                return;
                        }


                        for(;;){
                                //This call will wait until a datagram has been
➥received
                                try{
                                    PipeIn.receive(incoming);
                                }
                                catch(Exception e){
                                    System.out.println("Error recieving datagram - "
➥+ e);
                                }

                                //Convert the message to a string and print it out.
                                System.out.println(incoming.getAddress() + "::" +
                                    new String(incoming.getData()).trim());
                        }
                    }
                }

        public class ChatClient {

            public static void main(String args[]) {

                //Check how many parameters have been passed
```

```
        if(args.length < 2){
            System.out.println("Usage : ChatClient Partner
➥Port#");
            return;
        }

        //kick off the listening thread
        ListenForAPacket Listener = new ListenForAPacket();

        //Load the port number
        try{
            Listener.ListenToPort = (new Integer(args[1]))
➥.intValue();
        }
        catch(Exception e){
            System.out.println("Invalid Port Number - " + e);
            return;
        }
        Listener.start();

        //create the Datagram resource
        DatagramSocket PipeOut;
        try{
            //Set a datagram up to listen on the specifed port;
            PipeOut = new DatagramSocket();
        }
        catch(Exception e){
                System.out.println("Error creating datagram
➥object - "+
                    e);
                return;
        }

        //Loop until "exit is entered"
        //Limit 80 chars per line
        byte[] input = new byte[80];
```

continues

Listing 10.1　Continued

```
                      System.out.println("(Type \"Exit\" exit)");
                      for(;;)
                          try{
                              //clear the input byte[]
                              for(int i = 0;i < input.length;++i)
                                  input[i] = 0;

                              System.in.read(input);
                              String tmp = new String(input);
                              tmp = tmp.trim();
                              if(tmp.equalsIgnoreCase("exit"))
                                  return;
                              //Send the Packet
                              PipeOut.send(new DatagramPacket(input,input
➥.length,
                                  InetAddress.getByName(args[0]),
                                  Listener.ListenToPort));
                          }
                          catch (Exception e) {
                          return;
                          }
                      }
                  }
```

Figure 10.13 displays a sample chat session using the described UDP chat facility in Listing 10.1.

Figure 10.13

UDP Chat application output.

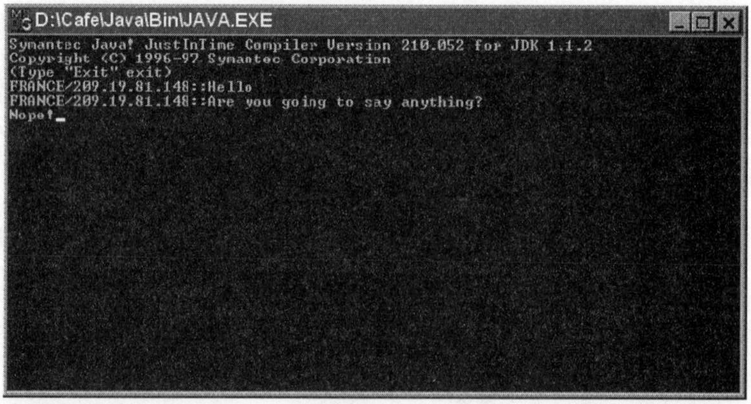

Example Chat Facility Using java.net.MulticastSocket

The previous example used standard UDP datagrams to create a chat application. However, standard UDP datagrams have a defined source and destination, which leads to a limitation in the chat application. Since the destination must be specified in the chat application, only two parties can chat at once. For this reason, the following presents an example chat application using standard UDP multicast datagrams. Figure 10.14 shows a general flow diagram describing the general application flow.

Figure 10.14

UDP Multicast Chat application flow diagram.

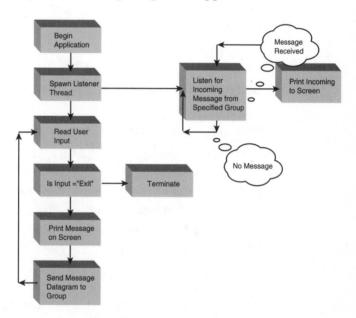

As Figure 10.14 shows, there are two distinct application flows: one for the main user loop and the other listens to the socket. In fact, this is identical to the flow of the previous UDP chat application, and, in reality, the code is very similar. The main difference is the use of an IP group instead of a destination IP address. Listing 10.2 provides a brief example of how IPC with UDP multicast datagrams can be facilitated. You can also find this application on the accompanying CD-ROM in the code/chapter10/multicast directory.

Listing 10.2 How IPC with UDP multicast datagrams can be facilitated.

```java
import java.net.DatagramSocket;
import java.net.MulticastSocket;
import java.net.DatagramPacket;
import java.net.InetAddress;

//Create a listiner thread.
class ListenForAPacket extends Thread{

    //Port to listen to
    public int ListenToPort = 0;

    //Line in
    public MulticastSocket PipeIn;

    //Sit in a loop waiting for a datagram
    public void run(){
        //The actual size of the incoming data will modify
        //the actual size, but an initial value still needs
        //to be supplied.
        DatagramPacket incoming = new DatagramPacket(new
➥byte[100],100);

        for(;;){
            //This call will wait until a datagram has been
➥received
            try{
                PipeIn.receive(incoming);
            }
            catch(Exception e){
                System.out.println("Error receiving datagram - "
➥+ e);
            }

            //Convert the message to a string and print it out.
```

```
                    System.out.println(incoming.getAddress() + "::" +
                        new String(incoming.getData()).trim());
            }
        }
    }

public class ChatClient {

    public static void main(String args[]) {

        //Check how many parameters have been passed
        if(args.length < 2){
            System.out.println("Usage : ChatClient Group Port#");
            return;
        }

        //kick off the listening thread
        ListenForAPacket Listener = new ListenForAPacket();

        //Load the port number
        try{
            Listener.ListenToPort = (new
➥Integer(args[1])).intValue();
        }
        catch(Exception e){
            System.out.println("Invalid Port Number - " + e);
            return;
        }

        //create the Datagram resource
        MulticastSocket PipeOut;
        InetAddress group;

        try{
            //Set a datagram up to listen on the specifed port;
```

continues

Listing 10.2   Continued

```
                        PipeOut = new MulticastSocket(Listener.ListenToPort);
                        //Get group IP
                        group = InetAddress.getByName(args[0]);
                        //Join the machine's group
                         PipeOut.joinGroup(group);
                                }
                catch(Exception e){
                        System.out.println("Error creating datagram
➡object - " + e);
                        return;
                }
                Listener.PipeIn = PipeOut;
                Listener.start();

                //Loop until "exit is entered"
                //Limit 80 chars per line
                byte[] input = new byte[80];
                System.out.println("(Type \"Exit\" exit)");
                for(;;)
                    try{
                        //clear the input byte[]
                        for(int i = 0;i < input.length;++i)
                            input[i] = 0;

                        System.in.read(input);
                        String tmp = new String(input);
                        tmp = tmp.trim();

                        if(tmp.equalsIgnoreCase("exit")){
                            PipeOut.leaveGroup(group);
                            break;
                        }

                        //Send the Packet
                        PipeOut.send(new
```

```
➥DatagramPacket(input,input.length,
                      group,Listener.ListenToPort));
            }
        catch (Exception e) {
            System.out.println("Error in main loop - " + e);
            return;
        }
    System.out.println("exiting");

    }

}
```

Figure 10.15 displays a sample chat session using the described UDP multicast chat facility in Listing 10.2.

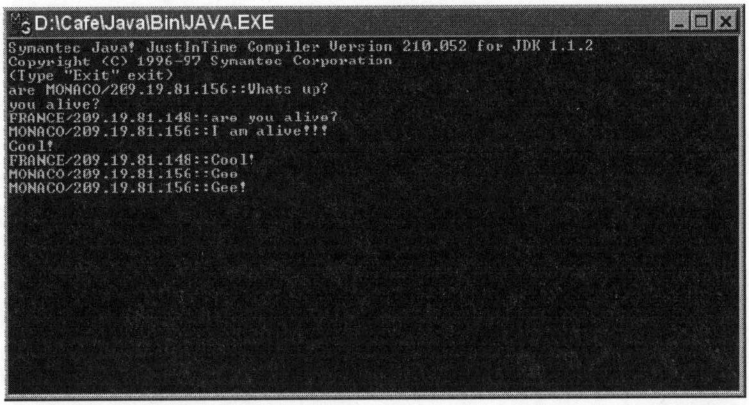

Figure 10.15

UDP Multicast Chat application output.

TCP/IP Socket-Based IPC

UDP datagrams are designed to facilitate a write-once-read-once communication. However, not all communications are that simple. For instance, a home banking application might require a client to enter a PIN to access some sort of financial history, and then provide a list of actions, like a transfer of funds.

Consider the case that UDP is used to facilitate such a conversation, as shown in Figure 10.16. A login datagram would be sent with the PIN, in response the financial history would be sent. Then, if a transfer of funds action is requested, the PIN would have to be re-submitted along with a request for a funds transfer. If all is transmitted correctly, the transaction is complete. In this way, UDP server applications do not have a concept of a client session. Rather, UDP servers live from one incoming datagram to the next. TCP/IP sockets provide a reliable, connection-oriented data transportation device.

Figure 10.16

UDP Home banking application.

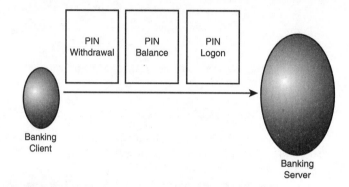

Figure 10.16 shows the general datagram communication style. The PIN is included with each request in an attempt to imply a banking session based on the PIN supplied. With TCP sockets, a unique session is established for each client connection, allowing the server to maintain a contextual conversation with a specific client, as shown in Figure 10.17.

Figure 10.17

TCP Home banking application.

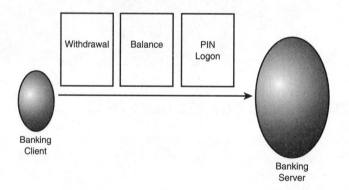

Figure 10.17 displays the inherit client and server roles of TCP/IP sockets. This is important to keep in mind because UDP datagrams do not have a notion of a client and a server. Rather, UDP datagrams are peers communicating on a shared media. In the section to follow, the client and server roles found in TCP/IP socket will be contextually explored and compared with Java's TCP/IP socket support.

Java TCP/IP Socket Support

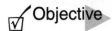 Objective

Java provides amazing facilities for the creation of TCP/IP client/ server applications. Knowledge of such facilities, and how to use them, is required knowledge to become a Certified Java Developer.

Java's TCP/IP socket support is provided by a set of two classes, `java.net.Socket` and `java.net.ServerSocket`. The difference between the two classes lies in the role of a client and server application. Client applications open a communication channel with a server of choice. Server applications maintain communication channels with multiple clients at once. `java.net.ServerSocket` facilitates a server application by spawning socket connections for each contextual client session.

A socket is a private communication channel between a client and server. However, one of the applications needs to initiate the socket connection. The responsibility of establishing the socket falls on the client, and the responsibility of accepting and waiting for the client request falls on the server applications. With that in mind the following sections present Java class facilities for creating and accepting TCP/IP socket communication devices.

java.net.Socket

`java.net.Socket` is the sole encapsulating device for all TCP/IP socket communication functionality. In being so, `java.net.Socket` has two distinct roles as a client- and server-connection facility. The following section focuses on the general use of the Socket class and discusses how the Socket object is used in a server application.

The following list of constructors presents the flexibility of `java.net.Socket`. Most of these are geared toward the creation of client-side application sockets. The following section, "`java.net.ServerSocket`," will explore the server side of the TCP/IP socket programming.

▶ public Socket(String host, int port) throws UnknownHostException, IOException   Creates a TCP/IP stream socket to the specified host (either IP address or host name) server listening on the provided port number. If the specified host cannot be found, an UnknownHostException is thrown. Likewise, if a socket construction error occurs, an IOexception is thrown.

▶ public Socket(InetAddress address, int port) throws IOException   Creates a TCP/IP stream socket to the server specified by the IP address and listening on the provided port number. If a socket construction error occurs, an IOexception is thrown. Note: the InetAddress class insures the validity of the specified host.

▶ public Socket(String host, int port, InetAddress localAddr, int localPort) throws IOException   Given the remote server's host name and port, the constructor creates a stream socket bound to the specified local port. By default, the system uses any available local port.

▶ public Socket(InetAddress address, int port, InetAddress localAddr, int localPort) throws IOException   Given the remote server's host name and port, the constructor creates a stream socket bound to the specified local port. By default, the system uses any available local port and machine's default IP address.

As you can see, there are many variations of TCP/IP stream sockets. However, the constructors fall in the 80/20 rule. That is, 80% of the time only 20% of the supplied variations are used. As demonstrated in the section "Example Distributed Prime Number Calculator Using TCP/IP Sockets," later in this chapter, only one of the provided constructors is used. The following is a complete list of all member methods supplied by java.net.Socket, of which only three are actually used in the example application.

▶ public InetAddress getInetAddress()   Returns the remote IP address to which the socket is connected.

▶ public InetAddress getLocalAddress()   Returns the IP address to which the socket is bound.

▶ `public int getPort()` Retrieves the remote port to which the socket is connected.

▶ `public int getLocalPort()` Retrieves the local port through which the socket is communicating.

▶ `public InputStream getInputStream() throws IOException`
Returns an input stream of data coming from the socket connections. An `IOException` is thrown if an input stream cannot be obtained.

▶ `public OutputStream getOutputStream() throws IOException`
Returns an output stream by which data can be transmitted across the open socket connections. An `IOException` is thrown if an output stream cannot be obtained.

▶ `public void setTcpNoDelay(boolean on) throws SocketException`
Specifies if all packets should be sent immediately. If `false`, all "tinygrams" are sent regardless of size. If `true`, "tinygrams" are held until the next client ACK following the Nagle algorithm. In this way, "tinygrams" packets that hold small amounts of data are packaged together in order to better optimize network performance. `SocketException` is thrown on error.

▶ `public boolean getTcpNoDelay() throws SocketException`
Returns `true` if Nagel algorithm is being used to optimize packet packaging, `false` if it is not. `SocketException` is thrown on error.

▶ `public void setSoLinger(boolean on, int val) throws SocketException` Enables/disables `SO_LINGER` with the specified linger time.

▶ `public int getSoLinger() throws SocketException` Returns setting for `SO_LINGER`. `-1` return implies that the option is disabled.

▶ `public int getSoLinger() throws SocketException` Returns the amount of time a read call will block before returning an error. A value of `-1` returns setting for `SO_LINGER`. `-1` returns implies that the option is disabled.

▶ `public synchronized void setSoTimeout(int timeout) throws SocketException` Determines the amount of time the socket will block waiting for data from the server. The specified time is in milliseconds. A value of -1 is interpreted as an infinite block interval. `SocketException` is thrown on error.

▶ `public synchronized int getSoTimeout() throws SocketException` Returns the amount of time a read call will block before returning. A value of -1 denotes an infinite block interval.

▶ `public synchronized void close() throws IOException` Closes the current thread.

▶ `public String toString()` Provides a string representation of the `Socket`-related data.

Only three methods are used for a large portion of development with `java.net.Socket`: `getInputStream()`, `getOutputStream()`, and `close()`. As you will see in "Example Distributed Prime Number Calculator Using TCP/IP Sockets," later in this chapter, these three methods allow you to treat the socket as if it were a local file. Input is obtained with primitive read methods, and output is transmitted with write methods. No magic, just a series of overhead calls which construct and previsions the communication channel for your use.

java.net.ServerSocket

Unlike UDP datagram, TCP/IP stream sockets have a notion of a server application. That is, with datagram the applications involved in the IPC communication are acting as peers. Datagrams are sent back and forth between applications, with no application taking a defined dominate role. However, TCP/IP stream sockets have distinct client/server application roles.

The previous section, "`java.net.Socket`," discussed the general use of the `Socket` object. Upon close examination of the constructors, the client socket nature of the object surfaces. That is, the Socket constructor provides the means to connect to a host. However, the `java.net.ServerSocket` provides means to create server application.

The following presents a complete list of constructors provided by the `java.net.ServerSocket` object. Each constructor provides a variable degree of flexibility in the creation of a server socket.

▶ `public ServerSocket(int port) throws IOException` Creates a TCP/IP stream server socket listing on the specified port. A port number of 0 denotes that any available port should be used. Note: In the case of a server with multiple IP addresses, the machine's default IP address will be used.

▶ `public ServerSocket(int port, int backlog) throws IOException` Creates a TCP/IP stream server socket listing on the specified port. A port number of 0 denotes that any available port should be used. The `backlog` parameter specifies how new client socket connections would be queued before they are refused. Note: In the case of a server with multiple IP addresses, the machine's default IP address will be used.

▶ `public ServerSocket(int port, int backlog, InetAddress bindAddr) throws IOException` Creates a TCP/IP stream server socket bound to the specified IP address listing on the specified port. A port number of 0 denotes that any available port should be used. The `backlog` parameter specifies how new client socket connections would be queued before they are refused.

Once the server socket has been created, the chief role of a server application is to accept and fulfill new client requests. To accomplish this feat, the `ServerSocket` object provides a single call named `accept()`. In the next section, "Example Distributed Prime Number Calculator Using TCP/IP Sockets," the `accept()` call will be used to accept incoming client requests. For now, the following provides a list of all member methods of the `ServerSocket` object, including the `accept()` call.

▶ `public InetAddress getInetAddress()` Returns the local address to which the server socket is bound.

▶ `public int getLocalPort()` Returns the port on which this socket is listening.

▶ `public Socket accept() throws IOException` Returns a `Socket` object connected to an incoming client request. The `accept()` call will block until a client request is available, or until a specified time-out has elapsed.

▶ `protected final void implAccept(Socket s) throws IOException` Provides the means to override the default accept characteristic to return a custom socket type.

▶ `public void close() throws IOException` Closes the server socket.

▶ `public synchronized void setSoTimeout(int timeout) throws SocketException` Specifies the maximum amount of time in milliseconds that an accept call will block. A time-out value of `0` is interpreted as an infinite time-out period.

▶ `public synchronized int getSoTimeout() throws IOException` Returns the time-out period for accept calls. A time-out value of `0` represents an infinite time-out period.

▶ `public String toString()` Returns a string representation of the pertinent server socket information, such as host address and port.

Example Distributed Prime Number Calculator Using TCP/IP Sockets

TCP/IP sockets are generally used to facilitate distributed computing solutions. Applications like Web servers and clients take advantage of the distributed computing model to present Web content. However, there are thousands of other distributed applications with various uses and roles. Several applications benefit from the distributed framework of TCP/IP sockets. In an effort to present an example that takes advantage of distributed computing, this section provides a distributed prime number calculator.

As seen through Java's support of TCP/IP sockets, both a client and a server application are required to facilitate an entire solution. The following sections present the prime number server and processing client using the `java.net.ServerSocket` and `java.net.Sockets` classes.

The Server

The primary role of any TCP/IP socket server application is to accept new client connections and fulfill the requests. However, there are two distinct development tasks which can be taken in creating such an application. The first is called a blocking server, or a server that can only process a single request at a time. The second, and more common of the two, is called a concurrent server, or a server that can fulfill multiple requests simultaneously. The difference between the two is how the `accept()` call is handled.

A call to `java.net.ServerSocket.accept()` blocks until it can return a new client connection. Once the connection is returned, it is up to the application to fulfill the client request. In a blocking server model, the new client request is fulfilled before a new connection is accepted. The downfall is that if a new client tries connecting to a server that is not currently waiting in an `accept()` call, the client connection will be refused. Server applications following the concurrent server model get around the problem of clients being refused by handing off the client request to another process/thread for execution. In this way, the server simply accepts the new client connection and hands it off to a thread for processing.

Listing 10.3 is an example TCP/IP socket server application that follows the concurrent model. As shown in Figure 10.18, the main application merely accepts the new client connection and then hands the session over to a fulfillment thread. In this way, the server application can accept all incoming client requests, as well as partition the application into more refined logical units of functionality.

Figure 10.18

*Prime Server
application flow.*

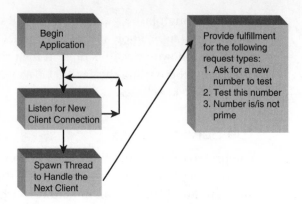

Listing 10.3 Concurrent model TCP/IP socket server application.

```
import java.util.Vector;

import java.math.BigInteger;

import java.io.*;

import java.net.ServerSocket;

import java.net.Socket;



//Static, synchronized storage device
class primeStorage {

    //Holds the primes which have been found;
    private static Vector PrimesFound= new Vector();

    //Holds the next number to test
    private static BigInteger NextToTest = new BigInteger("1");

    //Lagest number to test in bits
    public static int LargestNumberInBits = 40;

    //The Certainity factor that the number is a prime.
    public static int Certainty = 1;

    //Get the next number to test
    public synchronized static BigInteger getNextToTest(){
```

```
        if(LargestNumberInBits <= NextToTest.bitLength())
            return null;


        NextToTest = NextToTest.add(new BigInteger("1"));


        //return a copy of the NextToTest variable
        return NextToTest.add(new BigInteger("0"));
    }


    public synchronized static void foundPrime(BigInteger prime){
        PrimesFound.addElement(prime);
        System.out.println("Found a new Prime -" + prime);
    }


}

//Thread to maintain context with client
class clientCruncher extends Thread{

    //Message REQ IDs
    public static int GETCERT = 5;
    public static int NEWNUM = 10;
    public static int PRIMEFOUND = 20;

    //Message Response IDs
    public static int ACK = 10;
    public static int DIE = 20;



    private Socket ClientSocket;

    public clientCruncher(Socket client){
        ClientSocket = client;
    }

    public void run(){
```

continues

Listing 10.3 Continued

```
                        DataInputStream Din;
                        DataOutputStream Dout;

                try{
                        //Get the IN/OUT stream from the socket
                        Din = new DataInputStream(ClientSocket.getInput
        ➡Stream());
                        Dout = new DataOutputStream(ClientSocket.getOutput
        ➡Stream());

                }
                catch(Exception e){
                        System.out.println("Socket Stream Error - " + e);
                        return;
                }

                int packetType = 0;
                for(;;){
                        try{
                                //Get the request type.
                                packetType = Din.readInt();

                                //Client asked for the Certainity factor
                                if(packetType == GETCERT){
                                        Dout.writeInt(primeStorage.Certainty);
                                }
                                else
                                if(packetType == NEWNUM){
                                        BigInteger tmp = primeStorage.getNextTo
                ➡Test();

                                        //No more numbers to process
                                        if(tmp == null){
                                                Dout.writeInt(DIE);
                                                ClientSocket.close(); //Kill the socket
                                                return;
```

```
            }

            //Send Ack
            Dout.writeInt(ACK);

            //Send the size
            Dout.writeInt(tmp.toByteArray().length);

            //Send the next number to test;
            Dout.write(tmp.toByteArray());
        }
        else
        if(packetType == PRIMEFOUND){
            //Get length int
            int size = Din.readInt();
            //Declare storage
            byte tmpstore[] = new byte[size];
            //Get the data - block until all data is
➥ready
            Din.readFully(tmpstore);

            //Post the new prime
            primeStorage.foundPrime(new
➥BigInteger(tmpstore));

            //Send an Ack
            Dout.writeInt(ACK);
        }
        else
            System.out.println("Unknown Request Type ");
    }
    catch(Exception e){
        System.out.println("Socket IO Exception - " +e);
        break;
    }
}
```

continues

Listing 10.3   Continued

```
            }
        }


    public class PrimeServer {


        public static void main(String args[]) {

            ServerSocket ServSocket; //Main Server Socket

            Vector clients = new Vector(); //Vector of active clients

            try{
                //Create the server socket to listen on port 6789
                ServSocket = new ServerSocket(6789);
            }
            catch(Exception e){
                System.out.println("Server Bind Error - " + e);
                return;
            }

            //Set the largest number to test in bits
            primeStorage.LargestNumberInBits = 40;

            //Set the certainity factor that the number is a prime.
            primeStorage.Certainty = 10;


            //loop forever
            for(;;){
                try{

                    //block until a a client logs on.
                    clientCruncher tmp = new clientCruncher(Serv
➥Socket.accept());
```

```
            //Execute the thread to take care of the client
            tmp.start();
            clients.addElement(tmp);
        }
        catch(Exception e){
            System.out.println("Accept Error - " + e);
            break;
        }
    }
  }
}
```

As you can see from Listing 10.3, the application is broken down into three separate classes. The first, PrimeServer, is the main application entry point. From there, the second class is launched—clientCruncher. The clientCruncher class contains all application logic for dealing with a specific client session. In this way, the main application body, PrimeServer, creates a new instance and then hands the session off to the clientCruncher class for service. The third piece acts as merely a data storage unit for the executing client session treads.

The code for this TCP/IP server is straightforward. However, take a close look at the sections of code where the server is communicating directly with the client. This communication is an example of a small client/server protocol. As the number of fulfillment services a server provides grows, so does the complexity of the protocol. Later, the section on Java RMI, "RMI—the Next Generation of IPC," will explore how to eliminate client/server protocol heartache when communicating between JVMs.

The Client

Client applications without a GUI tend to be less complicated than server applications. The argument can be made that three-quarters of the battle of being a commercial software engineer is tied up in the GUI. For this reason, Listing 10.4 presents a GUI-less distributed prime number processing engine which connects to the server of the previous section.

Listing 10.4   Distributed prime calculator client.

```java
import java.math.BigInteger;
import java.io.*;
import java.net.Socket;

public class PrimeClient {

    //Message REQ IDs
    public static int GETCERT = 5;
    public static int NEWNUM = 10;
    public static int PRIMEFOUND = 20;

    //Message Response IDs
    public static int ACK = 10;
    public static int DIE = 20;

    public static void main(String args[]) {

        //Main Server Socket
        Socket ToServerSocket;
        //IO Streams
        DataInputStream Din;
        DataOutputStream Dout;

        //tmpVars
        int response = 0;
        BigInteger testMe;

        //Server Prime Certainty number
        int certfactor = 3;

        //Check to see if the host way provided
        if(args.length < 1){
            System.out.println("Server host must be provided");
            return;
        }
```

```
            //Create a socket to the specified host 6789
            try{
                ToServerSocket = new Socket(args[0],6789);
                Din  = new DataInputStream(ToServerSocket.get
➥InputStream());
                Dout = new DataOutputStream(ToServerSocket.getOutput
➥Stream());

                //Get the Certainty Number
                Dout.writeInt(GETCERT);      // Ask for the Certainty
➥factor
                certfactor = Din.readInt();  // Get IT.
                System.out.println("Certainty = " + certfactor);
            }
            catch(Exception e){
                System.out.println("Socket Creation Error - " + e);
                return;
            }

            //loop forever
            for(;;){
                try{
                    //Ask for a new number to test
                    Dout.writeInt(NEWNUM);

                    //get Response
                    response = Din.readInt();

                    //Check for no more numbers
                    if(response == DIE)
                        break;

                    response = Din.readInt();    //Get the byte size
                    byte tmp[] = new byte[response]; //Declare storage
                    Din.readFully(tmp);          //Get all bytes
                    testMe = new BigInteger(tmp);//Create the new
```

continues

Listing 10.4   Continued

```
➥value to test

                System.out.println("Working on " + testMe);

                //Check for a prime
                if(testMe.isProbablePrime(certfactor)){
                    //Prime found
                    Dout.writeInt(PRIMEFOUND);
                    Dout.writeInt(testMe.toByteArray().length); /
➥/Size
                    Dout.write(testMe.toByteArray()); //Data
                    Din.readInt();//Get Ack
                }
            }
            catch(Exception e){
                System.out.println("Main Loop Error - " + e);
                break;
            }
        }

        System.out.println("All Done");
        //Die Nicley
        try{
            ToServerSocket.close();
        }
        catch(Exception e){
            //Dying Anyway!
        }
    }
}
```

Within Listing 10.4, notice how much time is spent transmitting and receiving information from the socket connection. Data must be sent, as well as the size and a token to identify what the data is for, all of which, combined with synchronizing this communication on the server side, makes for some pretty tedious programming.

The next section explores how to eliminate client/server protocol heartache when communicating between JVMs.

RMI—the Next Generation of IPC

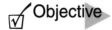 **Objective** RMI is the simplest and most powerful Java-to-Java IPC solution available. Knowledge of how to effectively use RMI can not only save you time, but is also required knowledge to become a Certified Java Developer.

Java's Remote Method Invocation (RMI) facility has been around since pre-JDK 1.02. However, RMI did not fully grow into its shoes until JDK 1.1, due to object serialization support. Today, RMI is a functional, stable, immensely useful, and really fun tool of the Java technology suite.

This chapter has thus far presented IPC in the context of using network devices such as datagrams and stream sockets. UDP datagrams and stream sockets still have their place in RMI; however, it is hidden. RMI uses TCP/IP sockets to communicate between JVM's, but, from a developer standpoint, that fact is not evident. The following sections explore how RMI functions, and how it can be used to facilitate Java-to-Java communications.

Register, Call, Notify

The way Java RMI works is simple. A registry on each JVM keeps a repository of all objects registered as servers. When a client Java application wishes to invoke a server object on a remote JVM, it simply asks the remote JVM for a reference to the server object and then uses that reference as if it were to a local object. This procedure for creating server objects, and then invoking them can be simplified to three words, registering, calling, and notifying.

As seen in Figure 10.19, each JVM holds a registry of server objects, each of which is connected to a transport at a level invisible to the developer. In this way, methods can be invoked, and values are returned, just as if the call occurred on the local JVM. The trick in making it all work is to know how to register an object and retrieve a remote reference. For this reason, the following sections spend some time discussing each step of provisioning an RMI resource.

Figure 10.19

RMI Framework.

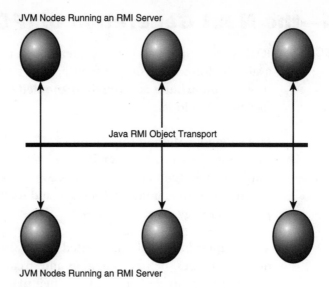

JVM Nodes Running an RMI Server

Java RMI Object Transport

JVM Nodes Running an RMI Server

Registering an Object

Registering an object with the RMI registry consists of a single call to the RMI engine. But if it were just that easy, this chapter would be shorter. In reality, registering a server object is as simple as a single call. However, before the registration call can be made, the following overhead tasks must be accomplished.

▶ Make sure the registry process is running.

▶ Create an interface for the server object.

▶ Implement the defined interface.

▶ Create RMI server stub classes.

▶ Register the server object.

The first overhead task is to make sure the RMI registry process is running. This process is responsible for maintaining a list of registered objects, as well as communicating directly with remote JVMs.

Java provides two means for kicking off the RMI registry. The first is via a command line tool named rmiregistry, which takes as a parameter the desired port on which to listen. The second alternative is to create the registry from within the server application. In both cases, a server application is required to register the object. The only difference is the following section of code would be admitted if the registry has already been started using the rmiregistry command line tool.

```
//Kick of the registry on port 6789
LocateRegistry.createRegistry(6789);
```

Once the registry is ready for objects to be registered, it's time to hit the code. In RMI terms, this means creating an interface of method services which the server will offer to remote clients, and an implementation of the defined interface. For example, the following defines an interface and provides an implementation for MyObject. The key things to study are the fact that the interface extends java.rmi.Remote, and the implementation class extends java.rmi.server.UnicastRemoteObject.

```
public interface MyObjectInterface extends java.rmi.Remote {
    void youCanCallMe(int someValue);
}

public class MyObject extends UnicastRemoteObject
implements MyObjectInterface {
    public void youCanCallMe(int someValue){
        System.out.println("This will print out on the Server!");
    }
}
```

The interface provides an implementation-free way for a client to access the server's published methods. That is, when deploying the client applications, the interface class file is all that is needed to make the remote call.

After the server implementation and interface have been compiled, a RMI stub must be created for all to work properly. This is achieved by executing JDK-provided rmic, the command line tool which will create two files. For example, the following command executes the `rmic` tool to create stubs for the `MyObject` server implementation. The two `.class` files generated must reside in the class path of the executing JVM.

```
rmic MyObject
```

The final step in registering the server object is to actually make the RMI call to register the object. As stated before, the actual process of registering an instance of the server object boils down to one call. However, the call takes on two forms, `bind` and `rebind`. The following provides an example of each of these regeneration forms.

```
Naming.rebind("//:6789/Hello.MyObject", server);
Naming.bind("Hello.MyObject", server);
```

The difference of these two calls can be implied by their names, bind and rebind. Both take in identical parameters. The first is an URL format identifier for the object, and the second is the object reference. However, `rebind` redefines the URL string to reference the passed object reference, and `bind` simply registers the URL mapped to the passed object.

Upon successfully completing all of the RMI overhead and server-side coding, it is time to begin work on the client. The "Example Distributed Prime Number Calculator using RMI" section, later in this chapter, provides a complete example of a functioning RMI server object implementation. However, you may wish to take some time and try your own hand at RMI. The concepts like registration of a server object and server interfaces become much clearer after you have manually coded the steps, and besides its fun.

Remotely Calling a Registered Method

With the server application in place, it is time to get a client going. What this entails is a name lookup of the server's registry to retrieve the remote object reference. A single method call to `java.rmi.Naming.lookup()` takes in as a parameter the desired object name and returns a reference to the specified remote object. The following provides an example lookup using the previously defined `MyObject` server.

```
//Get the remote resource - Name in //host:port/name format
MyObjectInterface rRef = (MyObjectInterface ) Naming.lookup("//"
+
    "//:6789/Hello.MyObject");

//Now you have the reference, make the method call
rRef.youCanCallMe(20);
```

As you can see, the call to `java.Naming.lookup()` returns an object reference to the server object registered in the remote registry. Once the reference is returned and cast into a usable format, the object reference can be used just as if the object had been instantiated locally.

Notify When Ready

The final aspect of RMI to master isn't mandatory for all applications. However, it is useful enough to demand some attention. As you have seen, a server registers an object instance with the register for remote access. What you haven't seen is the complimentary client-side technology. RMI provides a way for server object to remotely call into registered client object by means of client-side notification.

The post JDK 1.02 event model is implemented in a producer consumer fashion. That is, objects sign up to an event producer to be informed when the desired event occurs. This is achieved by an object that calls a registration method with a reference to itself. In this way, the producer keeps a running list of all references to notify when the specified event occurs.

If you extend this concept of object notification into the RMI space, what you end up with is a model by which a server can make a call into a client object. For example, in a chat application the server object keeps a reference of all parties in the chat room. Using remote notification, a chat client can register itself to be notified when a new party signs on, or when a party signs off, allowing the client to rely on the server pushing the data out, rather than the client pulling the data down.

To facilitate such a client notification mechanism, five things must be provisioned. First, the client must define and implement an interface by which the server can call into the object. Second, the rmic must be run on the client application, and the produced stubs must be in the client's class path. Third, the RMI registry must be started on the client machine. Fourth, the client must register itself with the local registry. Lastly, the server object must be modified to handle a client registration method.

The next section provides an example for each of these defined steps. However, you will find that the steps taken to create a server object are replicated in creating a callback client. In a sense, a client that expects a callback from a registered server is itself a server object.

Sample Distributed Prime Number Calculator using RMI

To provide a contrast to the TCP/IP socket implementation of the distributed prime calculator, the following section presents an RMI alternative implementation. Using RMI instead of a socket-based approach eliminates the costly chore of defining a client server protocol. Rather, RMI utilizes interfaces to publish remotely visible methods. In this way, a server would implement the interface, and the client simply casts a reference to the interface.

Including the server-defined interface, each RMI solution contains the following four pieces, which are discussed in the sections that follow.

- ▶ Server Interface
- ▶ Server Implementation
- ▶ Server Application
- ▶ Client Application

The Server Interface

The server interface provides an implementation free representation of the methods that the server object wishes to publish. In the following code, notice that `java.rmi.Remote` is extended by the `RMIPrimeServerInterface` interface definitions. This allows the object to be invoked remotely. Further, each published method must be declared to throw a `RemoteException`.

```java
import java.rmi.*;
import java.math.BigInteger;

public interface RMIPrimeServerInterface extends java.rmi.Remote {

    BigInteger getNumberToTest()throws RemoteException;
    void foundPrime(BigInteger isPrime)throws RemoteException;
    int getCertainty()throws RemoteException;

}
```

The Server Implementation

Once the server interface has been defined, the supporting functionally must be developed. In this particular case, Listing 10.5 implements the three methods defined by the `RMIPrimeServer-Interface`: `getNumberToTest()`, `foundPrime()`, and `getCertainty()`. Also, as an overhead note all server objects must extend `UnicastRemoteObject`.

Listing 10.5 RMI prime server.

```java
import java.rmi.*;
import java.rmi.server.*;
import java.util.Vector;
import java.math.BigInteger;

public class RMIPServer extends UnicastRemoteObject
implements RMIPrimeServerInterface{

    //Holds the primes which have been found;
    private static Vector PrimesFound= new Vector();
```

continues

Listing 10.5   Continued

```java
//Holds the next number to test
private static BigInteger NextToTest = new BigInteger("1");

//Lagest number to test in bits
public static int LargestNumberInBits = 40;

//The Certainty factor that the number is a prime.
public static int Certainty = 1;

//Token Constructor
public RMIPServer() throws RemoteException { }


//Get the prime Certainty
public int getCertainty(){
    return Certainty;
}

//Get the next number to test
public synchronized BigInteger getNumberToTest(){

    if(LargestNumberInBits <= NextToTest.bitLength())
        return null;

    NextToTest = NextToTest.add(new BigInteger("1"));

    //return a copy of the NextToTest variable
    return NextToTest.add(new BigInteger("0"));
}

public synchronized void foundPrime(BigInteger prime){
    PrimesFound.addElement(prime);
    System.out.println("Found a new Prime -" + prime);
}
}
```

The Server Application

After the server object has been developed and the rmic tool has generated the stubs, the main server application can be launched. It is completely legal to have a single application register and support multiple server objects. In Listing 10.6, a single-server object is registered and subsequently the main application execution thread is suspended. This type of application loader is necessary for all applications that create their own instance of the RMI registry.

Listing 10.6 RMI prime server loader application.

```java
import java.rmi.*;
import java.rmi.server.*;
import java.rmi.registry.LocateRegistry;
import java.rmi.registry.Registry;

public class PrimeServer extends Thread {

    public static void main(String args[]) {
        PrimeServer Prime = new PrimeServer();
        Prime.start();
    }

    public void run(){
        try{
        System.out.println("PrimeServer.main: creating
➥registry");
        LocateRegistry.createRegistry(6789);
        System.out.println("PrimeServer.main: creating server");
        RMIPServer server = new RMIPServer();
        server.Certainty = 8;
        System.out.println("PrimeServer.main: binding server ");
        Naming.rebind("//:6789/test.PrimeServer", server);
        System.out.println("PrimeServer.main: done");
        suspend();//hang out for a while
        }
```

continues

Listing 10.6   Continued

```
                catch(Exception e){
                    System.out.println("PrimeServer: " + e);
                }
            }
        }
```

The Client Application

Once all is fat and happy with the server registry, the client can be kicked off. As shown Listing 10.7, a RMI client looks up the desired object in the server registry, and uses the server's defined interface to access the desired methods. Take some time and look at how streamlined the RMI implementation is compared to the TCP/IP socket implementations.

Listing 10.7   RMI prime calculation client.

```
import java.rmi.*;
import java.rmi.server.*;
import java.rmi.registry.LocateRegistry;
import java.rmi.registry.Registry;
import java.awt.Frame;
import java.math.BigInteger;


public class PrimeClient {

    public static void main(String args[]) {

        //Check to see if the host way provided
        if(args.length < 1){
            System.out.println("Server host must be provided");
            return;
        }

        try{
```

```
        System.out.println("PrimeClient.main: Retrieving Ref");
            RMIPrimeServerInterface rRef;

            //Get the remote resource
        rRef = (RMIPrimeServerInterface)Naming.lookup("//
➡"+args[0]+
➡":6789/test.PrimeServer");
        //Make call to the server for the certainty factor
        int Certainty = rRef.getCertainty();
        System.out.println("Certainty - " + Certainty);
        BigInteger testMe;

        //Loop for a while
        for(;;){
            //Get the next number to test
          testMe = rRef.getNumberToTest();
          //Die if no more numbers
          if(testMe == null)
              break;

            System.out.println("Working on " + testMe);

            //Check for a prime
            if(testMe.isProbablePrime(Certainty)){
                //Prime found
                rRef.foundPrime(testMe);
            }
        }
      }
      catch(Exception e){
          System.out.println("PrimeServer: " + e);
      }
    }
  }
```

Sample Distributed Prime Number Calculator using RMI with Remote Notification

The following example is an extension of the previous RMI example, with a client-side notification hook. In this model, the client registers itself to receive a callback when a prime number has been found. The following is a complete list of all components for the client notification model, including a new client-side interface.

- ▶ Server Interface
- ▶ Server Implementation
- ▶ Server Application
- ▶ Client Interface
- ▶ Client Application

Server Interface

In the following code, the server interface has been modified to include a new callback registration method, `notifyMeOfPrime`.

```
import java.rmi.*;
import java.math.BigInteger;

public interface RMIPrimeServerInterface extends java.rmi.Remote {

    BigInteger getNumberToTest()throws RemoteException;
    void foundPrime(BigInteger isPrime)throws RemoteException;
    int getCertainty()throws RemoteException;
    void notifyMeOfPrime(PClientNotify ref)throws
RemoteException;
}
```

Server Implementation

In Listing 10.8, the server implementation has been modified to implement the registration method and to fire the callbacks upon notification of a new prime number.

Listing 10.8   Prime server implementation.

```java
import java.rmi.*;
import java.rmi.server.*;
import java.util.Vector;
import java.math.BigInteger;

public class RMIPServer extends UnicastRemoteObject
implements RMIPrimeServerInterface{

    //Holds the primes which have been found;
    private static Vector PrimesFound= new Vector();

    //Holds the next number to test
    private static BigInteger NextToTest = new BigInteger("1");

    //Lagest number to test in bits
    public static int LargestNumberInBits = 40;

    //The Certainty factor that the number is a prime.
    public static int Certainty = 1;

    //The Vector of registered prime recipients
    Vector notifyME = new Vector();

     //Token Constructor
    public RMIPServer() throws RemoteException { }


    //Get the prime Certainty
    public int getCertainty(){
        return Certainty;
    }

    //Get the next number to test
    public synchronized BigInteger getNumberToTest(){
```

continues

Listing 10.8   Continued

```
        if(LargestNumberInBits <= NextToTest.bitLength())
            return null;


    NextToTest = NextToTest.add(new BigInteger("1"));


    //return a copy of the NextToTest variable
    return NextToTest.add(new BigInteger("0"));
}


public synchronized void foundPrime(BigInteger prime){
    PrimesFound.addElement(prime);
    System.out.println("Found a new Prime -" + prime);
    //Tell all registered clients
    int len = notifyME.size();
    for(int i = 0;i < len; ++i){
        try{
        ((PClientNotify)notifyME.elementAt(i)).PrimeFound(prime);
        }
        catch(Exception e){
            //Remove the reference!
        }
    }
}


public void notifyMeOfPrime(PClientNotify ref){
    notifyME.addElement(ref);
}


}
```

Server Application

The server application does nothing more than create a registry,
and then registers the server object. For this reason, the server
application does not change with the addition of the callback
functionality. However, before the server application can be

successfully executed, the rmic tool must be re-run on the
RMIPServer class, as seen in Listing 10.9.

Listing 10.9   RMI prime server with callback loader.

```java
import java.rmi.*;
import java.rmi.server.*;
import java.rmi.registry.LocateRegistry;
import java.rmi.registry.Registry;

public class PrimeServer extends Thread {

    public static void main(String args[]) {
        PrimeServer Prime = new PrimeServer();
        Prime.start();
    }

    public void run(){
        try{
        System.out.println("PrimeServer.main: creating
➥registry");
        LocateRegistry.createRegistry(6789);
        System.out.println("PrimeServer.main: creating server");
        RMIPServer server = new RMIPServer();
        server.Certainty = 8;
        System.out.println("PrimeServer.main: binding server ");
        Naming.rebind("//:6789/test.PrimeServer", server);
        System.out.println("PrimeServer.main: done");
        suspend();//hang out for a while
        }
        catch(Exception e){
            System.out.println("PrimeServer: " + e);
        }
    }
}
```

Client Notification Interface

Just as the server interface provides the means for the client to call methods in the server object without implantation knowledge, the client interface does the same. With the client interface, the server object has a way to cast a generic Remote object into a specific method defined in an interface. For this reason, the following interface defines a method for the server to call when a new prime has been found.

```java
import java.rmi.*;
import java.math.BigInteger;

public interface PClientNotify extends java.rmi.Remote {
    void PrimeFound(BigInteger isPrime)throws RemoteException;
}
```

Client Application

To handle the new functionality of a client-side callback, the client application has taken on a face-lift of sorts. Specifically, in order for the client-side notification to work, the client application must be registered in with the local registry. To facilitate this, all application logic has been moved into a run method so that a new instance of the class can be executed. Once the new instance is created, the instance reference is published to the registry. However, unlike the server application, the client application relies on the RMI registry to be manually invoked with a call to rmiregistry, as seen in Listing 10.10.

Listing 10.10   RMI prime calculation client with server-side push.

```java
import java.rmi.*;
import java.rmi.server.*;
import java.awt.Frame;
import java.math.BigInteger;

public class PrimeClient implements PClientNotify {

    String host = "";
```

```
public void PrimeFound(BigInteger isPrime){
    System.out.println("New Prime Found - " + isPrime);
}

public void run(){

    try{
        UnicastRemoteObject.exportObject(this);
    System.out.println("PrimeClient.main: Retrieving Ref");
        RMIPrimeServerInterface rRef;

        //Get the remote resource
    rRef = (RMIPrimeServerInterface)Naming.lookup
➥("//"+host+":6789/test.PrimeServer");

        //Register for Prime notification
    rRef.notifyMeOfPrime(this);

        //Make call to the server for the certainty factor
    int Certainty = rRef.getCertainty();
    System.out.println("Certainty - " + Certainty);
    BigInteger testMe;

        //Loop for a while
    for(;;){
            //Get the next number to test
        testMe = rRef.getNumberToTest();
        //Die if no more numbers
        if(testMe == null)
            break;

            System.out.println("Working on " + testMe);

            //Check for a prime
            if(testMe.isProbablePrime(Certainty)){
```

continues

Listing 10.10 Continued

```
                        //Prime found
                        rRef.foundPrime(testMe);
                }
            }
        }
        catch(Exception e){
            System.out.println("PrimeServer: " + e);
        }


    }
    public static void main(String args[]) {

        //Check to see if the host way provided
        if(args.length < 1){
            System.out.println("Server host must be provided");
            return;
        }

        PrimeClient pc = new PrimeClient();
        pc.run();
        pc.host = args[0];
    }
}
```

Where To Go From Here

In this chapter, you learned how to use Java to communicate between process and machines. The fundamental transport concept of IP was presented as groundwork for UDP and TCP/IP. Likewise, RMI leverages TCP/IP to provide a powerful and intuitive model for inter JVM communication. All and all, this chapter covered a lot of ground, but none in vain. The Certified Java Developer Examination is a test of all aspects of advanced development, including creating distributed network applications.

In the chapters to follow, you will learn more about creating intelligent and documentable Java solutions. However, it is time well spent to revisit each Java IPC facility presented in this chapter, and try your hand at your own solutions. It is through experimentation that knowledge is validated, and you are urged to go play. After all, being a Java developer means knowing how to play hard.

Chapter 11
Creating Java APIs

Application Programming Interface has a historical connotation of being a flat, sometime cryptic set of functions to access the functionality embedded inside another application. However, Java provides the ability to present future development efforts with clear, documented, and extensible means for extending or accessing the functionality embedded inside an existing solution.

Back in the C/C++ days, a large portion of the APIs dealt with accessing libraries of compiled code. The reason for emphasis on compiled code is that most of the time developers did not have access to the actual implementation code. Rather, developers would have to decipher cryptic function names, and reams of useless documentation. Can you sense some personal frustration?

Then Java came, and it was good. JavaDoc presents APIs in a new and friendly way. Method and field declarations are presented for plain view with JavaDoc, leaving no good reason to scour through code. Further, Java drives home the true object-oriented view with entirely self-concept units of functionality. Java may have its shortcomings, but the language as a whole put the object-oriented paradigm into the hands of the main stream development community.

 Objectives

- ▶ Demonstrate Java programmatic style

- ▶ Properly partition a problem

- ▶ Implement stable and documentable solutions

- ▶ Master Java optimization

Note
> The Certified Developer Exam is much different than the Programmer Exam. To pass the Developer Exam you do not need to memorize facts, rather you need to understand broad concepts and show hands-on programming experience. For these reasons, there are not any Test Yourself quizzes or end-of-chapter questions in this section of the book.

The Java Way

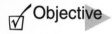**Objective** Forming and using a Javatrinsic programmatic style is a key focus of being a Certified Java Developer.

The common and instinctual habit for Java newcomers is to code Java as if it were a previously learned language. That is, most C/C++ programmers coding Java for the first time will try to make Java act and look like C/C++. However, Java is a fresh, new language that demands a new development mind-set.

If you talk to hardcore Java developers about the importance of Javatrinsic style, you might begin to hear church bells, for it is a religious issue. In many ways, the notion of the *right way*, instilled by James Gosling (Java's creator), rings in the ears of most Java developers. This *right way*, or the *Java Way*, of software development revolves around the following four goals. Granted, these goals are not unique to Java, but Java makes the goals achievable.

- Intuitive
- Useful
- Extensible
- Documentable

The following section takes an in-depth look at these four goals of Java development.

Intuitive

Putting a square peg in a round hole is not intuitive. Developing Javatrinsic solutions is about using the right tools to fulfill the job. Creating intuitive Javatrinsic solutions is about knowing what technologies are readily available, and making these technologies optimize your development effort. Without having a complete knowledge of the language, and the technology available in the Java technology suite, even the most talented developers can fall victim to un-intuitive designs. For example, the `java.io` package contains a powerful stream parsing class named `StreamTokenizer`. Without knowledge of this class, most developers would resort to a scratch-built parsing unit, leading to a costly and un-intuitive design.

Being a Java Certified Developer implies a complete mastery of the Java language, and the supplied class libraries. Creating intuitive designs stems from this fact. Knowing the language, and making Java work for you, is the difference between someone who can code Java and someone who can create intuitive Javatrinic solutions.

Useful

Unless you are in academia or the government, technology for technology's sake is not a valid reason for development. Academia and governmental organizations have the distinct privilege to develop applications for the sole reason that they can. However, the rest of us have to produce results to pay our bills. For this reason, every development effort should be grounded with a firm intention to create a useful solution.

An example of a non-useful development effort can be implied from a variety of life, and Dilbert situations. Marketing presents a requirement to engineering with the comment, "We need this because it is cool, and it is on our competitor's Web page." Having an application pour smoke out of a machine might be cool, but not all that useful. Further, if a competitor is boasting this feature, that doesn't mean they had intended smoke to be a feature. That is, firmly understanding the problem yourself is the first step in creating a useful solutions.

Getting to know a problem and then choosing the appropriate solution is the role of a developer. Creating intuitive designs forces you to take a step back to look at the big picture and partition the problem into granular pieces. Being a Certified Java Developer implies the ability to analyze each granule of functionality, and relate each piece to an actual Java implementation that leverages the Java technology suite.

Extensible

Part of the beauty of Java is its true object-oriented nature. Every class is designed to represent a discrete unit of functionality. However, by virtue of simply creating a class does not imply that all developers are adhering to Java's object-oriented paradigm. Java provides the means to create an extensible unit of functionality; it is up to you to implement the intent.

Possibly one of the greatest cases of a kludge program being re-used to death is the vi editor. For those of you that have never heard of vi, here is your chance to live a little. vi is a plain vanilla, non-graphical text editor usually found on the UNIX platforms. The author of vi simply needed a text editor for his own personal use. Fifteen years later people swear by the ease and raw power of vi. The point being, all kludge development efforts have the ability to be reused and extended. Each class you create should be developed with the extent of aiding future development, and therefore must be extensible.

In Java, everything is reusable, forcing the object-oriented paradigm onto all Java developers. Being a Certified Java Developer means using Java to its fullest potential in developing a solution. This includes creating extensible designs which leverage Java's pure object-oriented paradigm.

Documentable

A side effect of creating reusable and extensible solutions is an inherit need for documentation. Traditionally, this meant going into a trusty word processor and word smithing a document together. However, Java provides JavaDoc to quickly and efficiently code your work.

Chapter 6 "JDK Supplied Tools" presented JavaDoc as a tool, but didn't go into the implications of such a tool. JavaDoc runs through your actual source code and extracts contextual comments provided in your code. For example, in a class you introduce a method by a brief comment. JavaDoc will find the comment, notice that you were using that comment as an introduction for the method and produce HTML, including your comment and the method declaration. However, watch out for your spelling and other things you may think are just for your eyes. JavaDoc exposes a class's internals for all to see and analyze, so be cognizant of naming and commenting conventions.

Creating a documentable solution in Java equates to a solution that can be passed through JavaDoc. This might sound like a simple goal, but it is nevertheless important. The HTML pages produced by JavaDoc have become the industry standard of Java API documentation, and being a Certified Java Developer means adhering to this standard.

Creating a Java Solution

The previous section, "The Java Way," presented how to go about creating Javatrinsic solutions from a stylistic view. However, there is more to a solution than programmatic style. Creating an entire Java solution requires designing and implementing with the features and limitations of Java in mind.

Every programming language has its own set of exemplary attributes. C++ has brute power, Pascal likes strings, SmallTalk does objects, Visual Basic takes the programming out of development, and Ada is just Ada. A solution designed to be implemented in each of these languages will undoubtedly have a different flavor. Likewise, solutions designed in Java have a definite Java flavor.

When you take the Sun Certified Java Programmer examination, it is assumed that the syntactical issues of the Java language are not a stumbling block in your Java development. The Java Developer examination tests your ability to use Java to develop system-level solutions. The following list and sections provide a check list of design steps. These steps are not touted to be a definitive guide for proper object-oriented design. Rather, the list provides a mind-set of what the Sun Certified Java Developer examination evaluators are looking for in submitted solutions and design justifications.

- ▶ Packaging

- ▶ Objectizing

- ▶ Assessing the Design

- ▶ Implementation and Optimizing

The following sections explain and analyze each of these steps to provide a complete look at a structured design and implementation framework.

Packaging Functionality

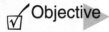 Objective

Using Java to properly partition a problem into packages and classes is a key element for a Sun Certified Java Developer.

Java provides two related means for packaging functionality. The first is the class object to provide the smallest form of functional encapsulation. The second is the package which holds a collection of classes. Knowing how to partition solution functionality into packages and classes is essential for Java development.

Before you can dissect a solution into class-size pieces of functionality, you must first figure out the larger functional breakdown. In Java, this means figuring out how to break the code into packages. Granted, not all solutions require a package breakdown. However, packages provide an elegant mechanism for distributing and grouping reusable code. For example, a utils package may contain a toolbox of custom-developed programming aids. All classes found in a utils package can be incorporated into other solutions with a single import statement. Further, Java requires that each package have its own sub-directory which provides streamlined file packaging distribution.

The easiest way to break a solution into packages is to draw the solutions. Draw not in the form of a flow diagram, but rather an architectural block diagram. If the solution can be broken into multiple packages, it will become visible by analyzing the architecture. Later, in the "Solution Example" section, a solution will be dissected into a series of packages. However, keep in mind that all good designs begin with a picture, and look for ways to package up general use utility classes.

Objectizing Into Functional Units

Once an architectural view has been laid out, the individual pieces of functionality can be broken into objects. Granted, objectization of functionality isn't always intuitively visible. It takes time, and analysis to create a true object-oriented, Javatrinisc design. Like most things, getting the hang of Java object partitioning takes a little getting used to. However, there are some tricks of Java design that will help you through the learning curve.

Objectifying functionality is really about breaking down, or grouping, functions into a common grouping of functionality. This might sound like a contradiction of terms, but it is relevant to the way you solve problems. For example, if you approach a problem from an architectural view and then drill down into specific functionality, you would use an object as the smallest unit of functionality (the methods and fields of an object are just a detail of the object's functionality.) On the other hand, if you approach problems from the bottom-up and define programmatic functions before looking at the big picture, an object is a way to group the functions into common groupings. It is true that objects are hierarchical in nature; however, the way the problem is approached depicts how the hierarchy is formed.

The following provides a few tips to aid your object layout with Java features in mind.

- ▶ Class and Method Visibility   If a class is only needed to facilitate the functionality found in a package, it should be declared as `protected`. Likewise, keep in mind what fields and methods you wish to make public.

- ▶ `static` Methods   `static` methods provide the ability for multiple classes and threads to access the same object state.

▶ abstract Methods abstract methods are used in a class that provides some implementation but requires others to be developed by extended classes. In this way, a class can be implemented, but also require specific implementation details from child classes.

▶ Interfaces Interfaces provide the means to create class templates. More specifically, an object reference can be cast into a specific interface in order to access required class members.

▶ final The final method not only provides a way to lock down an implementation, it also can be used as an optimization trick.

Taking a Final Look

With JavaDoc, the job of mapping out and analyzing object inter-action is a very helpful experience. Not everyone may think this process is fun, but when the end result is brought up on a Web browser no developer can stop themselves from saying, "Wow!" However, in order to use JavaDoc, class definitions and comments must be prototyped. Which leads to the equation: method proto-types plus documentation equals functional stubs.

Functional stubs are the foundation of a development effort. Each method and field is laid out and ready for implementation, from which the total design can be assessed and development can be-gin. Further, by creating functional stubs, JavaDoc can present an external view of the implementation to aid marketing and tangen-tial development efforts.

The creation of functional stubs is the most precise development road-map that can be created. Granted, not all development cy-cles can afford such detail, but they are nevertheless important as design and presentation tools. Besides, the Certified Developer Exam allows ample time for such development luxuries.

Implementing and Optimizing

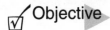

The ability to implement a stable, documentable Java solution is a part of being a Certified Java Developer.

With functional stubs in place, all that is left is to role up sleeves and start implementing. Sure, things might change a little. However, the goal of any design is to approximate design to implementation details. Issues like creating private variables, support methods, and optimization cannot be avoided. Optimization consideration is required in almost every Java development effort, and should be in the forefront of every developer's mind when implementing a solution. For this reason, the following provides a list of optimization tips to keep fresh while developing.

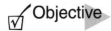

Knowing the Java optimization tricks and limitations is the role of a Certified Java Developer.

▶ A += 2 is 2 to 3 times faster than A = A + 2

▶ A++ is 3 to 4 times faster than A = A + 1

▶ Garbage is bad. Although in Java you have the ability to make objects right and left, that doesn't mean you should. Each created object has overhead associated with creation and reclamation.

▶ Create variables on the call stack instead of the garbage collection heap. Within the confines of a method body, primitive data types can be created in a temporal basis on the call stack.

▶ Optimize loop contents. That is, pull all assignments that are not affected by the loop outside of the loop body. For example, the following loop checks an array size for each loop interaction.

```
Hashtable myTable = new Hashtable(10);
for(int i = 0;i < myTable.size();++i){
}
```

Each time the loop iterates i < myTable.size()means another call on the call stack and processing time. A more optimized implementation would be as follows.

```
Hashtable myTable = new Hashtable(10);
Int size = myTable.size();
for(int i = 0;i < size;++i){
}
```

▶ Only create field assessor methods when required. Otherwise, simply make the field visible with a `public` declaration.

▶ Elaborate hierarchy trees may look cool, but are not efficient. That is, each method and field access must be resolved to a specific object in the tree. The shorter the tree, the faster the access.

▶ Use `synchronized` sparingly. `synchronized` is a very costly facility. All references must be serialized before entrance. Therefore, if you only have a small section of crucial code, only synchronize the code block.

▶ Exceptions are great, but they are only meant to convey an error. Every time an exception is thrown, the VM basically shuts down until the exception is caught.

▶ Use 64-bit data types sparingly, unless the target native architecture supports 64-bit instructions. However, keep in mind that the JVM stack is only 32-bits wide.

▶ Java does not have a pre-process, so be careful when debug statements are coded. If you create a `static final` debug flag, all evaluations deemed by the compiler to always be `false` will not be compiled into the final class.

Java can approach native performance, but not without effort. Someday Java compilers will stabilize and gain the intelligence to auto-optimize, but for now it is up to the developer.

Solution Example

The following sections provide a sample solution based on a fictitious requirement statement. From the requirement statement, an architectural diagram will be formed, which will then lead into development. This example is designed to not only mimic a real-world scenario, but to provide practice development exercises similar to the Sun Certified Java Developer examination.

The Requirements

An existing database server needs to be exposed to external applications. However, marketing wants this to be cool, and cool equates to the following requirements.

- ▶ All database-stored procedures must be made callable.

- ▶ Data returned to the application should employ server push technology.

- ▶ The administration interface is going to be changing with every strong breeze. Therefore, the client applications will need to get the admin GUI from the server as needed.

- ▶ All clients should know about one another.

- ▶ Clients should have the ability to communicate with one another.

- ▶ Provide a multi-threaded API.

As you can see, these requirements depict actual marketing requirements, vague and "buzzy." However, these requirements are specific enough to create an architecture form.

Proposed Architecture

From the requirements, a client/server architecture jumps right out. The server application must provide a set of callable functions to extend the value of the client application. Further, an existing database is provided to give some direction to the remotely accessible functionality. The solution can be logically divided into two distinct pieces: the database projector and the client enabler.

Granted, the names "database projector" and "client enabler" might seem a little premature. However, it is crucial to name the region of functionality, even if it is a code name. With names in place, you have the ability to more clearly present and encapsulate functionality. For example, Figure 11.1 provides a first-pass architectural diagram of the system using the names "database projector" and "client enabler" to iconize the functional reasons. Even if people don't know what the regions do, they now have a few buzz-words.

Figure 11.1

Solution architectural diagram.

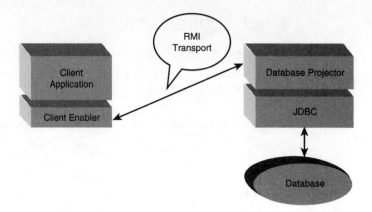

As discussed in Chapter 10, "Network Programming," RMI is the Java tool of choice for developing client/server applications. Based on the requirements to make the server-side facilities available to a client application, and to utilize server push technology, the solution will employ RMI. Therefore, given that RMI is to be the solution's transport mechanism, the "database projector" equates to an RMI server object, and the "client enabler" is an API to access the registered RMI facilities.

The structure of client/server applications is completely dependent on the transport device employed. Nailing down RMI as the base data transport facility for this solution allows the architecture to be expanded down to the class level. As Figure 11.2 presents, based on the choice to use RMI, the classes and packages are now pinned into place and are awaiting validation from the functional stubs.

Figure 11.2

RMI solution architectural diagram.

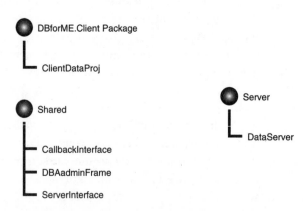

Functional Stubs

Creating the functional stubs of a solution is really the first phase of implementation. Given the architectural diagram presented in Figure 11.2, a functional class model can be constructed. In this way, functional stubs provide a proof of concept for the proposed solution.

The following sections present the functional stubs displayed through JavaDoc. Each package will be visited in turn, presenting all contained classes and including figures (Figures 11.3 to 11.7) that display the JavaDoc output for each stub. In this way, a complete look at each class and package of the solution can be viewed in context.

The Implementation

Once the functional stubs have been laid out and all associated issues are resolved, it is time to hit the code. If all is well with the design and the functional stubs, the implementation phase should be like clockwork. The functional stubs lay out the functional pieces in class level granularity, the implementation is merely the code holding the pieces together.

The sections provide a complete source listing from each class of the solution. The presented implementation has been developed with all optimization tips presented in the previous section, "Implementing and Optimizing." Additionally, the presented source code is available on the accompanying CD-ROM.

DBforME.Server.DataServer

```
package DBforME.Server;

import DBforME.Shared.*;
import java.rmi.*;
import java.rmi.server.*;
import java.rmi.registry.*;
import java.util.Hashtable;
import java.util.Properties;
import java.util.Enumeration;
```

```
/**
 * The DataServer provides an RMI server for the execution of
➥stored
 *procedures, * and facilitates inter client communications.
 * <BR>
 * Copyright (c) 1997 My Company, Inc. All Rights Reserved.
 * @author Cary A. Jardin
 * @version 1.0
 *
 */
public class DataServer extends UnicastRemoteObject
    implements ServerInterface{

    private Hashtable Clients   = new Hashtable(10);
    //The Name to associate with the remote object.
    private static String Name = "//:6789/DBforME.DataServer";
    //The port to bind the RMI registrary
    private static int port =  6789;


    public DataServer() throws RemoteException{}

//Methods - Remote Services
    /**
     * Remotely execute a stored procedure.
     * @param procName  The name of the stored procedure to
➥execute
     * @param params    The properties for the stored procedure
     * @param informMe  The client to whom the results should be
➥shipped to
     * @return    Returns the request ID value > 0 if successfull
➥execution,
     *                                  otherwise -1
     * @exception RemoteException   Thrown if a transport problem
➥occurs
     */
    public int execStoredProcedure(String procName, Properties
➥params,
        CallbackInterface informMe){
        //Code HERE!
        return 0;
    }

    /**
```

```
    * Return a list of all registerd clients
    * @return                      Returns a list of all
➥registed clients
    * @exception RemoteException   Thrown if a transport problem
➥occurs
   */
   public Properties getListOfClients(){
       return null;
   }


   /**
    * Returns a Class object defining the admin frame
    * @return                      Returns a Class def of the
➥Admin frame
    * @exception RemoteException   Thrown if a transport problem
➥occurs
   */
   public Class getAdminFrame(){
       return null;
   }


   /**
    * Send a byte stream to the specified client
    * @param from                  The reference to the message
➥creator
    * @param toClient              The messages "TO" address
    * @param data                  The data to send
    * @exception RemoteException   Thrown if a transport problem
➥occurs
   */
   public void sendInfoToClient(CallbackInterface from, String
➥toClient,
       byte[] data){
       CallbackInterface tmp;

       for(Enumeration e = Clients.keys();e.hasMoreElements();){
           tmp = (CallbackInterface)e.nextElement();
           if(toClient.equals((String)Clients.get(tmp))){
               try{
                 tmp.recvMessage((String)Clients.get(from),data);
               }
               catch(Exception ex){
                   System.out.println("DataServer.sendInfoToClient
➥" + "
```

```
                            "I think its DEAD " + ex);
                        unRegisterClient(tmp);
                    }
                    finally{
                        return;
                    }
                }
            }
        }


    /**
     * Send a byte stream to all registered clients
     * @param from                 The reference to the message
➥creator
     * @param data                 The data to send
     * @exception RemoteException  Thrown if a transport problem
➥occurs
     */
    public void sendInfoToAll(CallbackInterface from, byte[]
➥data){
        CallbackInterface tmp;

        for(Enumeration e = Clients.keys();e.hasMoreElements();){
            tmp = (CallbackInterface)e.nextElement();
            try{
                tmp.recvMessage((String)Clients.get(from),data);
            }
            catch(Exception ex){
                System.out.println("DataServer.sendInfoToClient"+
                    " I think its DEAD " + ex);
                unRegisterClient(tmp);
            }
        }
    }


//Methods - Remote Listener Reg
    /**
     * Registers a new Client
     * @param Host                 Client Host Name
     * @param clientRef            A reference to the client
➥object
     * @exception RemoteException  Thrown if a transport problem
➥occurs
     */
```

```
    public void registerClient(String Host,CallbackInterface
➥clientRef){
        Clients.put(clientRef,Host);
    }

//Methods - Remote Listener UnReg

    /**
     * Registers a new Client
     * @param clientRef            A reference to the client
➥object
     * @exception RemoteException   Thrown if a transport problem
➥occurs
     */
    public void unRegisterClient(CallbackInterface clientRef){
        Clients.remove(clientRef);
    }

    /**
     * Start up the stock server; also creates a registry so that
➥the
     * DataServer can lookup the server.
     */
    public static void main(String args[]){

        System.setSecurityManager(new RMISecurityManager());
        try {
            LocateRegistry.createRegistry(port);
            System.out.println("DataServer.main: creating
➥server");
            DataServer server = new DataServer();
            Naming.rebind(Name, server);
            System.out.println("DataServer.main: done");
        }
        catch (Exception e) {
            System.out.println("DataServer.main: an exception
➥occurred: "+
                    e.getMessage());
            e.printStackTrace();
        }
    }
}
```

Figure 11.3

JavaDoc output for DBforME. Server.DataServer.

All Packages   Class Hierarchy   This Package   Previous   Next   Index

Class DBforME.Server.DataServer

```
java.lang.Object
    |
    +----java.rmi.server.RemoteObject
            |
            +----java.rmi.server.RemoteServer
                    |
                    +----java.rmi.server.UnicastRemoteObject
                            |
                            +----DBforME.Server.DataServer
```

public class **DataServer**
extends UnicastRemoteObject

The DataServer provides an RMI server for the execution of stored procedures, and facilitates inter client communications.
Copyright (c) 1997 My Company, Inc. All Rights Reserved.

Constructor Index

○ **DataServer**()

Method Index

● **execStoredProcedure**(String, Properties, CallbackInterface)
     Remotely execute a stored procedure.
● **getAdminFrame**()
     Returns a Class object defining the admin frame
● **getListOfClients**()
     Return a list of all registerd clients
● **registerClient**(String, CallbackInterface)
     Registers a new Client
● **sendInfoToAll**(CallbackInterface, byte[])
     Send a byte stream to all registered clients
● **sendInfoToClient**(CallbackInterface, String, byte[])
     Send a byte stream to the specified client
● **unRegisterClient**(CallbackInterface)
     Registers a new Client

Constructors

◉ **DataServer**

public DataServer() throws RemoteException

Methods

● **execStoredProcedure**

```
public int execStoredProcedure(String procName,
                               Properties params,
                               CallbackInterface informMe)
```

Remotely execute a stored procedure.

Parameters:
     procName - The name of the stored procedure to execute
     params - The properties for the stored procedure
     informMe - The client to whom the results should be shipped to
Returns:
     Returns the request ID value > 0 if successfull execution, otherwise -1
Throws: RemoteException
     Thrown if a transport problem occurs

● **getListOfClients**

```
public Properties getListOfClients()
```

Return a list of all registerd clients

Returns:
Returns a list of all registed clients
Throws: RemoteException
Thrown if a transport problem occurs

● **getAdminFrame**

```
public Class getAdminFrame()
```

Returns a Class object defining the admin frame

Returns:
Returns a Class def of the Admin frame
Throws: RemoteException
Thrown if a transport problem occurs

● **sendInfoToClient**

```
public void sendInfoToClient(CallbackInterface from,
                             String toClient,
                             byte data[])
```

Send a byte stream to the specified client

Parameters:
from - The reference to the message creator
toClient - The messages "TO" address
data - The data to send
Throws: RemoteException
Thrown if a transport problem occurs

● **sendInfoToAll**

```
public void sendInfoToAll(CallbackInterface from,
                          byte data[])
```

Send a byte stream to all registered clients

Parameters:
from - The reference to the message creator
data - The data to send
Throws: RemoteException
Thrown if a transport problem occurs

● **registerClient**

```
public void registerClient(String Host,
                           CallbackInterface clientRef)
```

Registers a new Client

Parameters:
Host - Client Host Name
clientRef - A reference to the client object
Throws: RemoteException
Thrown if a transport problem occurs

● **unRegisterClient**

```
public void unRegisterClient(CallbackInterface clientRef)
```

Registers a new Client

Parameters:
clientRef - A reference to the client object
Throws: RemoteException
Thrown if a transport problem occurs

DBforME.Client.ClientDataProj

```java
package DBforME.Client;

import java.rmi.*;
import DBforME.Shared.*;
import java.rmi.server.*;
import java.util.Hashtable;
import java.util.Properties;
import java.net.InetAddress;

/**
 * The DataServer provides an RMI server for the execution of stored
 * procedures,
 * and facilitates inter client communications.
 * <BR>
 * Copyright (c) 1997 My Company, Inc. All Rights Reserved.
 * @author Cary A. Jardin
 * @version 1.0
 *
 */
public class ClientDataProj extends UnicastRemoteObject
    implements CallbackInterface{

    private static String Name = "//france:6789/DBforME.DataServer";
    private ServerInterface remoteServer = null;

    public ClientDataProj() throws RemoteException{
        //Export this Reference to recieve callbacks
            UnicastRemoteObject.exportObject(this);

        //Retrieve remote object
        try{
            remoteServer = (ServerInterface)Naming.lookup(Name);
            remoteServer.registerClient(
                InetAddress.getLocalHost().getHostName(),this);
        }
        catch(Exception e){
            //Throw an exception if a URL has a problem
            throw new RemoteException();
        }
    }

    public void finalize(){
        if(remoteServer != null)
            try{
                remoteServer.unRegisterClient(this);
            }
            catch(Exception e){}
    }
```

```
public synchronized byte[] getResultData(int reqID){
    //Something HERE!
    return null;
}

/**
 * Called remotely to feed resultant data into the client. Do
➥NOT call!
 * @param reqID           The request ID of the
➥incoming data
 * @param data            The result data
 * @exception RemoteException    Thrown if a transport problem
➥occurs
 */
public synchronized void resultData(int reqID, byte[] data){
    //Something HERE!
}

/**
 * Called remotely to feed data sent from another client. Do
➥NOT Call
 * @param from    The name of the client from which the data
➥originated
 * @param data    The message data
 * @exception RemoteException   Thrown if a transport problem
➥occurs
 */
public synchronized void recvMessage(String from, byte[]
➥data){
    //Something HERE!
}

//Methods - Remote Services
/**
 * Remotely execute a stored procedure.
 * @param procName    The name of the stored procedure to
➥execute
 * @param params      The properties for the stored
➥procedure
 * @return   Returns the request ID value > 0 if successfull
➥execution,
 *                              otherwise -1
 * @exception RemoteException   Thrown if a transport problem
➥occurs
 */
public synchronized int execStoredProcedure(String procName,
    Properties params){

    if(remoteServer == null)
        return -1;
```

```
                try{
                    return remoteServer.execStoredProcedure(procName,
➥params,
                        this);
                }
                catch(Exception e){
                    return -1;
                }
            }

        /**
         * Return a list of all registerd clients
         * @return                        Returns a list of all
➥registed clients,
         *                                or null if a problem
         * @exception RemoteException     Thrown if a transport problem
➥occurs
         */
        public synchronized Properties getListOfClients(){

            if(remoteServer == null)
                return null;

            try{
                return remoteServer.getListOfClients();
            }
            catch(Exception e){
                return null;
            }
        }

        /**
         * Returns a Class object defining the admin frame
         * @return                        Returns a Class def of the
➥Admin frame,
         *                                or null if a problem
         * @exception RemoteException     Thrown if a transport problem
➥occurs
         */
        public synchronized DBAdminFrame getAdminFrame(){

            if(remoteServer == null)
                return null;

            try{
                return (DBAdminFrame)(
                    remoteServer.getAdminFrame().newInstance());
            }
            catch(Exception e){
                return null;
```

```
        }
    }

    /**
     * Send a byte stream to the specified client
     * @param from                    The reference to the message
➡creator
     * @param toClient                The messages "TO" address
     * @param data                    The data to send
     * @exception RemoteException     Thrown if a transport problem
➡occurs
     */
    public synchronized void sendInfoToClient(String
➡toClient,byte[] data){

        if(remoteServer == null)
            return;

        try{
            remoteServer.sendInfoToClient(this,toClient,data);
        }
        catch(Exception e){
        }

        return;
    }

    /**
     * Send a byte stream to all registered clients
     * @param from                    The reference to the message
➡creator
     * @param data                    The data to send
     * @exception RemoteException     Thrown if a transport problem
➡occurs
     */
    public synchronized void sendInfoToAll(byte[] data){

        if(remoteServer == null)
            return;

        try{
            remoteServer.sendInfoToAll(this,data);
        }
        catch(Exception e){
        }

        return;
    }

}
```

Figure 11.4

JavaDoc output for DBforME. Client.Client DataProj.

All Packages   Class Hierarchy   This Package   Previous   Next   Index

Class DBforME.Client.ClientDataProj

```
java.lang.Object
   |
   +----java.rmi.server.RemoteObject
          |
          +----java.rmi.server.RemoteServer
                 |
                 +----java.rmi.server.UnicastRemoteObject
                        |
                        +----DBforME.Client.ClientDataProj
```

public class **ClientDataProj**
extends UnicastRemoteObject

The DataServer provides an RMI server for the execution of stored procedures, and facilitates inter client communications.
Copyright (c) 1997 My Company, Inc. All Rights Reserved.

Constructor Index

• **ClientDataProj**()

Method Index

• **execStoredProcedure**(String, Properties)
    Remotely execute a stored procedure.
• **finalize**()
• **getAdminFrame**()
    Returns a Class object defining the admin frame
• **getListOfClients**()
    Return a list of all registerd clients
• **getResultData**(int)
• **recvMessage**(String, byte[])
    Called remotely to feed data sent from another client.
• **resultData**(int, byte[])
    Called remotely to feed resultant data into the client.
• **sendInfoToAll**(byte[])
    Send a byte stream to all registered clients
• **sendInfoToClient**(String, byte[])
    Send a byte stream to the specified client

Constructors

◉ **ClientDataProj**

```
public ClientDataProj() throws RemoteException
```

Methods

◉ **finalize**

```
public void finalize()
```

> **Overrides:**
>   finalize in class Object

◉ **getResultData**

```
public synchronized byte[] getResultData(int reqID)
```

◉ **resultData**

```
public synchronized void resultData(int reqID,
                                    byte data[])
```

> Called remotely to feed resultant data into the client. Do NOT call!

> **Parameters:**
>   reqID - The request ID of the incoming data
>   data - The result data
> **Throws:** RemoteException
>   Thrown if a transport problem occurs

● **recvMessage**

```
public synchronized void recvMessage(String from,
                                     byte data[])
```

Called remotly to feed data sent from another client. Do NOT Call

Parameters:
> from - The name of the client from which the data originated
> data - The message data

Throws: RemoteException
> Thrown if a transport problem occurs

● **execStoredProcedure**

```
public synchronized int execStoredProcedure(String procName,
                                            Properties params)
```

Remotely execute a stored procedure.

Parameters:
> procName - The name of the stored procedure to execute
> params - The properties for the stored procedure

Returns:
> Returns the request ID value > 0 if successfull execution, otherwise -1

Throws: RemoteException
> Thrown if a transport problem occurs

● **getListOfClients**

```
public synchronized Properties getListOfClients()
```

Return a list of all registerd clients

Returns:
> Returns a list of all registed clients, or null if a problem

Throws: RemoteException
> Thrown if a transport problem occurs

● **getAdminFrame**

```
public synchronized DBAdminFrame getAdminFrame()
```

Returns a Class object defining the admin frame

Returns:
> Returns a Class def of the Admin frame, or null if a problem

Throws: RemoteException
> Thrown if a transport problem occurs

● **sendInfoToClient**

```
public synchronized void sendInfoToClient(String toClient,
                                          byte data[])
```

Send a byte stream to the specified client

Parameters:
> from - The reference to the message creator
> toClient - The messages "TO" address
> data - The data to send

Throws: RemoteException
> Thrown if a transport problem occurs

● **sendInfoToAll**

```
public synchronized void sendInfoToAll(byte data[])
```

Send a byte stream to all registered clients

Parameters:
> from - The reference to the message creator
> data - The data to send

Throws: RemoteException
> Thrown if a transport problem occurs

All Packages   Class Hierarchy   This Package   Previous   Next   Index

DBforME.Shared.CallbackInterface

```java
package DBforME.Shared;

import java.rmi.*;
import java.util.Vector;
import java.util.Properties;

/**
 * This interface defines callback hooks which the server can exploit to
 * transmit informaiton to the client<BR>
 * <BR>
 * Copyright (c)1997 My Company, Inc. All Rights Reserved.
 * @author Cary A. Jardin
 * @version 1.0
 *
 */
public interface CallbackInterface extends java.rmi.Remote {

    /**
     * Feeds the resultant data into the client
     * @param reqID              The request ID of the incoming data
     * @param data               The result data
     * @exception RemoteException    Thrown if a transport problem occurs
     */
    void resultData(int reqID, byte[] data) throws RemoteException;

    /**
     * Feed data sent from another client.
     * @param from  The name of the client from which the data originated
     * @param data   The message data
     * @exception RemoteException    Thrown if a transport problem occurs
     */
    void recvMessage(String from, byte[] data) throws RemoteException;

}
```

Figure 11.5

JavaDoc output for DBforME. Shared.Callback Interface.

All Packages   Class Hierarchy   This Package   Previous   Next   Index

Interface DBforME.Shared.CallbackInterface

public interface **CallbackInterface**
extends Remote

This interface defines callback hooks which the server can exploit to transmit informaiton to the client

Copyright (c)1997 My Company, Inc. All Rights Reserved.

Method Index

- **recvMessage**(String, byte[])
  Feed data sent from another client.
- **resultData**(int, byte[])
  Feeds the resultant data into the client

Methods

● **resultData**

```
public abstract void resultData(int reqID,
                                byte data[]) throws RemoteException
```

Feeds the resultant data into the client

Parameters:
reqID - The request ID of the incoming data
data - The result data
Throws: RemoteException
Thrown if a transport problem occurs

● **recvMessage**

```
public abstract void recvMessage(String from,
                                 byte data[]) throws RemoteException
```

Feed data sent from another client.

Parameters:
from - The name of the client from which the data originated
data - The message data
Throws: RemoteException
Thrown if a transport problem occurs

All Packages   Class Hierarchy   This Package   Previous   Next   Index

DBforME.Shared.DBAdminFrame

```java
package DBforME.Shared;

import java.awt.Frame;

/**
 * The DBAdminFrame is the base abstract class that must be used for
 * creating admin facilites.
 * <BR>
 * Copyright (c) 1997 My Company, Inc. All Rights Reserved.
 * @author Cary A. Jardin
 * @version 1.0
 *
 */
```

```
public abstract class DBAdminFrame extends Frame{

    /**
     * Upon constructing a new instance of the admin frame, this
     * method is called to inform the frame of its assoiciated
     * server host.
     * @param serverHostName        The host name of the origin server.
     */
    public abstract void setOrigin(String serverHostName);

}
```

Figure 11.6

JavaDoc output for DBforME. Shared. DBAdminFrame.

All Packages   Class Hierarchy   This Package   Previous   Next   Index

---

Class DBforME.Shared.DBAdminFrame

```
java.lang.Object
   |
   +----java.awt.Component
           |
           +----java.awt.Container
                   |
                   +----java.awt.Window
                           |
                           +----java.awt.Frame
                                   |
                                   +----DBforME.Shared.DBAdminFrame
```

---

public abstract class **DBAdminFrame**
extends Frame

The DBAdminFrame is the base abstract class that must be used for creating admin facilites.
Copyright (c) 1997 My Company, Inc. All Rights Reserved.

Constructor Index

• **DBAdminFrame**()

Method Index

• **setOrigin**(String)
  Upon constructing a new instance of the admin frame, this method is called to inform the frame of its assoiciated server host.

Constructors

● **DBAdminFrame**

```
public DBAdminFrame ()
```

Methods

● **setOrigin**

```
public abstract void setOrigin(String serverHostName)
```

Upon constructing a new instance of the admin frame, this method is called to inform the frame of its assoiciated server host.

Parameters:
serverHostName - The host name of the origin server.

All Packages   Class Hierarchy   This Package   Previous   Next   Index

DBforME.Shared.ServerInterface

```java
package DBforME.Shared;

import java.rmi.*;
import java.util.Properties;

/**
 * This interface defines the visible facilites provided to
 * client applications.<BR>
 * <BR>
 * Copyright (c)1997 My Company, Inc. All Rights Reserved.
 * @author Cary A. Jardin
 * @version 1.0
 *
 */
public interface ServerInterface extends java.rmi.Remote {

    /**
     * Remotely execute a stored procedure.
     * @param procName  The name of the stored procedure to
➥execute
     * @param params    The properties for the stored procedure
     * @param informMe  The client to whom the results should be
➥shipped to
     * @return   Returns the request ID value > 0 if successfull
➥execution,
     *                              otherwise -1
     * @exception RemoteException   Thrown if a transport problem
➥occurs
     */
    int execStoredProcedure(String procName, Properties params,
        CallbackInterface informMe) throws RemoteException;

    /**
     * Return a list of all registerd clients
     * @return                      Returns a list of all
➥registed clients
     * @exception RemoteException   Thrown if a transport problem
➥occurs
     */
    Properties getListOfClients() throws RemoteException;

    /**
     * Registers a new Client
     * @param Host                  Client Host Name
```

```
    * @param clientRef              A reference to the client
➥object
    * @exception RemoteException    Thrown if a transport problem
➥occurs
    */
   void registerClient(String Host,CallbackInterface clientRef)
     throws RemoteException;

   /**
    * Registers a new Client
    * @param clientRef              A reference to the client
➥object
    * @exception RemoteException    Thrown if a transport problem
➥occurs
    */
   void unRegisterClient(CallbackInterface clientRef)
➥throws RemoteException;

   /**
    * Returns a Class object defining the admin frame
    * @return                       Returns a Class def of the
➥Admin frame
    * @exception RemoteException    Thrown if a transport problem
➥occurs
    */
   Class getAdminFrame() throws RemoteException;

   /**
    * Send a byte stream to the specified client
    * @param from                   The reference to the message
➥creator
    * @param toClient               The messages "TO" address
    * @param data                   The data to send
    * @exception RemoteException    Thrown if a transport problem
➥occurs
    */
   void sendInfoToClient(CallbackInterface from, String
➥toClient,
     byte[] data) throws RemoteException;

   /**
    * Send a byte stream to all registered clients
    * @param from                   The reference to the message
➥creator
    * @param data                   The data to send
```

```
    * @exception RemoteException    Thrown if a transport problem
➡occurs
    */
    void sendInfoToAll(CallbackInterface from,
        byte[] data) throws RemoteException;
}
```

Figure 11.7

JavaDoc output for DBforME. Shared. ServerInterface.

All Packages   Class Hierarchy   This Package   Previous   Next   Index

Interface DBforME.Shared.ServerInterface

public interface **ServerInterface**
extends Remote

This interface defines the visible facilites provided to client applications.

Copyright (c)1997 My Company, Inc. All Rights Reserved.

Method Index

- **execStoredProcedure**(String, Properties, CallbackInterface)
  Remotely execute a stored procedure.
- **getAdminFrame**()
  Returns a Class object defining the admin frame
- **getListOfClients**()
  Return a list of all registerd clients
- **registerClient**(String, CallbackInterface)
  Registers a new Client
- **sendInfoToAll**(CallbackInterface, byte[])
  Send a byte stream to all registered clients
- **sendInfoToClient**(CallbackInterface, String, byte[])
  Send a byte stream to the specified client
- **unRegisterClient**(CallbackInterface)
  Registers a new Client

Methods

● **execStoredProcedure**

public abstract int execStoredProcedure (String procName,
                                         Properties params,
                                         CallbackInterface informMe) throws RemoteException

Remotely execute a stored procedure.

Parameters:
procName - The name of the stored procedure to execute
params - The properties for the stored procedure
informMe - The client to whom the results should be shipped to
Returns:
Returns the request ID value > 0 if successfull execution, otherwise -1
Throws: RemoteException
Thrown if a transport problem occurs

● **getListOfClients**

public abstract Properties getListOfClients() throws RemoteException

Return a list of all registerd clients

Returns:
Returns a list of all registed clients
Throws: RemoteException
Thrown if a transport problem occurs

● **registerClient**

```
public abstract void registerClient(String Host,
                                    CallbackInterface clientRef) throws RemoteException
```

Registers a new Client

Parameters:
Host - Client Host Name
clientRef - A reference to the client object
Throws: RemoteException
Thrown if a transport problem occurs

● **unRegisterClient**

```
public abstract void unRegisterClient(CallbackInterface clientRef) throws RemoteException
```

Registers a new Client

Parameters:
clientRef - A reference to the client object
Throws: RemoteException
Thrown if a transport problem occurs

● **getAdminFrame**

```
public abstract Class getAdminFrame() throws RemoteException
```

Returns a Class object defining the admin frame

Returns:
Returns a Class def of the Admin frame
Throws: RemoteException
Thrown if a transport problem occurs

● **sendInfoToClient**

```
public abstract void sendInfoToClient(CallbackInterface from,
                                      String toClient,
                                      byte data[]) throws RemoteException
```

Send a byte stream to the specified client

Parameters:
from - The reference to the message creator
toClient - The messages "TO" address
data - The data to send
Throws: RemoteException
Thrown if a transport problem occurs

● **sendInfoToAll**

```
public abstract void sendInfoToAll(CallbackInterface from,
                                   byte data[]) throws RemoteException
```

Send a byte stream to all registered clients

Parameters:
from - The reference to the message creator
data - The data to send
Throws: RemoteException
Thrown if a transport problem occurs

All Packages   Class Hierarchy   This Package   Previous   Next   Index

Where to Go From Here

Creating Java APIs is not a trivial task. The level of competency required to develop solid API architectures transcends simply programming with the language. This is not to say that knowing how to program Java is not a requirement for building the architecture for APIs. To the contrary, building solid Java API architectures mandates a firm background in Java development.

This chapter presented some general design and implementation procedures for creating optimized and efficient Java APIs. More importantly, this chapter brought you to a final step before becoming a Certified Java Developer. All that remains to round out your Java development knowledge is a survey of the Java technology suite presented in the next three chapters. After reading them, it's on to the examination.

12

JFC and Java
Media Kit

If you take a look at the progression of Java technology, the number of class libraries has grown exponentially, which makes sense. Originally, Java 1.02 provided the initial technology, and 1.1 delivered a full-fledged development platform to the extent that full featured 100% pure applications can be developed. This chapter focuses on two of the newest and most important sets of the enabling technologies: the Java Foundation Classes and Java Media Framework.

This chapter will provide the following resources for the Certified Java Developer Examination:

 Objectives

▶ Java Foundation Classes overview

▶ Java Media Kit overview

Note The Certified Developer Exam is much different than the Programmer Exam. To pass the Developer Exam you do not need to memorize facts, rather you need to understand broad concepts and show hands-on programming experience. For these reasons there are not any Test Yourself quizzes or end-of-chapter questions in this section of the book.

Java Foundation Classes

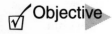

Objective Knowing the components of the Java Foundation Classes will aid in your application development, and help you pass the Sun Certified Java Developer programming exercise.

The AWT available with Java 1.02 did not measure up to the industry standard for GUI development. JDK 1.1 adopted a new event model in an effort to fix some of the ailments of the AWT. However, a new and more powerful GUI toolkit was just about to hit the scene. Beginning with AWT 1.1.4, the Java Foundation Classes (JFC) was shipped to provide a set of industrial-strength GUI development tools.

The JFC extends the original AWT facilities by providing a comprehensive set of GUI tool libraries. These libraries are comprised of completely portable tools, written 100% in Java unlike AWT, that relied on native GUI hooks for the screen presentation of an interface. The JFC employs a set of "lightweight components" which only use native calls to provide primitive drawing capabilities. The difference is in the look and flexibility. With the lightweight components, the GUI appears the same on any running platform.

The following section highlights the features of each of the JFC tool libraries. Additional information can be found at http://java.sun.com/products/jfc/.

Lightweight Components

Lightweight components directly equate to 100% pure Java GUI tools. That is, the traditional AWT components relied on the native platform for the presentation of GUI elements. For example, a button class, in the traditional AWT context, would be nothing more than a call to the native operating system to draw a button onto the canvas. A lightweight component does not utilize the native GUI components supplied by the platform. Rather, lightweight components draw themselves, using primitive platform-provided drawing facilities.

By drawing a button itself, a lightweight component is not bound to the look of the native platform. For example, MacOS GUIs have a different look and feel from Windows NT. By not relying on the underlying GUI facilities of the OS, the lightweight components can guarantee the look of a GUI component, regardless of OS.

The following is a list of provided lightweight GUI components. However, more are constantly being added. If you don't see something, visit http://java.sun.com/products/jfc/swingdoc-current/doc/index.html for more information.

▶ JButton	▶ JHTMLPane
▶ JCheckBox	▶ JInternalFrame
▶ JCheckBoxMenuItem	▶ JLabel
▶ JColorChooser	▶ JLayeredPane
▶ JComboBox	▶ JList
▶ JComponent	▶ JMenu
▶ JDesktopIcon	▶ JMenuBar
▶ JDesktopPane	▶ JMenuItem
▶ JDialog	▶ JOptionPane
▶ JDirectoryPane	▶ JPanel
▶ JFileChooser	▶ JPasswordField
▶ JFrame	▶ JPopupMenu

- ▶ JProgressBar
- ▶ JRadioButton
- ▶ JRadioButtonMenuItem
- ▶ JRootPane
- ▶ JScrollBar
- ▶ JScrollPane
- ▶ JSeparator
- ▶ JSlider
- ▶ JSplitPane
- ▶ JTabbedPane

- ▶ JTable
- ▶ JTextArea
- ▶ JTextField
- ▶ JTextPane
- ▶ JToggleButton
- ▶ JToolBar
- ▶ JToolTip
- ▶ JTree
- ▶ JViewport
- ▶ JWindow

Swing is Back!

It is almost impossible to talk about the JFC without talking about the Swing Set. All lightweight components were designed using the swing architecture, which essentially divides each component into three separate components. The first component holds the component state information, like that the button is pushed. The second is responsible for the presentation of the GUI component, with respect to the stored component state. Lastly, the third piece is responsible for dealing with user input. The combination of these pieces allows for a plugable GUI look and feel. Thus, the name Swing set, for you can swing between different GUI presentations on a variety of different platforms.

Increasing Accessibility

With the Swing set, the GUI look and feel can be changed at execution. This functionality not only provides the ability to morph a look and feel to blend with a native platform, but it also allows users to customize a GUI for their specific needs. Accessibility API provides a clean interface that allows assisting technologies to interact and communicate with the JFC components. Specifically, the Swing architecture allows for the GUI state, and GUI interaction, to be extrapolated from the GUI presentation. This provides the ability for existing interfaces to be useful to the physically challenged. With the Accessibility API, Java truly does provide a ubiquitously accessible technology suite.

2D API

The 2D API is the fruit of a joint development effort between Sun and Adobe Systems Inc. to provide display PostScript capability to Java. The Java 2D API extends the graphics and imaging classes defined by java.awt, while maintaining compatibility for existing programs. The Java 2D API enables developers to easily incorporate a two-dimensional imaging model for line art, text, and images that uniformly addresses color, spatial transformations, and compositing. With the Java 2D API, you use the same imaging model for both screen and print to provide a highly WYSIWYG (What You See Is What You Get) experience for the user.

Drag-and-Drop

Most commercial OS's are in the process of providing full Java support. This will provide Java application the capability to integrate directly with the native environment. However, if Java applications are to completely integrate with a native platform, it is crucial to support inter-application drag-and-drop.

Part of the post JDK 1.1 JavaBeans initiative, called the Glasgow specification, is to provide drag and drop between applications on a workstation's desktop. These facilities are achieved through libraries, and hooks found in the JFC. Beginning with JDK 1.2, full drag-and-drop support has been provided as a base tool for all 100% pure applications. In this way, Java GUIs can utilize the drag-and-drop facilities regardless of the execution platform

Java Media Kit

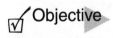 The Java Media Kit provides a few specialty pieces of functionality that are valuable to keep in mind during development and the Certified Developer Programming Exercise.

The Java Media and Communications APIs, also known as the Java Media Kit, contain a series of media-based tools. Specifically, the Java Media Kit was designed to provide a conglomeration of technologies to facilitate audio/video clips, animated presentations, 2D fonts, graphical display, images, 3D models, and telephony. By providing standard players and integrating these supporting technologies, the Java Media Kit enables developers to produce and distribute compelling, media-rich content.

The following section highlights the features of each of the Java Media Kit libraries. Additional information can be found at http://java.sun.com/products/jfc/.

Java 2D API

The 2D API is distributed as part of both JFC and the Java Media Kit. For a complete discussion, see "JFC and Java Media Kit," earlier in this chapter.

Java 3D API

The Java 3D API provides high-level facilities for the creation, manipulation, storage, and presentation of 3D geometry. The 3D API was jointly created by Intel Corporation, Silicon Graphics, Apple Computer, and Sun Microsystems to provide developers the capability to write stand-alone, three-dimensional graphics applications and Web-based 3D applets. The end result is a comprehensive model for the creation of entire 3D worlds.

Java Media Framework

The Java Media Framework (JMF) specifies a unified architecture, messaging protocol, and programming interface for media players, media capture, and conferencing. Video, audio, and various other media types can be played back, captured, and conference using the facilities found in the Java Media Framework

Java Sound

The Java Sound API provides a rich facility for the rendering and capturing of high quality audio. With full 32-channel capability, the Java Sound API is designed to bridge the gap between Java and the advanced sound facilities of most platforms.

Java Speech

The Java Speech API works in conjunction with the Java sound API to provide not only speech synthesizers, but also command/ control recognizers and dictation systems. These facilities can be broken down into the two primary regions of the Java Speech API: speech recognition and speech synthesis. Speech recognition is used to map spoken audio signals into text. Conversely, speech synthesis deals with the conversion of textual content into spoken audio signals. Together these two tools provide real-world capabilities to the Java Accessibility API and Java Telephony.

Java Telephony

The Java Telephony API, or JTAPI, provides a programmatic interface for the manipulation of computer telephony facilities. Every thing from making a call, to detailed call tracking and monitoring can be found in JTAPI. Using a layered object model, JTAPI calls for a pick and chooses the type of structure, with the available packages being the JTAPI Core, Call Control, Call Center, Call Media, Phone interface, and Capabilities. Through these facilities, the Java Telephony API is able to directly interface, monitor, and control existing and future computer telephony devices.

Where to Go From Here

The Java technology suit is large and growing. Knowing all of the tools in the proverbial Java technology tool-chest aids development. In this chapter, two new, key Java technologies were analyzed, JFC and the Java Media Kit. Keeping up-to-date with the latest Java technologies is the job of every Java developer, and a required skill for a Certified Java Developer.

Chapter 13

Enterprise Java, RMI, and JavaBeans

In the early days of Java, many believed Java to be synonymous with the Web. Since then, Java has grown into a full-fledged development environment. Java technologies have found a home in everything from embedded technologies to corporate applications. Specifically, the latest Java push has been in the enterprise space. With thin clients, scarce engineering resources, and a demand for more powerful applications, Java has provided a natural solution to enterprise applications.

The body of this chapter presents some key Java technologies that have paved the way for Java in the enterprise. At the minimum, a surface level knowledge of each presented technology is required for the Certified Developer Examination. These technologies are vast, and you are not expected to know every intricacy. However, you are expected to be aware of the technology and have the ability to utilize the technology to its greatest benefit.

This chapter will provide the following resources for the Certified Java Developer Examination:

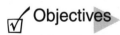 Objectives

- ▶ Java Management API overview

- ▶ JavaBeans overview

- ▶ Java Enterprise Beans overview

- ▶ Java Remote Method Invocation overview

Note

> The Certified Developer Exam is much different than the Programmer Exam. To pass the Developer Exam you do not need to memorize facts, rather you need to understand broad concepts and show hands-on programming experience. For these reasons there are not any Test Yourself quizzes or end-of-chapter questions in this section of the book.

JMAPI

Objective

The Java Management API provides the ability to create centrally administered interfaces for enterprise applications. This ability to facilitate such solutions is an invaluable skill for a Java developer, and an assumed talent found in a Certified Developer.

The Java Management API (JMAPI) is a newcomer to the Java technology suite. Simply put, JMAPI provides a common framework for the development of management interfaces. In an enterprise deployment with a router, Web server, DNS, database, and numerous other vital entities, management becomes confusing. If each entity has its own administration/management interface, the need for a interface manager becomes evident. JMAPI solves the multiple management interface dilemmas by providing a common, unifying management interface.

The following sections provide a brief description of the JMAPI facilities. Further information can be found at http://java.sun.com/products/JavaManagement/index.html.

Homogenizing Admin Interfaces

The JavaManagement API User Interface Style Guide contains specifications for developing JavaManagement API standard Java/Web-based user interfaces. Using any Java-enabled Web browser, administrators can troubleshoot and monitor network devices. Some of the JavaManagement API User Interface Style Guide components are listed below:

▶ Property book

▶ Page header

▶ Link label

▶ View configuration

An extension of the AWT (Abstract Windowing Toolkit), the Admin View Module (AVM) provides developers with user-interface components to create management type applications. The following lists some of the AVM components:

▶ Image button

▶ Multicolumn lists

▶ Scrolling windows and panels

▶ State button

▶ Toolbar

▶ Image canvas

▶ Convenience dialogs

▶ Busy tool

▶ Tables

▶ Hierarchy browser

▶ Charts, graphs, and meters

Base Object Interfaces

The Base Object Interfaces provide the facilities for modeling manageable units within an enterprise. Everything from routers to printers can be modeled with these interfaces, thus providing specific, manageable units. In this way JMAPI enabled interfaces can ubiquitously manage resources.

Managed Container Interfaces

JMAPI supports the notion of similar manageable units being grouped into a single, manageable container. The Managed Container Interfaces help the user perform more efficiently by modified shared properties of contained resources.

Managed Notification Interfaces

If something goes down, the JMAPI facility should know about it. For this reason, JMAPI provides the Managed Notification Interfaces to provide consistent event notification between managed objects or management applications. Using the Managed Notification Interfaces as a base, developers can create more complicated applications containing specific real-time event tacking and response behaviors.

Managed Protocol Interfaces

The Managed Protocol Interfaces facilitate management data transportation. These interfaces utilize standard Java IPC facilities, such as Sockets and RMI, to facilitate communication with various resources. In this way, various management protocols can be used in a management environment.

SNMP Interfaces

The Standard Network Management Protocol is by far the industry standard for the management of networkable resources. For this reason, the SNMP interfaces are standard with the JMAPI facility. This facility extends Managed Protocol Interfaces to provide interaction with SNMP-enabled Bas Objects.

Applet Integration Interfaces

By allowing integration between the JavaManagement API and a developer's Java applets, the Applet Integration Interfaces provide three integration levels. The developer may choose registered applets, management pages, or links.

JavaBeans

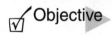 **Objective**   JavaBeans put the visual into Java visual development. Creating beans might not be on the plate for all Java developers, but it is a required skill for a Certified Developer.

Visual development optimizes programming efficiency by removing tedious development. JavaBeans is a format by which software components can be packaged into a single, visually accessible unit. That is, a JavaBean is an object that can be accessed from a visual development tool like Visual Café. JavaBeans is a packaging technology to standardize component architectures for visual development environments.

In the simplest case, a JavaBean is nothing more than an object in a ZIP file and a manifest file. This is not to say that bean development isn't complicated. Rather, as the following sections discuss, the complexity of a bean is a function of your presentation requirements. More information, and the complete Bean Development Kit (BDK) can be found at http://java.sun.com.

Visual Accessibility

In order for a visual development environment to take advantage of a custom component, the environment must first know how to *plug-in* the component. Visual development environments revolve around object properties, actions, and events. Therefore, plugging-in a component directly relates to finding out what properties, events, and actions are provided to the developer.

Things that are automatic are the epitome of simple. JavaBeans rely on the introspection capabilities of Java to provide an automatic mechanism for the presentation of an object's facilities. Beginning with JDK 1.1, a feature called introspection was shipped to provide object investigation facilities. With introspection, generic objects can be scanned for methods, fields, and constructors. In this way, the visual development environment can simply look at the bean and discover the object's events, actions, and properties. However, in order for the environment to decipher the object's facilities, the following naming and scope conventions must be adhered to.

- ▶ setX and getX pairs must be provided for all properties.

- ▶ isX must be used for boolean values.

- ▶ Bounded properties must throw PropertyVetoException.

- ▶ All publicly accessible methods not deemed to be associated with a property or event overhead are specified as actions.

- ▶ addX and removeX pairs must be provided for all thrown events.

The antitheses of automatic is manual. With introspection, Java-Bean developers have limited ability to specify the actions, events, and properties that will be presented to the visual development environment. As useful as automatic bean presentation is, it fails to provide commercial bean developers with the tools needed to create commercial-grade components. For this reason, JavaBeans provide the ability to override all or some of the default automatic presentation behaviors. In this way, beans can be developed in three different difficulty levels.

- ▶ Simple   Allowing the bean to automatically present its own interface

- ▶ Hard   Defining the entire bean interface presentation

- ▶ In Between   Using the default automatic presentation bean behavior and override behaviors as desired

Packaging

The packaging of a JavaBean is simple; zip(*Classes* + *Manifest*) = .jar. That is, once you have created all the class files that comprise the bean, use the jar command line tool to create the bean's .jar file. Or, you can use your favorite zip package to zip up the files and manually create the manifest file.

Enterprise JavaBeans

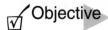 **Objective**

Enterprise JavaBeans rounds out the Java Enterprise technology suite. Knowledge of how to create enterprise beans is not a required skill for a Certified Developer, but knowing about them is.

As Java ages to maturity, the ubiquity pushes its way into enterprise applications. The Enterprise JavaBeans initiative provides an API optimized for building scaleable business applications as reusable server components. With Enterprise JavaBeans, developers can design and re-use small program elements to build powerful corporate applications. These "componentized" applications can run manufacturing, financial, inventory management, and data processing on any system or platform that is Java-enabled. Enterprise JavaBeans is an emerging standard, but nevertheless a technology that will unify the piecemeal enterprise environment.

RMI

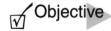 **Objective**

RMI is the only way to go from Java to Java communication. For this reason, it is a required skill for a Certified Developer.

Java's Remote Method Invocation (RMI) facility has been around since pre JDK 1.02. However, RMI did not fully grow into its shoes until JDK 1.1, due to object serialization support. Today, RMI is a functional, stable, immensely useful, and sadistically fun tool of the Java technology suite.

RMI uses TCP/IP sockets to communicate between JVMs. But from a developer standpoint, that fact is not evident. Chapter 10, "Network Programming," takes a complete look at the RMI technology, and its unsurpassed functionality in facilitating Java-to-Java communications.

Chapter 14

Additional Java Technologies

As the last two chapters illustrated, the Java technology suite is vast. Even the harshest skeptics of the Java movement, cannot devalue the pure development potential contained in the Java Development Kit. From object serialization to 3D graphics API, the JDK contains something for everyone. However, Java development isn't just about utilizing a rich embodiment of technology. The Java development craze has always been, and always will be, fueled by a strong and unified development culture.

The body of this chapter presents some key Java technologies and initiatives that embody the Java development culture. At the minimum, a surface level knowledge of each presented technology is required for the Certified Developer Examination. These technologies are vast, and you are not expected to know every intricacy. However, you are expected to be aware of the technologies and have the ability to justify your program design.

This chapter will provide the following resources for the Certified Java Developer Examination:

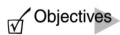 Objectives

- ▶ 100% Pure Java Development Overview

- ▶ Java Object Serialization Overview

- ▶ Java Database Connectivity Overview

- ▶ Java Electronic Commerce Framework (JECF) Overview

- ▶ Java IDL Overview

- ▶ Java Naming and Directory Interface (JNDI) Overview

Note

The Certified Developer Exam is much different than the Programmer Exam. To pass the Developer Exam you do not need to memorize facts, rather you need to understand broad concepts and show hands-on programming experience. For these reasons there are not any Test Yourself quizzes or end-of-chapter questions in this section of the book.

100% Pure Java Development

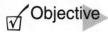Objective

100% Pure Java Development produces a "Write Once, Run Anywhere" application that assures everyone involved the product's portability and cross-platform compatibility.

100% Pure Java assures developers, customers, and end users that Java programs are portable. When buyers see the 100% Pure Java logo, they are seeing a guarantee for cross-platform compatibility. Besides the 100% Pure Java logo, the "Write Once, Run Anywhere" capability has several advantages. It decreases product development cycles, saves time and money, streamlines software development, and condenses delivery.

100% Pure Java applications *do not* contain or use the following:

- ▶ Native methods

- ▶ External dependencies (excluding external dependencies from the Core Java API)

- ▶ An undocumented part of a Java implementation

- ▶ "Tunnel" methods

- ▶ Hardwired platform constants

Getting an Application 100% Pure Java Certified

In order to facilitate 100% Pure Java certification, you need to know how much it will cost, when to start the certification process, and the steps involved in becoming certified.

100% Pure Java Certification Cost

In order to certify a product as 100% Pure Java, a small certification fee must be paid. The certification fee is low in comparison to the great benefits associated with having a 100% Pure Java product. Refer to the section titled "100% Pure Java Initiative," later in this chapter, to see why paying for the certification is worth every penny.

The initial product's certification costs $1000, and there are discounts for certifying multiple products. Re-certification, which costs $500 and excludes product maintenance releases, should be done for new features or functionality revisions.

100% Pure Java Certification Timing

As the old saying goes "Timing is everything." Being prepared and planning for certification will benefit you when you try to get your product 100% Pure Java certified. In the beginning of the Quality Assurance process, use JavaPureCheck to prepare for certification. The pure check is a Java supplied tool to test an application for non-%100 pure code. Any non pure code will be presented as a warning to aid in %100 pure certification.

Once the product has passed the JavaPureCheck facility, begin the certification process after the product's functionality is complete. If all is good with the JavaPureCheck, KeyLabs needs a maximum of one week to finish the 100% Pure Java certification.

100% Pure Java Certification Checklist

Follow the checklist below to get an application 100% Pure Java Certified. Refer to the URLs to guide you through each step.

1. Download and go over the 100% Pure Java Cookbook at http://www.suntest.com/100percent/cookbook.html.

2. Register product(s) for certification at KeyLabs at http://www.keylabs.com/100percent/.

3. Download the Certification Package at http://www.suntest.com/100percent/cert-guide.html.

4. Study the 100% Pure Java Certification Guide at http://www.suntest.com/100percent/cert-guide.html.

5. Run JavaPureCheck on the code and provide explanations at http://www.suntest.com/100percent/tools.html#jpc.

6. Create automated scripts for dynamic check and measure method coverage.

7. Build the Verification Package and submit to KeyLabs at http://www.keylabs.com/100percent/.

100% Pure Java Initiative

The 100% Pure Java Initiative is an industry-wide campaign to help software developers create, test, certify, market and sell 100% Pure Java applications.

The 100% Pure Java Initiative is supported by Sun, Apple, IBM, Novell, Netscape, and Oracle. Besides the large corporation support, getting an application certified has several marketing advantages, which are listed below.

▶ Use of the 100% Pure Java logo

▶ Event co-marketing

▶ Channel marketing

▶ Special advertising packages

▶ Direct access to a 100% Pure Java representative at Sun

▶ Inclusion in case studies

▶ Showcased in Java Partners Pavilions like JavaOne and Java Internet Business Expo

▶ Offered membership to Sun's Java Select Program

▶ Discount advertising with Ziff-Davis

▶ 100% Pure Java Hall of Fame

100% Pure Java Certified Applications

The number of 100% Pure Java applications is reaching 100. The following lists some of the companies with 100% Pure Java certified applications. For the latest updates on new 100% Pure Java certified applications check out http://java.sun.com/100percent/latestlist.html.

- ▶ Adaptivity   http://www.adaptivity.com/

- ▶ A-Frame Software Co., Inc.   http://www.a-frame.com/

- ▶ Agile Software   http://www.agilesoft.com/

- ▶ Applix, Inc.   http://www.applix.com/

- ▶ bidnask.com   http://www.bidnask.com/

- ▶ Bluestone Software, Inc.   http://www.bluestone.com/

- ▶ CBT Systems   http://www.cbtsys.com/

- ▶ Cereus Design   http://www.cereus7.com/HotTEA5.shtml

- ▶ Clearview Consulting, Inc.   http://www.clearvw.com/

- ▶ Corel, Inc.   http://www.corel.com/

- ▶ Digital Knowledge Assets   http://www.dkaweb.com/

- ▶ Equis International   http://www.equis.com/

- ▶ HOME Account Network, Inc.   http://www.homeaccount.com/

- ▶ IBM   http://www.ibm.com/

- ▶ I.digm   http://www.idigm.co.kr/

- ▶ ImaginOn, Inc.   http://www.imaginon.com/

- ▶ Infoscape, Inc.   http://www.infoscape.com/

- ▶ Infospace, Inc.   http://www.infospace-inc.com/

- ▶ Innotech Multimedia   http://www.netresults-search.com/

- Inso Corporation   http://www.inso.com/

- Interleaf, Inc.   http://www.interleaf.com/

- InterNetivity, Inc.   http://www.internetivity.com/

- IntraWeb Information Technologies   http://www.intraweb.de/

- InXight Software, Inc.   http://www.inxight.com/enter.htm

- ION Web Products, Inc.   http://www.ionsystems.com/

- i-Planet, Inc.   http://www.i-planet.com/

- IQ Net Corp   http://www.iqc.com/

- IQ Software   http://www.iqsoftware.com/

- Jstream   http://www.jstream.com/front.html

- Live Picture, Inc.   http://www.livepicture.com/

- Mark Watson Associates   http://www.markwatson.com/

- Maximum Computer Technologies, Inc.   http://www.maxtech.com/

- MerzCom   http://www.merzcom.com/

- Modultek Oy   http://www.modultek.com/PUBGUEST/owa/MST.MT_WWW_MAIN.MT_MAIN_PAGE?sLang=

- NEON, Inc.   http://www.neonsoft.com/

- NetAccent, Inc.   http://www.netaccent.com/

- NetFactory, Inc.   http://www.netcharts.com/

- Netmosphere   http://www.netmosphere.com/

- Netscape Communications Corporation   http://www.netscape.com/

- Novell Inc.   http://www.novell.com/

- Object Design, Inc.   http://www.odi.com/

- ▶ OpenConnect Systems   http://www.openconnect.com/

- ▶ Open Horizon   http://www.openhorizon.com/

- ▶ Optimus Solutions Pty Limited   http://www.magna.com.au/~optimus/

- ▶ Oracle   http://www.oracle.com/

- ▶ Persoft, Inc.   http://www.persoft.com/

- ▶ PHD—Professional Help Desk   http://www.PHD.com/

- ▶ Sanga International   http://www.sangacorp.com/

- ▶ Seagate Software   http://www.seagatesoftware.com/

- ▶ SensiView Corporation   http://www.sensiView.com/

- ▶ SoftPlus, Inc.   http://www.softplus.com/

- ▶ Software Builders International   http://www.softwarebuilders.com/

- ▶ Solid Information Technology Ltd   http://www.solidtech.com

- ▶ SQRIBE Technologies   http://www.sqribe.com/

- ▶ Sun Microsystems, Inc.   http://www.sun.com/

- ▶ Sybase, Inc.   http://www.sybase.com/

- ▶ Tendril Software, Inc.   http://www.tendril.com/tendril.html

- ▶ TRADE'ex Electronic Commerce Systems, Inc.   http://www.tradeex.com/

- ▶ U&I Interactive Software, Inc.   http://www.uandi.com/

- ▶ UniKix Technologies, Inc.   http://www.unikix.com/

- ▶ Verimation   http://www.verimation.se/

- ▶ Visualize, Inc.   http://www.visualizetech.com/

▶ Visual Numerics, Inc.   http://www.vni.com/index_hi.html

▶ Volano   http://www.volano.com/

▶ WebMan Technologies, Inc.   http://www.timecruiser.com/

▶ Wyatt River Software   http://www.wyattriver.com/

Java Object Serialization

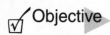 Object Serialization allows for based Java objects to be represented as a stream of bytes that can be later used to reconstitute equivalent objects.

Java is a truly object-oriented language. However, devices such as drives and network interfaces only understand the harsh reality of byte streams. For this reason, Java Object Serialization extends the core Java Input and Output classes to inter-operate with primitive computing devices. By encoding objects into a stream of bytes, Object Serialization supports the ability to read and write entire object hierarchies from a byte stream. This encoding is achieved by requiring each class to map its own statefull information into a byte array representation. In this way, facilities like RMI can transport and reconstitute objects across different virtual machines. For more information on Object Serialization and RMI check out http://java.sun.com/products/jdk/rmi/index.html.

Java Database Connectivity

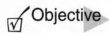 Java Database Connectivity (JDBC) furnishes programmers a standard interface to relational databases, and provides a familiar foundation for the building of higher-level tools and interfaces.

The JDBC API defines Java classes that represent database connections, SQL statements, result sets, database metadata, and so on. As the primary API for database access in Java, JDBC allows programmers to issue SQL statements and process the results.

To support multiple drivers connecting to different databases, the JDBC API is equipped with a driver manager. If JDBC drivers are written 100% in Java, they can be downloaded as part of an applet. If JDBC drivers are not written 100% in Java, they can use native methods to bridge to database access libraries, and will hinder the 100% pure certification process.

Java Electronic Commerce Framework (JECF)

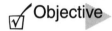 Objective

The JECF is a structured architecture for the development of Java electronic commerce applications.

Reducing developers' time and effort building electronic commerce applications, JECF is JavaSoft's architecture for supporting electronic commerce business transactions. The Java Electronic Commerce Framework is an extension to the core Java platform. Download the latest release of the Java Electronic Commerce Framework at http://java.sun.com/products/commerce/download.html.

Java Commerce APIs

Implementing basic services within the Java Electronic Commerce Framework, the Java Commerce APIs provide foundation services. The Java Commerce APIs allow developers to easily create new electronic commerce applications. The following lists what is allowed by the Java Commerce API classes.

▶ Easy, secure downloading and installation of cassettes

▶ Secure storage of private end-user information

▶ Rapid development of secure payment mechanisms

Tools

To help developers build sophisticated financial applications using the Java Developers Kit, The Java Electronic Commerce Framework provides tools using the Java Commerce APIs. The following tools let developers quickly and easily build electronic commerce applications.

> ▶ Java Wallet   User interface for on-line purchasing and other financial transactions

> ▶ Java Cassettes   Implements specific on-line transaction protocols such as credit card payments or electronic checks

> ▶ The Java Shopping Cart   Applet that can store a customer's selected items before completing an on- line purchase

Internal and Internet Use

By combining the tools listed previously, Java Commerce APIs, and the JDK, applications can be built for both internal corporate use and open systems like the Internet. However, by the nature of the Java Commerce APIs, all processing and security facilities must be supplied by third parties. That is, the Java Commerce APIs only provides a framework for developers to plug-in credit processing and secure transport facilities. Companies like Veriphone and RSA provide such facilities, that must be obtained separate from the Java Commerce APIs. In general, the Java Commerce APIs provide a framework for the development of following.

> ▶ Secure systems

> ▶ Flexible applications

> ▶ Applications can run universally

> ▶ Applications can be safely downloaded to any computer desktop over any network from a central server

Java IDL

The Java IDL provides interoperability with the industry standard for heterogeneous computing, CORBA.

As part of JavaSoft's platform APIs, Java IDL provides standards-based interoperability and connectivity with CORBA (Common Object Request Broker Architecture). CORBA is the open industry standard for heterogeneous computing. Java IDL allows Java to utilize the facilities of business/enterprise solutions written for a variety of different languages and platforms. Java IDL includes an IDL-to-Java compiler and a lightweight ORB that supports IIOP. For more information check out http://java.sun.com/products/jdk/idl/index.html.

Java Naming and Directory Interface (JNDI)

 Objective

The JNDI provides uniform, industry-standard, seamless connectivity from the Java platform to business information assets.

As a new addition to JavaSoft's platform APIs, JNDI allows developers to deliver Java applications with unified access to multiple naming and directory services across the enterprise. JNDI enables Java application to utilize the various enterprise naming and directory services. Because JNDI is part of the Java Enterprise API set, Java developers can create powerful and portable directory-enabled applications using this industry-standard interface. For more information on JNDI check out http://java.sun.com/products/jndi/index.html.

Where to Go From Here

The last three chapters hold only a glimpse of the entire Java technology offering. In the early days, Java developers could boast complete knowledge of all packages in the JDK, but those days are long gone. The technology found in the JDK is massive, and no one person is expected to have intimate knowledge of its contents. Nevertheless, Certified Java Developers are expected to be up to date with all Java technology offerings. Familiar, not to the extent of object or package familiarity, but rather familiar from a technological standpoint. This chapter, and the two prior to this, provide a snapshot of all key Java technologies to provide specific testable knowledge. However, before you proceed to the testing phase, take an hour and cruise around the JavaSoft Website (java.sun.com). Nothing is fresher than the source.

Chapter 15

Certified Developer Practice Test # 1

The Certified Java Developer examination covers far less ground than the Certified Java Programmer exam. The Certified Programmer exam must test language proficiency. The Certified Developer exam can assume language proficiency, and thus focuses on a handful of key Java development issues. A programmer writes code, which is why the Certified Programmer exam focuses on core Java language and runtime knowledge. On the other side of the coin, a Certified Developer is expected to possess the knowledge required to code an application, as well as the skills needed to design a reusable, extensible, and cost-effective implementation.

Both the Java Programmer and Java Developer certifications require a written examination, but only the Certified Developer requires you to prove Java mastery through an actual programming exercise. Ranging in complexity from a simple GUI exercise to a complex thread scheduling exercise, the assigned programming exercise tests the entire spectrum of Java technology knowledge. This chapter presents a practice programming exercise and examination to provide a final checkpoint before sitting for the Certified Developer Examination.

This chapter will provide the following resources for the Certified Java Developer Examination.

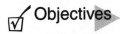 Objectives

- ▶ Study Guide and Checklist

- ▶ Practice Programming Exercise

- ▶ Practice Written Examination

- ▶ Solutions to the Programming Exercise and Written Examination

Countdown to Certification

With Chapters 10 through 14 behind you, you are ready to start thinking about sitting for the exam. For many, the idea of sitting for any exam instills an element of fear. But, at this stage in the game you are ready; it's just a question whether you are mentally ready.

The following sections set the stage for taking the Certified Developer Examination. When reading these sections, begin to mentally prepare yourself for what you can expect from the exam. Above all, relax.

The Programming Exercise

The first part of the Certified Developer Examination is a programming assignment. As the name implies, the programming assignment is to test your actual programming and development skills in a performance-based test. In this way, an assessment of your overall programming ability and style can be assessed. Remember, for a Certified Developer it is not enough to code a program. A Certified Developer engineers solutions.

Once you have contacted Sun Education, as described in Appendix A, and paid your money, the programming exercise can be obtained from http://www.sun.com/service/suned/cert/scjd_11.html. That's right, the programming exercise is a take-home test. Develop the solution however you like, with whatever you like, just make it clean and abide by all Java stylistic conventions.

The Written Exam

After you have completed the programming exercise, you can sit for the written portion. The Sun Certified Java Developer written examination is taken in the same manner as the Sun Certified Java Programmer examination. That is, you contact your local Sun Educational Services Office to purchase a voucher. After the voucher has been purchased, contact your local Sylvan Authorized Prometric Testing Center and register for the examination. However, unlike the Certified Programmer examination, the Developer examination takes four weeks to grade by a third party assessor.

Preparation Check-Off List

The following provides a checklist of topics that are covered in the Developer Certification exam. You should be comfortable with each of the topics found in the list, and ready to answer specific questions on each. Glance over the list both before you take the provided practice exam and before you sit for the actual test. This will get your Java gears turning, and put you in the proper mind-set to successfully complete the exam.

 Note

Forming a final checklist for Developer Certification will greatly aid exam preparation.

Developer Certification Exam Study Check-List:

▶ UDP Datagrams to facilitate IPC

▶ TCP/IP Sockets

▶ RMI-based IPC

▶ Object Serialization

▶ JFC and the Swing Set

▶ JavaBeans

▶ Enterprise Beans

▶ General Java Programmatic Style

▶ Proper Partitioning of a Problem

▶ JavaDoc Documentation

▶ Java Optimization

If you traversed the list with only a slight level of uncertainty, go ahead and dive into the practice programming exercise. On the other hand, if you are now questing your total Java knowledge, take some time and revisit the topics you are not quite sure of, and then take the test. As you can see, the test covers some advanced Java features and requires a fairly high level of knowledge.

Very few Java programmers could go through the above list and feel certain about each and every topic. Don't feel bad if you find yourself at a loss; it is a common feeling.

Practice Programming Exercise and Written Justification

The programming exercise is a test of your development and programming ability. The following sections provide a sample programming exercise and written exam, which mimics the actual Certified Java Developer Examination. Feel free to use external references when developing the programming exercise. However, you are on your own in the written sections.

One last note before you begin, the presented practice programming exercise does not go into GUI development. However, be prepared to create a GUI to harness the required functionality using AWT, and always write 100% pure code (see Chapter 14, "Additional Java Technologies").

 Note The requirements portion of the programming exercise forms the basis for what you are expected to implement.

The Original Requirements

An existing database server needs to be exposed to external applications. However, marketing wants this to be cool, and cool equates to the following requirements.

▶ All database stored procedures must be made callable.

▶ Data returned to the application should employ server push technology.

▶ The administration interface is going to be changing with every strong breeze. Therefore, the client applications will need to get the admin GUI from the server as needed.

▶ All clients should know about one another.

> ▶ Clients should have the ability to communicate with one another.

> ▶ Provide a Multi-Threaded API.

As you can see, these requirements depict actual marketing requirements, vague and "buzzy." However, these requirements are specific enough to derive the architecture shown in Figure 15.1.

FIG. 15.1

RMI Solution Architectural Diagram.

RMI Solution Package Diagram

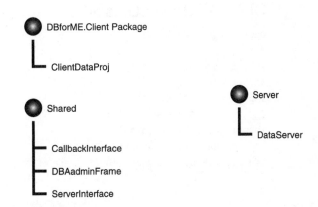

The New Requirements

After presenting an implementation of the stated requirements, marketing countered with the following list of requirement modifications.

> ▶ The server should keep a heart-beat with each client.

> ▶ Clients should have the ability to be informed of a client death.

> ▶ Once a client has died, all outstanding processes should be rolled back.

> ▶ Since some GUI's are implemented as an applet, a persistent object store is needed. That is, using object serialization provides each registered client the ability to store and retrieve objects.

▶ CPU space on the client is limited. Therefore, provide the facility for clients to remotely execute an object.

▶ Upon the completion of an executed client object, ship the object back to the client.

The following code presents the work done thus far on the project. All methods stating NYI (Not Yet Implemented) or "Something HERE" should be left as is.

DBforME.Server.DataServer

```
package DBforME.Server;

import DBforME.Shared.*;
import java.rmi.*;
import java.rmi.server.*;
import java.rmi.registry.*;
import java.util.Hashtable;
import java.util.Properties;
import java.util.Enumeration;

/**
 * The DataServer provides an RMI server for the execution of
➥stored
 * procedures,
 * and facilitates inter client communications.
 * <BR>
 * Copyright (c) 1997 My Company, Inc. All Rights Reserved.
 * @author Cary A. Jardin
 * @version 1.0
 *
 */
public class DataServer extends UnicastRemoteObject
implements ServerInterface{

    private Hashtable Clients   = new Hashtable(10);
    //The Name to associate with the remote object.
    private static String Name = "//:6789/DBforME.DataServer";
    //The port to bind the RMI registry
    private static int port =  6789;

    public DataServer() throws RemoteException{}
```

```
//Methods - Remote Services
    /**
    * Remotely execute a stored procedure.
    * @param procName    The name of the stored procedure to
➥execute
    * @param params      The properties for the stored procedure
    * @param informMe  The client to whom the results should be
➥shipped to
    * @return   Returns the request ID value > 0 if successful
➥execution,
    *                                otherwise -1
    * @exception RemoteException   Thrown if a transport problem
➥occurs
    */
    public int execStoredProcedure(String procName, Properties
➥params,
       CallbackInterface informMe){
         //Code HERE!
         return 0;
    }


    /**
    * Return a list of all registered clients
    * @return                    Returns a list of all
➥register clients
    * @exception RemoteException   Thrown if a transport problem
➥occurs
    */
    public Properties getListOfClients(){
        return null;
    }


    /**
    * Returns a Class object defining the admin frame
    * @return                    Returns a Class def of the
➥Admin frame
    * @exception RemoteException   Thrown if a transport problem
➥occurs
    */
    public Class getAdminFrame(){
        return null;
    }


    /**
```

```
     * Send a byte stream to the specified client
     * @param from                  The reference to the message
➥creator
     * @param toClient              The messages "TO" address
     * @param data                  The data to send
     * @exception RemoteException   Thrown if a transport problem
➥occurs
     */
    public void sendInfoToClient(CallbackInterface from, String
➥toClient,
        byte[] data){
        CallbackInterface tmp;

        for(Enumeration e = Clients.keys();e.hasMoreElements();){
            tmp = (CallbackInterface)e.nextElement();
            if(toClient.equals((String)Clients.get(tmp))){
                try{
                    tmp.recvMessage((String)Clients.get(from),data);
                }
                catch(Exception ex){
                    System.out.println("DataServer.sendInfoToClient"
+
                      " I think its DEAD " + ex);
                      unRegisterClient(tmp);
                }
                finally{
                    return;
                }
            }
        }
    }

    /**
     * Send a byte stream to all registered clients
     * @param from                  The reference to the message
➥creator
     * @param data                  The data to send
     * @exception RemoteException   Thrown if a transport problem
➥occurs
     */
    public void sendInfoToAll(CallbackInterface from, byte[]
➥data){
        CallbackInterface tmp;
```

```
            for(Enumeration e = Clients.keys();e.hasMoreElements();){
                tmp = (CallbackInterface)e.nextElement();
                try{
                    tmp.recvMessage((String)Clients.get(from),data);
                }
                catch(Exception ex){
                    System.out.println("DataServer.sendInfoToClient"+
                    " I think its DEAD " + ex);
                    unRegisterClient(tmp);
                }
            }
        }

//Methods - Remote Listener Reg
    /**
     * Registers a new Client
     * @param Host              Client Host Name
     * @param clientRef         A reference to the client
➥object
     * @exception RemoteException   Thrown if a transport problem
➥occurs
     */
    public void registerClient(String Host,CallbackInterface
➥clientRef){
        Clients.put(clientRef,Host);
    }

//Methods - Remote Listener UnReg

    /**
     * Registers a new Client
     * @param clientRef         A reference to the client
➥object
     * @exception RemoteException   Thrown if a transport problem
➥occurs
     */
    public void unRegisterClient(CallbackInterface clientRef){
        Clients.remove(clientRef);
    }

    /**
     * Start up the stock server; also creates a registry so that
➥the
     * DataServer can lookup the server.
```

```
        */
    public static void main(String args[]){

    System.setSecurityManager(new RMISecurityManager());
    try {
        LocateRegistry.createRegistry(port);
        System.out.println("DataServer.main: creating server");
        DataServer server = new DataServer();
        Naming.rebind(Name, server);
        System.out.println("DataServer.main: done");
    }
    catch (Exception e) {
        System.out.println("DataServer.main: an exception
➥occurred: "
                + e.getMessage());
        e.printStackTrace();
    }
    }
}
```

DBforME.Client.ClientDataProj

```
package DBforME.Client;

import java.rmi.*;
import DBforME.Shared.*;
import java.rmi.server.*;
import java.util.Hashtable;
import java.util.Properties;
import java.net.InetAddress;

/**
 * The DataServer provides an RMI server for the execution
 * of stored procedures,
 * and facilitates inter client communications.
 * <BR>
 * Copyright (c) 1997 My Company, Inc. All Rights Reserved.
 * @author Cary A. Jardin
 * @version 1.0
 *
 */
public class ClientDataProj extends UnicastRemoteObject
    implements CallbackInterface{
```

```
    private static String Name = "//france:6789/
➥DBforME.DataServer";
    private ServerInterface remoteServer = null;

    public ClientDataProj() throws RemoteException{
        //Export this Reference to receive callbacks
         UnicastRemoteObject.exportObject(this);

        //Retrieve remote object
        try{
            remoteServer = (ServerInterface)Naming.lookup(Name);
            remoteServer.registerClient(
                InetAddress.getLocalHost().getHostName(),this);
        }
        catch(Exception e){
            //Throw an exception if an URL has a problem
            throw new RemoteException();
        }
    }

    public void finalize(){
        if(remoteServer != null)
            try{
                remoteServer.unRegisterClient(this);
            }
            catch(Exception e){}
    }

    public synchronized byte[] getResultData(int reqID){
        //Something HERE!
        return null;
    }

    /**
     * Called remotely to feed resultant data into the client. Do
➥NOT call!
     * @param reqID           The request ID of the
➥incoming data
     * @param data            The result data
     * @exception RemoteException   Thrown if a transport problem
➥occurs
     */
    public synchronized void resultData(int reqID, byte[] data){
        //Something HERE!
    }
```

```
    /**
     * Called remotely to feed data sent from another client. Do
➥NOT Call
     * @param from  The name of the client from which the data
➥originated
     * @param data  The message data
     * @exception RemoteException   Thrown if a transport problem
➥occurs
     */
    public synchronized void recvMessage(String from, byte[]
➥data){
        //Something HERE!
    }


//Methods - Remote Services
    /**
     * Remotely execute a stored procedure.
     * @param procName  The name of the stored procedure to
➥execute
     * @param params    The properties for the stored procedure
     * @return   Returns the request ID value > 0 if successful
➥execution,
     *                                  otherwise -1
     * @exception RemoteException   Thrown if a transport problem
➥occurs
     */
    public synchronized int execStoredProcedure(String procName,
      Properties params){

        if(remoteServer == null)
            return -1;

        try{
            return remoteServer.execStoredProcedure(procName,
➥params,
                this);
        }
        catch(Exception e){
            return -1;
        }
    }

    /**
     * Return a list of all registered clients
     * @return                        Returns a list of all
```

```
➥register clients,
     *                                  or null if a problem
     * @exception RemoteException    Thrown if a transport problem
➥occurs
     */
    public synchronized Properties getListOfClients(){

        if(remoteServer == null)
            return null;

        try{
            return remoteServer.getListOfClients();
        }
        catch(Exception e){
            return null;
        }
    }

    /**
     * Returns a Class object defining the admin frame
     * @return                         Returns a Class def of
     *                                 the Admin frame, or null if a
➥problem
     * @exception RemoteException    Thrown if a transport problem
➥occurs
     */
    public synchronized DBAdminFrame getAdminFrame(){

        if(remoteServer == null)
            return null;

        try{
            return (DBAdminFrame)(
                    remoteServer.getAdminFrame().newInstance());
        }
        catch(Exception e){
            return null;
        }
    }

    /**
     * Send a byte stream to the specified client
     * @param from                    The reference to the message
➥creator
     * @param toClient                The messages "TO" address
```

```
     * @param data                  The data to send
     * @exception RemoteException    Thrown if a transport problem
➥occurs
     */
    public synchronized void sendInfoToClient(String
➥toClient,byte[] data){

        if(remoteServer == null)
            return;

        try{
            remoteServer.sendInfoToClient(this,toClient,data);
        }
        catch(Exception e){
        }

        return;
    }

    /**
     * Send a byte stream to all registered clients
     * @param from                   The reference to the message
➥creator
     * @param data                   The data to send
     * @exception RemoteException    Thrown if a transport problem
➥occurs
     */
    public synchronized void sendInfoToAll(byte[] data){

        if(remoteServer == null)
            return;

        try{
            remoteServer.sendInfoToAll(this,data);
        }
        catch(Exception e){
        }

        return;
    }

}
```

DBforME.Shared.CallbackInterface

```java
package DBforME.Shared;

import java.rmi.*;
import java.util.Vector;
import java.util.Properties;

/**
 * This interface defines callback hooks which the server can
➥exploit to
 * transmit information to the client<BR>
 * <BR>
 * Copyright (c)1997 My Company, Inc. All Rights Reserved.
 * @author Cary A. Jardin
 * @version 1.0
 *
 */
public interface CallbackInterface extends java.rmi.Remote {

    /**
     * Feeds the resultant data into the client
     * @param reqID              The request ID of the
➥incoming data
     * @param data               The result data
     * @exception RemoteException   Thrown if a transport problem
➥occurs
     */
    void resultData(int reqID, byte[] data) throws
➥RemoteException;

    /**
     * Feed data sent from another client.
     * @param from     The name of the client from which the data
➥originated
     * @param data     The message data
     * @exception RemoteException    Thrown if a transport problem
➥occurs
     */
    void recvMessage(String from, byte[] data) throws
➥RemoteException;

}
```

DBforME.Shared.DBAdminFrame

```
package DBforME.Shared;

import java.awt.Frame;

/**
 * The DBAdminFrame is the base abstract class that must be used
➥for
 * creating admin facilities.
 * <BR>
 * Copyright (c) 1997 My Company, Inc. All Rights Reserved.
 * @author Cary A. Jardin
 * @version 1.0
 *
 */
public abstract class DBAdminFrame extends Frame{

    /**
     * Upon constructing a new instance of the admin frame, this
     * method is called to inform the frame of its associated
     * server host.
     * @param serverHostName        The host name of the origin
server.
     */
    public abstract void setOrigin(String serverHostName);
}
```

DBforME.Shared.ServerInterface

```
package DBforME.Shared;

import java.rmi.*;
import java.util.Properties;

/**
 * This interface defines the visible facilities provided
 * to client applications.<BR>
 * <BR>
 * Copyright (c)1997 My Company, Inc. All Rights Reserved.
 * @author Cary A. Jardin
 * @version 1.0
 *
 */
public interface ServerInterface extends java.rmi.Remote {
```

```
    /**
     * Remotely execute a stored procedure.
     * @param procName  The name of the stored procedure to
➥execute
     * @param params    The properties for the stored procedure
     * @param informMe  The client to whom the results should be
➥shipped to
     * @return  Returns the request ID value > 0 if successful
➥execution,
     *                              otherwise -1
     * @exception RemoteException   Thrown if a transport problem
➥occurs
     */
    int execStoredProcedure(String procName, Properties params,
        CallbackInterface informMe) throws RemoteException;

    /**
     * Return a list of all registered clients
     * @return                      Returns a list of all
➥register clients
     * @exception RemoteException   Thrown if a transport problem
➥occurs
     */
    Properties getListOfClients() throws RemoteException;

    /**
     * Registers a new Client
     * @param Host                  Client Host Name
     * @param clientRef             A reference to the client
➥object
     * @exception RemoteException   Thrown if a transport problem
➥occurs
     */
    void registerClient(String Host,CallbackInterface clientRef)
        throws RemoteException;

    /**
     * Registers a new Client
     * @param clientRef             A reference to the client
➥object
     * @exception RemoteException   Thrown if a transport problem
➥occurs
     */
    void unRegisterClient(CallbackInterface clientRef)
```

```
          throws RemoteException;

   /**
    * Returns a Class object defining the admin frame
    * @return                     Returns a Class def of the
➥Admin frame
    * @exception RemoteException   Thrown if a transport problem
➥occurs
    */
   Class getAdminFrame() throws RemoteException;

   /**
    * Send a byte stream to the specified client
    * @param from                 The reference to the message
➥creator
    * @param toClient             The messages "TO" address
    * @param data                 The data to send
    * @exception RemoteException   Thrown if a transport problem
➥occurs
    */
   void sendInfoToClient(CallbackInterface from,
       String toClient,byte[] data) throws RemoteException;


   /**
    * Send a byte stream to all registered clients
    * @param from                 The reference to the message
➥creator
    * @param data                 The data to send
    * @exception RemoteException   Thrown if a transport problem
➥occurs
    */
   void sendInfoToAll(CallbackInterface from, byte[] data)
 throws RemoteException;
}
```

Practice Written Examination

 Note The written examination is a design justification for your implementation of the programming exercise. The questions are provided to make you think about the design you implement, to the extent of being able to justify it.

1. The solution developed in the programming solution combines database, client-to-client communication, persistent object storage, and distributed processing functionality.

    a) In paragraph form, discuss how you would re-partition these various different client services into a more granular approach.

    b) In paragraph form, discuss how you would implement a client solution that could take advantage of multiple servers offering replicated services.

2. The heart-beat feature is a possible CPU and bandwidth hog.

    a) Discuss how you could optimize the heart-beat implementation.

    b) If you believe that your implementation is optimal, discuss why. Otherwise, discuss why you choose to develop a non-optimal solution.

3. The original application chooses to use RMI.

    a) Discuss if you agree or disagree with this choice, and how you would have implemented the solution.

    b) In a high demand system, what possible problems can a RMI solution present?

4. The GUI portion of the application was not required in the programming example.

    a) Discuss how you would implement a GUI that can morph itself into the appearance of the native platform.

5. The code you wrote for the programming exercise was 100% pure.

    a) Discuss what writing 100% pure solutions means to you.

    b) Discuss the limitations of writing 100% pure code, and how to elegantly handle those instances.

 Note The written portion of the Certification process is a development justification for the programming exercise.

The Answers

The following sections provide possible solutions to the programming exercises and written examination. However, due to the subjectivity of the examination, your answers are not expected to be identical. Rather, this solution provides only one possible solution.

The Programming Exercise Solution

DbforME.Server.DataServer

```java
package DBforME.Server;

import DBforME.Shared.*;
import java.rmi.*;
import java.rmi.server.*;
import java.rmi.registry.*;
import java.util.Hashtable;
import java.util.Vector;
import java.util.Properties;
import java.util.Enumeration;
import java.util.Stack;
import java.io.*;

/**
 * The DataServer provides an RMI server for the execution of
➥stored
    procedures,
 * and facilitates inter client communications.
 * <BR>
 * Copyright (c) 1997 My Company, Inc. All Rights Reserved.
 * @author Cary A. Jardin
 * @version 1.0
 *
 */
public class DataServer extends UnicastRemoteObject
    implements ServerInterface, Runnable{

        private Hashtable Clients          = new Hashtable(10);
        private Vector ClientDeath         = new Vector(10);
        private Hashtable ClientProc       = new Hashtable(10);
        private Hashtable IDtoClient       = new Hashtable(10);
```

```
        private int NextProcID              = 1;
        private Object myLock               = new Object();

        //The Name to associate with the remote object.
        private static String Name          = "//:6789/
➥DBforME.DataServer";

        //The port to bind the RMI registry
        private static int port             = 6789;

        //Make the health call every 12000Ms
        private static int HealthInterval   =   12000;

        //Object File Extensions
        private static String ObjFileExt    =   ".pos";

        public DataServer() throws RemoteException{}


//Methods - Support Functions

        private Vector getClientVector(CallbackInterface clientRef){
            try{
                ObjectInputStream objIn = new ObjectInputStream(new
FileInputStream((String)Clients.get(clientRef) +
                    ObjFileExt));
                Vector cVect = (Vector)objIn.readObject();
                return cVect;
            }
            catch(Exception e){
                return new Vector();
            }
        }

        private void saveClientVector(CallbackInterface clientRef,
            Vector saveME){
            try{
                ObjectOutputStream objOut = new ObjectOutputStream(
                    new
FileOutputStream((String)Clients.get(clientRef) +
                    ObjFileExt));
                objOut.writeObject(saveME);
            }
            catch(Exception e){
```

```
        }
    }

    //Calls each registered client to make sure it is still
➥alive!
    private void makeHealthCalls(){

        //keep a stack of dead references;
        Stack cleanUp = new Stack();

        CallbackInterface tmpClient;
        for (Enumeration e = Clients.keys() ; e.hasMoreElements()
➥;) {
            tmpClient = (CallbackInterface)e.nextElement();
            try{
                tmpClient.heartBeat();
            }
            catch(Exception ex){
                cleanUp.push(tmpClient);
                System.out.println("Client Collected");
            }
        }
        killClients(cleanUp);
    }

    //Kills all client processes and unregisters the client
    private void killClients(Stack cleanme){
        //do cleanup
        CallbackInterface tmp;
        for(;!cleanme.empty();){
            tmp = (CallbackInterface)cleanme.pop();
            ClientDeath.removeElement(tmp);

            //Kill all outstanding process
            if(ClientProc.get(tmp) != null){
                Vector ProcessList = (Vector)ClientProc.get(tmp);
                int num = ProcessList.size();
                for(int i = 0;i < num;++i){
                    try{
                        ((Thread)ProcessList.elementAt(i)).stop();
                        if(ProcessList.elementAt(i) instanceof
➥RunJob){
                            IDtoClient.remove(
                    new
Integer(((RunJob)ProcessList.elementAt(i)).procID));
```

```
                                }
                            }
                            catch(Exception e){
                            //No Big
                            }
                        }
                        ProcessList.removeAllElements();
                    }
                    unRegisterClient(tmp);
                }
            }


            /**
             * Called by the RunJob Thread to inform that the
             * process has been completed
             */
            public final void jobDone(RunJob ref, int procID){

                CallbackInterface client =
        ➡(CallbackInterface)IDtoClient.get(
                    new Integer(procID));

                //inform the client
                try{
                    client.jobDone(ref, procID);

                    //clean up
                    IDtoClient.remove(new Integer(procID));
                    Vector tmpProc = (Vector)ClientProc.get(ref);
                    tmpProc.removeElement(ref);
                }
                catch(Exception e){
                }
            }


    //Methods - Remote Services
        /**
         * Executes the passed Thread on the server CPU.
         * @param runMe          The Thread to execute.
         * @param clientRef      The client to inform of the
    ➡completed job.
         * @exception RemoteException   Thrown if a transport problem
```

```
➥occurs
    */
    public int runJob(RunJob runMe, CallbackInterface
➥clientRef){

        synchronized(myLock){
            int id = NextProcID++;
            //Get the next id
            IDtoClient.put(new Integer(id),clientRef);

            //Set up the callback
            runMe.informMe = this;
            runMe.procID = id;

            //Save the process - accounting
            Vector tmpProc = (Vector)ClientProc.get(clientRef);
            if(tmpProc == null)
                tmpProc = new Vector(10);
            tmpProc.addElement(runMe);

            //kick it off
            runMe.start();
            return id;
        }
    }

    /**
     * Writes an object to the end of the client's persistent
➥storage
     *   device.
     * @param clientRef A reference to the client who is saving
➥the Object.
     * @param saveMe    The Object to save.
     * @exception RemoteException   Thrown if a transport problem
➥occurs
     */
    public void writeObject(CallbackInterface clientRef,Object
➥saveMe){
        Vector clientVect = getClientVector(clientRef);
        clientVect.addElement(saveMe);
        saveClientVector(clientRef,clientVect);
    }

    /**
```

```
         * Reads all Objects stored in the client's persistent storage
    ➥device.
         * @param clientRef A reference to the client who is reading
    ➥the Objects.
         * @return          Returns all Objects stored in the
    ➥specified client's
         *                             persistent storage device. null is
    ➥returned if
         *                             no Objects are found.
         * @exception RemoteException    Thrown if a transport problem
    ➥occurs
         * @exception IOException         Thrown if there is problem
    ➥reading
         *                             the Object file
         */
        public Vector readObjects(CallbackInterface clientRef){
            return getClientVector(clientRef);
        }


    /**
     * Purges all Objects in the client's persistent storage device.
     * @param clientRef  A reference to the client who is deleting
    ➥the Objects.
     * @exception RemoteException    Thrown if a transport problem
    ➥occurs
     */
        public void purgeObjectStore(CallbackInterface clientRef){
            Vector clientVect = getClientVector(clientRef);
            clientVect.removeAllElements();
            saveClientVector(clientRef,clientVect);
        }


    /**
        * Remotely execute a stored procedure.
        * @param procName  The name of the stored procedure to
    ➥execute
        * @param params     The properties for the stored procedure
        * @param informMe   The client to whom the results should be
    ➥shipped
        * @return           Returns the request ID value > 0 if
    ➥successful
        *                         execution, otherwise -1
        * @exception RemoteException    Thrown if a transport problem
    ➥occurs
```

```
        */
    public int execStoredProcedure(String procName, Properties
➥params,
        CallbackInterface informMe){
        //Code HERE!
        return 0;
    }

    /**
     * Return a list of all registered clients
     * @return                    Returns a list of all
➥register clients
     * @exception RemoteException   Thrown if a transport problem
➥occurs
     */
    public Properties getListOfClients(){
        return null;
    }

    /**
     * Returns a Class object defining the admin frame
     * @return                    Returns a Class def of the
➥Admin frame
     * @exception RemoteException   Thrown if a transport problem
➥occurs
     */
    public Class getAdminFrame(){
        return null;
    }

    /**
     * Send a byte stream to the specified client
     * @param from                The reference to the message
➥creator
     * @param toClient            The messages "TO" address
     * @param data                The data to send
     * @exception RemoteException   Thrown if a transport problem
➥occurs
     */
    public void sendInfoToClient(CallbackInterface from,
        String toClient,byte[] data){
        CallbackInterface tmp;

        for(Enumeration e = Clients.keys();e.hasMoreElements();){
```

```
                    tmp = (CallbackInterface)e.nextElement();
                    if(toClient.equals((String)Clients.get(tmp))){
                        try{
                            tmp.recvMessage((String)Clients.get(from),data);
                        }
                        catch(Exception ex){
                            System.out.println("DataServer.sendInfoToClient" +
                                " I think its DEAD " + ex);
                            unRegisterClient(tmp);
                        }
                        finally{
                            return;
                        }
                    }
                }
            }
        }

    /**
     * Send a byte stream to all registered clients
     * @param from                  The reference to the message
➥creator
     * @param data                  The data to send
     * @exception RemoteException   Thrown if a transport problem
➥occurs
     */
    public void sendInfoToAll(CallbackInterface from, byte[]
➥data){
        CallbackInterface tmp;

        for(Enumeration e = Clients.keys();e.hasMoreElements();){
            tmp = (CallbackInterface)e.nextElement();
            try{
                tmp.recvMessage((String)Clients.get(from),data);
            }
            catch(Exception ex){
                System.out.println("DataServer.sendInfoToClient" +
                    " I think its DEAD " + ex);
                unRegisterClient(tmp);
            }
        }
    }

//Methods - Remote Listener Reg
```

```
/**
 * Registers a client for the client death event.
 * @param clientRef   A reference to the client whom will be
➥informed.
 * @exception RemoteException    Thrown if a transport problem
➥occurs
 */
public void registerClientDeath(CallbackInterface clientRef){
    ClientDeath.addElement(clientRef);
}


/**
 * Registers a new Client
 * @param Host                Client Host Name
 * @param clientRef           A reference to the client
➥object
 * @exception RemoteException    Thrown if a transport problem
➥occurs
 */
public void registerClient(String Host,CallbackInterface
➥clientRef){
    Clients.put(clientRef,Host);
}

//Methods - Remote Listener UnReg

/**
 * Unregisters a client for the client death event.
 * @param clientRef   A reference to the client whom will be
➥informed.
 * @exception RemoteException    Thrown if a transport problem
➥occurs
 */
public void unRegisterClientDeath(CallbackInterface
➥clientRef){
    ClientDeath.removeElement(clientRef);
}

/**
 * Registers a new Client
 * @param clientRef              A reference to the client
➥object
 * @exception RemoteException    Thrown if a transport problem
```

```
➥occurs
   */
  public void unRegisterClient(CallbackInterface clientRef){
      //Get name
      String host = (String)Clients.get(clientRef);
      Clients.remove(clientRef);

      //Inform the registered listeners
      int num = ClientDeath.size();
      for(int i = 0;i < num;++i){
          try{
      ((CallbackInterface)ClientDeath.elementAt(i)).clientDeath(host);
          }
          catch(Exception e){
              //No Big
          }
      }
  }


  /**
   * Main run loop to make health calls
   */
  public void run(){
      for(;;){
          makeHealthCalls();
          try{
              Thread.sleep(HealthInterval);
          }
          catch(Exception e){}
      }
  }


  /**
   * Start up the stock server; also creates a registry so that
➥the
   * DataServer can lookup the server.
   */
  public static void main(String args[]){

  System.setSecurityManager(new RMISecurityManager());
  try {
      LocateRegistry.createRegistry(port);
      System.out.println("DataServer.main: creating server");
      DataServer server = new DataServer();
```

```
            Naming.rebind(Name, server);
            System.out.println("DataServer.main: done");
            System.out.println("DataServer.main: Executing health
➥thread");

            //Exec the Health Thread
            Thread mainHealthThread = new Thread(server);
            try{
                mainHealthThread.start();
            }
            catch(Exception e){
                System.out.println("DataServer.main:" +
                    " Error Exec Health Thread: Exiting " + e);
                return;
            }
        }
        catch (Exception e) {
            System.out.println("DataServer.main: an exception
➥occurred: " +
                e.getMessage());
            e.printStackTrace();
        }
    }
}
```

DBforME.Client.ClientDataProj

```
package DBforME.Client;

import java.rmi.*;
import DBforME.Shared.*;
import java.rmi.server.*;
import java.util.Hashtable;
import java.util.Properties;
import java.util.Vector;
import java.net.InetAddress;

/**
 * The DataServer provides an RMI server for the
 * execution of stored procedures,
 * and facilitates inter client communications.
 * <BR>
 * Copyright (c) 1997 My Company, Inc. All Rights Reserved.
 * @author Cary A. Jardin
```

```
     * @version 1.0
     *
     */
    public abstract class ClientDataProj implements
    ➥CallbackInterface{

        //Debug Flag
        private final static boolean DEBUG = false;
        //Remote Service
        private static String Name = "//france:6789/
    ➥DBforME.DataServer";
        //Remote Object Reference
        private ServerInterface remoteServer = null;

//Methods - Constructor
    public ClientDataProj() throws RemoteException{
        //Export this Reference to receive callbacks
         UnicastRemoteObject.exportObject(this);

        //Retrieve remote object
        try{
            remoteServer = (ServerInterface)Naming.lookup(Name);
            remoteServer.registerClient(
                InetAddress.getLocalHost().getHostName(),this);
        }
        catch(Exception e){
            //Throw an exception if a URL has a problem
            throw new RemoteException();
        }
    }

//Methods - Destructor
    public void finalize(){
        if(remoteServer != null)
            try{
                remoteServer.unRegisterClient(this);
            }
            catch(Exception e){}
    }

//Methods - Client callbacks
    /**
     * Called to validate that the Client is still alive.
     * @exception RemoteException   Thrown if a transport problem
```

```
➥occurs
     */
    public void heartBeat(){
        if(DEBUG)
            System.out.println("HeartBeart!!!");

    }

    /**
     * Called to inform the client of the death of another
➥client.
     * @param name                 The name of the client who
➥died.
     * @exception RemoteException   Thrown if a transport problem
➥occurs
     */
    public abstract void clientDeath(String name);

    /**
     * Called to inform that a client process has been completed.
     * @param result    A reference to the original Thread after
➥execution.
     * @param jobID       The job ID associated with the return
➥Thread.
     * @exception RemoteException   Thrown if a transport problem
➥occurs
     */
    public abstract void jobDone(RunJob result, int jobID);

    /**
     * Called remotely to feed resultant data into the client. Do
➥NOT call!
     * @param reqID                 The request ID of the
➥incoming data
     * @param data                  The result data
     * @exception RemoteException   Thrown if a transport problem
➥occurs
     */
    public abstract synchronized void resultData(int reqID,
➥byte[] data);

    /**
     * Called remotely to feed data sent from another client. Do
➥NOT Call
```

```
     * @param from      The name of the client from which the data
➥originated
     * @param data      The message data
     * @exception RemoteException    Thrown if a transport problem
➥occurs
     */
    public abstract void recvMessage(String from, byte[] data);

//Methods - Local accessor
    public synchronized byte[] getResultData(int reqID){
        //Something HERE!
        return null;
    }


//Methods - Remote Services
    /**
     * Remotely execute a stored procedure.
     * @param procName   The name of the stored procedure to
➥execute
     * @param params     The properties for the stored procedure
     * @return  Returns the request ID value > 0 if successful
➥execution,
     *                                   otherwise -1
     */
    public synchronized int execStoredProcedure(String procName,
        Properties params){

        if(remoteServer == null)
            return -1;

        try{
            return remoteServer.execStoredProcedure(procName,
➥params,
                this);
        }
        catch(Exception e){
            return -1;
        }
    }

    /**
     * Return a list of all registered clients
     * @return                         Returns a list of all
➥register clients,
```

```
    *                                  or null if a problem
    */
   public synchronized Properties getListOfClients(){

       if(remoteServer == null)
           return null;

       try{
           return remoteServer.getListOfClients();
       }
       catch(Exception e){
           return null;
       }
   }

   /**
    * Returns a Class object defining the admin frame
    * @return                    Returns a Class def of the
➥Admin frame,
    *                                  or null if a problem
    */
   public synchronized DBAdminFrame getAdminFrame(){

       if(remoteServer == null)
           return null;

       try{
       return
(DBAdminFrame)(remoteServer.getAdminFrame().newInstance());
       }
       catch(Exception e){
           return null;
       }
   }

   /**
    * Send a byte stream to the specified client
    * @param from                    The reference to the message
➥creator
    * @param toClient                The messages "TO" address
    * @param data                    The data to send
    */
   public synchronized void sendInfoToClient(String
toClient,byte[] data){
```

```java
        if(remoteServer == null)
            return;

        try{
            remoteServer.sendInfoToClient(this,toClient,data);
        }
        catch(Exception e){
        }

        return;
    }

    /**
     * Send a byte stream to all registered clients
     * @param from                The reference to the message
 creator
     * @param data                The data to send
     */
    public synchronized void sendInfoToAll(byte[] data){

        if(remoteServer == null)
            return;

        try{
            remoteServer.sendInfoToAll(this,data);
        }
        catch(Exception e){
        }

        return;
    }

    /**
     * Executes the passed Thread on the server CPU.
     * @param runMe               The Thread to execute.
     * @return                    Returns the Process ID > 0
     */
    public int runJob(RunJob runMe){

        if(remoteServer == null)
            return -1;

        try{
```

```
            return remoteServer.runJob(runMe,this);
        }
        catch(Exception e){
            return -1;
        }
    }


    /**
     * Writes an object to the end of the client's persistent
➥storage device.
     * @param saveMe              The Object to save.
     */
    public void writeObject(Object saveMe){
        if(remoteServer == null)
            return ;

        try{
            remoteServer.writeObject(this,saveMe);
        }
        catch(Exception e){
        }

        return;
    }


    /**
     * Reads all Objects stored in the client's persistent
➥storage device.
     * @return               Returns all Objects stored in the
➥specified client's
     *                       persistent storage device. null is
➥returned if
     *                       no Objects are found.
     */
    public Vector readObjects(){
        if(remoteServer == null)
            return null;

        try{
            return remoteServer.readObjects(this);
        }
        catch(Exception e){
            return null;
        }
```

```
        }

        /**
         * Purges all Objects in the client's persistent storage
➥device.
         */
        public void purgeObjectStore(){
            if(remoteServer == null)
                return;

            try{
                remoteServer.purgeObjectStore(this);
            }
            catch(Exception e){
            }
            return;
        }

    //Methods - Remote Listener Reg

        /**
         * Registers a client for the client death event.
         */
        public void registerClientDeath(){
            if(remoteServer == null)
                return;

            try{
                remoteServer.registerClientDeath(this);
            }
            catch(Exception e){
            }
            return;
        }

    //Methods - Remote Listener UnReg

        /**
         * Unregisters a client for the client death event.
         */
        public void unRegisterClientDeath(CallbackInterface
➥clientRef){
            if(remoteServer == null)
                return;
```

```
        try{
            remoteServer.unRegisterClientDeath(this);
        }
        catch(Exception e){
        }
        return;
    }
}
```

DBforME.Shared.CallbackInterface

```java
package DBforME.Shared;

import java.rmi.*;
import java.util.Vector;
import java.util.Properties;

/**
 * This interface defines callback hooks which the server can
➡exploit to
 * transmit information to the client<BR>
 * <BR>
 * Copyright (c)1997 My Company, Inc. All Rights Reserved.
 * @author Cary A. Jardin
 * @version 1.0
 *
 */
public interface CallbackInterface extends java.rmi.Remote {

    /**
     * Feeds the resultant data into the client
     * @param reqID              The request ID of the
➡incoming data
     * @param data               The result data
     * @exception RemoteException    Thrown if a transport problem
➡occurs
     */
    void resultData(int reqID, byte[] data) throws
➡RemoteException;

    /**
     * Feed data sent from another client.
     * @param from     The name of the client from which the data
```

```
➥originated
    * @param data     The message data
    * @exception RemoteException   Thrown if a transport problem
➥occurs
    */
   void recvMessage(String from, byte[] data) throws
➥RemoteException;

  /**
    * Called to validate that the Client is still alive.
    * @exception RemoteException   Thrown if a transport problem
➥occurs
    */
   void heartBeat() throws RemoteException;

  /**
    * Called to inform the client of the death of another
➥client.
    * @param name                The name of the client who
➥died.
    * @exception RemoteException   Thrown if a transport problem
➥occurs
    */
   void clientDeath(String name) throws RemoteException;

  /**
    * Called to inform that a client process has been completed.
    * @param result  A reference to the original Thread after
➥execution.
    * @param jobID   The job ID associated with the return
➥Thread.
    * @exception RemoteException   Thrown if a transport problem
➥occurs
    */
   void jobDone(RunJob result, int jobID);
}
```

DBforME.Shared.DBAdminFrame

```
package DBforME.Shared;

import java.awt.Frame;

/**
```

```
 * The DBAdminFrame is the base abstract class that must be used
➥for
 * creating admin facilities.
 * <BR>
 * Copyright (c) 1997 My Company, Inc. All Rights Reserved.
 * @author Cary A. Jardin
 * @version 1.0
 *
 */
public abstract class DBAdminFrame extends Frame{

    /**
     * Upon constructing a new instance of the admin frame, this
     * method is called to inform the frame of its associated
     * server host.
     * @param serverHostName        The host name of the origin
➥server.
     */
    public abstract void setOrigin(String serverHostName);
}
```

DBforME.Shared.ServerInterface

```
package DBforME.Shared;

import java.rmi.*;
import java.util.Properties;
import java.util.Vector;
import java.io.IOException;

/**
 * This interface defines the visible
 *   facilities provided to client applications.<BR>
 * <BR>
 * Copyright (c)1997 My Company, Inc. All Rights Reserved.
 * @author Cary A. Jardin
 * @version 1.0
 *
 */
public interface ServerInterface extends java.rmi.Remote {

    /**
     * Remotely execute a stored procedure.
     * @param procName  The name of the stored procedure to
```

```
➥execute
    * @param params    The properties for the stored procedure
    * @param informMe  The client to whom the results should be
➥shipped
    * @return    Returns the request ID value > 0 if successful
➥execution,
    *                                    otherwise -1
    * @exception RemoteException    Thrown if a transport problem
➥occurs
    */
    int execStoredProcedure(String procName, Properties params,
        CallbackInterface informMe) throws RemoteException;


    /**
     * Return a list of all registered clients
     * @return                      Returns a list of all
➥register clients
     * @exception RemoteException    Thrown if a transport problem
➥occurs
     */
    Properties getListOfClients() throws RemoteException;


    /**
     * Registers a new Client
     * @param Host               Client Host Name
     * @param clientRef          A reference to the client
➥object
     * @exception RemoteException    Thrown if a transport problem
➥occurs
     */
    void registerClient(String Host,CallbackInterface clientRef)
        throws RemoteException;


    /**
     * Registers a new Client
     * @param clientRef          A reference to the client
➥object
     * @exception RemoteException    Thrown if a transport problem
➥occurs
     */
    void unRegisterClient(CallbackInterface clientRef)
        throws RemoteException;


    /**
```

```
    * Returns a Class object defining the admin frame
    * @return                      Returns a Class def of the
➡Admin frame
    * @exception RemoteException   Thrown if a transport problem
➡occurs
    */
   Class getAdminFrame() throws RemoteException;

   /**
    * Send a byte stream to the specified client
    * @param from                  The reference to the message
➡creator
    * @param toClient               The messages "TO" address
    * @param data                   The data to send
    * @exception RemoteException   Thrown if a transport problem
➡occurs
    */
   void sendInfoToClient(CallbackInterface from, String
➡toClient,
     byte[] data) throws RemoteException;

   /**
    * Send a byte stream to all registered clients
    * @param from                  The reference to the message
➡creator
    * @param data                   The data to send
    * @exception RemoteException   Thrown if a transport problem
➡occurs
    */
   void sendInfoToAll(CallbackInterface from, byte[] data)
     throws RemoteException;

   /**
    * Executes the passed Thread on the server CPU.
    * @param runMe                  The Thread to execute.
    * @param clientRef              The client to inform of the
➡completed job.
    * @exception RemoteException   Thrown if a transport problem
➡occurs
    */
   int runJob(RunJob runMe, CallbackInterface clientRef)
     throws RemoteException;

   /**
```

```
    * Registers a client for the client death event.
    * @param clientRef    A reference to the client who will be
➥informed.
    * @exception RemoteException   Thrown if a transport problem
➥occurs
    */
   void registerClientDeath(CallbackInterface clientRef)
      throws RemoteException;


   /**
    * Unregisters a client for the client death event.
    * @param clientRef    A reference to the client who will be
➥informed.
    * @exception RemoteException   Thrown if a transport problem
➥occurs
    */
   void unRegisterClientDeath(CallbackInterface clientRef)
     throws RemoteException;


   /**
    * Writes an object to the end of the client's persistent
    * storage device.
    * @param clientRef             A reference to the client who
    * is saving the Object.
    * @param saveMe                The Object to save.
    * @exception RemoteException   Thrown if a transport problem
➥occurs
    */
   void writeObject(CallbackInterface clientRef,Object saveMe)
      throws RemoteException, IOException;
   /**
    * Reads all Objects stored in the client's persistent
➥storage device.
    * @param clientRef  A reference to the client who is reading
    *                     the Objects.
    * @return          Returns all Objects stored in the
➥specified client's
    *                       persistent storage device. null is
➥returned if
    *                       no Objects are found.
    * @exception RemoteException   Thrown if a transport problem
➥occurs
    * @exception IOException       Thrown if there is problem
➥reading the
```

```
     *   Object file
     */
    Vector readObjects(CallbackInterface clientRef) throws
➡RemoteException;

    /**
     * Purges all Objects in the client's persistent storage
➡device.
     * @param clientRef              A reference to the client who
     * is deleting the Objects.
     * @exception RemoteException    Thrown if a transport problem
➡occurs
     */
    void purgeObjectStore(CallbackInterface clientRef) throws
➡RemoteException;

}
```

DBforME.Shared.RunJob

```
package DBforME.Shared;

import DBforME.Server.DataServer;
import java.rmi.*;
import java.util.Vector;
import java.util.Properties;
import java.io.*;

/**
 * This class defines a process to be executed on a server
➡resource.
 * Since the
 * facility uses RMI, subclasses are responsible for providing
 * their own serialization.
 * <BR>
 * <BR>
 * Copyright (c)1997 My Company, Inc. All Rights Reserved.
 * @author Cary A. Jardin
 * @version 1.0
 *
 */
public abstract class RunJob extends Thread implements
➡Serializable{
```

```
/**
 * This will be set by the server to facilitate a callback
 * upon completion
 */
public DataServer informMe = null;

/**
 * This will be set by the server to facilitate a callback
 * upon completion
 */
public int procID = 0;


/**
 * Your code goes HERE. This method will be executed by the
 * newly created Thread
 */
public abstract void cpuJob();

/**
 * Standard Java serialization device responsible for
 * saving all state info.
 */
private abstract void writeObject(java.io.ObjectOutputStream
➡out)
    throws IOException;

/**
 * Standard Java serialization device responsible for
 * restoring all state info.
 */
private abstract void readObject(java.io.ObjectInputStream
➡in)
    throws IOException, ClassNotFoundException;

/**
 * Executed by the server to run the specified CPU job
 */
public final void run(){
    cpuJob();
    informMe.jobDone(this,procID);
}
}
```

Written Examination Answers

1. a)   Each of the discrete units of functionality should be partitioned into separate remote objects. In this way, clients can retrieve a listing of registered services. Placing all the facilities in a single object only makes sense if the services are not mutually exclusive and share common state information. Otherwise, each remote object should be partitioned in the same matter as local/standard objects. Object-oriented design holds even with remote objects.

1. b)   To the remote client, a server object is like any other object reference. To that extent, if the server objects are fully replicated on different servers, the client can simply destroy the failed server object and replace it with the alive server object. In this matter, an automatic rollover can take place, providing a greater degree of robustness.

2. a)   In the current heart-beat implementation, health call is made regardless if a piece of information has been sent to the client in question. That is, each communication with a client should be deemed as a health call. Therefore, making an actual heath call will only transpire if no other contact has been made with the clients.

   A second optimization technique is to eliminate RMI from the health call. The amount of data transmitted for each health call may far exceed a simple "I am Alive" flag. Therefore, a UDP solution could easily and efficiently handle such a heart-beat facility.

2. b)   The current implementation is not optimal. However, the implementation of an RMI call was the simplest and cleanest solution. As stated in answer 2.a, there are other, more optimal solutions, but this solution functions for the first round. If it turns out to be a problem, additional effort can be spent.

3. a)   RMI is slick, and it does expedite client/server solutions, but RMI client/solutions are not optimal in comparison to straight socket-level implementations. However, this is the same debate of whether to write code in assembly or a high-level language like Java. Sure, assembly might be faster, but

the development effort will be slower and less extensible. I fully agree with the use of RMI in this scenario, and believe in RMI for a wide range of client/server solutions.

3. b) There are two problems that plague RMI solutions in a high demand system. The first is the overhead for each connection, and the second is the amount of garbage produced for each RMI call. Such solutions implemented with pure sockets suffer from similar issues. However, writing directly to the wire gives ultimate control of optimization.

4. a) The Swing set of lightweight components allows GUIs to morph into various native execution platforms, and to custom appearances as well.

5. a) Writing a 100% pure solution means creating a solution that uses the strength of Java to assure cross-platform executions. To facilitate this, the general goal of writing 100% pure is to avoid the use of native application hooks.

5. b) When a solution requires native hooks, it should be implemented in a modular manner. That is, the native hooks should be wrapped in a class that can be replaced to enable the solution of various platforms.

Where to Go From Here

The Certified Developer Examination is a complete test of Java knowledge. As you saw in this chapter, the examination is divided into a performance-based programming exercise and a written examination. The combination provides a comprehensive assessment of your Java knowledge. This chapter provided a practice exam to help prepare you for the Certified Developer Examination.

Now that you have completed the content of this entire examination aid, you have three roads before you. If you FEEL you are ready, pay the money and begin the Certified Developer Process. If you are on the borderline of whether you should go for it or take some more time, email me your practice programming exercise and written exam at cjardin@servnow.com so that I can further direct you. If you do not think you are ready, take some time off and go play around at http://java.sun.com, and then take the other practice examination found in Chapter 16.

The Java Certification Process is by no means easy. The information covered in the Programmer and Developer examinations are grueling. However, you are a Certified Java Programmer on the verge of being a Certified Developer. All I can offer at this point is my email (cjardin@servnow.com) for any questions/comments. Feel free to use this resource, and I look forward to hearing from you.

Chapter **16**

Certified Developer Practice Test # 2

This chapter will provide the following resources for the Certified Java Developer Examination.

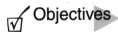 Objectives

- ▶ Study Guide and Checklist
- ▶ Practice Programming Exercise
- ▶ Practice Written Examination
- ▶ Solutions to the Programming Exercise and Written Examination

Practice Programming Exercise and Written Justification

See Chapter 15, "Certified Developer Practice Test # 1," for a complete description of the Developer Exam and notes to help you prepare. The Developer exam consists of two parts: a programming exercise and a written justification. The programming exercise is a test of your development and programming ability. The following sections provide a sample programming exercise and written exam, which mimic the actual Certified Java Developer Examination. Feel free to use external references when developing the programming exercise. However, you are on your own in the written sections.

One last note before you begin, the presented practice programming exercise does not go into GUI development. However, be prepared to create a GUI to utilize the required functionality using AWT, and always write 100% pure code (see Chapter 14, "Additional Java Technologies").

 Note
The requirements portion of the programming exercise forms the bases for what you are expected to implement.

The Original Requirements

An existing database server needs to be exposed to external applications. However, marketing wants this to be cool, and cool equates to the following requirements.

▶ All database stored procedures must be made callable.

▶ Data returned to the application should employ server push technology.

▶ The administration interface is going to be changing with every strong breeze. Therefore, the client applications will need to get the admin GUI from the server as needed.

▶ All clients should know about one another.

▶ Clients should have the ability to communicate with one another.

▶ Provide a Multi-Threaded API.

As you can see, these requirements depict actual marketing requirements, vague and "buzzy." However, these requirements are specific enough to derive the architecture shown in Figure 16.1 from.

FIG. 16.1

RMI Solution Architectural Diagram.

RMI Solution Package Diagram

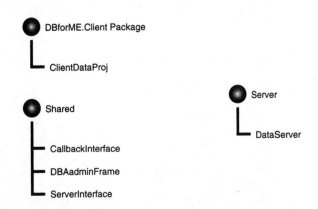

The New Requirements

After presenting an implementation of the stated requirements, marketing countered with the following list of requirement modifications.

▶ The clients need to have the ability to request an URL from the server. The server should then fetch the URL and send it back to the server. However, multiple requests can be submitted and delivered to the client as they become available.

▶ The server should keep a heart-beat with each client.

▶ Clients should have the ability to be informed of a client death.

▶ Once a client has died, all outstanding processes should be rolled back.

▶ Since some GUI's are implemented as an applet, a persistent object store is needed. That is, using object serialization provide each registered client the ability to store and retrieve objects.

▶ It is possible that future services may be offered to the client API. The server and client should be able to have open hooks for these new services.

The following code presents the work done this far on the project. All methods stating NYI (Not Yet Implemented) or "Something HERE" should be left as is.

DBforME.Server.DataServer

```
package DBforME.Server;

import DBforME.Shared.*;
import java.rmi.*;
import java.rmi.server.*;
import java.rmi.registry.*;
import java.util.Hashtable;
import java.util.Properties;
import java.util.Enumeration;

/**
 * The DataServer provides an RMI server for the execution of

 * stored procedures, and facilitates inter client
➡communications.
 * <BR>
 * Copyright (c) 1997 My Company, Inc. All Rights Reserved.
 * @author Cary A. Jardin
 * @version 1.0
 *
 */
public class DataServer extends UnicastRemoteObject
    implements ServerInterface{

    private Hashtable Clients   = new Hashtable(10);
    //The Name to associate with the remote object.
    private static String Name = "//:6789/DBforME.DataServer";
    //The port to bind the RMI registry
    private static int port =  6789;
```

```
     public DataServer() throws RemoteException{}

//Methods - Remote Services
    /**
    * Remotely execute a stored procedure.
    * @param procName  The name of the stored procedure to
➡execute
    * @param params    The properties for the stored procedure
    * @param informMe  The client to whom the results should be
➡shipped to
    * @return          Returns the request ID value > 0 if
➡successful
    *                          execution, otherwise -1
    * @exception RemoteException   Thrown if a transport problem
➡occurs
    */
    public int execStoredProcedure(String procName, Properties
➡params,
        CallbackInterface informMe){
          //Code HERE!
          return 0;
    }


    /**
    * Return a list of all registered clients
    * @return                      Returns a list of all
➡register clients
    * @exception RemoteException   Thrown if a transport problem
➡occurs
    */
    public Properties getListOfClients(){
        return null;
    }


    /**
    * Returns a Class object defining the admin frame
    * @return                      Returns a Class def of the
➡Admin frame
    * @exception RemoteException   Thrown if a transport problem
➡occurs
    */
    public Class getAdminFrame(){
        return null;
    }
```

```
    /**
     * Send a byte stream to the specified client
     * @param from                   The reference to the message
➥creator
     * @param toClient               The messages "TO" address
     * @param data                   The data to send
     * @exception RemoteException    Thrown if a transport problem
➥occurs
     */
    public void sendInfoToClient(CallbackInterface from,
        String toClient,byte[] data){
        CallbackInterface tmp;

        for(Enumeration e = Clients.keys();e.hasMoreElements();){
            tmp = (CallbackInterface)e.nextElement();
            if(toClient.equals((String)Clients.get(tmp))){
                try{
                    tmp.recvMessage((String)Clients.get(from),data);
                }
                catch(Exception ex){
                    System.out.println("DataServer.sendInfoToClient" +
                        I think its DEAD " + ex);
                     unRegisterClient(tmp);
                }
                finally{
                    return;
                }
            }
        }
    }

    /**
     * Send a byte stream to all registered clients
     * @param from                   The reference to the message
➥creator
     * @param data                   The data to send
     * @exception RemoteException    Thrown if a transport problem
➥occurs
     */
    public void sendInfoToAll(CallbackInterface from, byte[] data){
        CallbackInterface tmp;
```

```
        for(Enumeration e = Clients.keys();e.hasMoreElements();){
            tmp = (CallbackInterface)e.nextElement();
            try{
                tmp.recvMessage((String)Clients.get(from),data);
            }
            catch(Exception ex){
                System.out.println("DataServer.sendInfoToClient" +
                    "I think its DEAD " + ex);
                unRegisterClient(tmp);
            }
        }
    }

//Methods - Remote Listener Reg
    /**
     * Registers a new Client
     * @param Host                  Client Host Name
     * @param clientRef             A reference to the client
➥object
     * @exception RemoteException   Thrown if a transport problem
➥occurs
     */
    public void registerClient(String Host,CallbackInterface
➥clientRef){
        Clients.put(clientRef,Host);
    }

//Methods - Remote Listener UnReg

    /**
     * Registers a new Client
     * @param clientRef             A reference to the client
➥object
     * @exception RemoteException   Thrown if a transport problem
➥occurs
     */
    public void unRegisterClient(CallbackInterface clientRef){
        Clients.remove(clientRef);
    }

    /**
     * Start up the stock server; also creates a registry so that
➥the
     * DataServer can lookup the server.
```

```
    */
   public static void main(String args[]){

      System.setSecurityManager(new RMISecurityManager());
      try {
         LocateRegistry.createRegistry(port);
         System.out.println("DataServer.main: creating
➥server");
         DataServer server = new DataServer();
         Naming.rebind(Name, server);
         System.out.println("DataServer.main: done");
      }
      catch (Exception e) {
         System.out.println("DataServer.main: an exception
➥occurred: " +
            e.getMessage());
         e.printStackTrace();
      }
   }
}
```

DBforME.Client.ClientDataProj

```
package DBforME.Client;

import java.rmi.*;
import DBforME.Shared.*;
import java.rmi.server.*;
import java.util.Hashtable;
import java.util.Properties;
import java.net.InetAddress;

/**
 * The DataServer provides an RMI server for the execution of
 * stored procedures, and facilitates inter client
➥communications.
 * <BR>
 * Copyright (c) 1997 My Company, Inc. All Rights Reserved.
 * @author Cary A. Jardin
 * @version 1.0
 *
 */
public class ClientDataProj extends UnicastRemoteObject
   implements CallbackInterface{
```

```
    private static String Name = "//france:6789/
➡DBforME.DataServer";
    private ServerInterface remoteServer = null;

    public ClientDataProj() throws RemoteException{
        //Export this Reference to receive callbacks
       UnicastRemoteObject.exportObject(this);

        //Retrieve remote object
        try{
            remoteServer = (ServerInterface)Naming.lookup(Name);
            remoteServer.registerClient(
                InetAddress.getLocalHost().getHostName(),this);
        }
        catch(Exception e){
            //Throw an exception if a URL has a problem
            throw new RemoteException();
        }
    }

    public void finalize(){
        if(remoteServer != null)
            try{
                remoteServer.unRegisterClient(this);
            }
            catch(Exception e){}
    }

    public synchronized byte[] getResultData(int reqID){
        //Something HERE!
        return null;
    }

    /**
     * Called remotely to feed resultant data into the client. Do
➡NOT call!
     * @param reqID           The request ID of the
➡incoming data
     * @param data            The result data
     * @exception RemoteException   Thrown if a transport problem
➡occurs
     */
```

```
    public synchronized void resultData(int reqID, byte[] data){
        //Something HERE!
    }

    /**
     * Called remotely to feed data sent from another client. Do
➡NOT Call
     * @param from   The name of the client from which the data
➡originated
     * @param data   The message data
     * @exception RemoteException   Thrown if a transport problem
➡occurs
     */
    public synchronized void recvMessage(String from, byte[]
➡data){
        //Something HERE!
    }

//Methods - Remote Services
    /**
     * Remotely execute a stored procedure.
     * @param procName            The name of the stored
➡procedure to execute
     * @param params              The properties for the stored
➡procedure
     * @return   Returns the request ID value > 0 if successful
➡execution,
     *                            otherwise -1
     * @exception RemoteException   Thrown if a transport problem
➡occurs
     */
    public synchronized int execStoredProcedure(String procName,
        Properties params){

        if(remoteServer == null)
            return -1;

        try{
            return remoteServer.execStoredProcedure(procName,
➡params, this);
        }
        catch(Exception e){
            return -1;
        }
```

```
        }

    /**
     * Return a list of all registered clients
     * @return                    Returns a list of all
➥register clients,
     *                            or null if a problem
     * @exception RemoteException  Thrown if a transport problem
➥occurs
     */
    public synchronized Properties getListOfClients(){

        if(remoteServer == null)
            return null;


        try{
            return remoteServer.getListOfClients();
        }
        catch(Exception e){
            return null;
        }
    }


    /**
     * Returns a Class object defining the admin frame
     * @return                    Returns a Class def of the
➥Admin frame,
     *                            or null if a problem
     * @exception RemoteException  Thrown if a transport problem
➥occurs
     */
    public synchronized DBAdminFrame getAdminFrame(){

        if(remoteServer == null)
            return null;

        try{
         return (DBAdminFrame)(remoteServer.getAdminFrame().
➥newInstance());
        }
        catch(Exception e){
            return null;
        }
    }
```

```
/**
 * Send a byte stream to the specified client
 * @param from              The reference to the message
➡creator
 * @param toClient          The messages "TO" address
 * @param data              The data to send
 * @exception RemoteException  Thrown if a transport problem
➡occurs
 */
public synchronized void sendInfoToClient(String
➡toClient,byte[] data){

    if(remoteServer == null)
        return;

    try{
        remoteServer.sendInfoToClient(this,toClient,data);
    }
    catch(Exception e){
    }

    return;
}

/**
 * Send a byte stream to all registered clients
 * @param from              The reference to the message
➡creator
 * @param data              The data to send
 * @exception RemoteException  Thrown if a transport problem
➡occurs
 */
public synchronized void sendInfoToAll(byte[] data){

    if(remoteServer == null)
        return;

    try{
        remoteServer.sendInfoToAll(this,data);
    }
    catch(Exception e){
    }
```

```
        return;
    }

}


```

DBforME.Shared.CallbackInterface

```
package DBforME.Shared;

import java.rmi.*;
import java.util.Vector;
import java.util.Properties;

/**
 * This interface defines callback hooks which the server can
➥exploit to
 * transmit information to the client<BR>
 * <BR>
 * Copyright (c)1997 My Company, Inc. All Rights Reserved.
 * @author Cary A. Jardin
 * @version 1.0
 *
 */
public interface CallbackInterface extends java.rmi.Remote {

    /**
     * Feeds the resultant data into the client
     * @param reqID              The request ID of the
➥incoming data
     * @param data               The result data
     * @exception RemoteException    Thrown if a transport problem
➥occurs
     */
    void resultData(int reqID, byte[] data) throws
➥RemoteException;

    /**
     * Feed data sent from another client.
     * @param from  The name of the client from which the data
➥originated
     * @param data  The message data
     * @exception RemoteException    Thrown if a transport problem
➥occurs
     */
```

```
        void recvMessage(String from, byte[] data) throws
➥RemoteException;

}
```

DBforME.Shared.DBAdminFrame

```
package DBforME.Shared;

import java.awt.Frame;

/**
 * The DBAdminFrame is the base abstract class that must be used
➥for
 * creating admin facilities.
 * <BR>
 * Copyright (c) 1997 My Company, Inc. All Rights Reserved.
 * @author Cary A. Jardin
 * @version 1.0
 *
 */
public abstract class DBAdminFrame extends Frame{

    /**
     * Upon constructing a new instance of the admin frame, this
     * method is called to inform the frame of its associated
     * server host.
     * @param serverHostName      The host name of the origin
➥server.
     */
    public abstract void setOrigin(String serverHostName);
}
```

DBforME.Shared.ServerInterface

```
package DBforME.Shared;

import java.rmi.*;
import java.util.Properties;

/**
 * This interface defines the visible facilities provided
 * to client applications. <BR>
 * <BR>
```

```
 * Copyright (c)1997 My Company, Inc. All Rights Reserved.
 * @author Cary A. Jardin
 * @version 1.0
 *
 */
public interface ServerInterface extends java.rmi.Remote {

    /**
     * Remotely execute a stored procedure.
     * @param procName   The name of the stored procedure to
➥execute
     * @param params     The properties for the stored procedure
     * @param informMe   The client to whom the results should be
➥shipped to
     * @return   Returns the request ID value > 0 if successful
➥execution,
     *                                 otherwise -1
     * @exception RemoteException   Thrown if a transport problem
➥occurs
     */
    int execStoredProcedure(String procName, Properties params,
       CallbackInterface informMe) throws RemoteException;

    /**
     * Return a list of all registered clients
     * @return                       Returns a list of all
➥register clients
     * @exception RemoteException   Thrown if a transport problem
➥occurs
     */
    Properties getListOfClients() throws RemoteException;

    /**
     * Registers a new Client
     * @param Host                   Client Host Name
     * @param clientRef              A reference to the client
➥object
     * @exception RemoteException   Thrown if a transport problem
➥occurs
     */
    void registerClient(String Host,CallbackInterface clientRef)
       throws RemoteException;

    /**
```

```
   * Registers a new Client
   * @param clientRef              A reference to the client
➥object
   * @exception RemoteException    Thrown if a transport problem
➥occurs
   */
   void unRegisterClient(CallbackInterface clientRef) throws
➥RemoteException;

   /**
   * Returns a Class object defining the admin frame
   * @return                       Returns a Class def of the
➥Admin frame
   * @exception RemoteException    Thrown if a transport problem
➥occurs
   */
   Class getAdminFrame() throws RemoteException;

   /**
   * Send a byte stream to the specified client
   * @param from                   The reference to the message
➥creator
   * @param toClient               The messages "TO" address
   * @param data                   The data to send
   * @exception RemoteException    Thrown if a transport problem
➥occurs
   */
   void sendInfoToClient(CallbackInterface from,
      String toClient,byte[] data) throws RemoteException;

   /**
   * Send a byte stream to all registered clients
   * @param from                   The reference to the message
➥creator
   * @param data                   The data to send
   * @exception RemoteException    Thrown if a transport problem
➥occurs
   */
   void sendInfoToAll(CallbackInterface from, byte[] data)
➥throws RemoteException;
}
```

Practice Written Examination

Note

> The written examination is a design justification for your implementation of the programming exercise. The questions are provided to make you think about the design you implement, to the extent of being able to justify it.

1. The solution developed in the programming solution combines database, client-to-client communication, persistent object storage, and distributed processing functionality.

   a) In paragraph form, discuss how you would re-partition these various different client services into a more granular approach.

   b) In paragraph form, discuss how you would implement a client solution that could take advantage of multiple servers offering replicated services.

2. The heart-beat feature is a possible CPU and bandwidth hog.

   a) Discuss how you could optimize the heart-beat implementation.

   b) If you believe the your implementation is optimal, discuss why. Otherwise, discuss why you choose to develop a non-optimal solution.

3. The original application chooses to use RMI.

   a) Discuss if you agree or disagree with this choice, and how you would of implemented the solution.

   b) In a high demand system, what possible problems can a RMI solution present?

4. The clients have the ability to request URLs to be fetched by the server.

   a) Discuss how you use threads to implement multiple simultaneous requests.

5. The code you wrote for the programming exercise was 100% pure.

a) Discuss what writing 100% pure solutions means to you.

b) Discuss the limitations of writing 100% pure code, and how to elegantly handle those instances.

Note

The written portion of the Certification process is a development justification for the programming exercise.

The Answers

The following sections provide possible solutions to the programming exercises and written examination. However, due to the subjectivity of the examination, your answers are not expected to be identical. Rather, this solution provides only one possible solution.

The Programming Exercise Solution

DBforME.Server.DataServer

```
package DBforME.Server;

import DBforME.Shared.*;
import java.rmi.*;
import java.rmi.server.*;
import java.rmi.registry.*;
import java.util.Hashtable;
import java.util.Vector;
import java.util.Properties;
import java.util.Enumeration;
import java.util.Stack;
import java.io.*;
import java.net.URL;

/**
 * The DataServer provides an RMI server for the execution
 * of stored procedures,
 * and facilitates inter client communications.
 * <BR>
 * Copyright (c) 1997 My Company, Inc. All Rights Reserved.
 * @author Cary A. Jardin
 * @version 1.0
 *
 */
public class DataServer extends UnicastRemoteObject
    implements ServerInterface, Runnable{

    private Hashtable Clients          = new Hashtable(10);
    private Vector ClientDeath         = new Vector(10);
    private Hashtable ClientProc       = new Hashtable(10);
    private Hashtable IDtoClient       = new Hashtable(10);
    private int NextProcID             = 1;
```

```java
    private Object myLock            = new Object();

    //The Name to associate with the remote object.
    private static String Name       = "//:6789/
➥DBforME.DataServer";

    //The port to bind the RMI registry
    private static int port           = 6789;

    //Make the health call every 12000Ms
    private static int HealthInterval  =   12000;

    //Object File Extensions
    private static String ObjFileExt   =    ".pos";

    public DataServer() throws RemoteException{}


//Methods - Support Functions

    private Vector getClientVector(CallbackInterface clientRef){
        try{
            ObjectInputStream objIn = new ObjectInputStream(new
FileInputStream((String)Clients.get(clientRef) +
                ObjFileExt));
            Vector cVect = (Vector)objIn.readObject();
            return cVect;
        }
        catch(Exception e){
            return new Vector();
        }
    }

    private void saveClientVector(CallbackInterface clientRef,
        Vector saveME){
        try{
            ObjectOutputStream objOut = new
➥ObjectOutputStream(new
FileOutputStream((String)Clients.get(clientRef) +
                ObjFileExt));
            objOut.writeObject(saveME);
        }
        catch(Exception e){
        }
```

```
    }

    //Calls each registered client to make sure it is still
➥alive!
    private void makeHealthCalls(){

        //keep a stack of dead references;
        Stack cleanUp = new Stack();

        CallbackInterface tmpClient;
        for (Enumeration e = Clients.keys() ; e.hasMoreElements()
➥;) {
            tmpClient = (CallbackInterface)e.nextElement();
            try{
                tmpClient.heartBeat();
            }
            catch(Exception ex){
                cleanUp.push(tmpClient);
                System.out.println("Client Collected");
            }
        }
        killClients(cleanUp);
    }

    //Kills all client processes and unregisters the client
    private void killClients(Stack cleanme){
        //do cleanup
        CallbackInterface tmp;
        for(;!cleanme.empty();){
            tmp = (CallbackInterface)cleanme.pop();
            ClientDeath.removeElement(tmp);

            //Kill all outstanding process
            if(ClientProc.get(tmp) != null){
                Vector ProcessList = (Vector)ClientProc.get(tmp);
                int num = ProcessList.size();
                for(int i = 0;i < num;++i){
                    try{
                        ((Thread)ProcessList.elementAt(i)).stop();
                        if(ProcessList.elementAt(i) instanceof
➥FetchURL){
                            IDtoClient.remove(new
Integer(((FetchURL)ProcessList.elementAt(i)).procID));
                        }
```

```
                                            }
                                            catch(Exception e){
                                            //No Big
                                            }
                                    }
                                    ProcessList.removeAllElements();
                            }
                            unRegisterClient(tmp);
                    }
            }


            /**
             * Called by the FetchURL Thread to inform that the
             * process has been completed
             */
            public final void jobDone(FetchURL ref, int procID){

                    CallbackInterface client =
            ➥(CallbackInterface)IDtoClient.get(
                            new Integer(procID));

                    //inform the client
                    try{
            //          client.jobDone(ref, procID);

                            //clean up
                            IDtoClient.remove(new Integer(procID));
                            Vector tmpProc = (Vector)ClientProc.get(ref);
                            tmpProc.removeElement(ref);
                    }
                    catch(Exception e){
                    }
            }



    //Methods - Remote Services
        /**
         * Retrieves the passed URL.
         * @param getMe            The URL to fetch
         * @param clientRef        The client to inform of the
    ➥completed job.
         * @exception RemoteException    Thrown if a transport problem
    ➥occurs
         */
```

```
public int fetchURL(URL getMe, CallbackInterface clientRef){

    synchronized(myLock){
        int id = NextProcID++;
        FetchURL runMe = new FetchURL();
        //Get the next id
        IDtoClient.put(new Integer(id),clientRef);

        //Set up the callback
        runMe.informMe = this;
        runMe.procID = id;
        runMe.fetchThis = getMe;

        //Save the process - accounting
        Vector tmpProc = (Vector)ClientProc.get(clientRef);
        if(tmpProc == null)
            tmpProc = new Vector(10);
        tmpProc.addElement(runMe);

        //kick it off
        runMe.start();
        return id;
    }
}

/**
 * Writes an object to the end of the client's persistent
 * storage device.
 * @param clientRef A reference to the client who is saving
➡the Object.
 * @param saveMe    The Object to save.
 * @exception RemoteException   Thrown if a transport problem
➡occurs
 */
public void writeObject(CallbackInterface clientRef,Object
➡saveMe){
    Vector clientVect = getClientVector(clientRef);
    clientVect.addElement(saveMe);
    saveClientVector(clientRef,clientVect);
}

/**
 * Reads all Objects stored in the client's persistent
➡storage device.
```

```
      * @param clientRef A reference to the client who is reading
      * the Objects.
      * @return       Returns all Objects stored in the specified
➥client's
      *               persistent storage device. null is returned if
      *                           no Objects are found.
      * @exception RemoteException    Thrown if a transport problem
➥occurs
      * @exception IOException        Thrown if there is problem
➥reading
      * the Object file
      */
      public Vector readObjects(CallbackInterface clientRef){
         return getClientVector(clientRef);
      }


    /**
      * Purges all Objects in the client's persistent storage
➥device.
      * @param clientRef              A reference to the client who
➥is
      * deleting the Objects.
      * @exception RemoteException    Thrown if a transport problem
➥occurs
      */
      public void purgeObjectStore(CallbackInterface clientRef){
         Vector clientVect = getClientVector(clientRef);
         clientVect.removeAllElements();
         saveClientVector(clientRef,clientVect);
      }


    /**
      * Remotely execute a stored procedure.
      * @param procName               The name of the stored
➥procedure to execute
      * @param params                 The properties for the stored
➥procedure
      * @param informMe               The client to whom the
➥results should be shipped to
      * @return                       Returns the request ID value
➥> 0 if
      *                               successful execution,
      *                               otherwise -1
      * @exception RemoteException    Thrown if a transport problem
```

```
➥occurs
    */
   public int execStoredProcedure(String procName, Properties
➥params,
      CallbackInterface informMe){
      //Code HERE!
      return 0;
   }


   /**
    * Return a list of all registered clients
    * @return                    Returns a list of all
➥register clients
    * @exception RemoteException  Thrown if a transport problem
➥occurs
    */
   public Properties getListOfClients(){
      return null;
   }


   /**
    * Returns a Class object defining the admin frame
    * @return                    Returns a Class def of the
➥Admin frame
    * @exception RemoteException  Thrown if a transport problem
➥occurs
    */
   public Class getAdminFrame(){
      return null;
   }

   /**
    * Send a byte stream to the specified client
    * @param from                The reference to the message
➥creator
    * @param toClient            The messages "TO" address
    * @param data                The data to send
    * @exception RemoteException  Thrown if a transport problem
➥occurs
    */
   public void sendInfoToClient(CallbackInterface from,
      String toClient,byte[] data){
      CallbackInterface tmp;
```

```
        for(Enumeration e = Clients.keys();e.hasMoreElements();){
            tmp = (CallbackInterface)e.nextElement();
            if(toClient.equals((String)Clients.get(tmp))){
                try{
                    tmp.recvMessage((String)Clients.get(from),data);
                }
                catch(Exception ex){
                    System.out.println("DataServer.sendInfoToClient" +
                        "I think its DEAD " + ex);
                    unRegisterClient(tmp);
                }
                finally{
                    return;
                }
            }
        }
    }

    /**
     * Send a byte stream to all registered clients
     * @param from                    The reference to the message
➥creator
     * @param data                    The data to send
     * @exception RemoteException     Thrown if a transport problem
➥occurs
     */
    public void sendInfoToAll(CallbackInterface from, byte[] data){
        CallbackInterface tmp;

        for(Enumeration e = Clients.keys();e.hasMoreElements();){
            tmp = (CallbackInterface)e.nextElement();
            try{
                tmp.recvMessage((String)Clients.get(from),data);
            }
            catch(Exception ex){
                System.out.println("DataServer.sendInfoToClient" +
                    " I think its DEAD " + ex);
                unRegisterClient(tmp);
            }
        }
    }

    //Methods - Remote Listener Reg
```

```
    /**
     * Registers a client for the client death event.
     * @param clientRef          A reference to the client
     *                           whom will be informed.
     * @exception RemoteException    Thrown if a transport problem
➥occurs
     */
    public void registerClientDeath(CallbackInterface clientRef){
        ClientDeath.addElement(clientRef);
    }


    /**
     * Registers a new Client
     * @param Host               Client Host Name
     * @param clientRef          A reference to the client
➥object
     * @exception RemoteException    Thrown if a transport problem
➥occurs
     */
    public void registerClient(String Host,CallbackInterface
➥clientRef){
        Clients.put(clientRef,Host);
    }

//Methods - Remote Listener UnReg

    /**
     * Unregisters a client for the client death event.
     * @param clientRef          A reference to the client who
➥will
     *                                be informed.
     * @exception RemoteException    Thrown if a transport problem
➥occurs
     */
    public void unRegisterClientDeath(CallbackInterface
➥clientRef){
        ClientDeath.removeElement(clientRef);
    }


    /**
     * Registers a new Client
     * @param clientRef          A reference to the client
➥object
     * @exception RemoteException    Thrown if a transport problem
```

```
➥occurs
     */
    public void unRegisterClient(CallbackInterface clientRef){
        //Get name
        String host = (String)Clients.get(clientRef);
        Clients.remove(clientRef);

        //Inform the registered listeners
        int num = ClientDeath.size();
        for(int i = 0;i < num;++i){
            try{
    ((CallbackInterface)ClientDeath.elementAt(i)).clientDeath(host);
            }
            catch(Exception e){
                //No Big
            }
        }
    }

    /**
     * Main run loop to make health calls
     */
    public void run(){
        for(;;){
            makeHealthCalls();
            try{
                Thread.sleep(HealthInterval);
            }
            catch(Exception e){}
        }
    }

    /**
     * Start up the stock server; also creates a registry so that
➥the
     * DataServer can lookup the server.
     */
    public static void main(String args[]){

        System.setSecurityManager(new RMISecurityManager());
        try {
            LocateRegistry.createRegistry(port);
            System.out.println("DataServer.main: creating
➥server");
```

```
          DataServer server = new DataServer();
          Naming.rebind(Name, server);
          System.out.println("DataServer.main: done");
          System.out.println("DataServer.main: Executing health
➡thread");

              //Exec the Health Thread
              Thread mainHealthThread = new Thread(server);
              try{
                  mainHealthThread.start();
              }
              catch(Exception e){
                  System.out.println("DataServer.main:" +
                   " Error Exec Health Thread: Exiting " + e);
                  return;
              }
      }
      catch (Exception e) {
          System.out.println("DataServer.main: an exception
➡occurred: " +
                e.getMessage());
          e.printStackTrace();
      }
   }
}
```

DBforME.Client.ClientDataProj

```
package DBforME.Client;

import java.rmi.*;
import java.net.URL;
import DBforME.Shared.*;
import java.rmi.server.*;
import java.rmi.registry.*;
import java.util.Hashtable;
import java.util.Properties;
import java.util.Vector;
import java.net.InetAddress;

/**
 * The DataServer provides an RMI server for the execution
 * of stored procedures,
 * and facilitates inter client communications.
```

```
 * <BR>
 * Copyright (c) 1997 My Company, Inc. All Rights Reserved.
 * @author Cary A. Jardin
 * @version 1.0
 *
 */
public abstract class ClientDataProj implements
CallbackInterface{

    //Debug Flag
    private final static boolean DEBUG  = false;
    //Remote Service
    private static String HostName      = "france";
    private static int    HostPort      = 6789;
    private static String HostService   = "DBforME.DataServer";


    //Remote Object Reference
    private ServerInterface remoteServer = null;


//Methods - Constructor
    public ClientDataProj() throws RemoteException{
        //Export this Reference to receive callbacks
       UnicastRemoteObject.exportObject(this);

        //Retrieve remote object
        try{
            remoteServer = (ServerInterface)Naming.lookup("//"+
                HostName+":"+HostPort+"/"+HostService);
            remoteServer.registerClient(
                InetAddress.getLocalHost().getHostName(),this);
        }
        catch(Exception e){
            //Throw an exception if a URL has a problem
            throw new RemoteException();
        }
    }

//Methods - Destructor
    public void finalize(){
        if(remoteServer != null)
            try{
                remoteServer.unRegisterClient(this);
            }
```

```
            catch(Exception e){}
    }

//Methods - Client callbacks
    /**
     * Called to validate that the Client is still alive.
     * @exception RemoteException    Thrown if a transport problem
➥occurs
     */
    public void heartBeat(){
        if(DEBUG)
            System.out.println("HeartBeart!!!");

    }

    /**
     * Called to inform the client of the death of another
➥client.
     * @param name                   The name of the client who
➥died.
     * @exception RemoteException    Thrown if a transport problem
➥occurs
     */
    public abstract void clientDeath(String name);

    /**
     * Called to inform that a URL has been fetched
     * @param result                 A reference to the original
➥Thread
     *                                after execution.
     * @param jobID                  The jov ID associated with
➥the return Thread.
     * @exception RemoteException    Thrown if a transport problem
➥occurs
     */
    public abstract void URLDone(byte[] result, int jobID);

    /**
     * Called remotely to feed resultant data into the client. Do
➥NOT call!
     * @param reqID                  The request ID of the
➥incoming data
     * @param data                   The result data
```

```
   * @exception RemoteException   Thrown if a transport problem
➥occurs
   */
   public abstract synchronized void resultData(int reqID,
➥byte[] data);

   /**
   * Called remotely to feed data sent from another client. Do
➥NOT Call
   * @param from                  The name of the client from
   *                              which the data originated
   * @param data                  The message data
   * @exception RemoteException   Thrown if a transport problem
➥occurs
   */
   public abstract void recvMessage(String from, byte[] data);

//Methods - Local accessor
   public synchronized byte[] getResultData(int reqID){
       //Something HERE!
       return null;
   }

//Methods - Remote Services
   /**
   * Remotely execute a stored procedure.
   * @param procName              The name of the stored
➥procedure to execute
   * @param params                The properties for the stored
➥procedure
   * @return                      Returns the request ID value
➥> 0
   *                                 if successful execution,
   *                                 otherwise -1
   */
   public synchronized int execStoredProcedure(String procName,
       Properties params){

       if(remoteServer == null)
           return -1;

       try{
           return remoteServer.execStoredProcedure(procName,
➥params, this);
```

```
        }
        catch(Exception e){
            return -1;
        }
    }


    /**
     * Return a list of all registered clients
     * @return                  Returns a list of all
➥register clients,
     *                          or null if a problem
     */
    public synchronized Properties getListOfClients(){

        if(remoteServer == null)
            return null;

        try{
            return remoteServer.getListOfClients();
        }
        catch(Exception e){
            return null;
        }
    }


    /**
     * Returns a Class object defining the admin frame
     * @return                  Returns a Class def of the
➥Admin frame,
     *                          or null if a problem
     */
    public synchronized DBAdminFrame getAdminFrame(){

        if(remoteServer == null)
            return null;

        try{          return
➥(DBAdminFrame)(remoteServer.getAdminFrame().newInstance());
        }
        catch(Exception e){
            return null;
        }
    }
```

```
/**
 * Send a byte stream to the specified client
 * @param from              The reference to the message
➥creator
 * @param toClient          The messages "TO" address
 * @param data              The data to send
 */
public synchronized void sendInfoToClient(String
➥toClient,byte[] data){

    if(remoteServer == null)
        return;

    try{
        remoteServer.sendInfoToClient(this,toClient,data);
    }
    catch(Exception e){
    }

    return;
}

/**
 * Send a byte stream to all registered clients
 * @param from              The reference to the message
➥creator
 * @param data              The data to send
 */
public synchronized void sendInfoToAll(byte[] data){

    if(remoteServer == null)
        return;

    try{
        remoteServer.sendInfoToAll(this,data);
    }
    catch(Exception e){
    }

    return;
}

/**
 * Retrieves the specified URL
```

```
   * @param runMe                    The URL to fetch
   * @return                         Returns the Request ID > 0
   */
  public int getURL(URL getMe){

      if(remoteServer == null)
          return -1;

      try{
          return remoteServer.fetchURL(getMe,this);
      }
      catch(Exception e){
          return -1;
      }
  }


  /**
   * Writes an object to the end of the client's persistent
   * storage device.
   * @param saveMe                 The Object to save.
   */
  public void writeObject(Object saveMe){
      if(remoteServer == null)
          return ;

      try{
          remoteServer.writeObject(this,saveMe);
      }
      catch(Exception e){
      }

      return;
  }


  /**
   * Reads all Objects stored in the client's persistent
➥storage device.
   * @return        Returns all Objects stored in the
➥specified client's
   *                persistent storage device. null is
➥returned if
   *                no Objects are found.
   */
  public Vector readObjects(){
```

```
        if(remoteServer == null)
            return null;


        try{
            return remoteServer.readObjects(this);
        }
        catch(Exception e){
            return null;
        }
    }



    /**
     * Purges all Objects in the client's persistent storage
➥device.
     */
    public void purgeObjectStore(){
        if(remoteServer == null)
            return;


        try{
            remoteServer.purgeObjectStore(this);
        }
        catch(Exception e){
        }
        return;
    }


    /**
     * Returns the RMI registry from the server machine.
     * This way the Client has access to all registered objects
     * @return  Returns the Registry of the server
     */
    public Registry getRegistry(){
        try{
            return LocateRegistry.getRegistry(HostName,HostPort);
        }
        catch(Exception e){
            System.out.println("ClientDataProj.getISRegistry() -
➥"+ e);
            return null;
        }


    }
```

```
//Methods - Remote Listener Reg

    /**
     * Registers a client for the client death event.
     */
    public void registerClientDeath(){
        if(remoteServer == null)
            return;

        try{
            remoteServer.registerClientDeath(this);
        }
        catch(Exception e){
        }
        return;
    }

//Methods - Remote Listener UnReg

    /**
     * Unregisters a client for the client death event.
     */
    public void unRegisterClientDeath(CallbackInterface
➥clientRef){
        if(remoteServer == null)
            return;

        try{
            remoteServer.unRegisterClientDeath(this);
        }
        catch(Exception e){
        }
        return;
    }
}
```

DBforME.Shared.CallbackInterface

```
package DBforME.Shared;

import java.rmi.*;
import java.util.Vector;
import java.util.Properties;
```

```
/**
 * This interface defines callback hooks which the server can
➥exploit to
 * transmit information to the client<BR>
 * <BR>
 * Copyright (c)1997 My Company, Inc. All Rights Reserved.
 * @author Cary A. Jardin
 * @version 1.0
 *
 */
public interface CallbackInterface extends java.rmi.Remote {

    /**
     * Feeds the resultant data into the client
     * @param reqID            The request ID of the
➥incoming data
     * @param data             The result data
     * @exception RemoteException   Thrown if a transport problem
➥occurs
     */
    void resultData(int reqID, byte[] data) throws
➥RemoteException;


    /**
     * Feed data sent from another client.
     * @param from             The name of the client from
➥which the
     * data originated
     * @param data             The message data
     * @exception RemoteException   Thrown if a transport problem
➥occurs
     */
    void recvMessage(String from, byte[] data) throws
➥RemoteException;


    /**
     * Called to validate that the Client is still alive.
     * @exception RemoteException   Thrown if a transport problem
➥occurs
     */
    void heartBeat() throws RemoteException;


    /**
     * Called to inform the client of the death of another
➥client.
```

```
    * @param name                    The name of the client who
➡died.
    * @exception RemoteException    Thrown if a transport problem
➡occurs
    */
   void clientDeath(String name) throws RemoteException;


   /**
    * Called to inform that a URL has been fetched
    * @param result                 A reference to the original
➡Thread
    *                               after execution.
    * @param jobID                  The jov ID associated with
    *                               the return Thread.
    * @exception RemoteException    Thrown if a transport problem
➡occurs
    */
   void URLDone(byte[] result, int jobID);
}
```

DBforME.Shared.DBAdminFrame

```
package DBforME.Shared;

import java.awt.Frame;

/**
 * The DBAdminFrame is the base abstract class that must be used
➡for
 * creating admin facilities.
 * <BR>
 * Copyright (c) 1997 My Company, Inc. All Rights Reserved.
 * @author Cary A. Jardin
 * @version 1.0
 *
 */
public abstract class DBAdminFrame extends Frame{

    /**
     * Upon constructing a new instance of the admin frame, this
     * method is called to inform the frame of its associated
     * server host.
     * @param serverHostName         The host name of the origin
➡server.
```

```
     */
     public abstract void setOrigin(String serverHostName);
}
```

DBforME.Shared.ServerInterface

```
package DBforME.Shared;

import java.rmi.*;
import java.net.URL;
import java.util.Properties;
import java.util.Vector;
import java.io.IOException;

/**
 * This interface defines the visible facilities
 * provided to client applications.<BR>
 * <BR>
 * Copyright (c)1997 My Company, Inc. All Rights Reserved.
 * @author Cary A. Jardin
 * @version 1.0
 *
 */
public interface ServerInterface extends java.rmi.Remote {

    /**
     * Remotely execute a stored procedure.
     * @param procName  The name of the stored procedure to
➥execute
     * @param params    The properties for the stored procedure
     * @param informMe  The client to whom the results should be
➥shipped
     * @return    Returns the request ID value > 0 if successful
➥execution,
     *                              otherwise -1
     * @exception RemoteException   Thrown if a transport problem
➥occurs
     */
    int execStoredProcedure(String procName, Properties params,
        CallbackInterface informMe) throws RemoteException;
    /**
     * Return a list of all registered clients
     * @return                      Returns a list of all
➥register clients
```

```
     * @exception RemoteException    Thrown if a transport problem
➥occurs
     */
    Properties getListOfClients() throws RemoteException;

    /**
     * Registers a new Client
     * @param Host                   Client Host Name
     * @param clientRef              A reference to the client
➥object
     * @exception RemoteException    Thrown if a transport problem
➥occurs
     */
    void registerClient(String Host,CallbackInterface clientRef)
       throws RemoteException;
    /**
     * Registers a new Client
     * @param clientRef              A reference to the client
➥object
     * @exception RemoteException    Thrown if a transport problem
➥occurs
     */
    void unRegisterClient(CallbackInterface clientRef)
       throws RemoteException;

    /**
     * Returns a Class object defining the admin frame
     * @return                       Returns a Class def of the
➥Admin frame
     * @exception RemoteException    Thrown if a transport problem
➥occurs
     */
    Class getAdminFrame() throws RemoteException;

    /**
     * Send a byte stream to the specified client
     * @param from                   The reference to the message
➥creator
     * @param toClient               The messages "TO" address
     * @param data                   The data to send
     * @exception RemoteException    Thrown if a transport problem
➥occurs
     */
```

```
        void sendInfoToClient(CallbackInterface from, String
➥toClient,byte[] data)
            throws RemoteException;

        /**
         * Send a byte stream to all registered clients
         * @param from                  The reference to the message
➥creator
         * @param data                  The data to send
         * @exception RemoteException    Thrown if a transport problem
➥occurs
         */
        void sendInfoToAll(CallbackInterface from, byte[] data)
            throws RemoteException;

        /**
         * Retrieves the passed URL.
         * @param getMe          The URL to fetch.
         * @param clientRef      The client to inform of the
➥completed job.
         * @exception RemoteException    Thrown if a transport problem
➥occurs
         */
        int fetchURL(URL getMe, CallbackInterface clientRef)
            throws RemoteException;

        /**
         * Registers a client for the client death event.
         * @param clientRef             A reference to the client
         *     whom will be informed.
         * @exception RemoteException    Thrown if a transport problem
➥occurs
         */
        void registerClientDeath(CallbackInterface clientRef)
            throws RemoteException;

        /**
         * Unregisters a client for the client death event.
         * @param clientRef  A reference to the client whom will be
➥informed.
         * @exception RemoteException    Thrown if a transport problem
➥occurs
         */
        void unRegisterClientDeath(CallbackInterface clientRef)
            throws RemoteException;
```

```
    /**
     * Writes an object to the end of the client's persistent
➥storage device.
     * @param clientRef A reference to the client who is saving the
➥Object.
     * @param saveMe          The Object to save.
     * @exception RemoteException   Thrown if a transport problem
➥occurs
     */
    void writeObject(CallbackInterface clientRef,Object saveMe)
        throws RemoteException, IOException;


    /**
     * Reads all Objects stored in the client's persistent
➥storage device.
     * @param clientRef  A reference to the client who is reading
➥the Objects.
     * @return                Returns all Objects stored in
➥the
     *                        specified client's
     *                        persistent storage device. null
➥is
     *                        returned if
     *                        no Objects are found.
     * @exception RemoteException   Thrown if a transport problem
➥occurs
     * @exception IOException    Thrown if there is problem
➥reading
     *                        the Object file
     */
    Vector readObjects(CallbackInterface clientRef) throws
➥RemoteException;


    /**
     * Purges all Objects in the client's persistent storage
➥device.
     * @param clientRef  A reference to the client who is
➥deleting
     *     the Objects.
     * @exception RemoteException    Thrown if a transport problem
➥occurs
     */
    void purgeObjectStore(CallbackInterface clientRef)
        throws RemoteException;
}
```

DBforME.Shared.FetchURL

```
package DBforME.Shared;

import DBforME.Server.DataServer;
import java.rmi.*;
import java.util.Vector;
import java.util.Properties;
import java.io.*;
import java.net.URL;

/**
 * This class defines a process to be executed on a server
 * resource to fetch a URL.
 * <BR>
 * <BR>
 * Copyright (c)1997 My Company, Inc. All Rights Reserved.
 * @author Cary A. Jardin
 * @version 1.0
 *
 */
public class FetchURL extends Thread{

    /**
     * This will be set by the server to facilitate
     * a callback upon completion
     */
    public DataServer informMe = null;

    /**
     * This will be set by the server to facilitate a callback
     * upon completion
     */
    public int procID = 0;

    /**
     * The data retrieved from the URL
     */
    public byte[] data = null;

    /**
     * The URL to fetch
     */
    public URL fetchThis = null;
```

```
    /**
     * Executed by the server to run the specified fetch the URL
     */
    public final void run(){
        try{
            int size = fetchThis.openStream().available();
            DataInputStream inbuff = new DataInputStream(new
BufferedInputStream(fetchThis.openStream()));
            data = new byte[size];
            inbuff.readFully(data);
        }
        catch(Exception e){}
        informMe.jobDone(this,procID);
    }
}
```

Written Examination Answers

1. a)   Each of the discrete units of functionality should be
    partitioned into separate remote objects. In this way, clients
    can retrieve a listing of registered services. Placing all the
    facilities in a single object only makes sense if the services
    are not mutually exclusive and share common state informa-
    tion. Otherwise, each remote object should be partitioned in
    the same matter as local/standard objects. Object-oriented
    design holds even with remote objects.

1. b)   To the remote client a server object is like any other
    object reference. To the extent, if the server objects are fully
    replicated on different servers the client can simply destroy
    the failed server object and replace it with the alive server
    object. In this matter, an automatic rollover can take place,
    providing a greater degree of robustness.

2. a)   In the current heart-beat implementation, health call, is
    made regardless if a piece of information has been sent to
    the client in question. That is, each communication with a
    client should be deemed as a health call. Therefore, making
    an actual heath call will only transpire if no other contact has
    been made with the clients.

A second optimization technique is to eliminate RMI from the health call. The amount of data transmitted for each health call may far exceed a simple "I am Alive" flag. Therefore, a UDP solution could easily and efficiently handle such a heart-beat facility.

2. b)   The current implementation is not optimal. However, the implementation of an RMI call was the simplest and cleanest solution. As stated in answer 2.a, there are other, more optimal solutions, but this solution functions for the first round. If it turns out to be a problem, additional effort can be spent.

3. a)   RMI is slick, and it does expedite client/server solutions, but RMI client/solutions are not optimal in comparison to straight socket-level implementation. However, this is the same debate of whether to write code in assembly or a high-level language like Java. Sure, assembly might be faster, but the development effort will be slower and less extensible. I fully agree with the use of RMI in this scenario, and believe in RMI for a wide range of client/server solutions.

3. b)   There are two problems that plague RMI solutions in a high demand system. The first is the overhead for each connection, and the second is the amount of garbage produced for each RMI call. Such solutions implemented with pure sockets suffer from similar issues. However, writing directly to the wire gives ultimate control of optimization.

4. a)   When a client submits an URL request to the server object, the server object spawns a separate thread to fetch the URL. When the thread finishes its retrieval of the URL, the client is notified of completion with a byte array of the URL.

5. a)   Writing a 100% pure solution means creating a solution that uses the strength of Java to assure cross-platform executions. To facilitate this the general goal of writing 100% pure is to avoid the use of native application hooks.

5. b)   When a solution requires native hooks it should be implemented in a modular manner. That is, the native hooks

should be wrapped in a class that can be replaced to enable the solution of various platforms.

Where to Go From Here

The Certified Developer examination is a complete test of Java knowledge. As you saw in this chapter, the examination is divided into a performance-based programming exercise and a written examination. The combination provides a comprehensive assessment of your Java knowledge. This chapter provides a practice exam to help prepare you for the Certified Developer Examination.

Now that you have completed the content of this entire examination aid, you have three roads before you. If you FEEL you are ready, fork out the money and begin the Certified Developer Process. If you are on the borderline if you should go for it or take some more time, email me your practice programming exercise and written exam at cjardin@servnow.com so that I can further direct you. If you do not think you are ready, take some time off and go play around at http://java.sun.com.

The Java Certification Process is by no means easy. The information covered in the Programmer and Developer examinations are grueling. However, you are Certified Java Programmer on the verge of being a Certified Developer. All I can offer at this point is my email (cjardin@servnow.com) for any questions/comments. Feel free to use this resource, and I look forward to hearing from you.

P a r t **3**

Appendices

Appendix

Overview of the
Certification Process

To become a Sun Certified Java Programmer or Developer, you must pass a rigorous certification exam that is designed to measure your level of knowledge about Java. The two certifications that Sun offers are sequential: you must pass the Java Programmer exam before qualifying to take the Java Developer exam. These two exams measure very different things:

▶ **Sun Certified Java Programmer.** You must have a firm grasp of all Sun-provided development tools, especially the contents the JDK, JVM, and Runtime Environment. You must also show mastery of Java syntax, reserved words, declarations, language mechanics—such as object accessibility modifiers, the core APIs, and the issues involved in implementing applets and Java applications.

▶ **Sun Certified Java Developer.** To pass this exam, you must first have passed the Java Programmer exam. Then you must demonstrate knowledge of object-oriented design techniques, Java-related technologies—such as JDBC and IDL, and Java deployment issues. The final part of this exam is an actual programming assignment.

For up-to-date information about each type of certification, visit the Sun Educational Services Certification Programs Web site at http://www.sun.com/service/suned/cert/index.html

Sun Certified Java Programmer Exam

The Sun certification process is hierarchical in that the certification process contains two steps. The first step is the Sun Certified Java Programmer certification and the second is The Sun Certified Java Developer certification. This is not to say that the Certified Programmer certification is in any way easier than the Certified Developer certification. Rather, the information tested in the Certified Programmer is merely a prerequisite of the information required to pass the Certified Java Developer.

The amount of information covered in the Sun Certified Java Programmer examination is vast. Everything from JVM architecture to Graphic User Interface (GUI) event syntax is covered. That's a lot of information, and passing the exam is by no means a trivial task, but there is no need to worry. The examination content is broken down into distinct areas of study, which correlate directly to the chapters of this book.

If you take a step back and look at each of the Sun Certified Java Programmer Certification areas individually, each contains only a finite set of testable items. The following lists the specific regions of study for Java Programmer Certification and the associated chapter where relevant information can be found.

- ▶ Java Virtual Machine Specification—Chapter 1, "Java and the Java Virtual Machine (JVM)," provides in depth information on the JVM and class file structure.

- ▶ Language Syntax Knowledge—Chapter 2, "Java Language Internals," provides a detailed account of Java reserved words, conditionals, loops, object definitions, and visibility operators.

▶ Language Mechanics—Chapter 3, "Java Objects and Exceptions," focuses on vital Java topics such as interfaces, inheritance, packages, exceptions, and proper use of visibility operators.

▶ Java Thread Support—Chapter 4, "Threads in the Java Platform," is devoted to the sometimes confusing world of Java thread support.

▶ API Knowledge—Chapter 5, "Java API," explores each key package of the Java API library, including the Abstract Window Toolkit (AWT), and exception-specific syntax.

▶ Sun-Provided Development Tool Knowledge and Runtime Environment—Chapter 6, "JDK Supplied Tools," is devoted to the coverage of the Java Runtime Environment, the JDK supplied tools, coverage of the JVM architecture, and class file format.

Sun-Provided Development Tool Knowledge and Runtime Environment

Obtaining a firm knowledge of the Java technology begins at ground zero, the *Java Virtual Machine* (JVM). Java is more than a programming language; it is an entire set of technologies that have merged to form a ubiquitous development platform. Conveniently, Sun has packaged this suite of technologies into the *Java Development Kit* (JDK) and Java runtime environment.

Chapter 1, "Java and the Java Virtual Machine (JVM)," explains the entire Java technology from JVM architecture to the tools and runtime environment provided by Sun. With a bottom-up approach to the Java technology, you will see the entire picture of the Java technology phenomenon.

Language Syntax Knowledge

Programming efficiency is a function of the knowledge of the programming language, and a Java-certified programmer is required to be highly proficient in the Java language. A couple of common arguments against the requirement for rote memorization of a programming language syntax are, "If I really need to know it, I can look it up," and, "I know the theory of the language; syntax is just a detail." Both of these arguments hold merit, but they fail to address the issue of programming efficiency.

The intimate knowledge of a language provides a productive conduit through which ideas flow. Case in point: you may very well be able to ask for a restroom in a foreign tongue armed with a translating dictionary, but try explaining the design framework for a new application. You cannot expect to efficiently and elegantly code a new application without a firm understanding of that specific development language. The Java Certified Programmer exam tests language proficiency to a level that ensures language mastery. Chapter 2, "Java Language Internals" provides a detailed account of exactly what is required to be "proficient" in Java, including detailed discussions of proper syntax usage, language-reserved words, and declarations.

Language Mechanics

It's one thing to know all of the keywords of a language; it's quite another to know exactly how to use each of those words. This skill is often referred to as language mechanics. For example, take the sentence "Java is great." You can reconstruct the sentence into "Great is Java," and maintain the meaning, but you lose some of the eloquence. It is the goal of the Java Certified Programmer exam to test not only that you know what to say but how to say it.

Testing Java language syntax knowledge determines how well you know the keywords, or reserved words, of the language. Testing Java language mechanics validates knowledge of Java as an entire development language. For example, Java provides four object accessibility modifiers which are `public`, `private`, default, and `protected`. Each of these modifiers has drastically different effects on developed objects, but all are syntactically correct.

Firm knowledge of language mechanics ensures solid, scaleable, and extensible implementations. Chapters 3 and 4 provide an in-depth Java language mechanics lesson, and Chapter 4, "Threads in the Java Platform," will dive into the specific Java mechanics of Java thread support. After you have completed Chapters 3–5, you will have a firm understanding of the mechanics of the entire Java language, as well as the knowledge required to become a Sun-Certified Java Programmer.

Java API Knowledge

A good measure of Java's popularity can be attributed to its vast API libraries. Everything from basic math functions to public key security can be found in the Java API libraries. For the Java developer, these libraries are the life blood of Java development, and the key to the programming simplicity that many programmers have come to love about Java.

Application Programming Interfaces (APIs) provide functionality above and beyond the facilities the languages provide. That is, you probably would not expect a language to enable pictures to be displayed. But you would definitely expect a language add-on to provide such a service. In this manner, APIs can be viewed as leveraging the work others have done to simplify development. This concept is not a new one introduced by Java; however, it is a concept that Java mastered.

Knowing the Java-supplied APIs is like a carpenter knowing what tools are in his or her tool box. With such knowledge, the carpenter can look at a problem and choose the tools that will expedite the completion of the task. In Java, knowledge of the supplied APIs is not only a requirement to become a Certified Java Programmer, but it is also crucial to productive Java programming.

Specific Applet and Application Implementation Issues

Many newcomers to Java believe an applet to be synonymous with Java, and for good reason. Java's main marketing push, and chief distinguishing technology, is and has been applets. It has not been until recently that Java applications and enterprise solutions have begun to take center stage. Nevertheless, the fact remains that

Java application deployment can take two discrete routes, each with separate associated issues.

Applets are Web-deployed applications, and Java applications are stand-alone program executables. The key difference between the two lies in what the executable calls home. That is, an applet's home is inside a Web browser that dictates the applet's operating environment. A Java application's home is in the executing computer's operating system. Each deployment offers its own set of attributes, with neither being superior to the other. Rather, the deployments have their own qualities and abilities. The key is to know which one fits your need most precisely.

During the discussion of the Java runtime environment in Chapter 1, you will be exposed to the differences between applets and applications. The differences are not vast, but they are great enough to justify the distinction as required knowledge to become a Certified Java Programmer.

Sun Certified Java Developer Exam

It's one thing to be a programmer; it's another to be an engineer. The difference is more than a play on words. A programmer writes code, which is why the Certified Programmer exam focuses on core Java language proficiency and runtime knowledge. An engineer not only holds the knowledge to code an application, but also possesses the skills needed to design a reusable, extensible, and cost-effective implementation.

An engineer is a programmer who can justify a design. This is the reason for the certification hierarchy. In order to sit for the Certified Java Developer exam, you must first complete the Certified Java Programmer exam. In this way, the Certified Developer exam focuses only on specific Java design and implementation issues.

The Certified Developer exam focuses on a handful of key Java development issues; it also involves an actual programming assignment that ranges in complexity from a simple GUI exercise to a complex thread scheduling. However, with a firm grasp of the Certified Programmer examination content and mastery of the following areas of Java development, you will be amply prepared for anything thrown at you.

The following lists the specific regions of study for Java Developer Certification, and the associated chapter where relevant information can be found.

- ▶ Network Programming—Chapters 10, "Network Programming," introduces network programming using the provided Java facilities, including RMI.

- ▶ Object-Oriented Design—Chapter 11, "Creating Java APIs," explores OOD with a Java flavor, including issues such as extensible object abstraction, persistent object storage, and autonomous object design.

- ▶ Java-Related Technologies—Chapters 12, "JFC and Java Media Kit," through 14, "Additional Java Technologies," provide a menu of the Java technology suite, including discussions of RMI, JavaBeans, JDBC, and CORBA interaction.

Object-Oriented Design

Object Oriented Design (OOD) is a relatively new concept in the development community, but it is one that Java has mastered. When you get into OOD theory, you begin treading on delicate and sensitive personal preferences. Developers with C++ background hold their paradigm to be pure, as do the SmallTalk and Ada communities. Without stepping on any toes, a safe and correct statement to sum up Java Object capabilities is "Java provides an ample canvas for development and implementation of true OOD."

Unlike C++, which needed to maintain compatibility with C, Java was created without any such prerequisite. In fact, Java was created with the sole intention of implementing a truly *Object Oriented Programming* (OOP) language. The result was Java's self-contained, adaptive, and extensible Object model and Object Naming Space.

In Chapter 11, "Creating Java APIs," you will find a detailed discussion of the Java Object model, as well as the information required for the Certified Java Developer Exam. At this level, the information presented transcends rote memorization and provides useful information for all aspects of software development.

Java-Related Technologies

In the early days of Java, Java was used solely for presentation of dynamic content on the Web. Since then, the Java suite of technologies and APIs has ranged from 2D and 3D graphic APIs to a component framework for enterprise-level distributed computing. The Java technology suite has grown and will continue to grow. It is the job of a Certified Developer to know the available technologies.

Java has exploded. The original JDK 1.0 beta contained the bare necessity technologies. Things such as JDBC, JavaBeans, and RMI were just a glimmer in some engineer's eye. The suite of Java technologies has grown exponentially, and some day the growth will plateau. However, for the time being, Java technology growth is just like the Energizer bunny: "It just keeps going, and going, and going…"

Where there was once one Java technology there now are many, and keeping abreast of the technologies is a full-time job in itself. Chapter 12 through 14 will present all the key technologies that make up the Java technology suite. With this content, the chapters will provide not only vital information for the Certified Java Developer exam, but also a one-stop-shopping experience for all that is and will be hot in the Java development community.

Java Deployment Issues

"Write once, run anywhere!" That has been the battle cry of Java since its inception. But life is not that cut-and-dried. Applets run in browsers, and Java applications run from within the native operating system. The downside of this story is that applets must reside inside a browser, and Java applications cannot function inside a browser. So the slogan "Write once, run anywhere!" does have some exceptions, and where there are exceptions there are deployment issues.

In developing a new Java program, the decision to implement the program as either an applet or an application may seem like a logical first step. Nevertheless, it is usually the exception and not the rule that such a step is considered, resulting in large amounts of development resources being wasted due to misinformation. To avoid wasting development cycles and ensure proper design rationales, the Java Certified Developer exam tests for knowledge of key Java deployment issues.

Chapter 11, "Creating Java APIs," will explore the various Java deployment issues, including the JDK 1.1 test suite. Knowing what to expect and what to plan for might not always be possible. What is possible and vital to a project is knowing what to watch out for. That is the reason for knowing Java deployment issues.

Registering for the Exams

The Sun Java Certification exams are proctored by Sylvan Prometric, a division of Sylvan Learning Systems (which acquired Drake Prometric in 1995). Sylvan Prometric has a large set of international testing facilities.

When you're ready to take the exam, contact your local Sun Educational Services Office to purchase a voucher. You can locate the nearest Sun office by visiting http://www.hibbertco.com/sun/suncontacts/contacts.html.

Once the voucher has been purchased, you will be directed to the local Sylvan Authorized Prometric Testing Center to register for your examination.

The Sun Java Certified Programmer exam consists of a "written" test that is administered on a computer. Answers are a combination of multiple choice and short answer. The testing software included on the CD-ROM with this book mimics the testing environment and will help you practice and feel confident for your exam. You will have your test results within minutes of completing the exam.

After you pass the Programmer exam, you can try to take the Developer exam. The Developer exam consists of two parts. The first part is a programming exercise that you download from the Web, complete at your own speed, and then upload again for grading.

It will take approximately 4 weeks to get your results. The second part of the exam is a series of multiple choice and short answer questions administered in the same way as the Programmer exam.

Each written exam costs $150.00. The programming exercise for the Developer Certification costs $250.00. That is, assuming you pass each exam the first time, completing the Certified Java Programmer certification costs $150.00 and the Certified Java Developer certification costs $400.00 ($150.00 + $250.00).

It is the goal of this book to provide the tools you need to pass the entire suite of certification tests.

Appendix B

Using the CD-ROM

The *Java 1.1 Certification Training Guide* CD-ROM is a hybrid CD-ROM that will run on Windows 95/NT, UNIX, and Macintosh systems. To access the latest installation information and links to technical advice for this book, open the readME.htm file found at the root directory of the disk.

The following subdirectories are contained within a \WIN, \SOLARIS, and \MAC folder and each subdirectory contains:

- ▶ /TestApp The Java test engine and examination questions.

- ▶ /Code A listing of code discussed in the book, organized by chapters.

Using the Test Application

The Java Certification test engine on the CD-ROM is written entirely in Java, and was created specifically for this book. The test engine was specially designed to mimic the functionality found at the Certification testing centers, so by practicing with the test engine you not only test your Java knowledge, but you also become comfortable with the testing environment. Because Sun periodically changes the coverage of the test and the mix of certain types of questions, we have built a Web site to support this book. The Web site contains additional test questions. The test engine is designed to automatically gather questions from the Web site. In this way, we can keep you up-to-date and give you new questions with which to.

Because the test engine is a Java applet, you can use any Java-enabled computer that runs, at minimum, the JDK version 1.1.4 (Windows/Solaris) or MRJ 1.5.1 (Macintosh).

Note

Due to the "essay" nature of the developer examination, answers cannot be graded by a test engine. The test engine only presents simulated questions and programming tasks.

For installation instructions, please see the ReadMe.htm file in the root directory of the CD-ROM. As an example, here are the approximate steps you'll go through to install the test engine on a Windows 95 system:

1. Verify that your JDK is 1.1.4 or higher for Windows/Solaris or 1.5.1 for Macintosh—just as long as it is past JDK 1.1.

2. Copy the /TestApp directory onto a local drive (for example, c:\) so that there exists a \TestApp Directory on your computer.

3. Add the three files found in \TestApp\AddToClassPath to the JVM's classpath.

Note

JDK uses the Environment variable named CLASSPATH.

For Windows 95/NT, add the following line in your AUTOEXEC.BAT file (note that *XXXX* is the directory where your JDK is installed):

```
CLASSPATH=%CLASSPATH%,;C:\XXXX\lib\classes.zip;
➡C:\TestApp\AddToClassPath\symclass.zip;C:\TestApp\
➡AddToClassPath\icebrowserbean.jar;C:\TestApp\
➡AddToClassPath\symbeans.jar
```

Make sure that the path statement in your AUTOEXEC.BAT file also points to the \bin subdirectory where your JDK is installed, and that it also points to:

```
c:\TestApp
```

Symantec Cafe and Visual Cafe users should modify their ../bin/sc.ni files as follows:

```
CLASSPATH=.;%@P%\..\JAVA\LIB\CLASSES.ZIP;C:\TestApp\
➥AddToClassPath\symclass.zip;C:\TestApp\AddToClassPath\
➥icebrowserbean.jar;C:\TestApp\AddToClassPath\symbeans.jar
```

4. Modify the TestApp/test.ini file's LocalPath property to point to the local drive location where you have the test engine installed. By default this is (note the trailing /):

```
LocalPath=C:/TestApp/
```

5. Modify the TestApp/test.ini file's GetNetQuest property to true if you have net access and would like to use the most recent test data available from the Web site supporting this book.

```
GetNetQuest=true
```

6. Open a DOS window, switch to the c:\TestApp directory, and type:

```
java MainTestFrame
```

When the test engine is started, it will randomly select 90 questions from the contents of the CD-ROM and the active question repository at http://www.xprime.com.

Once the test engine has been started, the clock is ticking. As you can see from Figure B.1, the test application is fairly straight forward. The current question is displayed in the large center screen text panel. The buttons on the bottom of the window allow you to skip or flag the current question so that you can answer it later. When you flag a question, a colored square will appear in the top righthand corner to remind you that you haven't answered that question. A scrolling text bar on the top left corner of the screen displays the total number of completed questions, flagged questions, and the total time left for the quiz.

Figure B.1

Java Test Application.

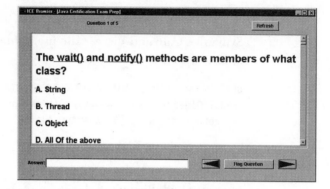

Once the quiz has been completed, all flagged questions will be revisited one last time. Once you answer all questions, or time runs out, the test engine will give you your score.

The test engine is designed to provide the most up-to-date testing data possible. With a live question repository, the test composition will change as new information becomes available. Feel free to drop me a line, at Cjaridn@servnow.com, if you need help or have questions.

One last thing. The test application uses the amazing freeware HTML bean provided by Jeremy Cook available at http://www.bgnett.no/datatech/ICEBrowser/index.html. Thanks Jeremy for making a truly useful tool.

Index

E

G

M

N

O

P

U